PRINCIPLES OF BIG DATA

PRINCIPLES OF BIG DATA

Preparing, Sharing, and Analyzing Complex Information

Jules J. Berman, Ph.D., M.D.

AMSTERDAM • BOSTON • HEIDELBERG • LONDON
NEW YORK • OXFORD • PARIS • SAN DIEGO
SAN FRANCISCO • SINGAPORE • SYDNEY • TOKYO

Morgan Kaufmann is an imprint of Elsevier

Acquiring Editor: *Andrea Dierna*
Editorial Project Manager: *Heather Scherer*
Project Manager: *Punithavathy Govindaradjane*
Designer: *Russell Purdy*

Morgan Kaufmann is an imprint of Elsevier
225 Wyman Street, Waltham, MA 02451, USA

Library of Congress Cataloging-in-Publication Data
Berman, Jules J.
    Principles of big data : preparing, sharing, and analyzing complex information / Jules J Berman.
      pages cm
    ISBN 978-0-12-404576-7
    1. Big data. 2. Database management. I. Title.
    QA76.9.D32B47 2013
    005.74–dc23

                                                                                        2013006421

British Library Cataloguing-in-Publication Data
A catalogue record for this book is available from the British Library

Printed and bound in the United States of America
13   14   15   16   17   10 9 8 7 6 5 4 3 2 1

For information on all MK publications visit our website at *www.mkp.com*

Dedication

To my father, Benjamin

Contents

8. Simple but Powerful Big Data Techniques

9. Analysis

10. Special Considerations in Big Data Analysis

11. Stepwise Approach to Big Data Analysis

12. Failure

13. Legalities

14. Societal Issues

15. The Future

Acknowledgments

I thank Roger Day, and Paul Lewis who resolutely poured through the entire manuscript, placing insightful and useful comments in every chapter. I thank Stuart Kramer, whose valuable suggestions for the content and organization of the text came when the project was in its formative stage. Special thanks go to Denise Penrose, who worked on her very last day at Elsevier to find this title a suitable home at Elsevier's Morgan Kaufmann imprint. I thank Andrea Dierna, Heather Scherer, and all the staff at Morgan Kaufmann who shepherded this book through the publication and marketing processes.

Author Biography

Jules Berman holds two Bachelor of Science degrees from MIT (Mathematics, and Earth and Planetary Sciences), a Ph.D. from Temple University, and an M.D. from the University of Miami. He was a graduate researcher in the Fels Cancer Research Institute at Temple University and at the American Health Foundation in Valhalla, New York. His postdoctoral studies were completed at the U.S. National Institutes of Health, and his residency was completed at the George Washington University Medical Center in Washington, DC. Dr. Berman served as Chief of Anatomic Pathology, Surgical Pathology and Cytopathology at the Veterans Administration Medical Center in Baltimore, Maryland, where he held joint appointments at the University of Maryland Medical Center and at the Johns Hopkins Medical Institutions. In 1998, he became the Program Director for Pathology Informatics in the Cancer Diagnosis Program at the U.S. National Cancer Institute, where he worked and consulted on Big Data projects. In 2006, Dr. Berman was President of the Association for Pathology Informatics. In 2011, he received the Lifetime Achievement Award from the Association for Pathology Informatics. He is a coauthor on hundreds of scientific publications. Today, Dr. Berman is a freelance author, writing extensively in his three areas of expertise: informatics, computer programming, and pathology.

Preface

Data pours into millions of computers every moment of every day. It is estimated that the total accumulated data stored on computers worldwide is about 300 exabytes (that's 300 billion gigabytes). Data storage increases at about 28% per year. The data stored is peanuts compared to data that is transmitted without storage. The annual transmission of data is estimated at about 1.9 zettabytes (1900 billion gigabytes, see Glossary item, Binary sizes).[1] From this growing tangle of digital information, the next generation of data resources will emerge.

As the scope of our data (i.e., the different kinds of data objects included in the resource) and our data timeline (i.e., data accrued from the future and the deep past) are broadened, we need to find ways to fully describe each piece of data so that we do not confuse one data item with another and so that we can search and retrieve data items when needed. Astute informaticians understand that if we fully describe everything in our universe, we would need to have an ancillary universe to hold all the information, and the ancillary universe would need to be much much larger than our physical universe.

In the rush to acquire and analyze data, it is easy to overlook the topic of data preparation. If data in our Big Data resources (see Glossary item, Big Data resource) are not well organized, comprehensive, and fully described, then the resources will have no value. The primary purpose of this book is to explain the principles upon which serious Big Data resources are built. All of the data held in Big Data resources must have a form that supports search, retrieval, and analysis. The analytic methods must be available for review, and the analytic results must be available for validation.

Perhaps the greatest potential benefit of Big Data is the ability to link seemingly disparate disciplines, for the purpose of developing and testing hypotheses that cannot be approached within a single knowledge domain. Methods by which analysts can navigate through different Big Data resources to create new, merged data sets are reviewed.

What exactly is Big Data? Big Data can be characterized by the three V's: volume (large amounts of data), variety (includes different types of data), and velocity (constantly accumulating new data).[2] Those of us who have worked on Big Data projects might suggest throwing a few more V's into the mix: vision (having a purpose and a plan), verification (ensuring that the data conforms to a set of specifications), and validation (checking that its purpose is fulfilled; see Glossary item, Validation).

Many of the fundamental principles of Big Data organization have been described in the "metadata" literature. This literature deals with the formalisms of data description (i.e., how to describe data), the syntax of data description (e.g., markup languages such as eXtensible Markup Language, XML), semantics (i.e., how to make computer-parsable statements that convey meaning), the syntax of semantics (e.g., framework specifications such as Resource Description Framework, RDF, and Web Ontology Language, OWL), the creation of data objects that hold data values and self-descriptive information, and the deployment of ontologies, hierarchical class systems whose members are data objects (see Glossary items, Specification, Semantics, Ontology, RDF, XML).

The field of metadata may seem like a complete waste of time to professionals who have succeeded very well in data-intensive fields, without resorting to metadata formalisms. Many computer scientists, statisticians, database managers, and network specialists have no trouble handling large amounts of data and may not see the need to create a strange new data model for Big Data resources. They might feel that all they really need is greater storage capacity, distributed over more powerful computers, that work in parallel with one another. With this kind of computational power, they can store, retrieve, and analyze larger and larger quantities of data. These fantasies only apply to systems that use relatively simple data or data that can be represented in a uniform and standard format. When data is highly complex and diverse, as found in Big Data resources, the importance of metadata looms large. Metadata will be discussed, with a focus on those concepts that must be incorporated into the organization of Big Data resources. The emphasis will be on explaining the relevance and necessity of these concepts, without going into gritty details that are well covered in the metadata literature.

When data originates from many different sources, arrives in many different forms, grows in size, changes its values, and extends into the past and the future, the game shifts from data computation to data management. It is hoped that this book will persuade readers that faster, more powerful computers are nice to have, but these devices cannot compensate for deficiencies in data preparation. For the foreseeable future, universities, federal agencies, and corporations will pour money, time, and manpower into Big Data efforts. If they ignore the fundamentals, their projects are likely to fail. However, if they pay attention to Big Data fundamentals, they will discover that Big Data analyses can be performed on standard computers. The simple lesson, that data trumps computation, is repeated throughout this book in examples drawn from well-documented events.

There are three crucial topics related to data preparation that are omitted from virtually every other Big Data book: **identifiers, immutability**, and **introspection.**

A thoughtful identifier system ensures that all of the data related to a particular data object will be attached to the correct object, through its identifier, and to no other object. It seems simple, and it is, but many Big Data resources assign identifiers promiscuously, with the end result that information related to a unique object is scattered throughout the resource, or attached to other objects, and cannot be sensibly retrieved when needed. The concept of object identification is of such overriding importance that a Big Data resource can be usefully envisioned as a collection of unique identifiers to which complex data is attached. Data identifiers are discussed in Chapter 2.

Immutability is the principle that data collected in a Big Data resource is permanent and can never be modified. At first thought, it would seem that immutability is a ridiculous and impossible constraint. In the real world, mistakes are made, information changes, and the methods for describing information change. This is all true, but the astute Big Data manager knows how to accrue information into data objects without changing the pre-existing data. Methods for achieving this seemingly impossible trick are described in detail in Chapter 6.

Introspection is a term borrowed from object-oriented programming, not often found in the Big Data literature. It refers to the ability of data objects to describe themselves when interrogated. With introspection, users of a Big Data resource can quickly determine the content of data objects and the hierarchical organization of data objects within the Big Data resource. Introspection allows users to see the types of data relationships that can be analyzed within the resource and clarifies how disparate resources can interact with one another. Introspection is described in detail in Chapter 4.

Another subject covered in this book, and often omitted from the literature on Big Data, is data indexing. Though there are many books written on the art of science of so-called back-of-the-book indexes, scant attention has been paid to the process of preparing indexes for large and complex data resources. Consequently, most Big Data resources have nothing that could be called a serious index. They might have a Web page with a few links to explanatory documents or they might have a short and crude "help" index, but it would be rare to find a Big Data resource with a comprehensive index containing a thoughtful and updated list of terms and links. Without a proper index, most Big Data resources have utility for none but a few cognoscenti. It seems odd to me that organizations willing to spend hundreds of millions of dollars on a Big Data resource will balk at investing some thousands of dollars on a proper index.

Aside from these four topics, which readers would be hard-pressed to find in the existing Big Data literature, this book covers the usual topics relevant to Big Data design, construction, operation, and analysis. Some of these topics include data quality, providing structure to unstructured data, data deidentification, data standards and interoperability issues, legacy data, data

reduction and transformation, data analysis, and software issues. For these topics, discussions focus on the underlying principles; programming code and mathematical equations are conspicuously inconspicuous. An extensive Glossary covers the technical or specialized terms and topics that appear throughout the text. As each Glossary term is "optional" reading, I took the liberty of expanding on technical or mathematical concepts that appeared in abbreviated form in the main text. The Glossary provides an explanation of the practical relevance of each term to Big Data, and some readers may enjoy browsing the Glossary as a stand-alone text.

The final four chapters are nontechnical—all dealing in one way or another with the consequences of our exploitation of Big Data resources. These chapters cover legal, social, and ethical issues. The book ends with my personal predictions for the future of Big Data and its impending impact on the world. When preparing this book, I debated whether these four chapters might best appear in the front of the book, to whet the reader's appetite for the more technical chapters. I eventually decided that some readers would be unfamiliar with technical language and concepts included in the final chapters, necessitating their placement near the end. Readers with a strong informatics background may enjoy the book more if they start their reading at Chapter 12.

Readers may notice that many of the case examples described in this book come from the field of medical informatics. The health care informatics field is particularly ripe for discussion because every reader is affected, on economic and personal levels, by the Big Data policies and actions emanating from the field of medicine. Aside from that, there is a rich literature on Big Data projects related to health care. As much of this literature is controversial, I thought it important to select examples that I could document, from reliable sources. Consequently, the reference section is large, with over 200 articles from journals, newspaper articles, and books. Most of these cited articles are available for free Web download.

Who should read this book? This book is written for professionals who manage Big Data resources and for students in the fields of computer science and informatics. Data management professionals would include the leadership within corporations and funding agencies who must commit resources to the project, the project directors who must determine a feasible set of goals and who must assemble a team of individuals who, in aggregate, hold the requisite skills for the task: network managers, data domain specialists, metadata specialists, software programmers, standards experts, interoperability experts, statisticians, data analysts, and representatives from the intended user community. Students of informatics, the computer sciences, and statistics will discover that the special challenges attached to Big Data, seldom discussed in university classes, are often surprising and sometimes shocking.

By mastering the fundamentals of Big Data design, maintenance, growth, and validation, readers will learn how to simplify the endless tasks engendered by Big Data resources. Adept analysts can find relationships among data objects held in disparate Big Data resources, if the data is prepared properly. Readers will discover how integrating Big Data resources can deliver benefits far beyond anything attained from stand-alone databases.

Introduction

It's the data, stupid. **Jim Gray**

Back in the mid-1960s, my high school held pep rallies before big games. At one of these rallies, the head coach of the football team walked to the center of the stage, carrying a large box of printed computer paper; each large sheet was folded flip-flop style against the next sheet, all held together by perforations. The coach announced that the athletic abilities of every member of our team had been entered into the school's computer (we were lucky enough to have our own IBM-360 mainframe). Likewise, data on our rival team had also been entered. The computer was instructed to digest all of this information and to produce the name of the team that would win the annual Thanksgiving Day showdown. The computer spewed forth the aforementioned box of computer paper; the very last output sheet revealed that we were the preordained winners. The next day, we sallied forth to yet another ignominious defeat at the hands of our long-time rivals.

Fast forward about 50 years to a conference room at the National Cancer Institute in Bethesda, Maryland. I am being briefed by a top-level science administrator. She explains that disease research has grown in scale over the past decade. The very best research initiatives are now multi-institutional and data-intensive. Funded investigators are using high-throughput molecular methods that produce mountains of data for every tissue sample in a matter of minutes. There is only one solution: we must acquire supercomputers and a staff of talented programmers who can analyze all our data and tell us what it all means!

The NIH leadership believed, much as my high school's coach believed, that if you have a really big computer and you feed it a huge amount of information then you can answer almost any question.

That day, in the conference room at NIH, circa 2003, I voiced my concerns, indicating that you cannot just throw data into a computer and expect answers to pop out. I pointed out that, historically, science has been a reductive process, moving from complex, descriptive data sets to simplified generalizations. The idea of developing an expensive supercomputer facility to work with increasing quantities of biological data, at higher and higher levels of complexity, seemed impractical and unnecessary (see Glossary item, Supercomputer). On that day, my concerns were not well received. High-performance supercomputing was a very popular topic, and still is.

Nearly a decade has gone by since the day that supercomputer-based cancer diagnosis was envisioned. The diagnostic supercomputer facility was never built. The primary diagnostic tool used in hospital laboratories is still the microscope, a tool invented circa 1590. Today, we learn from magazines and newspapers that scientists can make important diagnoses by inspecting the full sequence of the DNA that composes our genes. Nonetheless, physicians rarely order whole genome scans; nobody understands how to use the data effectively. You can find lots of computers in hospitals and medical offices, but the computers do not calculate your diagnosis. Computers in the medical workplace are largely relegated to the prosaic tasks of collecting, storing, retrieving, and delivering medical records.

Before we can take advantage of large and complex data sources, we need to think deeply about the meaning and destiny of Big Data.

DEFINITION OF BIG DATA

Big Data is defined by the three V's:

1. Volume—large amounts of data
2. Variety—the data comes in different forms, including traditional databases, images, documents, and complex records
3. Velocity—the content of the data is constantly changing, through the absorption of complementary data collections, through the introduction of previously archived data or legacy collections, and from streamed data arriving from multiple sources

It is important to distinguish Big Data from "lotsa data" or "massive data." In a Big Data Resource, all three V's must apply. It is the size, complexity, and restlessness of Big Data resources that account for the methods by which these resources are designed, operated, and analyzed.

The term "lotsa data" is often applied to enormous collections of simple-format records, for example, every observed star, its magnitude and its location; every person living in the United Stated and their telephone numbers; every cataloged living species and its phylogenetic lineage; and so on. These very large data sets are often glorified lists. Some are catalogs whose purpose is to store and retrieve information. Some "lotsa data" collections are spreadsheets (two-dimensional tables of columns and rows), mathematically equivalent to an immense matrix. For scientific purposes, it is sometimes necessary to analyze all of the data in a matrix, all at once. The analyses of enormous matrices are computationally intensive and may require the resources of a supercomputer. This kind of global analysis on large matrices is not the subject of this book.

Big Data resources are not equivalent to a large spreadsheet, and a Big Data resource is not analyzed in its totality. Big Data analysis is a multistep process whereby data is extracted, filtered, and transformed, with analysis often proceeding in a piecemeal, sometimes recursive, fashion. As you read this book, you will find that the gulf between "lotsa data" and Big Data is profound; the two subjects can seldom be discussed productively within the same venue.

BIG DATA VERSUS SMALL DATA

Big Data is not small data that has become bloated to the point that it can no longer fit on a spreadsheet, nor is it a database that happens to be very large. Nonetheless, some professionals who customarily work with relatively small data sets harbor the false impression that they can apply their spreadsheet and database skills directly to Big Data resources without mastering new skills and without adjusting to new analytic paradigms. As they see things, when the data gets bigger, only the computer must adjust (by getting faster, acquiring more volatile memory, and increasing its storage capabilities); Big Data poses no special problems that a supercomputer could not solve.

This attitude, which seems to be prevalent among database managers, programmers, and statisticians, is highly counterproductive. It leads to slow and ineffective software, huge investment losses, bad analyses, and the production of useless and irreversibly defective Big Data resources.

Let us look at a few of the general differences that can help distinguish Big Data and small data.

1. Goals

   small data—Usually designed to answer a specific question or serve a particular goal.

   Big Data—Usually designed with a goal in mind, but the goal is flexible and the questions posed are protean. Here is a short, imaginary funding announcement for Big Data grants designed "to combine high-quality data from fisheries, Coast Guard, commercial shipping, and coastal management agencies for a growing data collection that can be used to support a variety of governmental and commercial management studies in the lower peninsula." In this fictitious case, there is a vague goal, but it is obvious that there really is no way to completely specify what the Big Data resource will contain and how the various types of data held in the resource will be organized, connected to other data resources, or usefully analyzed. Nobody can specify, with any degree of confidence, the ultimate destiny of any Big Data project; it usually comes as a surprise.

2. Location

   small data—Typically, small data is contained within one institution, often on one computer, sometimes in one file.

   Big Data—Typically spread throughout electronic space, typically parceled onto multiple Internet servers, located anywhere on earth.

3. Data structure and content

   small data—Ordinarily contains highly structured data. The data domain is restricted to a single discipline or subdiscipline. The data often comes in the form of uniform records in an ordered spreadsheet.

   Big Data—Must be capable of absorbing unstructured data (e.g., such as free-text documents, images, motion pictures, sound recordings, physical objects). The subject matter of the resource may cross multiple disciplines, and the individual data objects in the resource may link to data contained in other, seemingly unrelated, Big Data resources.

4. Data preparation

   small data—In many cases, the data user prepares her own data, for her own purposes.

   Big Data—The data comes from many diverse sources, and it is prepared by many people. People who use the data are seldom the people who have prepared the data.

5. Longevity

   small data—When the data project ends, the data is kept for a limited time (seldom longer than 7 years, the traditional academic life span for research data) and then discarded.

   Big Data—Big Data projects typically contain data that must be stored in perpetuity. Ideally, data stored in a Big Data resource will be absorbed into another resource when the original resource terminates. Many Big Data projects extend into the future and the past (e.g., legacy data), accruing data prospectively and retrospectively.

6. Measurements

   small data—Typically, the data is measured using one experimental protocol, and the data can be represented using one set of standard units (see Glossary item, Protocol).

   Big Data—Many different types of data are delivered in many different electronic formats. Measurements, when present, may be obtained by many different protocols. Verifying the quality of Big Data is one of the most difficult tasks for data managers.

7. Reproducibility
   small data—Projects are typically repeatable. If there is some question about the quality of the data, reproducibility of the data, or validity of the conclusions drawn from the data, the entire project can be repeated, yielding a new data set.
   Big Data—Replication of a Big Data project is seldom feasible. In most instances, all that anyone can hope for is that bad data in a Big Data resource will be found and flagged as such.

8. Stakes
   small data—Project costs are limited. Laboratories and institutions can usually recover from the occasional small data failure.
   Big Data—Big Data projects can be obscenely expensive. A failed Big Data effort can lead to bankruptcy, institutional collapse, mass firings, and the sudden disintegration of all the data held in the resource. As an example, an NIH Big Data project known as the "NCI cancer Biomedical Informatics Grid" cost at least $350 million for fiscal years 2004 to 2010 (see Glossary item, Grid). An ad hoc committee reviewing the resource found that despite the intense efforts of hundreds of cancer researchers and information specialists, it had accomplished so little and at so great an expense that a project moratorium was called.[3] Soon thereafter, the resource was terminated.[4] Though the costs of failure can be high in terms of money, time, and labor, Big Data failures may have some redeeming value. Each failed effort lives on as intellectual remnants consumed by the next Big Data effort.

9. Introspection
   small data—Individual data points are identified by their row and column location within a spreadsheet or database table (see Glossary item, Data point). If you know the row and column headers, you can find and specify all of the data points contained within.
   Big Data—Unless the Big Data resource is exceptionally well designed, the contents and organization of the resource can be inscrutable, even to the data managers (see Glossary item, Data manager). Complete access to data, information about the data values, and information about the organization of the data is achieved through a technique herein referred to as introspection (see Glossary item, Introspection).

10. Analysis
    small data—In most instances, all of the data contained in the data project can be analyzed together, and all at once.
    Big Data—With few exceptions, such as those conducted on supercomputers or in parallel on multiple computers, Big Data is ordinarily analyzed in incremental steps (see Glossary items, Parallel computing, MapReduce). The data are extracted, reviewed, reduced, normalized, transformed, visualized, interpreted, and reanalyzed with different methods.

WHENCE COMEST BIG DATA?

Often, the impetus for Big Data is entirely ad hoc. Companies and agencies are forced to store and retrieve huge amounts of collected data (whether they want to or not).

Generally, Big Data come into existence through any of several different mechanisms.

1. An entity has collected a lot of data, in the course of its normal activities, and seeks to organize the data so that materials can be retrieved, as needed. The Big Data effort is intended to streamline the regular activities of the entity. In this case, the data is just waiting to be used. The entity is not looking to discover anything or to do anything new. It simply wants to use the data to do what it has always been doing—only better. The typical medical center is a good example of an "accidental" Big Data resource. The day-to-day activities of caring for patients and recording data into hospital information systems results in terabytes of collected data in forms such as laboratory reports, pharmacy orders, clinical encounters, and billing data. Most of this information is generated for a one-time specific use (e.g., supporting a clinical decision, collecting payment for a procedure). It occurs to the administrative staff that the collected data can be used, in its totality, to achieve mandated goals: improving quality of service, increasing staff efficiency, and reducing operational costs.

2. An entity has collected a lot of data in the course of its normal activities and decides that there are many new activities that could be supported by their data. Consider modern corporations—these entities do not restrict themselves to one manufacturing process or one target audience. They are constantly looking for new opportunities. Their collected data may enable them to develop new products based on the preferences of their loyal customers, to reach new markets, or to market and distribute items via the Web. These entities will become hybrid Big Data/manufacturing enterprises.

3. An entity plans a business model based on a Big Data resource. Unlike the previous entities, this entity starts with Big Data and adds a physical component secondarily. Amazon and FedEx may fall into this category, as they began with a plan for providing a data-intense service (e.g., the Amazon Web catalog and the FedEx package-tracking system). The traditional tasks of warehousing, inventory, pickup, and delivery had been available all along, but lacked the novelty and efficiency afforded by Big Data.

4. An entity is part of a group of entities that have large data resources, all of whom understand that it would be to their mutual advantage to federate their data resources.[5] An example of a federated Big Data resource would be hospital databases that share electronic medical health records.[6]

5. An entity with skills and vision develops a project wherein large amounts of data are collected and organized to the benefit of themselves and their user-clients. Google, and its many services, is an example (see Glossary items, Page rank, Object rank).

6. An entity has no data and has no particular expertise in Big Data technologies, but it has money and vision. The entity seeks to fund and coordinate a group of data creators and data holders who will build a Big Data resource that can be used by others. Government agencies have been the major benefactors. These Big Data projects are justified if they lead to important discoveries that could not be attained at a lesser cost, with smaller data resources.

THE MOST COMMON PURPOSE OF BIG DATA IS TO PRODUCE SMALL DATA

If I had known what it would be like to have it all, I might have been willing to settle for less. Lily Tomlin

Imagine using a restaurant locater on your smartphone. With a few taps, it lists the Italian restaurants located within a 10 block radius of your current location. The database being queried is big and complex (a map database, a collection of all the restaurants in the world, their longitudes and latitudes, their street addresses, and a set of ratings provided by patrons, updated continuously), but the data that it yields is small (e.g., five restaurants, marked on a street map, with pop-ups indicating their exact address, telephone number, and ratings). Your task comes down to selecting one restaurant from among the five and dining thereat.

In this example, your data selection was drawn from a large data set, but your ultimate analysis was confined to a small data set (i.e., five restaurants meeting your search criteria). The purpose of the Big Data resource was to proffer the small data set. No analytic work was performed on the Big Data resource—just search and retrieval. The real labor of the Big Data resource involved collecting and organizing complex data so that the resource would be ready for your query. Along the way, the data creators had many decisions to make (e.g., Should bars be counted as restaurants? What about take-away only shops? What data should be collected? How should missing data be handled? How will data be kept current?).

Big Data is seldom, if ever, analyzed in toto. There is almost always a drastic filtering process that reduces Big Data into smaller data. This rule applies to scientific analyses.

The Australian Square Kilometre Array of radio telescopes,[7] WorldWide Telescope, CERN's Large Hadron Collider, and the Panoramic Survey Telescope and Rapid Response System array of telescopes produce petabytes of data every day (see Glossary items, Square Kilometer Array, Large Hadron Collider, WorldWide Telescope). Researchers use these raw data sources to produce much smaller data sets for analysis.[8]

Here is an example showing how workable subsets of data are prepared from Big Data resources. Blazars are rare supermassive black holes that release jets of energy moving at near-light speeds. Cosmologists want to know as much as they can about these strange objects. A first step to studying blazars is to locate as many of these objects as possible. Afterward, various measurements on all of the collected blazars can be compared and their general characteristics can be determined. Blazars seem to have a gamma ray signature not present in other celestial objects. The Wide-field Infrared Survey Explorer (WISE) collected infrared data on the entire observable universe. Researchers extracted from the WISE data every celestial body associated with an infrared signature in the gamma ray range that was suggestive of blazars—about 300 objects. Further research on these 300 objects led researchers to believe that about half were blazars (about 150).[9] This is how Big Data research typically works—by constructing small data sets that can be productively analyzed.

OPPORTUNITIES

Make no mistake. Despite the obstacles and the risks, the potential value of Big Data is inestimable. A hint at future gains from Big Data comes from the National Science

Foundations (NSF) 2012 solicitation for grants in core techniques for Big Data (BIGDATA NSF12499). The NSF aims to

> advance the core scientific and technological means of managing, analyzing, visualizing, and extracting useful information from large, diverse, distributed and heterogeneous data sets so as to: accelerate the progress of scientific discovery and innovation; lead to new fields of inquiry that would not otherwise be possible; encourage the development of new data analytic tools and algorithms; facilitate scalable, accessible, and sustainable data infrastructure; increase understanding of human and social processes and interactions; and promote economic growth and improved health and quality of life. The new knowledge, tools, practices, and infrastructures produced will enable breakthrough discoveries and innovation in science, engineering, medicine, commerce, education, and national security.[10]

The NSF envisions a Big Data future with the following pay-offs:

> Responses to disaster recovery empower rescue workers and individuals to make timely and effective decisions and provide resources where they are most needed;
> Complete health/disease/genome/environmental knowledge bases enable biomedical discovery and patient-centered therapy; the full complement of health and medical information is available at the point of care for clinical decision-making;
> Accurate high-resolution models support forecasting and management of increasingly stressed watersheds and eco-systems;
> Access to data and software in an easy-to-use format are available to everyone around the globe;
> Consumers can purchase wearable products using materials with novel and unique properties that prevent injuries;
> The transition to use of sustainable chemistry and manufacturing materials has been accelerated to the point that the US leads in advanced manufacturing;
> Consumers have the information they need to make optimal energy consumption decisions in their homes and cars;

> Civil engineers can continuously monitor and identify at-risk man-made structures like bridges, moderate the impact of failures, and avoid disaster;
> Students and researchers have intuitive real-time tools to view, understand, and learn from publicly available large scientific data sets on everything from genome sequences to astronomical star surveys, from public health databases to particle accelerator simulations and their teachers and professors use student performance analytics to improve that learning; and
> Accurate predictions of natural disasters, such as earthquakes, hurricanes, and tornadoes, enable life-saving and cost-saving preventative actions.[10]

Many of these hopes for the future may come true if we manage our Big Data resources wisely.

BIG DATA MOVES TO THE CENTER OF THE INFORMATION UNIVERSE

> Physics is the universe's operating system.
> *Steven R. Garman*

In prior times, scientists followed a well-trodden path towards truth: hypothesis, then experiment, then data, then analysis, then publication. The manner in which a scientist analyzed his or her data was crucial because other scientists would not have access to the same data and could not reanalyze the data for themselves. Basically, the final manuscript was the scientific product. Scientific knowledge was built on trust.

In the Big data paradigm, the concept of a final manuscript has little meaning. Big Data resources are permanent, and the data within the resource is immutable (see Chapter 6). Any scientist's analysis of the data does not need to be the final word; another scientist can access and reanalyze the same data over and over again.

On September 3, 1976, the Viking Lander 2 landed on the planet Mars, where it remained operational for the next 3 years, 7 months, and 8 days. Soon after landing, it performed an interesting remote-controlled experiment. Using samples of Martian dirt, astrobiologists measured the conversion of radioactively labeled precursors into more complex carbon-based molecules—the so-called Labeled-Release study. For this study, control samples of dirt were heated to a high temperature (i.e., sterilized) and likewise exposed to radioactively labeled precursors, without producing complex carbon-containing molecules. The tentative conclusion, published soon thereafter, was that Martian organisms in the samples of dirt had built carbon-based molecules through a metabolic pathway.[11] As you might expect, the conclusion was immediately challenged and remains controversial, to this day, nearly 32 years later.

How is the Viking Lander experiment of any relevance to the topic of Big Data? In the years since 1976, long after the initial paper was published, the data from the Labeled-Release study has been available to scientists for reanalysis. New analytic techniques have been applied to the data, and new interpretations have been published.[11] As additional missions have reached Mars, more data has emerged (i.e., the detection of water and methane), also supporting the conclusion that there is life on Mars. None of the data is conclusive; Martian organisms have not been isolated. The point made here is that the Labeled-Release data is accessible and permanent and can be studied again and again, compared or combined with new data, and argued ad nauseum.

Today, hundreds or thousands of individuals might contribute to a Big Data resource. The data in the resource might inspire dozens of major scientific projects, hundreds of manuscripts, thousands of analytic efforts, or billions of search and retrieval operations. The Big Data resource has become the central, massive object around which universities, research laboratories, corporations, and federal agencies orbit. These orbiting objects draw information from the Big Data resource, and they use the information to support analytic studies and to publish manuscripts. Because Big Data resources are permanent, any analysis can be critically examined, with the same set of data, or reanalyzed anytime in the future. Because Big Data resources are constantly growing forward in time (i.e., accruing new information) and backward in time (i.e., absorbing legacy data sets), the value of the data is constantly increasing.

Big Data resources are the stars of the modern information universe. All matter in the physical universe comes from heavy elements created inside stars, from lighter elements. All data in the informational universe is complex data built from simple data. Just as stars can exhaust themselves, explode, or even collapse under their own weight to become black holes, Big Data resources can lose funding and die, release their contents and burst into nothingness, or collapse under their own weight, sucking everything around them into a dark void. It's an interesting metaphor. The following chapters show how a Big Data resource can be designed and operated to ensure stability, utility, growth, and permanence; features you might expect to find in a massive object located in the center of the information universe.

CHAPTER

1

Providing Structure to Unstructured Data

I was working on the proof of one of my poems all the morning, and took out a comma. In the afternoon I put it back again. **Oscar Wilde**

BACKGROUND

In the early days of computing, data was always highly structured. All data was divided into fields, the fields had a fixed length, and the data entered into each field was constrained to a predetermined set of allowed values. Data was entered into punch cards, with preconfigured rows and columns. Depending on the intended use of the cards, various entry and read-out methods were chosen to express binary data, numeric data, fixed-size text, or programming instructions (see Glossary item, Binary data). Key-punch operators produced mountains of punch cards. For many analytic purposes, card-encoded data sets were analyzed without the assistance of a computer; all that was needed was a punch card sorter. If you wanted the data card on all males, over the age of 18, who had graduated high school, and had passed their physical exam, then the sorter would need to make four passes. The sorter would pull every card listing a male, then from the male cards it would pull all the cards of people over the age of 18, and from this double-sorted substack it would pull cards that met the next criterion, and so on. As a high school student in the 1960s, I loved playing with the card sorters. Back then, all data was structured data, and it seemed to me, at the time, that a punch-card sorter was all that anyone would ever need to analyze large sets of data.

Of course, I was completely wrong. Today, most data entered by humans is unstructured, in the form of free text. The free text comes in e-mail messages, tweets, documents, and so on. Structured data has not disappeared, but it sits in the shadows cast by mountains of unstructured text. Free text may be more interesting to read than punch cards, but the venerable punch card, in its heyday, was much easier to analyze than its free-text descendant. To get much informational value from free text, it is necessary to impose some structure. This may involve translating the text to a preferred language, parsing the text into sentences, extracting and normalizing the conceptual terms contained in the sentences, mapping terms to a standard nomenclature (see Glossary items, Nomenclature, Thesaurus), annotating the terms with codes from one or more standard nomenclatures, extracting and standardizing data values from the text, assigning data values to specific classes of data belonging to a classification system, assigning the classified data to a storage and retrieval system (e.g., a database), and indexing the data in the system. All of these activities are difficult to do on a small scale and virtually impossible to do on a large scale. Nonetheless, every Big Data project that uses unstructured data must deal with these tasks to yield the best possible results with the resources available.

MACHINE TRANSLATION

The purpose of narrative is to present us with complexity and ambiguity. *Scott Turow*

The term unstructured data refers to data objects whose contents are not organized into arrays of attributes or values (see Glossary item, Data object). Spreadsheets, with data distributed in cells, marked by a row and column position, are examples of structured data. This paragraph is an example of unstructured data. You can see why data analysts prefer spreadsheets over free text. Without structure, the contents of the data cannot be sensibly collected and analyzed. Because Big Data is immense, the tasks of imposing structure on text must be automated and fast.

Machine translation is one of the better known areas in which computational methods have been applied to free text. Ultimately, the job of machine translation is to translate text from one language into another language. The process of machine translation begins with extracting sentences from text, parsing the words of the sentence into grammatic parts, and arranging the grammatic parts into an order that imposes logical sense on the sentence. Once this is done, each of the parts can be translated by a dictionary that finds equivalent terms in a foreign language to be reassembled by applying grammatic positioning rules appropriate for the target language. Because this process uses the natural rules for sentence constructions in a foreign language, the process is often referred to as natural language machine translation.

It all seems simple and straightforward. In a sense, it is—if you have the proper look-up tables. Relatively good automatic translators are now widely available. The drawback of all these applications is that there are many instances where they fail utterly. Complex sentences, as you might expect, are problematic. Beyond the complexity of the sentences are other problems, deeper problems that touch upon the dirtiest secret common to all human languages— languages do not make much sense. Computers cannot find meaning in sentences that have no meaning. If we, as humans, find meaning in the English language, it is only because we impose our own cultural prejudices onto the sentences we read, to create meaning where none exists.

It is worthwhile to spend a few moments on some of the inherent limitations of English. Our words are polymorphous; their meanings change depending on the context in which they occur. Word polymorphism can be used for comic effect (e.g., "Both the martini and the bar patron were drunk"). As humans steeped in the culture of our language, we effortlessly invent the intended meaning of each polymorphic pair in the following examples: "a bandage wound around a wound," "farming to produce produce," "please present the present in the present time," "don't object to the data object," "teaching a sow to sow seed," "wind the sail before the wind comes," and countless others.

Words lack compositionality; their meaning cannot be deduced by analyzing root parts. For example, there is neither pine nor apple in pineapple, no egg in eggplant, and hamburgers are made from beef, not ham. You can assume that a lover will love, but you cannot assume that a finger will "fing." Vegetarians will eat vegetables, but humanitarians will not eat humans. Overlook and oversee should, logically, be synonyms, but they are antonyms.

For many words, their meanings are determined by the case of the first letter of the word. For example, Nice and nice, Polish and polish, Herb and herb, August and august.

It is possible, given enough effort, that a machine translator may cope with all the aforementioned impedimenta. Nonetheless, no computer can create meaning out of ambiguous gibberish, and a sizable portion of written language has no meaning, in the informatics sense (see Glossary item, Meaning). As someone who has dabbled in writing machine translation tools, my favorite gripe relates to the common use of reification—the process whereby the subject of a sentence is inferred, without actually being named (see Glossary item, Reification). Reification is accomplished with pronouns and other subject references.

Here is an example, taken from a newspaper headline: "Husband named person of interest in slaying of mother." First off, we must infer that it is the husband who was named as the person of interest, not that the husband suggested the name of the person of interest. As anyone who follows crime headlines knows, this sentence refers to a family consisting of a husband, wife, and at least one child. There is a wife because there is a husband. There is a child because there is a mother. The reader is expected to infer that the mother is the mother of the husband's child, not the mother of the husband. The mother and the wife are the same person. Putting it all together, the husband and wife are father and mother, respectively, to the child. The sentence conveys the news that the husband is a suspect in the slaying of his wife, the mother of the child. The word "husband" reifies the existence of a wife (i.e., creates a wife by implication from the husband–wife relationship). The word "mother" reifies a child. Nowhere is any individual husband or mother identified; it's all done with pointers pointing to other pointers. The sentence is all but meaningless; any meaning extracted from the sentence comes as a creation of our vivid imaginations.

Occasionally, a sentence contains a reification of a group of people, and the reification contributes absolutely nothing to the meaning of the sentence. For example, "John married aunt Sally." Here, a familial relationship is established ("aunt") for Sally, but the relationship does not extend to the only other person mentioned in the sentence (i.e., Sally is not John's aunt). Instead, the word "aunt" reifies a group of individuals; specifically, the group of people who have Sally as their aunt. The reification seems to serve no purpose other than to confuse.

Here is another example, taken from a newspaper article: "After her husband disappeared on a 1944 recon mission over Southern France, Antoine de Saint-Exupery's widow sat down and wrote this memoir of their dramatic marriage." There are two reified persons in the sentence: "her husband" and "Antoine de Saint-Exupery's widow." In the first phrase, "her husband" is a relationship (i.e., "husband") established for a pronoun (i.e., "her") referenced to the person in the second phrase. The person in the second phrase is reified by a relationship to Saint-Exupery (i.e., "widow"), who just happens to be the reification of the person in the first phrase (i.e., "Saint-Exupery is her husband").

We write self-referential reifying sentences every time we use a pronoun: "It was then that he did it for them." The first "it" reifies an event, the word "then" reifies a time, the word "he" reifies a subject, the second "it" reifies some action, and the word "them" reifies a group of individuals representing the recipients of the reified action.

Strictly speaking, all of these examples are meaningless. The subjects of the sentence are not properly identified and the references to the subjects are ambiguous. Such sentences cannot be sensibly evaluated by computers.

A final example is "Do you know who I am?" There are no identifiable individuals; everyone is reified and reduced to an unspecified pronoun ("you," "I"). Though there are just a few words in the sentence, half of them are superfluous. The words "Do," "who," and "am" are merely fluff, with no informational purpose. In an object-oriented world, the question would be transformed into an assertion, "You know me," and the assertion would be sent a query message, "true?" (see Glossary item, Object-oriented programming). We are jumping ahead. Objects, assertions, and query messages will be discussed in later chapters.

Accurate machine translation is beyond being difficult. It is simply impossible. It is impossible because computers cannot understand nonsense. The best we can hope for is a translation that allows the reader to impose the same subjective interpretation of the text in the translation language as he or she would have made in the original language. The expectation that sentences can be reliably parsed into informational units is fantasy. Nonetheless, it is possible to compose meaningful sentences in any language, if you have a deep understanding of informational meaning. This topic will be addressed in Chapter 4.

AUTOCODING

The beginning of wisdom is to call things by their right names. *Chinese proverb*

Coding, as used in the context of unstructured textual data, is the process of tagging terms with an identifier code that corresponds to a synonymous term listed in a standard nomenclature (see Glossary item, Identifier). For example, a medical nomenclature might contain the term renal cell carcinoma, a type of kidney cancer, attaching a unique identifier code for the term, such as "C9385000." There are about 50 recognized synonyms for "renal cell carcinoma." A few of these synonyms and near-synonyms are listed here to show that a single concept can be expressed many different ways, including adenocarcinoma arising from kidney, adenocarcinoma involving kidney, cancer arising from kidney, carcinoma of kidney,

Grawitz tumor, Grawitz tumour, hypernephroid tumor, hypernephroma, kidney adenocarcinoma, renal adenocarcinoma, and renal cell carcinoma. All of these terms could be assigned the same identifier code, "C9385000."

The process of coding a text document involves finding all the terms that belong to a specific nomenclature and tagging the term with the corresponding identifier code.

A nomenclature is a specialized vocabulary, usually containing terms that comprehensively cover a well-defined and circumscribed area (see Glossary item, Vocabulary). For example, there may be a nomenclature of diseases, or celestial bodies, or makes and models of automobiles. Some nomenclatures are ordered alphabetically. Others are ordered by synonymy, wherein all synonyms and plesionyms (near-synonyms, see Glossary item, Plesionymy) are collected under a canonical (i.e., best or preferred) term. Synonym indexes are always corrupted by the inclusion of polysemous terms (i.e., terms with multiple meanings; see Glossary item, Polysemy). In many nomenclatures, grouped synonyms are collected under a code (i.e., a unique alphanumeric string) assigned to all of the terms in the group (see Glossary items, Uniqueness, String). Nomenclatures have many purposes: to enhance interoperability and integration, to allow synonymous terms to be retrieved regardless of which specific synonym is entered as a query, to support comprehensive analyses of textual data, to express detail, to tag information in textual documents, and to drive down the complexity of documents by uniting synonymous terms under a common code. Sets of documents held in more than one Big Data resource can be harmonized under a nomenclature by substituting or appending a nomenclature code to every nomenclature term that appears in any of the documents.

In the case of "renal cell carcinoma," if all of the 50+ synonymous terms, appearing anywhere in a medical text, were tagged with the code "C938500," then a search engine could retrieve documents containing this code, regardless of which specific synonym was queried (e.g., a query on Grawitz tumor would retrieve documents containing the word "hypernephroid tumor"). The search engine would simply translate the query word, "Grawitz tumor," into its nomenclature code, "C938500," and would pull every record that had been tagged by the code.

Traditionally, nomenclature coding, much like language translation, has been considered a specialized and highly detailed task that is best accomplished by human beings. Just as there are highly trained translators who will prepare foreign language versions of popular texts, there are highly trained coders, intimately familiar with specific nomenclatures, who create tagged versions of documents. Tagging documents with nomenclature codes is serious business. If the coding is flawed, the consequences can be dire. In 2009, the Department of Veterans Affairs sent out hundreds of letters to veterans with the devastating news that they had contracted amyotrophic lateral sclerosis, also known as Lou Gehrig's disease, a fatal degenerative neurologic condition. About 600 of the recipients did not, in fact, have the disease. The VA retracted these letters, attributing the confusion to a coding error.[12] Coding text is difficult. Human coders are inconsistent, idiosyncratic, and prone to error. Coding accuracy for humans seems to fall in the range of 85 to 90%[13] (see Glossary item, Accuracy and precision).

When dealing with text in gigabyte and greater quantities, human coding is simply out of the question. There is not enough time, or money, or talent to manually code the textual data contained in Big Data resources. Computerized coding (i.e., autocoding) is the only practical solution.

Autocoding is a specialized form of machine translation, the field of computer science dealing with drawing meaning from narrative text, or translating narrative text from one language to another. Not surprisingly, autocoding algorithms have been adopted directly from the field of machine translation, particularly algorithms for natural language processing (see Glossary item, Algorithm). A popular approach to autocoding involves using the natural rules of language to find words or phrases found in text, and matching them to nomenclature terms. Ideally the correct text term is matched to its equivalent nomenclature term, regardless of the way that the term is expressed in the text. For instance, the term "adenocarcinoma of lung" has much in common with alternate terms that have minor variations in word order, plurality, inclusion of articles, terms split by a word inserted for informational enrichment, and so on. Alternate forms would be "adenocarcinoma of the lung," "adenocarcinoma of the lungs," "lung adenocarcinoma," and "adenocarcinoma found in the lung." A natural language algorithm takes into account grammatic variants, allowable alternate term constructions, word roots (stemming), and syntax variation (see Glossary item, Syntax). Clever improvements on natural language methods might include string similarity scores, intended to find term equivalences in cases where grammatic methods come up short.

A limitation of the natural language approach to autocoding is encountered when synonymous terms lack etymologic commonality. Consider the term "renal cell carcinoma." Synonyms include terms that have no grammatic relationship with one another. For example, hypernephroma and Grawitz tumor are synonyms for renal cell carcinoma. It is impossible to compute the equivalents among these terms through the implementation of natural language rules or word similarity algorithms. The only way of obtaining adequate synonymy is through the use of a comprehensive nomenclature that lists every synonym for every canonical term in the knowledge domain.

Setting aside the inability to construct equivalents for synonymous terms that share no grammatic roots (e.g., renal cell carcinoma, Grawitz tumor, and hypernephroma), the best natural language autocoders are pitifully slow. The reason for the slowness relates to their algorithm, which requires the following steps, at a minimum: parsing text into sentences; parsing sentences into grammatic units, rearranging the units of the sentence into grammatically permissible combinations, expanding the combinations based on stem forms of words, allowing for singularities and pluralities of words, and matching the allowable variations against the terms listed in the nomenclature.

A good natural language autocoder parses text at about 1 kilobyte per second. This means that if an autocoder must parse and code a terabyte of textual material, it would require 1000 million seconds to execute, or about 30 years. Big Data resources typically contain many terabytes of data; thus, natural language autocoding software is unsuitable for translating Big Data resources. This being the case, what good are they?

Natural language autocoders have value when they are employed at the time of data entry. Humans type sentences at a rate far less than 1 kilobyte per second, and natural language autocoders can keep up with typists, inserting codes for terms, as they are typed. They can operate much the same way as autocorrect, autospelling, look-ahead, and other commonly available crutches intended to improve or augment the output of plodding human typists. In cases where a variant term evades capture by the natural language algorithm, an astute typist might supply the application with an equivalent (i.e., renal cell carcinoma = rcc) that can be stored by the application and applied against future inclusions of alternate forms.

It would seem that by applying the natural language parser at the moment when the data is being prepared, all of the inherent limitations of the algorithm can be overcome. This belief, popularized by developers of natural language software and perpetuated by a generation of satisfied customers, ignores two of the most important properties that must be preserved in Big Data resources: longevity and curation (see Glossary item, Curator).

Nomenclatures change over time. Synonymous terms and their codes will vary from year to year as new versions of old nomenclature are published and new nomenclatures are developed. In some cases, the textual material within the Big Data resource will need to be re-annotated using codes from nomenclatures that cover informational domains that were not anticipated when the text was originally composed.

Most of the people who work within an information-intensive society are accustomed to evanescent data; data that is forgotten when its original purpose was served. Do we really want all of our old e-mails to be preserved forever? Do we not regret our earliest blog posts, Facebook entries, and tweets? In the medical world, a code for a clinic visit, a biopsy diagnosis, or a reportable transmissible disease will be used in a matter of minutes or hours—maybe days or months. Few among us place much value on textual information preserved for years and decades. Nonetheless, it is the job of the Big Data manager to preserve resource data over years and decades. **When we have data that extends back, over decades, we can find and avoid errors that would otherwise reoccur in the present, and we can analyze trends that lead us into the future.**

To preserve its value, data must be constantly curated, adding codes that apply to currently available nomenclatures. There is no avoiding the chore—the entire corpus of textual data held in the Big Data resource needs to be recoded again and again, using modified versions of the original nomenclature or using one or more new nomenclatures. This time, an autocoding application will be required to code huge quantities of textual data (possibly terabytes), quickly. Natural language algorithms, which depend heavily on regex operations (i.e., finding word patterns in text) are too slow to do the job (see Glossary item, Regex).

A faster alternative is so-called lexical parsing. This involves parsing text, word by word, looking for exact matches between runs of words and entries in a nomenclature. When a match occurs, the words in the text that matched the nomenclature term are assigned the nomenclature code that corresponds to the matched term. Here is one possible algorithmic strategy for autocoding the sentence "Margins positive malignant melanoma." For this example, you would be using a nomenclature that lists all of the tumors that occur in humans. Let us assume that the terms "malignant melanoma" and "melanoma" are included in the nomenclature. They are both assigned the same code, for example, "Q5673013," because the people who wrote the nomenclature considered both terms to be biologically equivalent.

Let's autocode the diagnostic sentence "Margins positive malignant melanoma":

1. Begin parsing the sentence, one word at a time. The first word is "Margins." You check against the nomenclature and find no match. Save the word "margins." We'll use it in step 2.
2. You go to the second word, "positive," and find no matches in the nomenclature. You retrieve the former word "margins" and check to see if there is a two-word term, "margins positive." There is not. Save "margins" and "positive" and continue.

3. You go to the next word, "malignant." There is no match in the nomenclature. You check to determine whether the two-word term "positive malignant" and the three-word term "margins positive malignant" are in the nomenclature. They are not.
4. You go to the next word, "melanoma." You check and find that melanoma is in the nomenclature. You check against the two-word term "malignant melanoma," the three-word term "positive malignant melanoma," and the four-word term "margins positive malignant melanoma." There is a match for "malignant melanoma" but it yields the same code as the code for "melanoma."
5. The autocoder appends the code "Q5673013" to the sentence and proceeds to the next sentence, where it repeats the algorithm.

The algorithm seems like a lot of work, requiring many comparisons, but it is actually much more efficient than natural language parsing. A complete nomenclature, with each nomenclature term paired with its code, can be held in a single variable, in volatile memory (see Glossary item, Variable). Look-ups to determine whether a word or phrase is included in the nomenclature are also fast. As it happens, there are methods that will speed things along much faster than our sample algorithm. My own previously published method can process text at a rate more than 1000-fold faster than natural language methods.[14] With today's fast desktop computers, lexical autocoding can recode all of the textual data residing in most Big Data resources within a realistic time frame.

A seemingly insurmountable obstacle arises when the analyst must integrate data from two separate Big Data resources, each annotated with a different nomenclature. One possible solution involves on-the-fly coding, using whatever nomenclature suits the purposes of the analyst.

Here is a general algorithm for on-the-fly coding.[15] This algorithm starts with a query term and seeks to find every synonym for the query term, in any collection of Big Data resources, using any convenient nomenclature.

1. The analyst starts with a query term submitted by a data user. The analyst chooses a nomenclature that contains his query term, as well as the list of synonyms for the term. Any vocabulary is suitable so long as the vocabulary consists of term/code pairs, where a term and its synonyms are all paired with the same code.
2. All of the synonyms for the query term are collected together. For instance, the 2004 version of a popular medical nomenclature, the Unified Medical Language System, had 38 equivalent entries for the code C0206708, nine of which are listed here:

> C0206708 | Cervical Intraepithelial Neoplasms
> C0206708 | Cervical Intraepithelial Neoplasm
> C0206708 | Intraepithelial Neoplasm, Cervical
> C0206708 | Intraepithelial Neoplasms, Cervical
> C0206708 | Neoplasm, Cervical Intraepithelial
> C0206708 | Neoplasms, Cervical Intraepithelial
> C0206708 | Intraepithelial Neoplasia, Cervical
> C0206708 | Neoplasia, Cervical Intraepithelial
> C0206708 | Cervical Intraepithelial Neoplasia

If the analyst had chosen to search on "Cervical Intraepithelial Neoplasia," his term will be attached to the 38 synonyms included in the nomenclature.

3. One by one, the equivalent terms are matched against every record in every Big Data resource available to the analyst.

4. Records are pulled that contain terms matching any of the synonyms for the term selected by the analyst.

In the case of this example, this would mean that all 38 synonymous terms for "Cervical Intraepithelial Neoplasms" would be matched against the entire set of data records. The benefit of this kind of search is that data records that contain any search term, or its nomenclature equivalent, can be extracted from multiple data sets in multiple Big Data resources, as they are needed, in response to any query. There is no pre-coding, and there is no need to match against nomenclature terms that have no interest to the analyst. The drawback of this method is that it multiplies the computational task by the number of synonymous terms being searched, 38-fold in this example. Luckily, there are simple and fast methods for conducting these synonym searches.[15]

INDEXING

Knowledge can be public, yet undiscovered, if independently created fragments are logically related but never retrieved, brought together, and interpreted. *Donald R. Swanson*[16]

Individuals accustomed to electronic media tend to think of the Index as an inefficient or obsolete method for finding and retrieving information. Most currently available e-books have no index. It's far easier to pull up the "Find" dialog box and enter a word or phrase. The e-reader can find all matches quickly, provide the total number of matches, and bring the reader to any or all of the pages containing the selection. As more and more books are published electronically, the Index, as we have come to know it, will cease to be.

It would be a pity if indexes were to be abandoned by computer scientists. A well-designed book index is a creative, literary work that captures the content and intent of the book and transforms it into a listing wherein related concepts, found scattered throughout the text, are collected under common terms and keyed to their locations. It saddens me that many people ignore the book index until they want something from it. Open a favorite book and read the index, from A to Z, as if you were reading the body of the text. You will find that the index refreshes your understanding of the concepts discussed in the book. The range of page numbers after each term indicates that a concept has extended its relevance across many different chapters. When you browse the different entries related to a single term, you learn how the concept represented by the term applies itself to many different topics. You begin to understand, in ways that were not apparent when you read the book as a linear text, the versatility of the ideas contained in the book. When you've finished reading the index, you will notice that the indexer exercised great restraint when selecting terms. Most indexes are under 20 pages (see Glossary item, Indexes). The goal of the indexer is not to create a concordance (i.e., a listing of every word in a book, with its locations), but to create a keyed encapsulation of concepts, subconcepts, and term relationships.

The indexes we find in today's books are generally alphabetized terms. In prior decades and prior centuries, authors and editors put enormous effort into building indexes, sometimes producing multiple indexes for a single book. For example, a biography might contain a traditional alphabetized term index, followed by an alphabetized index of the names of the people included in the text. A zoology book might include an index specifically for animal names, with animals categorized according to their taxonomic order (see Glossary item, Taxonomy). A geography index might list the names of localities subindexed by country, with countries subindexed by continent. A single book might have five or more indexes. In 19th century books, it was not unusual to publish indexes as stand-alone volumes.

You may be thinking that all this fuss over indexes is quaint, but it cannot apply to Big Data resources. Actually, Big Data resources that lack a proper index cannot be utilized to their full potential. Without an index, you never know what your queries are missing. Remember, in a Big Data resource, it is the relationship among data objects that are the keys to knowledge. Data by itself, even in large quantities, tells only part of a story. The most useful Big Data resource has electronic indexes that map concepts, classes, and terms to specific locations in the resource where data items are stored. An index imposes order and simplicity on the Big Data resource. Without an index, Big Data resources can easily devolve into vast collections of disorganized information.

The best indexes comply with international standards (ISO 999) and require creativity and professionalism.[17] Indexes should be accepted as another device for driving down the complexity of Big Data resources. Here are a few of the specific strengths of an index that cannot be duplicated by "find" operations on terms entered into a query box.

1. An index can be read, like a book, to acquire a quick understanding of the contents and general organization of the data resource.
2. When you do a "find" search in a query box, your search may come up empty if there is nothing in the text that matches your query. This can be very frustrating if you know that the text covers the topic entered into the query box. Indexes avoid the problem of fruitless searches. By browsing the index you can find the term you need, without foreknowledge of its exact wording within the text.
3. Index searches are instantaneous, even when the Big Data resource is enormous. Indexes are constructed to contain the results of the search of every included term, obviating the need to repeat the computational task of searching on indexed entries.
4. Indexes can be tied to a classification. This permits the analyst to know the relationships among different topics within the index and within the text.
5. Many indexes are cross-indexed, providing relationships among index terms that might be extremely helpful to the data analyst.
6. Indexes from multiple Big Data resources can be merged. When the location entries for index terms are annotated with the name of the resource, then merging indexes is trivial, and index searches will yield unambiguously identified locators in any of the Big Data resources included in the merge.
7. Indexes can be created to satisfy a particular goal, and the process of creating a made-to-order index can be repeated again and again. For example, if you have a Big Data resource devoted to ornithology, and you have an interest in the geographic location of species, you might want to create an index specifically keyed to localities, or you might want to add a locality subentry for every indexed bird name in your original index. Such indexes can be constructed as add-ons, as needed.

8. Indexes can be updated. If terminology or classifications change, there is nothing stopping you from rebuilding the index with an updated specification. In the specific context of Big Data, you can update the index without modifying your data (see Chapter 6).

9. Indexes are created after the database has been created. In some cases, the data manager does not envision the full potential of the Big Data resource until after it is created. The index can be designed to facilitate the use of the resource, in line with the observed practices of users.

10. Indexes can serve as surrogates for the Big Data resource. In some cases, all the data user really needs is the index. A telephone book is an example of an index that serves its purpose without being attached to a related data source (e.g., caller logs, switching diagrams).

TERM EXTRACTION

There's a big difference between knowing the name of something and knowing something. Richard Feynman

One of my favorite movies is the parody version of "Hound of the Baskervilles," starring Peter Cooke as Sherlock Holmes and Dudley Moore as his faithful hagiographer, Dr. Watson. Sherlock, preoccupied with his own ridiculous pursuits, dispatches Watson to the Baskerville family manse, in Dartmoor, to undertake urgent sleuth-related activities. The hapless Watson (Dudley Moore), standing in the great Baskerville Hall, has no idea how to proceed with the investigation. After a moment of hesitation, he turns to the incurious maid and commands, "Take me to the clues!"

Building an index is a lot like solving a fiendish crime—you need to know how to find the clues. Likewise, the terms in the text are the clues upon which the index is built. Terms in a text file do not jump into your index file—you need to find them. There are several available methods for finding and extracting index terms from a corpus of text,[18] but no method is as simple, fast, and scalable as the "stop" word method[19] (see Glossary items, Term extraction algorithm, Scalable).

Text is composed of words and phrases that represent specific concepts that are connected together into a sequence, known as a sentence.

Consider the following: "The diagnosis is chronic viral hepatitis." This sentence contains two very specific medical concepts: "diagnosis" and "chronic viral hepatitis." These two concepts are connected to form a meaningful statement with the words "the" and "is," and the sentence delimiter, "." "The," "diagnosis," "is," "chronic viral hepatitis," "."

A term can be defined as a sequence of one or more uncommon words that are demarcated (i.e., bounded on one side or another) by the occurrence of one or more common words, such as "is," "and," "with," "the."

Here is another example: "An epidural hemorrhage can occur after a lucid interval." The medical concepts "epidural hemorrhage" and "lucid interval" are composed of uncommon words. These uncommon word sequences are bounded by sequences of common words or of sentence delimiters (i.e., a period, semicolon, question mark, or exclamation mark indicating the end of a sentence or the end of an expressed thought). "An," "epidural hemorrhage," "can occur after a," "lucid interval," "."

If we had a list of all the words that were considered common, we could write a program that extracts all the concepts found in any text of any length. The concept terms would consist of all sequences of uncommon words that are uninterrupted by common words. An algorithm for extracting terms from a sentence follows.

1. Read the first word of the sentence. If it is a common word, delete it. If it is an uncommon word, save it.
2. Read the next word. If it is a common word, delete it and place the saved word (from the prior step, if the prior step saved a word) into our list of terms found in the text. If it is an uncommon word, append it to the word we saved in step one and save the two-word term. If it is a sentence delimiter, place any saved term into our list of terms and stop the program.
3. Repeat step two.

This simple algorithm, or something much like it, is a fast and efficient method to build a collection of index terms. To use the algorithm, you must prepare or find a list of common words appropriate to the information domain of your Big Data resource. To extract terms from the National Library of Medicine's citation resource (about 20 million collected journal articles), the following list of common words is used: "about, again, all, almost, also, although, always, among, an, and, another, any, are, as, at, be, because, been, before, being, between, both, but, by, can, could, did, do, does, done, due, during, each, either, enough, especially, etc, for, found, from, further, had, has, have, having, here, how, however, i, if, in, into, is, it, its, itself, just, kg, km, made, mainly, make, may, mg, might, ml, mm, most, mostly, must, nearly, neither, no, nor, obtained, of, often, on, our, overall, perhaps, pmid, quite, rather, really, regarding, seem, seen, several, should, show, showed, shown, shows, significantly, since, so, some, such, than, that, the, their, theirs, them, then, there, therefore, these, they, this, those, through, thus, to, upon, use, used, using, various, very, was, we, were, what, when, which, while, with, within, without, would."

Such lists of common words are sometimes referred to as "stop word lists" or "barrier word lists," as they demarcate the beginnings and endings of extraction terms.

Notice that the algorithm parses through text sentence by sentence. This is a somewhat awkward method for a computer to follow, as most programming languages automatically cut text from a file line by line (i.e., breaking text at the newline terminator). A computer program has no way of knowing where a sentence begins or ends, unless the programmer finds sentences, as a program subroutine.

There are many strategies for determining where one sentence stops and another begins. The easiest method looks for the occurrence of a sentence delimiter immediately following a lowercase alphabetic letter, that precedes one or two space characters, that precede an uppercase alphabetic character.

Here is an example: "I like pizza. Pizza likes me." Between the two sentences is the sequence "a. P," which consists of a lowercase "a" followed by a period, followed by two spaces, followed by an uppercase "P". This general pattern (lowercase, period, one or two spaces, uppercase) usually signifies a sentence break. The routine fails with sentences that break at the end of a line or at the last sentence of a paragraph (i.e., where there is no intervening space). It also fails to demarcate proper sentences captured within one sentence (i.e., where a semicolon ends an expressed thought, but is not followed by an uppercase letter). It might falsely demarcate a sentence in an outline, where a lowercase letter is followed by a period, indicating a new subtopic. Nonetheless, with a few tweaks providing for exceptional types of sentences, a programmer can whip up a satisfactory subroutine that divides unstructured text into a set of sentences.

Once you have a method for extracting terms from sentences, the task of creating a true index, associating a list of locations with each term, is child's play for programmers. Basically, as you collect each term (as described above), you attach the term to the location at which it was found. This is ordinarily done by building an associative array, also called a hash or a dictionary depending on the programming language used. When a term is encountered at subsequent locations in the Big Data resource, these additional locations are simply appended to the list of locations associated with the term. After the entire Big Data resource has been parsed by your indexing program, a large associative array will contain two items for each term in the index: the name of the term and the list of locations at which the term occurs within the Big Data resource. When the associative array is displayed as a file, your index is completed! No, not really.

Using the described methods, an index can be created for any corpus of text. However, in most cases, the data manger and the data analyst will not be happy with the results. The index will contain a huge number of terms that are of little or no relevance to the data analyst. The terms in the index will be arranged alphabetically, but an alphabetic representation of the concepts in a Big Data resource does not associate like terms with like terms.

Find a book with a really good index. You will see that the indexer has taken pains to unite related terms under a single subtopic. In some cases, the terms in a subtopic will be divided into subtopics. Individual terms will be linked (cross-referenced) to related terms elsewhere in the index.

A good index, whether it is created by a human or by a computer, will be built to serve the needs of the data manager and of the data analyst. The programmer who creates the index must exercise a considerable degree of creativity, insight, and elegance. Here are just a few of the questions that should be considered when an index is created for unstructured textual information in a Big Data resource.

1. Should the index be devoted to a particular knowledge domain? You may want to create an index of names of persons, an index of geographic locations, or an index of types of transactions. Your choice depends on the intended uses of the Big Data resource.
2. Should the index be devoted to a particular nomenclature? A coded nomenclature might facilitate the construction of an index if synonymous index terms are attached to their shared nomenclature code.
3. Should the index be built upon a scaffold that consists of a classification? For example, an index prepared for biologists might be keyed to the classification of living organisms. Gene data has been indexed to a gene ontology and used as a research tool.[20]
4. In the absence of a classification, might proximity among terms be included in the index? Term associations leading to useful discoveries can sometimes be found by collecting the distances between indexed terms.[21,22] Terms that are proximate to one another (i.e., co-occurring terms) tend to have a relational correspondence. For example,

if "aniline dye industry" co-occurs often with the seemingly unrelated term "bladder cancer," then you might start to ask whether aniline dyes can cause bladder cancer.

5. Should multiple indexes be created? Specialized indexes might be created for data analysts who have varied research agendas.

6. Should the index be merged into another index? It is far easier to merge indexes than to merge Big Data resources. It is worthwhile to note that the greatest value of Big Data comes from finding relationships among disparate collections of data.

2

Identification, Deidentification, and Reidentification

Many errors, of a truth, consist merely in the application the wrong names of things. **Baruch Spinoza**

BACKGROUND

Data identification is certainly the most underappreciated and least understood Big Data issue. Measurements, annotations, properties, and classes of information have no informational meaning unless they are attached to an identifier that distinguishes one data object from all other data objects and that links together all of the information that has been or will be associated with the identified data object (see Glossary item, Annotation). The method of identification and the selection of objects and classes to be identified relates fundamentally to the organizational model of the Big Data resource. If data identification is ignored or implemented improperly, the Big Data resource cannot succeed.

This chapter will describe, in some detail, the available methods for data identification and the minimal properties of identified information (including uniqueness, exclusivity, completeness, authenticity, and harmonization). The dire consequences of inadequate identification will be discussed, along with real-world examples. Once data objects have been properly identified, they can be deidentified and, under some circumstances, reidentified (see Glossary item, Deidentification, Reidentification). The ability to deidentify data objects confers enormous advantages when issues of confidentiality, privacy, and intellectual property emerge (see Glossary items, Privacy and confidentiality, Intellectual property). The ability to reidentify deidentified data objects is required for error detection, error correction, and data validation.

A good information system is, at its heart, an identification system: a way of naming data objects so that they can be retrieved by their name and a way of distinguishing each object from every other object in the system. If data managers properly identified their data and did absolutely nothing else, they would be producing a collection of data objects with more informational value than many existing Big Data resources. Imagine this scenario. You show up for treatment in the hospital where you were born and in which you have been seen for various ailments over the past three decades. One of the following events transpires.

1. The hospital has a medical record of someone with your name, but it's not you. After much effort, they find another medical record with your name. Once again, it's the wrong person. After much time and effort, you are told that the hospital cannot produce your medical record. They deny losing your record, admitting only that they cannot retrieve the record from the information system.
2. The hospital has a medical record of someone with your name, but it's not you. Neither you nor your doctor is aware of the identity error. The doctor provides inappropriate treatment based on information that is accurate for someone else, but not for you. As a result of this error, you die, but the hospital information system survives the ordeal, with no apparent injury.
3. The hospital has your medical record. After a few minutes with your doctor, it becomes obvious to both of you that the record is missing a great deal of information, relating to tests and procedures done recently and in the distant past. Nobody can find these missing records. You ask your doctor whether your records may have been inserted into the electronic chart of another patient or of multiple patients. The doctor shrugs his or her shoulders.
4. The hospital has your medical record, but after a few moments, it becomes obvious that the record includes a variety of tests done on patients other than yourself. Some of the other patients have your name. Others have a different name. Nobody seems to understand how these records pertaining to other patients got into your chart.
5. You are informed that the hospital has changed its hospital information system and your old electronic records are no longer available. You are asked to answer a long list of questions concerning your medical history. Your answers will be added to your new medical chart. Many of the questions refer to long-forgotten events.
6. You are told that your electronic record was transferred to the hospital information system of a large multihospital system. This occurred as a consequence of a complex acquisition and merger. The hospital in which you are seeking care has not yet been deployed within the information structure of the multihospital system and has no access to your records. You are assured that your records have not been lost and will be accessible within the decade.

7. You arrive at your hospital to find that the once-proud edifice has been demolished and replaced by a shopping mall. Your electronic records are gone forever, but you console yourself with the knowledge that J.C. Penney has a 40% off sale on jewelry.

Hospital information systems are prototypical Big Data resources. Like most Big Data resources, records need to be unique, accessible, complete, uncontaminated (with records of other individuals), permanent, and confidential. This cannot be accomplished without an adequate identifier system.

FEATURES OF AN IDENTIFIER SYSTEM

An object identifier is an alphanumeric string associated with the object. For many Big Data resources, the objects that are of greatest concern to data managers are human beings. One reason for this is that many Big Data resources are built to store and retrieve information about individual humans. Another reason for the data manager's preoccupation with human identifiers relates to the paramount importance of establishing human identity, with absolute certainty (e.g., banking transactions, blood transfusions). We will see, in our discussion of immutability (see Chapter 6), that there are compelling reasons for storing all information contained in Big Data resources within data objects and providing an identifier for each data object (see Glossary items, Immutability, Mutability). Consequently, one of the most important tasks for data managers is the creation of a dependable identifier system.[23]

The properties of a good identifier system are the following:

1. *Completeness*. Every unique object in the Big Data resource must be assigned an identifier.
2. *Uniqueness*. Each identifier is a unique sequence.
3. *Exclusivity*. Each identifier is assigned to a unique object, and to no other object.
4. *Authenticity*. The objects that receive identification must be verified as the objects that they are intended to be. For example, if a young man walks into a bank and claims to be Richie Rich, then the bank must ensure that he is, in fact, who he says he is.
5. *Aggregation*. The Big Data resource must have a mechanism to aggregate all of the data that is properly associated with the identifier (i.e., to bundle all of the data that belong to the uniquely identified object). In the case of a bank, this might mean collecting all of the transactions associated with an account. In a hospital, this might mean collecting all of the data associated with a patient's identifier: clinic visit reports, medication transactions, surgical procedures, and laboratory results. If the identifier system performs properly, aggregation methods will always collect all of the data associated with an object and will never collect any data that is associated with a different object.
6. *Permanence*. The identifiers and the associated data must be permanent. In the case of a hospital system, when the patient returns to the hospital after 30 years of absence, the record system must be able to access his identifier and aggregate his data. When a patient dies, the patient's identifier must not perish.
7. *Reconciliation*. There should be a mechanism whereby the data associated with a unique, identified object in one Big Data resource can be merged with the data held in another resource, for the same unique object. This process, which requires comparison, authentication, and merging, is known as reconciliation. An example of reconciliation is

found in health record portability. When a patient visits a hospital, it may be necessary to transfer her electronic medical record from another hospital (see Glossary item, Electronic medical record). Both hospitals need a way of confirming the identity of the patient and combining the records.

8. *Immutability*. In addition to being permanent (i.e., never destroyed or lost), the identifier must never change (see Chapter 6).[24] In the event that two Big Data resources are merged, or that legacy data is merged into a Big Data resource, or that individual data objects from two different Big Data resources are merged, a single data object will be assigned two identifiers—one from each of the merging systems. In this case, the identifiers must be preserved as they are, without modification. The merged data object must be provided with annotative information specifying the origin of each identifier (i.e., clarifying which identifier came from which Big Data resource).

9. *Security*. The identifier system is vulnerable to malicious attack. A Big Data resource with an identifier system can be irreversibly corrupted if the identifiers are modified. In the case of human-based identifier systems, stolen identifiers can be used for a variety of malicious activities directed against the individuals whose records are included in the resource.

10. *Documentation and quality assurance*. A system should be in place to find and correct errors in the patient identifier system. Protocols must be written for establishing the identifier system, for assigning identifiers, for protecting the system, and for monitoring the system. Every problem and every corrective action taken must be documented and reviewed. Review procedures should determine whether the errors were corrected effectively, and measures should be taken to continually improve the identifier system. All procedures, all actions taken, and all modifications of the system should be thoroughly documented. This is a big job.

11. *Centrality*. Whether the information system belongs to a savings bank, an airline, a prison system, or a hospital, identifiers play a central role. You can think of information systems as a scaffold of identifiers to which data is attached. For example, in the case of a hospital information system, the patient identifier is the central key to which every transaction for the patient is attached.

12. *Autonomy*. An identifier system has a life of its own, independent of the data contained in the Big Data resource. The identifier system can persist, documenting and organizing existing and future data objects even if all of the data in the Big Data resource were to suddenly vanish (i.e., when all of the data contained in all of the data objects are deleted).

REGISTERED UNIQUE OBJECT IDENTIFIERS

Uniqueness is one of those concepts that everyone thoroughly understands; explanations would seem unnecessary. Actually, uniqueness in computational sciences is a somewhat different concept than uniqueness in the natural world. In computational sciences, uniqueness is achieved when a data object is associated with a unique identifier (i.e., a character string that has not been assigned to any other data object). Most of us, when we think of a data object, are probably thinking of a data record, which may consist of the name of a person followed by a list of feature values (height, weight, age, etc.) or a sample of blood followed by laboratory values (e.g., white blood cell count, red cell count, hematocrit, etc.). For computer scientists, a data object is a holder for data values (the so-called encapsulated data), descriptors of the data, and properties of the holder (i.e., the class of objects to which the instance belongs). Uniqueness is achieved when the data object is permanently bound to its own identifier sequence.

Unique objects have three properties:

1. A unique object can be distinguished from all other unique objects.
2. A unique object cannot be distinguished from itself.
3. Uniqueness may apply to collections of objects (i.e., a class of instances can be unique).

Registries are trusted services that provide unique identifiers to objects. The idea is that everyone using the object will use the identifier provided by the central registry. Unique object registries serve a very important purpose, particularly when the object identifiers are persistent. It makes sense to have a central authority for Web addresses, library acquisitions, and journal abstracts. Some organizations that issue identifiers are listed here:

DOI, Digital object identifier
PMID, PubMed identification number
LSID (Life Science Identifier)
HL7 OID (Health Level 7 Object Identifier)
DICOM (Digital Imaging and Communications in Medicine) identifiers
ISSN (International Standard Serial Numbers)
Social Security Numbers (for U.S. population)
NPI, National Provider Identifier, for physicians
Clinical Trials Protocol Registration System
Office of Human Research Protections Federal Wide Assurance number
Data Universal Numbering System (DUNS) number
International Geo Sample Number
DNS, Domain Name Service

In some cases, the registry does not provide the full identifier for data objects. The registry may provide a general identifier sequence that will apply to every data object in the resource. Individual objects within the resource are provided with a registry number and a suffix sequence, appended locally. Life Science Identifiers serve as a typical example of a registered identifier. Every LSID is composed of the following five parts: Network Identifier, root DNS name of the issuing authority, name chosen by the issuing authority, a unique object identifier assigned locally, and an optional revision identifier for versioning information.

In the issued LSID identifier, the parts are separated by a colon, as shown: urn:lsid:pdb .org:1AFT:1. This identifies the first version of the 1AFT protein in the Protein Data Bank. Here are a few LSIDs:

urn:lsid:ncbi.nlm.nih.gov:pubmed:12571434

This identifies a PubMed citation.

urn:lsid:ncbi.nlm.nig.gov:GenBank:T48601:2

This refers to the second version of an entry in GenBank.

An object identifier (OID) is a hierarchy of identifier prefixes. Successive numbers in the prefix identify the descending order of the hierarchy. Here is an example of an OID from HL7, an organization that deals with health data interchanges: 1.3.6.1.4.1.250.

Each node is separated from the successor by a dot. A sequence of finer registration details leads to the institutional code (the final node). In this case, the institution identified by the HL7 OID happens to be the University of Michigan.

The final step in creating an OID for a data object involves placing a unique identifier number at the end of the registered prefix. OID organizations leave the final step to the institutional data managers. The problem with this approach is that the final within-institution data object identifier is sometimes prepared thoughtlessly, corrupting the OID system.[25]

Here is an example. Hospitals use an OID system for identifying images—part of the DICOM (Digital Imaging and Communications in Medicine) image standard. There is a prefix consisting of a permanent, registered code for the institution and the department and a suffix consisting of a number generated for an image, as it is created.

A hospital may assign consecutive numbers to its images, appending these numbers to an OID that is unique for the institution and the department within the institution. For example, the first image created with a computed tomography (CT) scanner might be assigned an identifier consisting of the OID (the assigned code for institution and department) followed by a separator such as a hyphen, followed by "1".

In a worst-case scenario, different instruments may assign consecutive numbers to images, independently of one another. This means that the CT scanner in room A may be creating the same identifier (OID+image number) as the CT scanner in room B for images on different patients. This problem could be remedied by constraining each CT scanner to avoid using numbers assigned by any other CT scanner. This remedy can be defeated if there is a glitch anywhere in the system that accounts for image assignments (e.g., if the counters are reset, broken, replaced, or simply ignored).

When image counting is done properly and the scanners are constrained to assign unique numbers (not previously assigned by other scanners in the same institution), each image may indeed have a unique identifier (OID prefix + image number suffix). Nonetheless, the use of consecutive numbers for images will create havoc, over time. Problems arise when the image service is assigned to another department in the institution, when departments merge, or when institutions merge. Each of these shifts produces a change in the OID (the institutional and departmental prefix) assigned to the identifier. If a consecutive numbering system is used, then you can expect to create duplicate identifiers if institutional prefixes are replaced after the merge. The old records in both of the merging institutions will be assigned the same prefix and will contain replicate (consecutively numbered) suffixes (e.g., image 1, image 2, etc.).

Yet another problem may occur if one unique object is provided with multiple different unique identifiers. A software application may be designed to ignore any previously assigned unique identifier, and to generate its own identifier, using its own assignment method. Doing so provides software vendors with a strategy that insulates them from bad identifiers created by their competitor's software and potentially nails the customer to their own software (and identifiers).

In the end, the OID systems provide a good set of identifiers for the institution, but the data objects created within the institution need to have their own identifier systems. Here is the HL7 statement on replicate OIDs: "Though HL7 shall exercise diligence before assigning an OID in the HL7 branch to third parties, given the lack of a global OID registry mechanism, one cannot make absolutely certain that there is no preexisting OID assignment for such third-party entity." [26]

There are occasions when it is impractical to obtain unique identifiers from a central registry. This is certainly the case for ephemeral transaction identifiers such as the tracking codes that follow a blood sample accessioned into a clinical laboratory.

The Network Working Group has issued a protocol for a Universally Unique IDentifier (UUID, also known as GUID, see Glossary item, UUID) that does not require a central registrar. A UUID is 128 bits long and reserves 60 bits for a string computed directly from a computer time stamp.[27] UUIDs, if implemented properly, should provide uniqueness across space and time. UUIDs were originally used in the Apollo Network Computing System and were later adopted in the Open Software Foundation's Distributed Computing Environment. Many computer languages (including Perl, Python, and Ruby) have built-in routines for generating UUIDs.[19]

There are enormous advantages to an identifier system that uses a long random number sequence, coupled to a time stamp. Suppose your system consists of a random sequence of 20 characters followed by a time stamp. For a time stamp, we will use the so-called Unix epoch time. This is the number of seconds that have elapsed since midnight, January 1, 1970. An example of an epoch time occurring on July 21, 2012, is 1342883791.

A unique identifier could be produced using a random character generator and an epoch time measurement, both of which are easily available routines built into most programming languages. Here is an example of such an identifier: mje03jdf8ctsSdkTEWfk-1342883791.

The characters in the random sequence can be uppercase or lowercase letters, roman numerals, or any standard keyboard characters. These comprise about 128 characters, the so-called seven-bit ASCII characters (see Glossary item, ASCII). The chance of two selected 20-character random sequences being identical is 128 to the -20 power. When we attach a time stamp to the random sequence, we place the added burden that the two sequences have the same random number prefix and that the two identifiers were created at the same moment in time (see Glossary item, Time stamp).

A system that assigns identifiers using a long, randomly selected sequence followed by a time-stamp sequence can be used without worrying that two different objects will be assigned the same identifier.

Hypothetically, though, suppose you are working in a Big Data resource that creates trillions of identifiers every second. In all those trillions of data objects, might there not be a duplication of identifiers that might someday occur? Probably not, but if that is a concern for the data manager, there is a solution. Let's assume that there are Big Data resources that are capable of assigning trillions of identifiers every single second that the resource operates. For each second that the resource operates, the data manager keeps a list of the new identifiers that are being created. As each new identifier is created, the list is checked to ensure that the new identifier has not already been assigned. In the nearly impossible circumstance that a duplicate exists, the system halts production for a fraction of a second, at which time a new epoch time sequence has been established and the identifier conflict resolves itself.

Suppose two Big Data resources are being merged. What do you do if there are replications of assigned identifiers in the two resources? Again, the chances of identifier collisions are so remote that it would be reasonable to ignore the possibility. The faithfully obsessive data manager may select to compare identifiers prior to the merge. In the exceedingly unlikely event that there is a match, the replicate identifiers would require some sort of annotation describing the situation.

It is technically feasible to create an identifier system that guarantees uniqueness (i.e., no replicate identifiers in the system). Readers should keep in mind that uniqueness is just 1 of 12 design requirements for a good identifier system.

REALLY BAD IDENTIFIER METHODS

I always wanted to be somebody, but now I realize I should have been more specific. *Lily Tomlin*

Names are poor identifiers. Aside from the obvious fact that they are not unique (e.g., surnames such as Smith, Zhang, Garcia, Lo, and given names such as John and Susan), a single name can have many different representations. The sources for these variations are many. Here is a partial listing.

1. Modifiers to the surname (du Bois, DuBois, Du Bois, Dubois, Laplace, La Place, van de Wilde, Van DeWilde, etc.).
2. Accents that may or may not be transcribed onto records (e.g., acute accent, cedilla, diacritical comma, palatalized mark, hyphen, diphthong, umlaut, circumflex, and a host of obscure markings).
3. Special typographic characters (the combined "æ").
4. Multiple "middle names" for an individual that may not be transcribed onto records, for example, individuals who replace their first name with their middle name for common usage while retaining the first name for legal documents.
5. Latinized and other versions of a single name (Carl Linnaeus, Carl von Linne, Carolus Linnaeus, Carolus a Linne).
6. Hyphenated names that are confused with first and middle names (e.g., Jean-Jacques Rousseau or Jean Jacques Rousseau; Louis-Victor-Pierre-Raymond, 7th duc de Broglie, or Louis Victor Pierre Raymond Seventh duc deBroglie).
7. Cultural variations in name order that are mistakenly rearranged when transcribed onto records. Many cultures do not adhere to the western European name order (e.g., given name, middle name, surname).
8. Name changes, through legal action, aliasing, pseudonymous posing, or insouciant whim.

Aside from the obvious consequences of using names as record identifiers (e.g., corrupt database records, impossible merges between data resources, impossibility of reconciling legacy record), there are nonobvious consequences that are worth considering. Take, for example, accented characters in names. These word decorations wreak havoc on orthography and on alphabetization. Where do you put a name that contains an umlauted character? Do you pretend the umlaut isn't there and put it in alphabetic order with the plain characters? Do you order based on the ASCII-numeric assignment for the character, in which the umlauted letter may appear nowhere near the plain-lettered words in an alphabetized list? The same problem applies to every special character.

A similar problem exists for surnames with modifiers. Do you alphabetize de Broglie under "D," under "d," or "B?" If you choose B, then what do you do with the concatenated form of the name, "deBroglie?"

When it comes down to it, it is impossible to satisfactorily alphabetize a list of names. This means that searches based on proximity in the alphabet will always be prone to errors.

I have had numerous conversations with intelligent professionals who are tasked with the responsibility of assigning identifiers to individuals. At some point in every conversation, they will find it necessary to explain that although an individual's name cannot serve as an identifier, the combination of name plus date of birth provides accurate identification in almost every instance. They sometimes get carried away, insisting that the combination of name plus date of birth plus social security number provides perfect identification, as no two people will share all three identifiers: same name, same date of birth, and same social security number. This argument rises to the height of folly and completely misses the point of identification. As we will see, it is relatively easy to assign unique identifiers to individuals and to any data object, for that matter. For managers of Big Data resources, the larger problem is ensuring that each unique individual has only one identifier (i.e., denying one object multiple identifiers).

Let us see what happens when we create identifiers from the name plus birthdate. We will examine name + birthdate + social security number later in this section.

Consider this example. Mary Jessica Meagher, born June 7, 1912, decided to open a separate bank account in each of 10 different banks. Some of the banks had application forms, which she filled out accurately. Other banks registered her account through a teller, who asked her a series of questions and immediately transcribed her answers directly into a computer terminal. Ms. Meagher could not see the computer screen and could not review the entries for accuracy.

Here are the entries for her name plus date of birth:

1. Marie Jessica Meagher, June 7, 1912 (the teller mistook Marie for Mary).
2. Mary J. Meagher, June 7, 1912 (the form requested a middle initial, not name).
3. Mary Jessica Magher, June 7, 1912 (the teller misspelled the surname).
4. Mary Jessica Meagher, Jan 7, 1912 (the birth month was constrained, on the form, to three letters; Jun, entered on the form, was transcribed as Jan).
5. Mary Jessica Meagher, 6/7/12 (the form provided spaces for the final two digits of the birth year. Through the miracle of bank registration, Mary, born in 1912, was reborn a century later).
6. Mary Jessica Meagher, 7/6/2012 (the form asked for day, month, year, in that order, as is common in Europe).
7. Mary Jessica Meagher, June 1, 1912 (on the form, a 7 was mistaken for a 1).
8. Mary Jessie Meagher, June 7, 1912 (Marie, as a child, was called by the informal form of her middle name, which she provided to the teller).
9. Mary Jessie Meagher, June 7, 1912 (Marie, as a child, was called by the informal form of her middle name, which she provided to the teller and which the teller entered as the male variant of the name).
10. Marie Jesse Mahrer, 1/1/12 (an underzealous clerk combined all of the mistakes on the form and the computer transcript and added a new orthographic variant of the surname).

For each of these 10 examples, a unique individual (Mary Jessica Meagher) would be assigned a different identifier at each of 10 banks. Had Mary reregistered at one bank, 10 times, the results may have been the same.

If you toss the social security number into the mix (name + birthdate + social security number), the problem is compounded. The social security number for an individual is anything but unique. Few of us carry our original social security cards. Our number changes due to false memory ("You mean I've been wrong all these years?"), data entry errors ("Character trasnpositoins, I mean transpositions, are very common"), intention to deceive ("I don't want to give those people my real number"), or desperation ("I don't have a number, so I'll invent one"), or impersonation ("I don't have health insurance, so I'll use my friend's social security number"). Efforts to reduce errors by requiring patients to produce their social security cards have not been entirely beneficial.

Beginning in the late 1930s, the E. H. Ferree Company, a manufacturer of wallets, promoted their product's card pocket by including a sample social security card with each wallet sold. The display card had the social security number of one of their employees. Many people found it convenient to use the card as their own social security number. Over time, the wallet display number was claimed by over 40,000 people. Today, few institutions require individuals to prove their identity by showing their original social security card. Doing so puts an unreasonable burden on the honest patient (who does not happen to carry his/her card) and provides an advantage to criminals (who can easily forge a card).

Entities that compel individuals to provide a social security number have dubious legal standing. The social security number was originally intended as a device for validating a person's standing in the social security system. More recently, the purpose of the social security number has been expanded to track taxable transactions (i.e., bank accounts, salaries). Other uses of the social security number are not protected by law. The Social Security Act (Section 208 of Title 42 U.S. Code 408) prohibits most entities from compelling anyone to divulge his/her social security number.

Considering the unreliability of social security numbers in most transactional settings, and considering the tenuous legitimacy of requiring individuals to divulge their social security numbers, a prudently designed medical identifier system will limit its reliance on these numbers. The thought of combining the social security number with name and date of birth will virtually guarantee that the identifier system will violate the strict one-to-a-customer rule.

EMBEDDING INFORMATION IN AN IDENTIFIER: NOT RECOMMENDED

Most identifiers are not purely random numbers—they usually contain some embedded information that can be interpreted by anyone familiar with the identification system. For example, they may embed the first three letters of the individual's family name in the identifier. Likewise, the last two digits of the birth year are commonly embedded in many types of identifiers. Such information is usually included as a crude "honesty" check by people "in the know." For instance, the nine digits of a social security number are divided into an area code (first three digits), a group number (the next two digits), followed by a serial number (last four digits). People with expertise in the social security numbering system can pry considerable information from a social security number and can determine whether certain numbers are bogus based on the presence of excluded subsequences.

Seemingly inconsequential information included in an identifier can sometimes be used to discover confidential information about individuals. Here is an example. Suppose every client transaction in a retail store is accessioned under a unique number, consisting of the year of the accession, followed by the consecutive count of accessions, beginning with the first accession of the new year. For example, accession 2010-3518582 might represent the 3,518,582nd purchase transaction occurring in 2010. Because each number is unique, and because the number itself says nothing about the purchase, it may be assumed that inspection of the accession number would reveal nothing about the transaction.

Actually, the accession number tells you quite a lot. The prefix (2010) tells you the year of the purchase. If the accession number had been 2010-0000001, then you could safely say that accession represented the first item sold on the first day of business in the year 2010. For any subsequent accession number in 2010, simply divide the suffix number (in this case 3,518,512) by the last accession number of the year, multiply by 365 (the number of days in a nonleap year), and you have the approximate day of the year that the transaction occurred. This day can easily be converted to a calendar date.

Unimpressed? Consider this scenario. You know that a prominent member of the President's staff had visited a Washington, DC, hospital on February 15, 2005, for the purpose of having a liver biopsy. You would like to know the results of that biopsy. You go to a Web site that lists the deidentified pathology records for the hospital for the years 2000 to 2010. Though no personal identifiers are included in these public records, the individual records are sorted by accession numbers. Using the aforementioned strategy, you collect all of the surgical biopsies performed on or about February 15, 2005. Of these biopsies, only three are liver biopsies. Of these three biopsies, only one was performed on a person whose gender and age matched the President's staff member. The report provides the diagnosis. You managed to discover some very private information without access to any personal identifiers.

The alphanumeric character string composing the identifier should not expose the patient's identity. For example, a character string consisting of a concatenation of the patient's name, birthdate, and social security number might serve to uniquely identify an individual, but it could also be used to steal an individual's identity. The safest identifiers are random character strings containing no information whatsoever.

ONE-WAY HASHES

A one-way hash is an algorithm that transforms a string into another string in such a way that the original string cannot be calculated by operations on the hash value (hence the term "one-way" hash). Popular one-way hash algorithms are MD5 and Standard Hash Algorithm. A one-way hash value can be calculated for any character string, including a person's name, a document, or even another one-way hash. For a given input string, the resultant one-way hash will always be the same.

Here are a few examples of one-way hash outputs performed on a sequential list of input strings, followed by their one-way hash (MD5 algorithm) output.

Jules Berman ⇒ Ri0oaVTIAilwnS8 + nvKhfA
"Whatever" ⇒ n2YtKKG6E4MyEZvUKyGWrw
Whatever ⇒ OkXaDVQFYjwkQ + MOC8dpOQ
jules berman ⇒ SlnuYpmyn8VXLsxBWwO57Q
Jules J. Berman ⇒ i74wZ/CsIbxt3goH2aCS + A
Jules J Berman ⇒ yZQfJmAf4dIYO6Bd0qGZ7g
Jules Berman ⇒ Ri0oaVTIAilwnS8 + nvKhfA

The one-way hash values are a seemingly random sequence of ASCII characters (the characters available on a standard keyboard). Notice that a small variation among input strings (e.g., exchanging an uppercase for a lowercase character, adding a period or quotation mark) produces a completely different one-way hash output. The first and the last entry (Jules Berman) yield the same one-way hash output (Ri0oaVTIAilwnS8 + nvKhfA) because the two input strings are identical. A given string will always yield the same hash value so long as the hashing algorithm is not altered. Each one-way hash has the same length (22 characters for this particular MD5 algorithm), regardless of the length of the input term. A one-way hash output of the same length (22 characters) could have been produced for a string, file, or document of any length.

One-way hash values can substitute for identifiers in individual data records. This permits Big Data resources to accrue data, over time, to a specific record, even when the record is deidentified. Here is how it works.[28] A record identifier serves as the input value for a one-way hash. The primary identifier for the record is now a one-way hash sequence. The data manager of the resource, looking at such a record, cannot determine the individual associated with the record because the original identifier has been replaced with an unfamiliar sequence.

An identifier will always yield the same one-way hash sequence whenever the hash algorithm is performed. When the patient revisits the hospital at some future time, another transactional record is created, with the same patient identifier. The new record is deidentified, and the original patient identifier for the record is substituted with its one-way hash value. The recorded new deidentified record can now be combined with prior deidentified records that have the same one-way hash value. Using this method, deidentified records produced for an individual can be combined, without knowing the name of the individual whose records are being collected. Methods for record deidentification will be described in a later section in this chapter.

Implementation of one-way hashes carries certain practical problems. If anyone happens to have a complete listing of all of the original identifiers, then it would be a simple matter to perform one-way hashes on every listed identifier. This would produce a look-up table that can match deidentified records back to the original identifier, a strategy known as a dictionary attack. For deidentification to work, the original identifier sequences must be kept secret.

USE CASE: HOSPITAL REGISTRATION

Imagine a hospital that maintains two separate registry systems: one for dermatology cases and another for psychiatry cases. The hospital would like to merge records from the two services under a carefully curated index of patients (the master patient index). Because of sloppy identifier practices, a sample patient has been registered 10 times in the dermatology system and 6 times in the psychiatry system, each time with different addresses, social security numbers, birthdates, and spellings of the name, producing 16 differently registered records. The data manager uses an algorithm designed to reconcile multiple registrations under a single identifier from a master patient index. One of the records from the dermatology service is matched positively against one of the records from the psychiatry service. Performance studies on the algorithm indicate that the two merged records have a 99.8% chance of belonging to the correct patient listed in the master patient index. Though the two merged records correctly point to the same patient, the patient still has 14 unmatched records, corresponding to the remaining 14 separate registrations. The patient's merged record will not contain his complete set of records. If all of the patient's records were deidentified, the set of one patient's multiply registered records would produce a misleading total for the number of patients included in the data collection.

Consider these words, from the Healthcare Information and Management Systems Society,[29] "A local system with a poorly maintained or 'dirty' master person index will only proliferate and contaminate all of the other systems to which it links."

Here are just a few examples of the kinds of problems that can result when hospitals misidentify patients:

1. Bill sent to incorrectly identified person.
2. Blood transfusion provided to incorrectly identified person.
3. Correctly identified medication provided to incorrectly identified person.
4. Incorrectly identified dosage of correct medication provided to correctly identified person.
5. Incorrectly identified medication provided to correctly identified person.
6. Incorrectly identified patient treated for another patient's illness.
7. Report identified with wrong person's name.
8. Report provided with diagnosis intended for different person.
9. Report sent to incorrectly identified physician.
10. Wrong operation performed on incorrectly identified patient.[30]

Patient identification in hospitals is further confounded by a natural reluctance among some patients to comply with the registration process. A patient may be highly motivated to provide false information to a registrar, or to acquire several different registration identifiers, or to seek a false registration under another person's identity (i.e., commit fraud), or to circumvent the registration process entirely. In addition, it is a mistake to believe that honest patients are able to fully comply with the registration process. Language and cultural barriers, poor memory, poor spelling, and a host of errors and misunderstandings can lead to duplicative or otherwise erroneous identifiers. It is the job of the registrar to follow hospital policies that overcome these difficulties.

Registration in hospitals should be conducted by a trained registrar who is well versed in the registration policies established by the institution. Registrars may require patients to provide a full legal name, any prior held names (e.g., maiden name), date of birth, and a government-issued photo id card (e.g., driver's license or photo id card issued by the department of motor vehicles). In my opinion, registration should require a biometric identifier [e.g., fingerprints, retina scan, iris scan, voice recording, photograph, DNA markers[31,32] (see Glossary item, CODIS)]. If you accept the premise that hospitals have the responsibility of knowing who it is that they are treating, then obtaining a sample of DNA from every patient, at the time of registration, is reasonable. That DNA can be used to create a unique patient profile from a chosen set of informative loci; a procedure used by the CODIS system developed for law enforcement agencies. The registrar should document any distinguishing and permanent physical features that are plainly visible (e.g., scars, eye color, colobomas, tattoos).

Neonatal and pediatric identifiers pose a special set of problems for registrars. It is quite possible that a patient born in a hospital and provided with an identifier will return, after a long hiatus, as an adult. An adult should not be given a new identifier when a pediatric identifier was issued in the remote past. Every patient who comes for registration should be matched against a database of biometric data that does not change from birth to death (e.g., fingerprints, DNA). **Registration is a process that should occur only once per patient. Registration should be conducted by trained individuals who can authenticate the identity of patients**.

DEIDENTIFICATION

Deidentification is the process of stripping information from a data record that might link the record to the public name of the record's subject. In the case of a patient record, this would involve stripping any information from the record that would enable someone to connect the record to the name of the patient. The most obvious item to be removed in the deidentification process is the patient's name. Other information that should be removed would be the patient's address (which could be linked to the name), the patient's date of birth (which narrows down the set of individuals to whom the data record might pertain), and the patient's social security number. In the United States, patient privacy regulations include a detailed discussion of record deidentification, and this discussion recommends 18 patient record items for exclusion from deidentified records.[33]

Before going any further, it is important to clarify that deidentification is not achieved by removing an identifier from a data object. In point of fact, nothing good is ever achieved by simply removing an identifier from a data object; doing so simply invalidates the data object (i.e., every data object, identified or deidentified, must have an identifier). As discussed earlier in the chapter, identifiers can be substituted with a one-way hash value, thus preserving the uniqueness of the record. Deidentification involves removing information contained in the data object that reveals something about the publicly known name of the data object. This kind of information is often referred to as identifying information, but it would be much less confusing if we used another term for such data, such as "name-linking information." The point here is that we do not want to confuse the identifier of a data object with the information contained in a data object that can link the object to its public name.

It may seem counterintuitive, but there is very little difference between an identifier and a deidentifier; under certain conditions the two concepts are equivalent. Here is how a dual identification/deidentification system might work:

1. Collect data on unique object: "Joe Ferguson's bank account contains $100."
2. Assign a unique identifier: "Joe Ferguson's bank account is 7540038947134."

3. Substitute name of object with its assigned unique identifier: "754003894713 contains $100."
4. Consistently use the identifier with data.
5. Do not let anyone know that Joe Ferguson owns account "754003894713."

The dual use of an identifier/deidentifier is a tried-and-true technique. Swiss bank accounts are essentially unique numbers (identifiers) assigned to a person. You access the bank account by producing the identifier number. The identifier number does not provide information about the identity of the bank account holder (i.e., it is a deidentifier).

The purpose of an identifier is to tell you that whenever the identifier is encountered, it refers to the same unique object, and whenever two different identifiers are encountered, they refer to different objects. The identifier, by itself, contains no information that links the data object to its public name.

It is important to understand that the process of deidentification can succeed only when each record is properly identified (i.e., there can be no deidentification without identification). Attempts to deidentify a poorly identified data set of clinical information will result in replicative records (multiple records for one patient), mixed-in records (single records composed of information on multiple patients), and missing records (unidentified records lost in the deidentification process).

The process of deidentification is best understood as an algorithm performed on the fly, in response to a query from a data analyst. Here is how such an algorithm might proceed.

1. The data analyst submits a query requesting a record from a Big Data resource. The resource contains confidential records that must not be shared, unless the records are deidentified.
2. The Big Data resource receives the query and retrieves the record.
3. A copy of the record is parsed, and any of the information within the data record that might link the record to the public name of the subject of the record (usually the name of an individual) is deleted from the copy. This might include the aforementioned name, address, date of birth, social security number, and so on.
4. A pseudo-identifier sequence is prepared for the deidentified record. The pseudo-identifier sequence might be generated by a random number generator, or it might be generated by encrypting the original identifier, or through a one-way hash algorithm, or by other methods chosen by the Big Data manager.
5. A transaction record is attached to the original record that includes the pseudo-identifier, the deidentified record, the time of the transaction, and any information pertaining to the requesting entity (e.g., the data analyst who sent the query) that is deemed fit and necessary by the Big Data resource data manager.
6. A record is sent to the data analyst that consists of the deidentified record and the unique pseudo-identifier created for the record.

Because the deidentified record and its unique pseudo-identifier are stored with the original record, subsequent requests for the record can be returned with the prepared information, at the discretion of the Big Data manager. This general approach to data deidentification will apply to requests for a single record or a million records.

At this point, you might be asking yourself the following question: "What gives the data manager the right to distribute parts of a confidential record, even if it happens to be deidentified?" You might think that if you tell someone a secret, under the strictest confidence, then you would not want any part of that secret to be shared with anyone else. The whole notion of sharing confidential information that has been deidentified may seem outrageous and unacceptable.

We will discuss the legal and ethical issues of Big Data in Chapters 13 and 14. For now, readers should know that there are several simple and elegant principles that justify sharing deidentified data.

Consider the statement "Jules Berman has a blood glucose level of 85." This would be considered a confidential statement because it tells people something about my medical condition. Consider the phrase "blood glucose 85." When the name "Jules Berman" is removed, we are left with a disembodied piece of data. "Blood glucose 85" is no different from "Temperature 98.6," "Apples 2," or "Terminator 3." They are simply raw data belonging to nobody in particular.

The act of deidentification renders the data harmless by transforming information about a person or data object into information about nothing in particular. Because the use of deidentified data poses no harm to human subjects, U.S. regulations allow the unrestricted use of such data for research purposes.[33,34] Other countries have similar provisions.

DATA SCRUBBING

Data scrubbing is sometimes used as a synonym for deidentification. It is best to think of data scrubbing as a process that begins where deidentification ends. A data scrubber will remove unwanted information from a data record, including information of a personal nature, and any information that is not directly related to the purpose of the data record. For example, in the case of a hospital record, a data scrubber might remove the names of physicians who treated the patient, the names of hospitals or medical insurance agencies, addresses, dates, and any textual comments that are inappropriate, incriminating, irrelevant, or potentially damaging.

In medical data records, there is a concept known as "minimal necessary" that applies to shared confidential data[33](see Glossary item, Minimal necessary). It holds that when records are shared, only the minimum necessary information should be released. Any information not directly relevant to the intended purposes of the data analyst should be withheld. The process of data scrubbing gives data managers the opportunity to render a data record free of information that would link the record to its subject and free of extraneous information that the data analyst does not actually require.

There are many methods for data scrubbing. Most of these methods require the data manager to develop an exception list of items that should not be included in shared records (e.g., cities, states, zip codes, names of people, and so on). The scrubbing application moves through the records, extracting unnecessary information along the way. The end product is cleaned, but not sterilized. Though many undesired items can be successfully removed, this approach never produces a perfectly scrubbed set of data. In a Big Data resource, it is simply impossible for the data manager to anticipate every objectionable item and to include it in an exception list. Nobody is that smart.

There is, however, a method whereby data records can be cleaned, without error. This method involves creating a list of data (often in the form of words and phrases) that is acceptable for inclusion in a scrubbed and deidentified data set. Any data that is not in the list of acceptable information is automatically deleted. Whatever is left is the scrubbed data. This method can be described as a reverse scrubbing method. Everything is in the data set is automatically deleted, unless it is an approved "exception."

This method of scrubbing is very fast and can produce an error-free deidentified and scrubbed output.[19,35,36] An example of the kind of output produced by a reverse scrubber is shown:

> "Since the time when * * * * * * * * his own * and the * * * *, the anomalous * * have been * and persistent * * *; and especially * true of the construction and functions of the human *, indeed, it was the anomalous that was * * * in the * the attention, * * that were * to develop into the body * * which we now * *. As by the aid * * * * * * * * * our vision into the * * * has emerged *, we find * * and even evidence of *. To the highest type of * * it is the * the ordinary * * * * *. * to such, no less than to the most *, * * * is of absorbing interest, and it is often * * that the * * the most * into the heart of the mystery of the ordinary. * * been said, * * * * *. * * dermoid cysts, for example, we seem to * * * the secret * of Nature, and * out into the * * of her clumsiness, and * of her * * * *, *, * tell us much of * * * used by the vital * * * * even the silent * * * upon the * * *."

The reverse scrubber requires the preexistence of a set of approved terms. One of the simplest methods for generating acceptable terms involves extracting them from a nomenclature that comprehensively covers the terms used in a knowledge domain. For example, a comprehensive listing of living species will not contain dates or zip codes or any of the objectionable language or data that should be excluded from a scrubbed data set. In a method that I have published, a list of approved doublets (approximately 200,000 two-word phrases collected from standard nomenclatures) are automatically collected for the scrubbing application.[19] The script is fast, and its speed is not significantly reduced by the size of the list of approved terms.

REIDENTIFICATION

For scientists, deidentification serves two purposes:

1. To protect the confidentiality and the privacy of the individual (when the data concerns a particular human subject)
2. To remove information that might bias the experiment (e.g., to blind the experimentalist to patient identities)

Because confidentiality and privacy concerns always apply to human subject data and because issues of experimental bias always apply when analyzing data, it would seem imperative that deidentification should be an irreversible process (i.e., the names of the subjects and samples should be held a secret, forever).

Scientific integrity does not always accommodate irreversible deidentification. On occasion, experimental samples are mixed up; samples thought to come from a certain individual, tissue, record, or account may, in fact, come from another source. Sometimes major findings in science need to be retracted when a sample mix-up has been shown to occur.[37–41] When samples are submitted, without mix-up, the data is sometimes collected improperly. For example, reversing electrodes on an electrocardiogram may yield spurious and misleading results. Sometimes data is purposefully fabricated and otherwise corrupted to suit the personal agendas of dishonest scientists. When data errors occur, regardless of reason, it is important to retract the publications.[42,43] To preserve scientific integrity, it is sometimes necessary to discover the identity of deidentified records.

In some cases, deidentification stops the data analyst from helping individuals whose confidentiality is being protected. Imagine you are conducting an analysis on a collection of deidentified data and you find patients with a genetic marker for a disease that is curable, if treated at an early stage; or you find a new biomarker that determines which patients would benefit from surgery and which patients would not. You would be compelled to contact the subjects in the database to give them information that could potentially save their lives. An irreversibly deidentified data set precludes any intervention with subjects—nobody knows their identities.

Deidentified records can, under strictly controlled circumstances, be reidentified. Reidentification is typically achieved by entrusting a third party with a confidential list that maps individuals to their deidentified records. Obviously, reidentification can only occur if the Big Data resource keeps a link connecting the identifiers of their data records to the identifiers of the corresponding deidentified record. The act of assigning a public name to the deidentified record must always involve strict oversight. The data manager must have in place a protocol that describes the process whereby approval for reidentification is obtained. Reidentification provides an opportunity whereby confidentiality can be breached and human subjects can be harmed. Consequently, stewarding the reidentification process is one of the most serious responsibilities of Big Data managers.

LESSONS LEARNED

Everything has been said before, but since nobody listens we have to keep going back and beginning all over again. *Andre Gide*

Identification issues are often ignored by Big Data managers who are accustomed to working on small data projects. It is worthwhile to repeat the most important ideas described in this chapter, many of which are counterintuitive and strange to those whose lives are spent outside the confusing realm of Big Data.

1. All Big Data resources can be imagined as an identifier system for data objects and data-related events (i.e., timed transactions). The data in a big data resource can be imagined as character sequences that are attached to identifiers.
2. Without an adequate identification system, a Big Data resource has no value. The data within the resource cannot be trusted.
3. An identifier is a unique alphanumeric sequence assigned to a data object.

4. A data object is a collection of data that contains self-describing information, and one or more data values. Data objects should be associated with a unique identifier.

5. Deidentification is the process of stripping information from a data record that might link the record to the public name of the record's subject.

6. Deidentification should not be confused with the act of stripping a record of an identifier. A deidentified record must have an associated identifier, just as an identified data record must have an identifier.

7. Where there is no identification, there can be no deidentification and no reidentification.

8. Reidentification is the assignment of the public name associated with a data record to the deidentified record. Reidentification is sometimes necessary to verify the contents of a record or to provide information that is necessary for the well-being of the subject of a deidentified data record. Reidentification always requires approval and oversight.

9. When a deidentified data set contains no unique records (i.e., every record has one or more additional records from which it cannot be distinguished, aside from its assigned identifier sequence), then it becomes impossible to maliciously uncover a deidentified record's public name.

10. Data scrubbers remove unwanted information from a data record, including information of a personal nature, and any information that is not directly related to the purpose of the data record. Data deidentification is a process whereby links to the public name of the subject of the record are removed (see Glossary items, Data cleaning, Data scrubbing).

11. The fastest known method of data scrubbing involves preparing a list of approved words and phrases that can be retained in data records and removing every word or phrase that is not found in the approved list.

3

Ontologies and Semantics

Order and simplification are the first steps toward the mastery of a subject. **Thomas Mann**

BACKGROUND

Information has limited value unless it can take its place within our general understanding of the world. When a financial analyst learns that the price of a stock has suddenly dropped, he cannot help but wonder if the drop of a single stock reflects conditions in other stocks in the same industry. If so, the analyst may check to ensure that other industries are following a downward trend. He may wonder whether the downward trend represents a shift in the national or global economies. There is a commonality to all of the questions posed by the financial analyst. In every case, the analyst is asking a variation on a single question: "How does this thing relate to that thing?"

Big Data resources are complex. When data is simply stored in a database, without any general principles of organization, it is impossible to discover the relationships among the data objects. To be useful, the information in a Big Data resource must be divided into classes of data. Each data object within a class shares a set of properties chosen to enhance our ability to relate one piece of data with another.

Ontologies are formal systems that assign data objects to classes and that relate classes to other classes. When the data within a Big Data resource is classified within an ontology, data analysts can determine whether observations on a single object will apply to other objects in the same class. Similarly, data analysts can begin to ask whether observations that hold true for a class of objects will relate to other classes of objects. Basically, ontologies help scientists fulfill one of their most important tasks—determining how things relate to other things. This chapter will describe how ontologies are constructed and how they are used for scientific discovery in Big Data resources. The discussion will begin with a discussion of the simplest form of ontology—classification.

CLASSIFICATIONS, THE SIMPLEST OF ONTOLOGIES

The human brain is constantly processing visual and other sensory information collected from the environment. When we walk down the street, we see images of concrete and asphalt and millions of blades of grass, birds, dogs, other persons, and so on. Every step we take conveys a new world of sensory input. How can we process it all? The mathematician and philosopher Karl Pearson (1857–1936) has likened the human mind to a "sorting machine."[44] We take a stream of sensory information, sort it into a set of objects, and then assign the individual objects to general classes. The green stuff on the ground is classified as "grass," and the grass is subclassified under some larger grouping, such as "plants." A flat stretch of asphalt and concrete may be classified as a "road," and the road might be subclassified under "man-made constructions." If we lacked a culturally determined classification of objects for our world, we would be overwhelmed by sensory input, and we would have no way to remember what we see and no way to draw general inferences about anything. Simply put, without our ability to classify, we would not be human.[45]

Every culture has some particular way to impose a uniform way of perceiving the environment. In English-speaking cultures, the term "hat" denotes a universally recognized object. Hats may be composed of many different types of materials and they may vary greatly in size, weight, and shape. Nonetheless, we can almost always identify a hat when we see one, and we can distinguish a hat from all other types of objects. An object is not classified as a hat simply because it shares a few structural similarities with other hats. A hat is classified as a hat because it has a class relationship; all hats are items of clothing that fit over the head. Likewise, all biological classifications are built by relationships, not by similarities.[45,46]

Aristotle was one of the first experts in classification. His greatest insight came when he correctly identified a dolphin as a mammal. Through observation, he knew that a large group of animals was distinguished by a gestational period in which a developing embryo is nourished by a placenta, and the offspring are delivered into the world as formed but small versions of the adult animals (i.e., not as eggs or larvae), and the newborn animals feed from milk excreted from nipples, overlying specialized glandular organs (mammae). Aristotle knew that these features, characteristic of mammals, were absent in all other types of animals. He also knew that dolphins had all these features; fish did not. He correctly reasoned that dolphins were a type of mammal, not a type of fish. Aristotle was ridiculed by his contemporaries for whom it was obvious that dolphins were a type of fish. Unlike Aristotle, they based their classification on similarities, not on relationships. They saw that dolphins looked like fish and dolphins swam in the ocean like fish, and this was all the proof they needed to conclude that dolphins were indeed fish. For about 2000 years following the death of Aristotle, biologists persisted in their belief that dolphins were a type of fish. For the past several hundred years, biologists have acknowledged that Aristotle was correct after all—dolphins are mammals. Aristotle discovered and taught the most important principle of classification: that classes are built on relationships among class members, not by counting similarities.[45] We will see in later chapters that methods of grouping data objects by similarity can be very misleading and should not be used as the basis for constructing a classification or an ontology.

A classification is a very simple form of ontology, in which each class is limited to one parent class. To build a classification, the ontologist must do the following: (1) define classes (i.e., find the properties that define a class and extend to the subclasses of the class), (2) assign instances to classes, (3) position classes within the hierarchy, and (4) test and validate all of the above.

The constructed classification becomes a hierarchy of data objects conforming to a set of principles:

1. The classes (groups with members) of the hierarchy have a set of properties or rules that extend to every member of the class and to all of the subclasses of the class, to the exclusion of unrelated classes. A subclass is itself a type of class wherein the members have the defining class properties of the parent class plus some additional property(ies) specific to the subclass.
2. In a hierarchical classification, each subclass may have no more than one parent class. The root (top) class has no parent class. The biological classification of living organisms is a hierarchical classification.
3. At the bottom of the hierarchy is the class instance. For example, your copy of this book is an instance of the class of objects known as "books."
4. Every instance belongs to exactly one class.
5. Instances and classes do not change their positions in the classification. As examples, a horse never transforms into a sheep and a book never transforms into a harpsichord.
6. The members of classes may be highly similar to one another, but their similarities result from their membership in the same class (i.e., conforming to class properties), and not the other way around (i.e., similarity alone cannot define class inclusion).

Classifications are always simple; the parental classes of any instance of the classification can be traced as a simple, nonbranched list, ascending through the class hierarchy. As an example, here is the lineage for the domestic horse (*Equus caballus*) from the classification of living organisms:

Equus caballus
Equus subg. *Equus*
Equus
Equidae
Perissodactyla
Laurasiatheria
Eutheria
Theria
Mammalia
Amniota

Tetrapoda
Sarcopterygii
Euteleostomi
Teleostomi
Gnathostomata
Vertebrata
Craniata
Chordata
Deuterostomia
Coelomata
Bilateria
Eumetazoa
Metazoa
Fungi/Metazoa group
Eukaryota
cellular organisms

The words in this zoologic lineage may seem strange to laypersons, but taxonomists who view this lineage instantly grasp the place of domestic horses in the classification of all living organisms.

A classification is a list of every member class, along with their relationships to other classes. Because each class can have only one parent class, a complete classification can be provided when we list all the classes, adding the name of the parent class for each class on the list. For example, a few lines of the classification of living organisms might be:

Craniata, subclass of Chordata
Chordata, subclass of Deuterostomia
Deuterostomia, subclass of Coelomata
Coelomata, subclass of Bilateria
Bilateria, subclass of Eumetazoa

Given the name of any class, a programmer can compute (with a few lines of code) the complete ancestral lineage for the class by iteratively finding the parent class assigned to each ascending class.[19]

A taxonomy is a classification with the instances "filled in." This means that for each class in a taxonomy, all the known instances (i.e., member objects) are explicitly listed. For the taxonomy of living organisms, the instances are named species. Currently, there are several million named species of living organisms, and each of these several million species is listed under the name of some class included in the full classification.

Classifications drive down the complexity of their data domain because every instance in the domain is assigned to a single class and every class is related to the other classes through a simple hierarchy.

It is important to distinguish a classification system from an identification system. An identification system puts a data object into its correct slot within the classification. For example, a fingerprint-matching system may look for a set of features that puts a fingerprint into a special subclass of all fingerprints, but the primary goal of fingerprint matching is to establish the identity of an instance (i.e., to show that two sets of fingerprints belong to the same person). In the realm of medicine, when a doctor renders a diagnosis on a patient's diseases, she is not classifying the disease—she is finding the correct slot within the preexisting classification of diseases that holds her patient's diagnosis.

ONTOLOGIES, CLASSES WITH MULTIPLE PARENTS

Ontologies are constructions that permit an object to be a direct subclass of more than one class. In an ontology, the class "horse" might be a subclass of Equus, a zoologic term, as well as a subclass of "racing animals," "farm animals," and "four-legged animals." The class "book" might be a subclass of "works of literature," as well as a subclass of "wood-pulp materials" and "inked products." Ontologies are unrestrained classifications.

Ontologies are predicated on the belief that a single object or class of objects might have multiple different fundamental identities and that these different identities will often place one class of objects directly under more than one superclass.

Data analysts sometimes prefer ontologies over classifications because they permit the analyst to find relationships among classes of objects that would have been impossible to find under a classification. For example, a data analyst might be interested in determining the relationships among groups of flying animals, such as butterflies, birds, bats, and so on. In the classification of living organisms, these animals occupy classes that are not closely related to one another—no two of the different types of flying animals share a single parent class. Because classifications follow relationships through a lineage, they cannot connect instances of classes that fall outside the line of descent.

Ontologies are not subject to the analytic limitations imposed by classifications. In an ontology, a data object can be an instance of many different kinds of classes; thus, the class does not define the essence of the object as it does in a classification. In an ontology, the assignment of an object to a class and the behavior of the members of the objects of a class are determined by rules. An object belongs to a class when it behaves like the other members of the class, according to a rule created by the ontologist. Every class, subclass, and superclass is defined by rules, and rules can be programmed into software.

Classifications were created and implemented at a time when scientists did not have powerful computers that were capable of handling the complexities of ontologies. For example, the classification of all living organisms on earth was created over a period of two millennia. Several million species have been assigned to the classification. It is currently estimated that we will need to add another 10 to 50 million species before we come close to completing the taxonomy of living organisms. Prior generations of scientists could cope with a simple classification, wherein each class of organisms falls under a single superclass; they could not cope with a complex ontology of organisms.

The advent of powerful and accessible computers has spawned a new generation of computer scientists who have developed powerful methods for building complex ontologies. It is the goal of these computer scientists to analyze data in a manner that allows us to find and understand ontologic relationships among data objects.

In simple data collections, such as spreadsheets, data is organized in a very specific manner that preserves the relationships among specific types of data. The rows of the spreadsheet are the individual data objects (i.e., people, experimental samples, class of information, etc.). The left-hand field of the row is typically the name assigned to the data object, and the cells of the row are the attributes of the data object (e.g., quantitative measurements, categorical data, and other information). Each cell of each row occurs in a specific order, and the order determines the kind of information contained in the cell. Hence, every column of the spreadsheet has a particular type of information in each spreadsheet cell.

Big Data resources are much more complex than spreadsheets. The set of features belonging to an object (i.e., the values, sometimes called variables, belonging to the object, corresponding to the cells in a spreadsheet row) will be different for different classes of objects. For example, a member of Class Automobile may have a feature such as "average miles per gallon in city driving," whereas a member of Class Mammal would not. Every data object must be assigned membership in a class (e.g., Class Persons, Class Tissue Samples, Class Bank Accounts), and every class must be assigned a set of class properties. In Big Data resources that are based on class models, the data objects are not defined by their location in a rectangular spreadsheet—they are defined by their class membership. Classes, in turn, are defined by their properties and by their relations to other classes.

The question that should confront every Big Data manager is "Should I model my data as a classification, wherein every class has one direct parent class, or should I model the resource as an ontology, wherein classes may have multiparental inheritance?"

CHOOSING A CLASS MODEL

The simple and fundamental question "Can a class of objects have more than one parent class?" lies at the heart of several related fields: database management, computational informatics, object-oriented programming, semantics, and artificial intelligence (see Glossary item, Artificial intelligence). Computer scientists are choosing sides, often without acknowledging the problem or fully understanding the stakes. For example, when a programmer builds object libraries in the Python or the Perl programming languages, he is choosing to program in a permissive environment that supports multiclass object inheritance. In Python and Perl, any object can have as many parent classes as the programmer prefers. When a programmer chooses to program in the Ruby programming language, he shuts the door on multiclass inheritance. A Ruby object can have only one direct parent class. Most programmers are totally unaware of the liberties and restrictions imposed by their choice of programming language until they start to construct their own object libraries or until they begin to use class libraries prepared by another programmer.

In object-oriented programming, the programming language provides a syntax whereby a named method is "sent" to data objects, and a result is calculated. The named methods are functions and short programs contained in a library of methods created for a class. For example, a "close" method, written for file objects, typically shuts a file so that it cannot be accessed for read or write operations. In object-oriented languages, a "close" method is sent to an instance of class "File" when the programmer wants to prohibit access to the file. The programming language, upon receiving the "close" method, will look for a method named "close" somewhere in the library of methods prepared for the "File" class. If it finds the "close" method in the "File" class library, it will apply the method to the object to which the method was sent. In simplest terms, the specified file would be closed.

If the "close" method were not found among the available methods for the "File" class library, the programming language would automatically look for the "close" method in the parent class of the "File" class. In some languages, the parent class of the "File" class is the "Input/Output" class. If there were a "close" method in the "Input/Output" class, the method would be sent to the "File" Object. If not, the process of looking for a "close" method would be repeated for the parent class of the "Input/Output" class. You get the idea. Object-oriented languages search for methods by moving up the lineage of ancestral classes for the object instance that receives the method.

In object-oriented programming, every data object is assigned membership to a class of related objects. Once a data object has been assigned to a class, the object has access to all of the methods available to the class in which it holds membership and to all of the methods in all the ancestral classes. This is the beauty of object-oriented programming. If the object-oriented programming language is constrained to single parental inheritance (e.g., the Ruby programming language), then the methods available to the programmer are restricted to a tight lineage. When the object-oriented language permits multiparental inheritance (e.g., Perl and Python programming languages), a data object can have many different ancestral classes spread horizontally and vertically through the class libraries.

Freedom always has its price. Imagine what happens in a multiparental object-oriented programming language when a method is sent to a data object and the data object's class library does not contain the method. The programming language will look for the named method in the library belonging to a parent class. Which parent class library should be searched? Suppose the object has two parent classes, and each of those two parent classes has a method of the same name in their respective class libraries? The functionality of the method will change depending on its class membership (i.e., a "close" method may have a different function within class "File" than it may have within class "Transactions" or class "Boxes"). There is no way to determine how a search for a named method will traverse its ancestral class libraries; hence, the output of a software program written in an object-oriented language that permits multiclass inheritance is unpredictable.

The rules by which ontologies assign class relationships can become computationally difficult. When there are no restraining inheritance rules, a class within the ontology might be an ancestor of a child class that is an ancestor of its parent class (e.g., a single class might be a grandfather and a grandson to the same class). An instance of a class might be an instance of two classes, at once. The combinatorics and the recursive options can become computationally difficult or impossible.

Those who use ontologies that allow multiclass inheritance will readily acknowledge that they have created a system that is complex and unpredictable. The ontology expert justifies his complex and unpredictable model on the observation that reality itself is complex and unpredictable (see Glossary item, Modeling). A faithful model of reality cannot be created with a simple-mined classification. With time and effort, modern approaches to complex systems will isolate and eliminate computational impedimenta; these are the kinds of problems that computer scientists are trained to solve. For example, recursiveness within an ontology can be avoided if the ontology is acyclic (i.e., class relationships are not permitted to cycle back onto themselves). For every problem created by an ontology, an adept computer scientist will find a solution. Basically, ontologists believe that the task of organizing and understanding information no longer resides within the ancient realm of classification.

For those nonprogrammers who believe in the supremacy of classifications over ontologies, their faith has nothing to do with the computational dilemmas incurred with multiclass parental inheritance. They base their faith on epistemological grounds—on the nature of objects. They hold that an object can only be one thing. You cannot pretend that one thing is really two or more things simply because you insist that it is so. One thing can only belong to one class. One class can only have one ancestor class; otherwise, it would have a dual nature. Assigning more than one parental class to an object is a sign that you have failed to grasp the essential nature of the object. The classification expert believes that ontologies (i.e., classifications that permit one class to have more than one parent class and that permit one object to hold membership in more than one class) do not accurately represent reality.

At the heart of classical classification is the notion that everything in the universe has an essence that makes it one particular thing, and nothing else. This belief is justified for many different kinds of systems. When an engineer builds a radio, he knows that he can assign names to components, and these components can be relied upon to behave in a manner that is characteristic of its type. A capacitor will behave like a capacitor, and a resistor will behave like a resistor. The engineer need not worry that the capacitor will behave like a semiconductor or an integrated circuit.

What is true for the radio engineer may not hold true for the Big Data analyst. In many complex systems, the object changes its function depending on circumstances. For example, cancer researchers discovered an important protein that plays a very important role in the development of cancer. This protein, p53, was considered to be the primary cellular driver for human malignancy. When p53 mutated, cellular regulation was disrupted, and cells proceeded down a slippery path leading to cancer. In the past few decades, as more information was obtained, cancer researchers have learned that p53 is just one of many proteins that play some role in carcinogenesis, but the role changes depending on the species, tissue type, cellular microenvironment, genetic background of the cell, and many other factors. Under one set of circumstances, p53 may play a role in DNA repair, whereas under another set of circumstances, p53 may cause cells to arrest the growth cycle.[47,48] It is difficult to classify a protein that changes its primary function based on its biological context.

Simple classifications cannot be built for objects whose identities are contingent on other objects not contained in the classification. Compromise is needed. In the case of protein classification, bioinformaticians have developed GO, the Gene Ontology. In GO, each protein is assigned a position in three different systems: cellular component, biological process, and molecular function. The first system contains information related to the anatomic position of the protein in the cell (e.g., cell membrane). The second system contains the biological pathways in which the protein participates (e.g., tricarboxylic acid cycle), and the third system describes its various molecular functions. Each ontology is acyclic to eliminate the occurrences of class relationships that cycle back to the same class (i.e., parent class cannot be its own child class). GO allows biologists to accommodate the context-based identity of proteins by providing three different ontologies, combined into one. One protein fits into the cellular component ontology, the biological process ontology, and the molecular function ontology. The three ontologies are combined into one controlled vocabulary that can be ported into the relational model for a Big Data resource. Whew!

As someone steeped in the ancient art of classification, and as someone who has written extensively on object-oriented programming, I am impressed, but not convinced, by arguments on both sides of the ontology/classification debate. As a matter of practicality, complex ontologies are not successfully implemented in Big Data projects. The job of building and operating a Big Data resource is always difficult. Imposing a complex ontology framework onto a Big Data resource tends to transform a tough job into an impossible job. Ontologists believe that Big Data resources must match the complexity of their data domain. They would argue that the dictum "keep it simple, stupid" only applies to systems that are simple at the outset (see Glossary item, KISS). I would comment here that one of the problems with ontology builders is that they tend to build ontologies that are much more complex than reality. They do so because it is actually quite easy to add layers of abstraction to an ontology, without incurring any immediate penalty.

Without stating a preference for single-class inheritance (classifications) or multiclass inheritance (ontologies), I would suggest that when modeling a complex system, you should always strive to design a model that is as simple as possible. The wise ontologist will settle for a simplified approximation of the truth. Regardless of your personal preference, you should learn to recognize when an ontology has become too complex. **Here are the danger signs of an overly complex ontology.**

1. Nobody, even the designers, fully understands the ontology model.
2. You realize that the ontology makes no sense. The solutions obtained by data analysts are absurd, or they contradict observations. The ontologists perpetually tinker with the model in an effort to achieve a semblance of reality and rationality. Meanwhile, the data analysts tolerate the flawed model because they have no choice in the matter.
3. For a given problem, no two data analysts seem able to formulate the query the same way, and no two query results are ever equivalent.
4. The time spent on ontology design and improvement exceeds the time spent on collecting the data that populates the ontology.
5. The ontology lacks modularity. It is impossible to remove a set of classes within the ontology without reconstructing the entire ontology. When anything goes wrong, the entire ontology must be fixed or redesigned.
6. The ontology cannot be fitted into a higher level ontology or a lower level ontology.
7. The ontology cannot be debugged when errors are detected.
8. Errors occur without anyone knowing that the error has occurred.

Simple classifications are not flawless. **Here are a few danger signs of an overly simple classification.**

1. The classification is too granular to be of much value in associating observations with particular instances within a class or with particular classes within the classification.
2. The classification excludes important relationships among data objects. For example, dolphins and fish both live in water. As a consequence, dolphins and fish will both be subject to some of the same influences (e.g., ocean pollutants, water-borne infectious agents, and so on). In this case, relationships that are not based on species ancestry are simply excluded from the classification of living organisms and cannot be usefully examined.

3. The classes in the classification lack inferential competence. Competence in the ontology field is the ability to infer answers based on the rules for class membership. For example, in an ontology you can subclass wines into white wines and red wines, and you can create a rule that specifies that the two subclasses are exclusive. If you know that a wine is white, then you can infer that the wine does not belong to the subclass of red wines. Classifications are built by understanding the essential features of an object that make it what it is; they are not generally built on rules that might serve the interest of the data analyst or the computer programmer. Unless a determined effort has been made to build a rule-based classification, the ability to draw logical inferences from observations on data objects will be sharply limited.

4. The classification contains a "miscellaneous" class. A formal classification requires that every instance belongs to a class with well-defined properties. A good classification does not contain a "miscellaneous class" that includes objects that are difficult to assign. Nevertheless, desperate taxonomists will occasionally assign objects of indeterminate nature to a temporary class, waiting for further information to clarify the object's correct placement. In the classification of living organisms, two prominent examples come to mind: the fungal deuteromycetes and the eukaryotic protists. These two groups of organisms never really qualified as classes; each were grab-bag collections containing unrelated organisms that happened to share some biological similarities. Over the decades, these pseudo-classes have insinuated their way into standard biology textbooks. The task of repairing the classification, by creating and assigning the correct classes for the members of these unnatural groupings, has frustrated biologists through many decades and is still a source of some confusion.[49]

5. The classification may be unstable. Simplistic approaches may yield a classification that serves well for a limited number of tasks, but fails to be extensible to a wider range of activities or fails to integrate well with classifications created for other knowledge domains. All classifications require review and revision, but some classifications are just awful and are constantly subjected to major overhauls.

It seems obvious that in the case of Big Data, a computational approach to data classification is imperative, but a computational approach that consistently leads to failure is not beneficial. It is my impression that most of the ontologies that have been created for data collected in many of the fields of science have been ignored or abandoned by their intended beneficiaries. They are simply too difficult to understand and too difficult to implement.

INTRODUCTION TO RESOURCE DESCRIPTION FRAMEWORK SCHEMA

Is there a practical method whereby any and all data can be intelligibly organized into classes and shared over the Internet? There seems to be a solution waiting for us. The W3C consortium (the people behind the World Wide Web) has proposed a framework for representing Web data that encompasses a very simple and clever way to assign data to identified data objects, to represent information in meaningful statements, and to assign instances to classes of objects with defined properties. The solution is known as Resource Description Framework (RDF). Using RDF, Big Data resources can design a scaffold for their information that can be understood by humans, parsed by computers, and shared by other Big Data resources. This solution transforms every RDF-compliant Web page into an accessible database whose contents can be searched, extracted, aggregated, and integrated along with all the data contained in every existing Big Data resource.

Without jumping ahead of the game, it is appropriate to discuss in this chapter the marvelous "trick" that RDF Schema employs that solves many of the complexity problems of ontologies and many of the oversimplification issues associated with classifications. It does so by introducing the new concept of class property. The class property permits the developer to assign features that can be associated with a class and its members. A property can apply to more than one class and may apply to classes that are not directly related (i.e., neither an ancestor class nor a descendant class). The concept of the assigned class property permits developers to create simple ontologies by reducing the need to create classes to account for every feature of interest to the developer. Moreover, the concept of the assigned property permits classification developers the ability to relate instances belonging to unrelated classes through their shared property features. The RDF Schema permits developers to build class structures that preserve the best qualities of both complex ontologies and simple classifications. We will discuss RDF at greater length in Chapter 4. In this section, we will restrict our attention to one aspect of RDF—its method of defining classes of objects and bestowing properties on classes that vastly enhance the manner in which class models can be implemented in Big Data resources.

How do the Class and Property definitions of RDF Schema work? The RDF Schema is a file that defines Classes and Properties. When an RDF Schema is prepared, it is simply posted onto the Internet, as a public Web page, with a unique Web address.

An RDF Schema contains a list of classes, their definition(s), and the names of the parent class (es). This is followed by a list of properties that apply to one or more classes in the Schema. The following example is an example of RDF Schema written in plain English, without formal RDF syntax.

Plain-English RDF Schema

Class: Fungi
Definition: Contains all fungi
Subclass of: Class Opisthokonta (described in another RDF Schema)

Class: Plantae
Definition: Includes multicellular organisms such as flowering plants, conifers, ferns, and mosses
Subclass of: Class Archaeplastida (described in another RDF Schema)

Property: Stationary existence
Definition: Adult organism does not ambulate under its own power
Range of classes: Class Fungi, Class Plantae

Property: Soil habitation
Definition: Lives in soil
Range of classes: Class Fungi, Class Plantae

Property: Chitinous cell wall
Definition: Chitin is an extracellular material often forming part of the matrix surrounding cells
Range of classes: Class Opisthokonta

Property: Cellulosic cell wall
Definition: Cellulose is an extracellular material often forming part of the matrix
surrounding cells
Range of classes: Class Archaeplastida

This Schema defines two classes: Class Fungi, containing all fungal species, and Class Plantae, containing the flowering plants, conifers, and mosses. The Schema defines four properties. Two of the properties (Property Stationary existence and Property Soil habitation) apply to two different classes. Two of the properties (Property Chitinous cell wall and Property Cellulosic cell wall) apply to only one class.

By assigning properties that apply to several unrelated classes, we keep the class system small, but we permit property comparisons among unrelated classes. In this case, we defined Property Stationary growth, and we indicated that the property applied to instances of Class Fungi and Class Plantae. This schema permits databases that contain data objects assigned to Class Fungi or data objects assigned to Class Plantae to include data object values related to Property Stationary growth. Data analysts can collect data from any plant or fungus data object and examine these objects for data values related to Property Stationary growth.

Property Soil habitation applies to Class Fungi and to Class Plantae. Objects of either class may include a soil habitation data value. Data objects from two unrelated classes (Class Fungi and Class Plantae) can be analyzed by a shared property.

The schema lists two other properties: Property Chitinous cell wall and Property Cellulosic cell wall. In this case, each property is assigned to one class only. Property Chitinous cell wall applies to Class Opisthokonta. Property Cellulosic cell wall applies to Class Archaeplastida. These two properties are exclusive to their class. If a data object is described as having a cellulosic cell wall, it cannot be a member of Class Opisthokonta. If a data object is described as having a chitinous cell wall, then it cannot be a member of Class Archaeplastida.

A property assigned to a class will extend to every member of every descendant class. Class Opisthokonta includes Class Fungi, and it also includes Class Animalia, the class of all animals. This means that all animals may have the property of a chitinous cell wall. In point of fact, chitin is distributed widely throughout the animal kingdom, but is not found in mammals.

RDF seems like a panacea for ontologists, but it is seldom used in Big Data resources. The reason for its poor acceptance is largely due to its strangeness. Savvy data mangers who have led successful careers using standard database technologies are understandably reluctant to switch over to an entirely new paradigm of information management. Realistically, a novel and untested approach to data description, such as RDF, will take decades to catch on. Whether RDF succeeds as a data description standard is immaterial. The fundamental principles upon which RDF is built are certain to dominate the world of Big Data. Everyone who works with Big Data should be familiar with the power of RDF. In the next chapter, you will learn how data formatted using RDF syntax can be assigned to classes defined in public RDF Schema documents and how the data can be integrated with any RDF-formatted data sets.

COMMON PITFALLS IN ONTOLOGY DEVELOPMENT

Do ontologies serve a necessary role in the design and development of Big Data resources? Yes. Because every Big Data resource is composed of many different types of information, it becomes important to assign types of data into groups that have similar properties: images, music, movies, documents, and so forth. The data manager needs to distinguish one type of data object from another and must have a way of knowing the set of properties that apply to the members of each class. When a query comes in asking for a list of songs written by a certain composer or performed by a particular musician, the data manager will need to have a software implementation wherein the features of the query are matched to the data objects for which those features apply. The ontology that organizes the Big Data resource may be called by many other names (class systems, tables, data typing, database relationships, object model), but it will always come down to some way of organizing information into groups that share a set of properties.

Despite the importance of ontologies to Big Data resources, the process of building an ontology is seldom undertaken wisely. There is a rich and animated literature devoted to the limitations and dangers of ontology building.[50,51] Here are just a few pitfalls that you should try to avoid.

1. **Don't build transitive classes.** Class assignment is permanent. If you assign your pet beagle to the "dog" class, you cannot pluck him from this class and reassign him to the "feline" class. Once a dog, always a dog. This may seem like an obvious condition for an ontology, but it can be very tempting to make a class known as "puppy." This practice is forbidden because a dog assigned to class "puppy" will grow out of his class when he becomes an adult. It is better to assign "puppy" as a property of Class Dog, with a property definition of "age less than 1 year."

2. **Don't build miscellaneous classes.** Even experienced ontologists will stoop to creating a "miscellaneous" class as an act of desperation. The temptation to build a "miscellaneous" class arises when you have an instance (of a data object) that does not seem to fall into any of the well-defined classes. You need to assign the instance to a class, but you do not know enough about the instance to define a new class for the instance. To keep the project moving forward, you invent a "miscellaneous" class to hold the object until a better class can be created. When you encounter another object that does not fit into any of the defined classes, you simply assign it to the "miscellaneous" class. Now you have two objects in the "miscellaneous" class. Their only shared property is that neither object can be readily assigned to any of the defined classes. In the classification of living organisms, Class Protoctista was invented in the mid-19th century to hold, temporarily, some of the organisms that could not be classified as animal, plant, or fungus. It has taken a century for taxonomists to rectify the oversight, and it may take another century for the larger scientific community to fully adjust to the revisions. Likewise, mycologists (fungus experts) have accumulated a large group of unclassifiable fungi. A pseudoclass of fungi, deuteromyctetes (spelled with a lowercase "d", signifying its questionable validity as a true biologic class), was created to hold these indeterminate organisms until definitive classes can be assigned. At present, there are several thousand such fungi, sitting in taxonomic limbo, until they can be placed into a definitive taxonomic class.[52]

Sometimes, everyone just drops the ball and miscellaneous classes become permanent.[53] Successive analysts, unaware that the class is illegitimate, assumed that the "miscellaneous" objects were related to one another (i.e., related through their "miscellaneousness"). Doing so led to misleading interpretations (e.g., finding similarities among unrelated data objects and failing to see relationships that would have been obvious had the objects been assigned to their correct classes). The creation of an undefined "miscellaneous" class is an example of a general design flaw known as "ontological promiscuity."[50] When an ontology is promiscuous, the members of one class cannot always be distinguished from members of other classes.

3. **Don't invent classes and properties if they have already been invented.**[54] Time-pressured ontologists may not wish to search, find, and study the classes and properties created by other ontologists. It is often easier to invent classes and properties as you need them, defining them in your own Schema document. If your ambitions are limited to using your own data for your own purposes, there really is no compelling reason to hunt for external ontologies. Problems will surface when you need to integrate your data objects with the data objects held in other Big Data resources. If every resource invented its own set of classes and properties, then there could be no sensible comparisons among classes, and the relationships among the data objects from the different resources cannot be explored.

Most data records, even those that are held in seemingly unrelated databases, contain information that applies to more than one type of data. A medical record, a financial record, and a music video may seem to be heterogeneous types of data, but each is associated with the name of a person, and each named person might have an address (see Glossary item, Heterogeneous data). The classes of information that deal with names and addresses can be integrated across resources if they all fit into the same ontology, and if they all have the same intended meanings in each resource.

4. **Use a simple data description language.** If you decide to represent your data objects as triples, you will have a choice of languages, each with its own syntax, with which to describe your data objects, roughly listed here in order of increasing complexity: Notation 3, Turtle, RDF, DAML/OIL, and OWL (see Glossary items, RDF, Triple, Notation 3). Experience suggests that syntax languages start out simple; complexity is added as users demand additional functionalities. The task of expressing objects in an ontology language has gradually become a job for highly trained specialists who work in the obscure field of descriptive logic. As the complexity of the descriptive language increases, the number of people who can understand and operate the resource tends to diminish. In general, complex descriptive languages should only be used by well-staffed and well-funded Big Data resources capable of benefiting from the added bells and whistles.

5. **Do not confuse properties with your classes.** When I lecture on the topic of classifications and ontologies, I always throw out the following question: "Is a leg a subclass of the human body?" Most people answer yes. The reason they give is that the normal human body contains a leg; hence leg is a subclass of the human body. They forget that a leg is not a type of human body and is therefore not a subclass of the human body. As a part of the human body, "leg" is a property of a class. Furthermore, lots of different classes of things have legs (e.g., dogs, cows, tables). The "leg" property can be applied to many different classes and is usually asserted with a "has_a" descriptor (e.g., "Fred has_a leg"). The fundamental difference between classes and properties is one of the more difficult concepts in the field of ontology.

Introspection

All science is description and not explanation. **Karl Pearson**[44]*(see Glossary item, Pearson's correlation)*

BACKGROUND

Not very long ago, a cancer researcher sent me one of his published papers. For his study, he used a publicly available collection of gene microarray data collected on tumors. He knew that I was a longtime proponent of open access scientific data sets and that I had been encouraging my colleagues to use these available data sources for various analytic projects (see Glossary item, Open access). I read the paper with admiration, but the "methods" section of the paper did not provide much description of the human lung cancer tissues that were used to generate the microarray data.

I called the researcher and asked, perhaps a bit undiplomatically, the following question: "The methods section indicates that data on 12 lung cancer tissues, provided by the repository, were studied. How do you distinguish whether these were 12 lung cancer samples from 12 different patients or 12 samples of tissue all taken from one lung cancer in one patient?" If it were the former (12 lung cancers from each of 12 patients), his study conclusions would have applied to a sampling of different tumors and might reasonably apply to lung cancers in general. If it were the latter (12 samples of one tumor), then his generalized conclusion was unjustified.

There was a pause on the line, and I was told that he had neglected to include that information in the manuscript, but the paper included a link to the repository Web site, where the detailed sample information was stored.

After our conversation, I visited the Web site and found that information linking samples to source was omitted. There was a sample number, followed by the name of a type of cancer (lung cancer, in this case), and then there was the raw gene-array data. There was simply no way of determining whether different samples of a given type were derived from different patients or from one patient. I recontacted the researcher and reiterated the problem. He agreed that the people at the repository should have been more attentive to data annotation. It has been my experience that some data analysts believe that their professional responsibility begins with the received data. In their opinion, preanalytic issues, such as those described above, do not fall under their professional jurisdiction; that's the job of the data manager. This approach to Big Data analysis is an invitation to disaster. **Studies emanating from Big Data resources have no scientific value, and the Big Data resources are all a waste of time and money if data analysts cannot find, or fail to comprehend, the basic information that describes the data held in the resources.**

KNOWLEDGE OF SELF

The aforementioned story serves as an introduction to the concept of introspection, a term that is not commonly applied to Big Data resources, but should be. Introspection is a term taken from the field of object-oriented programming, and it refers to the ability of data objects to describe themselves, when called upon. In object-oriented programming languages, everything is objectified. Variables are objects, parameters are objects, methods are objects, and so on. Every object carries around its own data values, as well as an identifier, and self-descriptive information, including its class assignment (i.e., the name of the class of objects to which it belongs). An object can have its own methods (similar to subroutines), and it has access to a library of methods built for its class (i.e., class methods) and from the ancestor classes in its lineage (i.e., superclass methods).

Most object-oriented programming languages have methods that can ask an object to describe itself. To illustrate, let us see how Ruby, a popular object-oriented programming language, implements introspection.

First, let's create a new object, "x"; we will assign "hello world" to the object:

```
x = "hello world"      yields "hello world"
```

Ruby knows that "hello world" is a string and automatically assigns "x" to Class String. We can check any object to determine its class by sending the "class" method to the object, as shown:

```
x.class      yields String
```

When we send the "class" method to x, Ruby outputs its class assignment, "String." Every class (except the top level class in the hierarchy) has a single parent class, also known as a superclass. We can learn the name of the superclass of Class String by sending the superclass method, as shown:

```
x.class.superclass        yields Object
```

Ruby tells us that the superclass of Class String is Class Object.

Ruby assigns a unique identifier to every created object. We can find the object identifier by sending "x" the object_id method:

```
x.object_id        yields 22502910
```

The unique object identifier for "x" is 22502910.

If we ever need to learn the contents of "x", we can send the inspect method to the object:

```
x.inspect        yields "hello world"
```

Ruby reminds us that "x" contains the string "hello world."

Every data object in Ruby inherits dozens of class methods. We can generate a list of methods available to "x" by sending it the "methods" method:

```
x.methods
```

Ruby yields a list of dozens of methods, including a few that we can try out here: "length," "is_a?," "upcase," "downcase," "capitalize," and "reverse":

```
x.length        yields 11
```

The length method, sent to "x", yields the number of characters in "hello world":

```
x.is_a?(String)        yields true
```

When ruby uses the is_a? method to determine if x is a member of Class String, it yields "true":

```
x.is_a?(Integer)        yields false
```

When ruby uses the is_a? method to determine if x is a member of Class Integer, it yields "false":

```
x.upcase        yields "HELLO WORLD"
x.downcase        yields "hello world"
x.capitalize        yields "Hello world"
x.reverse        yields "dlrow olleh"
```

String methods sent to the "x" object return appropriate values, as shown above.

What happens when we send "x" a method from a library of methods build for some other class?

The "nonzero?" method tests to see whether an object of Class Integer is zero. This method is useful for members of Class Integer to avoid division by zero.

Let us see what happens when we send "x" the "nonzero?" method:

```
x.nonzero?        Yields NoMethodError: undefined method
           'nonzero?' for "hello world":String
```

Ruby sends us an error message, indicating that "nonzero?" is an undefined method for an object of Class String.

How does introspection, a feature of object-oriented programming languages, apply to Big Data? In principle, Big Data resources must have the same features of introspection that are automatically provided by object-oriented programming languages. Specifically, all data pertaining to the object must be encapsulated within the object to include the raw data, a description for the raw data (the so-called metadata), the name of the class to which the data object belongs, and a unique identifier that distinguishes the data object from all other data objects.

I must admit that most Big Data resources lack introspection. Indeed, most Big Data managers are unfamiliar with the concept of introspection as it applies to Big Data. When you speak to the people who manage Big Data, you may be surprised to learn that they are happy, even ecstatic, about their introspection-free resource. As far as they are concerned, their resource functions just fine, without introspection. When pressed on the subject of data introspection, data managers may confess that their Big Data resources may fall short of perfection, but their users have accommodated themselves to minor deficiencies.

There is always a price to pay when Big Data resources lack introspection. Symptoms of an introspection-free Big Data resource include the following.

1. The resource is used for a narrow range of activities, somewhat less than was originally proposed when the resource was initiated.
2. The resource is used by a small number of domain experts; to all others, the resource is inscrutable.
3. The data records for the resource cannot be verified. It is impossible to eliminate the possibility that records may have been duplicated or that data may have been mistakenly inserted into the wrong records (i.e., the data records may have been corrupted).
4. The resource cannot merge its data with data contained in other Big Data resources.
5. The resource cannot match its record identifiers with record identifiers from other resources. For example, if each of two Big Data resources has a record on the same individual, the resources cannot sensibly combine the two records into a single record.
6. The resource cannot accrue legacy data, collected by its own institution on older software, into the current Big Data resource.
7. Despite employing a crew of professionals for the resource, only one individual seems to be privy to the properties of data objects in the largely undocumented system. When he is absent, the system tends to crash.

Introspection is not a feature that you can attach to a Big Data resource as an afterthought. Introspection is a foundational component of well-designed resources. Most Big Data resources will never attain the level of introspection available in object-oriented programming languages, but some introspective features would seem essential. For the remainder of this chapter, and for the next few chapters, we will discuss the first step in introspection—describing data.

eXTENSIBLE MARKUP LANGUAGE

When you think about it, numbers are meaningless. The number "8" has no connection to anything in the physical realm until we attach some information to the number (e.g., 8 candles, 8 minutes). Some numbers, such as "0" or "−5," have no physical meaning under any set of circumstances. There really is no such thing as "0 dollars"; it is an abstraction indicating the absence of a positive number of dollars. Likewise, there is no such thing as "−5 walnuts"; it is an abstraction that we use to make sense of subtractions (5 − 10 = −5).

XML (eXtensible Markup Language) is a syntax for attaching descriptors (so-called metadata) to data values (see Glossary item, Metadata).

When we write "8 walnuts," "walnuts" is the metadata that tells us what is being referred to by the data, in this case the number "8".

When we write "8 o'clock," "8" is the data and "o'clock" is the metadata.

In XML, descriptors are commonly known as tags.

XML has its own syntax—a set of rules for expressing data/metadata pairs. Every data value is flanked by a start tag and an end tag. Enclosing angle brackets, "<>", and the end-tag marker, "/", are hallmarks of XML markup. For example:

```
<name>Tara Raboomdeay</name>
```

This simple but powerful relationship between metadata and data allows us to use every metadata/data pair as a miniscule database that can be combined with related metadata/data pairs from the same XML document or from different XML documents.

It is impossible to overstate the importance of XML (eXtensible Markup Language) as a data organization tool. With XML, every piece of data tells us something about itself. When a data value has been annotated with metadata, it can be associated with other, related data, even when the other data is located in a seemingly unrelated database (see Glossary item, Integration).

When all data is flanked by metadata, it is relatively easy to port the data into spreadsheets, where the column headings correspond to the metadata tags, and the data values correspond to the values found in the cells of the spreadsheet. The rows correspond to the record numbers.

A file that contains XML markup is considered a proper XML document only if it is well formed. Here are the properties of a well-formed XML document.

1. The document must have a proper XML header. The header can vary somewhat, but it usually looks something like <?xml version = "1.0"?>.
2. XML files are ASCII files, consisting of characters available to a standard keyboard.
3. Tags in XML files must conform to composition rules (e.g., spaces are not permitted within a tag, and tags are case sensitive).
4. Tags must be properly nested (i.e., no overlapping). For example,

```
<chapter><chapter_title>Introspection</chapter_title>
 </chapter> is properly nested XML.
<chapter><chapter_title>Introspection</chapter>
 </chapter_title> is improperly nested.
```

Web browsers will not display XML files that are not well formed.

The actual structure of an XML file is determined by another XML file known as an XML Schema. The XML Schema file lists the tags and determines the structure for those XML files that are intended to comply with a specific Schema document. A valid XML file conforms to the rules of structure and content defined in its assigned XML Schema.

Every XML file valid for the same XML Schema will contain data described with the same tags, permitting data integration among those files. This is one of the great strengths of XML.

The greatest drawback of XML is that data/metadata pairs are not assigned to a unique object. XML describes its data, but it does not tell us the object of the data. This gaping hole in XML was filled by Resource Description Framework (RDF), a modified XML syntax designed to associate every data/metadata pair with a unique data object. Before we can begin to understand RDF, we need to understand the concept of "meaning" in the context of information science.

INTRODUCTION TO MEANING

Metadata gives structure to data values, but it does not tell us anything about how the data value relates to anything else. For example,

```
<height_in_feet_inches>5'11"</height_in_feet_inches>
```

What does it mean to know that 5'11" is height value, expressed in feet and inches? Nothing really. The metadata/data pair seems to be meaningless.

This brings us to the question: What is the meaning of meaning? In informatics, meaning is achieved when described data (i.e., a metadata/data pair) is bound to the unique identifier of a data object. For example, consider this sentence: "Jules J. Berman's height is five feet eleven inches."

This sentence has meaning because there is data (five feet eleven inches), and it is described (person's height), and it is bound to a unique individual (Jules J. Berman).

If this data were entered into a Big Data resource, it would need a unique identifier (to distinguish a particular instance of a person named Jules J. Berman from all the other persons named Jules J. Berman). The statement would also benefit from a formal system that ensures that the metadata makes sense (e.g., what exactly is height and does Jules J. Berman actually have a height?) and that the data is appropriate (e.g., is 5 feet 11 inches an allowable measure of a person's height?).

A statement with meaning does not need to be a true statement (e.g., the height of Jules J. Berman was not 5 feet 11 inches when Jules J. Berman was an infant).

Semantics is the study of meaning. In the context of Big Data, semantics is the technique of creating meaningful assertions about data objects. All meaningful assertions can be structured as a three-item list consisting of an identified data object, a data value, and a descriptor for the data value, for example,

```
<Jules J. Berman> <height_in_feet_inches> <5'11">
```

These three-item assertions are referred to as "triples."

In practical terms, semantics involves making assertions about data objects (i.e., making triples), combining assertions about data objects (i.e., aggregating triples), and assigning data objects to classes—hence relating triples to other triples. As a word of warning, few informaticians would define semantics in these terms, but I would suggest that all definitions for semantics are functionally equivalent to the definition offered here. For example, every cell in a spreadsheet is a data value that has a descriptor (the column header) and a subject (the row identifier). A spreadsheet can be pulled apart and reassembled as a set of triples (known as a triple store) equal in number to the number of cells contained in the original spreadsheet. Each triple would be an assertion consisting of the following:

```
<row identifier> <column header> <content of cell>
```

Likewise, any relational database, no matter how many relational tables are included, can be decomposed into a triple store. The primary keys of the relational tables would correspond to the identifier of the RDF triple. Column header and cell contents complete the triple.

Triple stores can serve as native databases, or as a large relational table, or as preindexed tables. Regardless, the final database products have the same potential functionality as any popular database engine.[55] The advantage of the triple store is that every statement has meaning, every statement is self-descriptive, and any triple can be aggregated with any other triple.

NAMESPACES AND THE AGGREGATION OF MEANINGFUL ASSERTIONS

A namespace is the metadata realm in which a metadata tag applies (see Glossary item, Namespace). The purpose of a namespace is to distinguish metadata tags that have the same name, but a different meaning. For example, within a single XML file, the metadata term "date" may be used to signify a calendar date, a fruit, or a social engagement. To avoid confusion, the metadata term is given a prefix that is associated with a Web document that defines the term within an assigned Web location. For example, an XML page might contain three date-related values, and their metadata descriptors:

```
<calendar:date>June 16, 1904</caldendar:date>
<agriculture:date>Thoory</agriculture:date>
<social:date>Pyramus and Thisbe<social:date>
```

At the top of the XML document you would expect to find a list of three locations (Web addresses) where the namespaces used in the XML page are described. In this example, there would be a namespace address for "calendar:, agriculture:, and social:".

The relevance of namespaces to Big Data resources relates to the heterogeneity of information contained in or linked to a resource. Every description of a value must be provided a unique namespace. With namespaces, a single data object residing in a Big Data resource can be associated with assertions (i.e., object-metadata-data triples) that include descriptors of the same name, without losing the intended sense of the assertions. Furthermore, triples held in different Big Data resources can be merged, with their proper meanings preserved.

Here is an example wherein two resources are merged, with their data arranged as assertion triples:

Big Data resource 1
    29847575938125 calendar:date   February 4, 1986
    83654560466294 calendar:date   June 16, 1904

Big Data resource 2
    57839109275632 social:date   Jack and Jill
    83654560466294 social:date   Pyramus and Thisbe
Merged Big Data resource 1+2
    29847575938125 calendar:date February 4, 1986
    57839109275632 social:date   Jack and Jill
    83654560466294 social:date   Pyramus and Thisbe
    83654560466294 calendar:date June 16, 1904

There you have it. The object identified as 83654560466294 is associated with a "date" metadata tag in both resources. When the resources are merged, the unambiguous meaning of the metadata tag is conveyed through the appended namespaces (i.e., social: and calendar:)

RESOURCE DESCRIPTION FRAMEWORK TRIPLES

If you want to represent data as triples, you will need to use a standard grammar and syntax. RDF is a dialect of XML designed to convey triples. Providing detailed instruction in RDF syntax, or its dialects, lies far outside the scope of this book (see Glossary item, Notation 3). However, every Big Data manager must be aware of those features of RDF that enhance the value of Big Data resources. These would include the following.

1. The ability to express any triple in RDF (i.e., the ability to make RDF statements).
2. The ability to assign the subject of an RDF statement to a unique, identified, and defined class of objects (i.e., the ability to assign the object of a triple to a class).
3. The ability for all data developers to choose the same publicly available RDF Schemas and namespace documents with which to describe their data, thus supporting data integration over multiple Big Data resources. This last feature allows us to turn the Web into a worldwide Big Data resource composed of RDF documents.

We will briefly examine each of these three features in RDF. First, consider the following triple: pubmed:8718907, creator, Bill Moore

Every triple consists of an identifier (the subject of the triple), followed by metadata, followed by a value. In RDF syntax, the triple is flanked by metadata indicating the beginning and end of the triple. This is the <rdf:description> tag and its end tag </rdf:description>. The identifier is listed as an attribute within the <rdf:description> tag and is described with the rdf:about tag, indicating the subject of the triple. There follows a metadata descriptor, in this case <author>, enclosing the value, "Bill Moore":

```
<rdf:description rdf:about="urn:pubmed:8718907">
  <creator>Bill Moore</creator>
</rdf:description>
```

The RDF triple tells us that Bill Moore wrote the manuscript identified with the PubMed number 8718907. The PubMed number is the National Library of Medicine's unique identifier assigned to a specific journal article. We could express the title of the article in another triple:

pubmed:8718907, title, "A prototype Internet autopsy database. 1625 consecutive fetal and neonatal autopsy facesheets spanning 20 years."

In RDF, the same triple is expressed as

```
<rdf:description rdf:about="urn:pubmed:8718907">
  <title>A prototype Internet autopsy database. 1625
      consecutive fetal and neonatal autopsy facesheets
      spanning 20 years</title>
</rdf:description>
```

Resource Description Framework permits us to nest triples if they apply to the same unique object:

```
<rdf:description rdf:about="urn:pubmed:8718907">
  <author>Bill Moore</author>
  <title>A prototype Internet autopsy database. 1625
      consecutive fetal and neonatal autopsy facesheets spanning
      20 years</title>
</rdf:description>
```

Here we see that the PubMed manuscript identified as 8718907 was written by Bill Moore (the first triple) and is titled "A prototype Internet autopsy database. 1625 consecutive fetal and neonatal autopsy facesheets spanning 20 years" (a second triple).

What do we mean by the metadata tag "title"? How can we be sure that the metadata term "title" refers to the name of a document and does not refer to an honorific (e.g., The Count of Monte Cristo or the Duke of Earle). We append a namespace to the metadata. Namespaces were described in an earlier section of this chapter.

```
<rdf:description rdf:about="urn:pubmed:8718907">
  <dc:creator>Bill Moore</dc:creator>
  <dc:title>A prototype Internet autopsy database. 1625
      consecutive fetal and neonatal autopsy facesheets spanning
      20 years</dc:title>
</rdf:description>
```

In this case, we appended "dc:" to our metadata. By convention, "dc:" refers to the Dublin Core metadata set at http://dublincore.org/documents/2012/06/14/dces/.

The Dublin Core is a set of metadata elements developed by a group of librarians at a workshop in Dublin, Ohio, in 1995. It would be very useful if every electronic document were annotated with the Dublin Core elements.

The most popular Dublin Core metadata properties are:

contributor - the entity that contributes to the document
coverage - the general area of information covered in the document
creator - entity primarily responsible for creating the document
date - a time associated with an event relevant to the document
description - description of the document
format - file format

identifier - a character string that uniquely and unambiguously identifies the document
language - the language of the document
publisher - the entity that makes the resource available
relation - a pointer to another related document, typically the identifier of the related document
rights - the property rights that apply to the document
source - an identifier linking to another document from which the current document was derived
subject - topic of the document
title - title of the document
type - genre of the document

Resource Description Framework was developed as a semantic framework for the Web. The object identifier system for RDF was created to describe Web addresses or unique resources that are available through the Internet. The identification of unique addresses is done through the use of a Uniform Resource Name (URN). In many cases, the object of a triple designed for the Web will be a Web address. In other cases, the URN will be an identifier, such as the PubMed reference number in the example above. In this case, we appended the "urn:" prefix to the PubMed reference in the "about" declaration for the object of the triple:

```
<rdf:description rdf:about="urn:pubmed:8718907">
```

Let us create an RDF triple whose subject is an actual Web address:

```
<rdf:Description rdf:about="http://www.usa.gov/">
  <dc:title>USA.gov: The U.S. Government's Official Web
    Portal</dc:title>
</rdf:Description>
```

Here we make a triple wherein the object is uniquely identified by the Web address http://www.usa.gov/, and the title of the Web page is "USA.gov: The U.S. Government's Official Web Portal."

How can we assign a data object to a class of objects? We do this with the "rdf:type" declaration:

```
<rdf:description rdf:about=http://www.usa.gov/">
  <rdf:type resource="http://dublincore.org/documents/2012/
    06/14/dcmi-terms/?v=terms#FileFormat">
</rdf:description>
```

This RDF statement tells us that the Web address "http://www.usa.gov" is a type of FileFormat (i.e., is a member of Class FileFormat). Information about Class FileFormat is available in a Schema document at the following address: http://dublincore.org/documents/2012/06/14/dcmi-terms/?v=terms#FileFormat.

Resource Description Framework Schemas were introduced in Chapter 3. A Schema is a document that contains definitions of Classes and Properties. These classes and properties can be linked from other documents. If we reviewed the Schema information at the provided Web address, we would find that FileFormat is a Class and is defined as "A digital resource format."

If everyone were to assign classes to their data objects, and if everyone used the same set of Schemas to define their classes, then the Web would become a worldwide Big Data resource. This is the principle underlying the concept of the Semantic Web popularized in recent years by the World Wide Web Consortium (W3C). Currently, Semantic Web devotees are restricted to a small group of stalwarts, but hope springs eternal. In the next few decades, the Semantic Web may grow to become the backbone of a new information age based on integrating triples whose objects belong to classes defined in Schemas. Enormous databases composed of simple triples, so-called triplestores, may become the celestial bodies occupying the Big Data universe. In the meantime, RDF faces a great number of compliance hurdles. These will be discussed in Chapter 5.

REFLECTION

Reflection is a programming technique wherein a computer program will modify itself, at run time, based on information it acquires through introspection. For example, a computer program may iterate over a collection of data objects, examining the self-descriptive information for each object in the collection (i.e., object introspection). If the information indicates that the data object belongs to a particular class of objects, the program might call a method appropriate for the class. The program executes in a manner determined by descriptive information obtained during run time, metaphorically reflecting upon the purpose of its computational task. Because introspection is a property of well-constructed Big Data resources, reflection is an available technique to programmers who deal with Big Data.

USE CASE: TRUSTED TIME STAMP

A time stamp is a data value that contains the time that an event occurred and can be expressed as the date plus Greenwich Mean Time. The time stamp is irreversibly and immutably linked to an event or any data object. Because the time stamp is a data value, it should be attached to metadata. A few triples can clarify how time stamps can be used.

```
882773 is_a "patient"
882773 has_a 73002548367
73002548367 is_a "lab test"
73002548367 GMT_accession_time "2012-6-28 01:01:36"
73002548367 GMT_validation_time "2012-6-28 01:10:42"
```

These triples assert that there is a patient who has the unique identifier 882773. This patient has a lab test with the unique identifier 73002548367. The request for the test was accessioned into the laboratory at 2012-6-28 01:01:36, Greenwich Mean Time. The final results were released and validated 9 minutes and 6 seconds later, at 2012-6-28 01:10:42, Greenwich Mean Time. The same test could have many other triples, asserting the type of test, the result of the test, the range of normal values for the test, and so on. The two time stamps included here were generated by a short program that converted the computer's internally measured time into Greenwich Mean Time.

Time stamps are not tamper proof. In many instances, changing a recorded time residing in a file or data set requires nothing more than viewing the data on your computer screen and substituting one date and time for another. Dates that are automatically recorded, by your computer system, can also be altered. Operating systems permit users to reset the system date and time. Because the timing of events can be altered, scrupulous data managers employ a trusted time-stamp protocol by which a time stamp can be verified.

Here is a description of how a trusted time-stamp protocol might work. You have just created a message and you need to document that the message existed on the current date. You create a one-way hash on the message (a fixed-length sequence of seemingly random alphanumeric characters, see Glossary item, One-way hash). You send the one-way hash sequence to your city's newspaper, with instructions to publish the sequence in the classified section of that day's late edition. You're done. Anyone questioning whether the message really existed on that particular date can perform their own one-way hash on the message and compare the sequence with the sequence that was published in the city newspaper on that date. The sequences will be identical to each other.

Today, newspapers are seldom used in trusted time-stamp protocols. A time authority typically receives the one-way hash value on the document, appends a time, and encrypts a message containing the one-way hash value and the appended time, using a private key. Anyone receiving this encrypted message can decrypt it using the time authority's public key. The only messages that can be decrypted with the time authority's public key are messages that were encrypted using the time authority's private key, hence establishing that the message had been sent by the time authority. The decrypted message will contain the one-way hash (specific for the document) and the time that the authority received the document. This time-stamp protocol does not tell you when the message was created; it tells you when the message was stamped.

SUMMARY

Introspection refers to the ability of a data object to describe itself. In practical terms, a data analyst should be able to determine the data contents of every data object, the descriptors that apply to each data element, the identifier of the data object, the class assignment for the data object, and the properties that apply to the assigned class, as well as the names and properties of the classes that are related to the class assigned to the data object.

Meaning is achieved by binding a metadata–data pair to an identified subject, forming a triple; for example, pubmed:8718907 (the subject), creator (the metadata), Bill Moore (the data).

Metadata tags need to be defined, and this can be accomplished with the use of a prefix attached to the metadata. The prefix is linked to a document known as a namespace that contains definitions for metadata tags. If everyone were to use the same namespace documents as sources for their metadata tags, then the metadata and the data contained in triple statements could be integrated over multiple documents.

Every data object must be assigned a unique identifier, consisting of an alphanumeric sequence that is always associated with the unique data object and which is not associated with any other objects. When identifiers are reconciled across Big Data resources, and the metadata/data tags are selected from the same namespaces, then every data object held in multiple Big Data resources can be merged.

Resource Description Framework is a formal syntax for triples. The subjects of triples can be assigned to classes of objects defined in RDF Schemas and linked from documents composed of RDF triples. When data objects are assigned to classes, the data analysts can discover new relationships among the objects that fall into a class and can also determine relationships among different related classes (i.e., ancestor classes and descendant classes, also known as superclasses and subclasses). RDF triples plus RDF Schemas provide a semantic structure that supports introspection.

Data Integration and Software Interoperability

The nice thing about standards is that you have so many to choose from. **Andrew S. Tanenbaum**

BACKGROUND

Everyone is taught, at an early age, the standard composition of a written letter. You start with the date, then you include the name and address of your correspondent, then you write a salutation (e.g., "Dear Abby,"), then comes the body of the letter, followed by a closing (e.g., "Best wishes,"), and your name and signature on the next lines. It's all rather rigid, and anyone can recognize a page of correspondence, from across the room, just by the configuration of lines and paragraphs on the page.

Now, consider the reminder notes that you leave for yourself. You might jot a thought down on a Post-it, hanging your Post-it notes on your refrigerator, or you might use a small paper notepad. You might write something on your computer or your smartphone. You might carry a little voice recorder for this purpose. The point is that there are an endless variety of methods whereby people leave notes for themselves, yet there is only one format for writing a letter to a friend.

The reason for this disparity in available options relates to the important distinction between self and nonself. When you write a note to yourself, you're free to do as you please. When you write a note to another person, you must conform to a standard.

The entire concept of data integration and software interoperability draws from the same basic rule. If you intend to create your own data, to serve your own purposes, then you need not be concerned with data integration and software interoperability. Everyone else must toe the line.

Until the last decade or two, most data systems were created for use within one organization or corporation. The last thing on anyone's mind was providing access to outsiders. All this has changed. Today, data means very little if it cannot be integrated with related data sources. Today's software protocols operate with standard application programming interfaces that mediate the interchange of data over operating systems and networks.

In small data projects, a single standard will often support the successful interchange of data. In a Big Data project, data integration and system interoperability might involve the use of multiple standards, with data conforming to multiple versions of each standard. Sharing the data across networks may involve the use of many different interchange protocols. The purpose of this chapter is to familiarize data managers with standards issues that are important to Big Data resources.

THE COMMITTEE TO SURVEY STANDARDS

When I was a program director at the National Institutes of Health (NIH), I had the opportunity to sit on many different committees. On one occasion, I was asked to sit on a committee to assess the collected standards used by the various divisions at the National Cancer Institute (NCI). The purpose of the committee, as best I can remember, was to determine whether the various divisions and branches of the institute might benefit from a centralized approach to the usage of standards.

For the most part, the standards consisted of coded nomenclatures, consisting of synonyms for common terms collected under a common identifier (i.e., the code for the term). There must have been over 100 different nomenclatures in use: nursing terms, cancer terms, veterinary pathology terms, administrative terms, etc. Many of these nomenclatures had been bundled into one composite nomenclature by the National Library of Medicine. This omnibus nomenclature is called the Unified Medical Language System (UMLS).

The UMLS contained nomenclatures that had been created by various medical organizations. Some of these nomenclatures could be used freely. Others came with encumbrances (see Glossary item, DMCA). Users of UMLS were expected to know the legal restrictions associated with any of the 100+ nomenclatures they might use.

Here is an example of a licensing statement that had been associated with just one of the nomenclatures contained in the UMLS: "LICENSEE's right to use material from the source vocabulary is restricted to internal use at the LICENSEE's site(s) for research, product development, and statistical analysis only." At another point, the agreement prohibits the "incorporation of material from these copyrighted sources in any publicly accessible computer-based information system."[56]

The problem here is obvious. The standard had been made available for use within a single institution. It was not intended for use in Big Data resources, for which data annotations are distributed to users around the world and shared with other Big Data resources.

The National Cancer Institute had obtained the 100+ nomenclatures contained in the UMLS and had purchased other nomenclatures for specialized purposes. Many of these nomenclatures had restrictive licenses. During committee discussions, I was astonished to learn that several of the committee members had no problem with the licenses. It seemed that all of the licenses permitted use for scientific purposes, within the institution. Because the NCI conducted research and because the research would be conducted on the premises, the license restrictions would not apply within the NCI. The committee members neglected to consider that NCI had an obligation to share its data with other institutions.

In the past decade, the deluge of data has fundamentally changed the nature of science. Today, science is no longer conducted by an individual, in a single laboratory. The results of scientific work cannot be distilled into a small table in a journal article. Science today involves sharing data across institutions and supplementing publications with large and complete sets of data. Science has no validity unless all of the data is freely available to the public. Distributing the raw data and the processed data that supports a scientific conclusion would violate the licenses for the nomenclatures that were used to collect and annotate the data. In short, restrictive licenses on nomenclatures effectively block the scientific value of Big Data.

In the case of the NCI committee, my recommendation was to chuck every nomenclature that restricted the free distribution of annotated data. The UMLS contained several excellent restriction-free nomenclatures, including the National Library of Medicine's Medical Subject Headings. I wrote a short Perl script that extracted the restriction-free nomenclatures from the UMLS corpus.[56] The task of building a composite nomenclature for the National Cancer Institute eventually fell under the aegis of the ill-fated Cancer Bioinformatics Grid (see Chapter 12).

STANDARD TRAJECTORY

Standards are sometimes touted as the solution to every data integration issue. When implemented as intended, they can support the exchange of data between heterogeneous systems.[57] Such exchanges may involve nonequivalent databases (i.e., databases with different data models, different software, and nonequivalent types of data). Exchanges may also involve information transfer between humans and databases or between software agents and mechanical devices. Any exchanges between one data source and another data source can benefit from standards for describing the data and standards for transferring the data.

Whereas a single, all-purpose, unchanging, and perpetual standard is a blessing for Big Data managers, an assortment of incompatible standards can be a curse. The utility of data standards has been undermined by the proliferation of standards, the frequent versioning of data standards, the intellectual property encumbrances placed upon standards, the tendency for standards to increase in complexity over time, the abandonment of unpopular standards, and the idiosyncratic ways in which standards are implemented by data managers.

Looking upon the field of information science, and the growing role of Big Data in science and society, it is tempting to believe that the profusion of standards that we see today is the result of rapid growth in a new field. As the field matures, there will be a filtering-out process wherein the weaker standards are replaced by the strongest, most useful standards, until we reach a point when a few tested and stable standards dominate. This scenario will probably never happen. To the contrary, there is every indication that the number of standards will increase, that the newly created standards will not serve their intended purposes, and that future revisions of these early and inadequate standards will be more complex and less useful than their inadequate predecessors.

Of course, the future need not be so dreary, but it is worth taking a look at some of the scientific, economic, legal, and social forces that push us to create more and more standards of lower and lower quality.

1. **There is no guiding force that has the authority or the popular support to limit the flood of new standards.** They just keep coming. Today, there are thousands of organizations that develop standards; these are called Standards Development Organizations (SDOs). The development of standards has become part of the culture of technology. SDOs are supported by layers of oversight. SDOs may become members of a Standards Activities Organization, such as the American National Standards Institute (ANSI), which coordinates between Standards Development Organizations and Standards Organizations, providing guidance and procedures to move from a recommended specification to a certified new standard. ANSI has advisory boards that facilitate the development and implementation of standards within specific fields of endeavor. Above the Standards Activities Organizations are the standards certifying agencies. The two most important are International Organization for Standardization (ISO) and International Electrochemical Commission (IEC).

Aside from SDOs, there are independent-minded groups that create their own standards without following the aforementioned route. These groups often develop standards for their members or for their own private consumption. They see no reason to follow a path to the ISO or the IEC. There is no way to count the number of independent standards that are being created.

In addition to the standards produced by SDOs and independent groups, there are the de facto standards that seem to arise out of thin air, and rapidly gain in popularity. These represent the "better mousetraps" that somebody builds and to which the world beats a path. In the long run, de facto standards such as Transfer Control Protocol/Internet Protocol (TCP/IP), the C programming language, QWERTY keyboards, PDF files, and Microsoft Word DOC documents will have a much greater influence than any official standards.

2. **Standards can be easy to create.** Many standards are created for a niche audience. I have personally been involved in projects to develop specialized standards for tissue microarrays and for in situ hybridization data.[58,59] When the topic is very narrow, a standard can be developed in under a month through the part-time efforts of a few motivated individuals. The time-consuming component of the standards process is vetting—getting your committee members and your user community to read, understand, approve, support, and use the finished product. For the technically minded, the vetting process can be an insurmountable object. The creators of the standard may not have the stamina, social skill, money, or friends to produce a popular and widely implemented standard. Nonetheless, it is relatively easy to write a standards document and publish it as a journal article or as a Web posting, vetted or not.

3. **Standards are highly profitable, with many potential revenue streams.** When there is no industry standard for data representation, then each vendor may prepare its own

proprietary data model and format to establish "vendor lock-in." The customer's data is held in the format provided by the vendor. Because the format is proprietary, competing vendors cannot appropriate the format in their own hardware and software. The customer becomes locked into the vendor's original system, upgrades, and add-ons. Proprietary systems provide vendors with an opportunity to gain customer loyalty, without necessarily producing a superior product.

One of the purposes of industry-wide standards is to abolish proprietary systems. The hope is that if every vendor's software, hardware, and data models were equivalent, then buyers could break away from locked-in systems—the free market would prevail.

Who sits on standards development committees? Who has the time to invest in the vetting process? Who has the expertise to write a standard? Who can afford to send representatives across the globe to attend committee meetings? Vendors—vendors write the standards, vendors vet the standards, and vendors implement the standards. Large corporations can afford to send a delegation of standards experts to a standards committee. Furthermore, the corporation that sends delegates will pay for membership in the committee. Consequently, the standards committee becomes dependent on the corporation to finance the standards process, and this dependence strengthens the corporation's influence. The corporation will work to create a standard that can be technically supported by their products in place or under development. The corporation thus secures an advantage over corporations that are not present in the standards committee and who cannot anticipate the outcome of the standards process or who cannot comply with the technical specification for reasons of system incompatibility or simply because the proposed standard is technically beyond the capacity of its staff.

It is one of the great ironies of informatics that standards are written by the people who are the standard's intended targets of restraint. Vendors are clever and have learned to benefit from the standards-making process.

In some cases, a member of a standards committee may knowingly insert a fragment of patented property into the standard. After the standard is released and implemented in many different vendor systems, the patent holder rises to assert the hidden patent. In this case, all those who implemented the standard may find themselves required to pay a royalty for the use of some intellectual property sequestered within the standard. The practice of hiding intellectual property within a standard or device is known as patent farming or patent ambushing.[60] The patent farmer plants seeds in the standard and harvests his crop when the standard has grown to maturity—a rustic metaphor for some highly sophisticated and cynical behavior.

Savvy standards committees take measures to reduce patent farming. This often takes the form of an agreement, signed by all members of the standards committee, to refrain from asserting patent claims on the users of the standards. There are several ways to circumvent these agreements. If a corporation holds patents on components of a standard, the corporation can sell their patents to a third party. The third party would be a so-called patent-holding company that buys patents in selected technologies with the intention of eventually asserting patents over an array of related activities.[61] If the patent holder asserts the patent, the corporation might profit from patent farming, through their sale of the patent, without actually breaking the agreement (see Glossary item, Patent farming).

Corporations can profit from standards indirectly by obtaining patents on the uses of the standard, not on the patent itself. For example, an open standard may have been created that can be obtained at no cost, that is popular among its intended users, and that contains no hidden intellectual property. An interested corporation or individual may discover a use for the standard that is nonobvious, novel, and useful; these are the three criteria for awarding patents. The corporation or individual can patent the use of the standard, without needing to patent the standard itself. The patent holder will have the legal right to assert the patent over anyone who uses the standard for the purpose claimed by the patent. This patent protection will apply even when the standard is free and open.

The world of standards is a very strange place. Big Data managers are particularly vulnerable to the legal trappings associated with standards because Big Data is complex and diverse and requires different standards for different types of data and for different types of software.

4. **Standards are popular (everyone wants one of their own).** Having your own standard is somewhat of a status symbol. Whenever a team of scientists develops a new method, or a variant of an old method, and an organized way of collecting the data produced by the method, there will be a natural urge to legitimize and aggrandize these efforts with a new standard. The standard will dictate how the method is used and how the data is collected, labeled, and stored. In the late 1990s, the most favored way to represent data was through a new markup language, basically a list of XML tags, and a schema that dictated the nesting hierarchy of the tags. In almost every case, these markup languages were self-contained constructs that did not reuse tags from related markup languages. For example, many different markup languages contained an equivalent tag that described the sample name or the sample identifier, but these markup languages did not refer to preexisting equivalent tags in other Schemas (i.e., they did not make use of established namespaces). Consequently, a Babel of markup languages sprang into existence, with no attempt at harmonizing the languages or sharing content among the different languages. Thankfully, the markup language fad has passed, but a basic problem persists. Deep down, scientists believe that their way of organizing their own data should be the standard for the entire world. This irrational belief accounts for much of the unchecked proliferation of personalized standards.

5. **Most standards are created for reasons that applied in the past, but that do not apply in the Big Data era.** For the last half-century, the purpose of a standard was to ensure that everyone who created a particular type of object (e.g., a physical object, a document, or a collection of a specific type of information) would do so in the same way so that the objects could be compared and categorized.

For example, imagine an international standard for death certificates. You would naturally want each license to contain the same information, including the name of the deceased, identifying information (e.g., date of birth, gender, race), causes of death, and contributing factors, all coded in accordance with a standard nomenclature. With the cause of death, you would want to find details of the circumstances of the death (e.g., date and time of death, time at which the certificate was signed). Regarding format, you might want every country to list the contents of the document in the same order, numbered identically, so that item 4 in a Portuguese death certificate would correspond to item 4 in an Australian certificate. You might want the layout of the documents to be identical (e.g., name of deceased in the upper left, date of birth of deceased in the upper right). These restrictions are intended to facilitate comparing death certificates worldwide. **This detailed approach to layout is terribly outdated and largely irrelevant to the purposes of standards in Big Data resources. In the Big Data**

universe, the purpose of a standard is not to compare one document with another document of the same kind; the purpose of a standard is to enable data analysts to relate data objects within a document to data objects contained in documents of a different kind.

This last point is the most difficult for people to understand, particularly those people who have been supporters of data standards and who have used them to good effect in their work. It is a near-impossible task to convince someone to abandon a paradigm that has served them well. But it's worth a try!

Let us reexamine the role of the standard death certificate in Big Data analysis. The list of diseases contains the primary cause of death plus any diseases that contributed to the primary cause of death. Another database, in a hospital information system, might list various diseases that coexist in living patients. By comparing data in the database of death certificates with data in a hospital information system, it may be possible to find sets of diseases that co-occur with a high risk of death. By comparing the average age at which a particular disease is associated with death, it may be possible to predict when a disease under treatment is likely to lead to death. The occurrence of diseases in particular racial groups included in death certificate data may lead to disparities found in the occurrence of the same diseases in a living population. These are extremely simple examples wherein data values included in one standard data set (death certificates) are compared with data values in another standard data set (hospital information system records). The comparisons are made between selected data values in heterogeneous data sets; the comparisons are not made between two documents that conform to the same standard.

The phenomenon of data integration over heterogeneous sources is repeated in virtually every Big Data effort. A real estate property with a known address is matched against crime statistics collected for its listed zip code. A planting chart based on a list of popular flowers and vegetables within a locality is matched against a climate zone data set matched to geographic region. In both cases, the comparisons are made for data values held in heterogeneous data sets.

In an earlier era, standards served to create data homogeneity. In the Big Data era, standards serve to find the data relationships in heterogeneous data sources.

SPECIFICATIONS AND STANDARDS

Good specifications will always improve programmer productivity far better than any programming tool or technique. *Milt Bryce*

The two terms "standards" and "specifications" are used interchangeably in the informatics literature, but they are different from one another in very important ways. A "standard" is a set of construction rules that tells you how to represent a required set of information. For a given subject (i.e., an image, a movie, a legal certificate, a programming language), the standard tells you exactly how the contents must be organized, from top to bottom, what contents must be included, and how those contents are expressed. For a standard to have value, it generally requires approval from a standards-certifying organization (such as the ISO) or from some large and influential industry group.

A "specification" is a general way of describing objects (i.e., physical objects such as nuts and bolts or symbolic objects such as numbers) so that anyone can fully understand your intended meaning. Specifications do not force you to include specific types of information and do not impose a specific order on the data contained in the document. Specifications are not generally certified by a standards organization. Their legitimacy depends on their popularity. Examples of specifications are Resource Description Framework (RDF), produced by the World Wide Web Consortium (W3C), and TCP/IP, maintained by the Internet Engineering Task Force.

The strength of a standard is that it imposes uniformity; the weakness of a standard is that it has no flexibility and impedes innovation. An engineer might want to manufacture a cup with a very wide bottom rim and a narrow top rim, with no handle, with three handles, or with an attached computer chip. If the standard prohibits the bottom rim diameter to exceed the top rim diameter, requires exactly one handle, or has no method for describing ancillary attachments, then the innovator cannot comply with the standard.

The strength of the specification is that it is highly flexible; the weakness of the specification is that its flexibility allows designers to omit some of the information required to fully specify the object. In practice, proper implementation of specifications is ensured by usability tests. If everyone seems to understand your implementation of a specification and if your implementation functions adequately and operates with other systems without problems, then the specification has served its intended purpose.

Both standards and specifications suffer from the following.

1. **New versions may appear, without much notice, and the new versions may not be fully compatible with older versions.** For example, Python 3.x has a somewhat different syntax than Python 2.x. Your Python 2.x programs will not necessarily run in a Python 3.x environment, and your Python 3.x programs may not run in a Python 2.x environment. Incompatible programs may run for a while and then stop when a conflict arises. Because the glitch is caused by a language incompatibility, not a programming error, you may find the debugging process exasperating.
2. **Standards and specifications may be overly complex.** It is easy for a standards committee to create a complex standard or for an organization to develop a specification language that contains thousands of metadata tags. A complex standard or specification can easily exceed human comprehension. Data managers may be hesitant to stake their resource on tools that they cannot understand.
3. **There are too many standards and specifications from which to choose.** Big Data managers would like to stay in conformance with industry standards. The problem is that Big Data serves many different purposes and must comply with many different standards, all at the same time.

After a standard has been created, there follows a Darwinian struggle for supremacy. Standards committees sometimes display group behavior that can be described as antisocial or even sociopathic. They want their standard to be the only standard used in a data domain. If there are other standards in the data domain, they sometimes use coercive methods to force everyone to use their standard.

The most common coercive argument involves threatening colleagues with the inflated claim that everyone will be using the standard; failing to switch to the standard will result in a loss of business opportunities. The proponents of a standard may suggest that those who fail to adopt the standard will be ostracized and marginalized by their colleagues. I've personally heard coercive arguments from some of my colleagues who, in every other respect, are decent and altruistic individuals. The reason for their nastiness often comes down to economics. Vendors and Big Data managers select a standard in the full knowledge that a poor choice may bring financial ruin. If the vendor builds a data model to fit a standard, and the standard is not adopted by their market, then they will not be able to sell their software. If a Big Data manager annotates terabytes of data in conformance with an ontology that is soon to be abandoned by its user community, then the value of the resource will plummet. Nevertheless, there can be no excuses for bad behavior; coercion should not be tolerated.

A few commonsense measures might help the data manager:

1. Learn how to decompose the standard document into an organized collection of data objects that can be merged with other data object collections or inserted into a preferred data model.
2. If feasible, avoid using any standard as your data object model for the resource. It is often best to model your own data in a simple but flexible format that can be ported into any selected standard, as needed.
3. Know the standards you use. Read the license agreements. Keep your legal staff apprised of your pending decisions.
4. Try your best to use standards that are open source or that belong to the public domain (see Glossary item, Public domain).

VERSIONING

An idea can be as flawless as can be, but its execution will always be full of mistakes. **Brent Scowcroft**

In 2000, I attended a workshop in San Diego whose purpose was to introduce pathologists to new, standardized protocols for describing different types of cancer specimens (e.g., cancer of the adrenal gland, cancer of the prostate, cancer of the lung, etc.). This wasn't the first such standardization effort of its kind. Over the past decade, several groups had been pushing for standards that would ensure that pathology reports prepared in any U.S. hospital would contain the same kind of information for a given type of specimen. Having a reporting standard seemed like a good idea, but as I looked at the protocols I saw lots of problems. Lists of required items seemed incomplete, and many of the descriptors were poorly defined. Some of the descriptors were nonqualitative and required subjective data. The final reports would not be highly reproducible between laboratories or within a single laboratory. These deficiencies are par for the course in any standards effort. I asked the chairman how she planned to deal with producing and controlling new versions of the standard. She replied that because the protocols had been prepared by experts and thoroughly tested by a panel of implementers, there would be no need to develop new versions. She was telling me that the new standard had been born perfect! More than a decade has passed, during which the standards have been subjected to unceasing modifications.

For most types of standards and specifications, versioning is a requirement. Nomenclatures in every area of science and technology are constantly being updated. Every year, the Medical Subject Headings comes out with an updated version. Some nomenclatures are actually named according to the version (e.g., ICD-10 is the 10th version of the International Classification of Diseases). New versions of nomenclatures are not simple expansions of older versions. Aside from the addition of new terms, old terms must be retired and new coding sequences are sometimes created. The relationships among terms (i.e., the class or classes to which a term belongs) might change.

Without exception, all large nomenclatures are unstable. Changes in a nomenclature may have a ripple effect, changing the meaning of terms that are not included in the nomenclature. Here is an example from the world of mycology (the study of fungi). When the name of a fungus changes, so must the name of the associated disease. Consider *Allescheria boydii*. People infected with this organism were said to suffer from the disease known as allescheriasis. When the organism's name was changed to *Petriellidium boydii*, the disease name was changed to petriellidosis. When the fungal name was changed, once more, to *Pseudallescheria boydii*, the disease name was changed to pseudallescheriasis.[52] All three names appear in the literature (past and present). In this case, changes in the fungal nomenclature necessitate reciprocal changes in every disease nomenclature. Such changes may require months, years, or even decades to adjudicate and finalize in the newer versions of the nomenclatures. Within this period, the term may change again, and the corrected versions of the disease nomenclatures may be obsolete on their release date.

The horticultural nomenclature is riddled with naming conventions that date back to specific eras. Cultivars are plant varieties produced by breeding. Before 1959, cultivars were given Latin names exclusively. After 1959, Latin forms were forbidden for cultivar names, but any modern language would suffice. Consequently, post-1959, botanists must know each cultivar in the language chosen by the plant's breeder, for example,

Chamaecyparis lawsoniana 'Aureomarginata' (pre-1959 name, Latin in form)
Chamaecyparis lawsoniana 'Golden Wonder' (post-1959 name, English language)
Pinus densiflora 'Akebono' (post-1959 name, Japanese language)

Regarding animal names, a specific synonym may map to more than one concept term (i.e., a term may have different meanings depending on the circumstances for which it is applied). For example, *Enterobius vermicularis* is called a pinworm in the United States and a threadworm in the United Kingdom, while *Strongyloides stercoralis* is just the opposite, a threadworm in the United States and a pinworm in the United Kingdom. The only way to escape this transatlantic confusion is to translate the common name of an organism back to its standard Latin binomial.

Malcolm Duncan has posted an insightful and funny essay entitled "The Chocolate Teapot (Version 2.3)."[62] In this essay, he shows how new versions of nomenclatures may unintentionally alter the meanings of classes of terms contained in earlier versions, making it impossible to compare or sensibly aggregate and interpret terms and concepts contained in any of the versions. The essay is a must-read for anyone seriously interested in terminologies, but we can examine a few of the points raised by Duncan.

Suppose you have a cookware terminology with a "teapot" item. If the nomenclature is somewhat dated (e.g., circa 1857), teapots were made of porcelain, and porcelain came in two colors: white and blue. Version 2 of the terminology might accommodate the two subtypes: blue teapot and white teapot. If a teapot were neither blue nor white, it would presumably be coded under the parent term, "teapot." Suppose version 3 expands to accommodate some new additions to the teapot pantheon: chocolate teapot, ornamental teapot, china teapot, and industrial teapot. Now the teapot world is shaken by a tempest of monumental proportions. The white and the blue teapots, implicitly considered to be made of porcelain, like all china teapots, stand divided across the subtypes. How does one deal with a white porcelain teapot that is not a china teapot? If we had previously assumed that a teapot was an item in which tea is made, how do we adjust, conceptually, to the new term "ornamental teapot"? If the teapot is ornamental, then it has no tea-making functionality, and if it cannot be used to make tea, how can it be a teapot? Must we change our concept of the teapot to include anything that looks like a teapot? If so, how can we deal with the new term "industrial teapot," which is likely to be a big stainless steel vat that has more in common, structurally, with a microbrewery fermenter than with an ornamental teapot? What is the meaning of a chocolate teapot? Is it something made of chocolate, is it chocolate colored, or does it brew chocolate-flavored tea? Suddenly we have lost the ability to map terms in version 3 to terms in versions 1 and 2. We no longer understand the classes of objects (i.e., teapots) in the various versions of our cookware nomenclature. We cannot unambiguously attach nomenclature terms to objects in our data collection (e.g., blue china teapot). We no longer have a precise definition of a teapot or of the subtypes of teapot.

We discussed classifications and ontologies in Chapter 3. Classifications have a very strong advantage over ontologies with regard to the ease of versioning. Because each class in a classification is restricted to a single parent, the hierarchical tree of a classification is simple. When a class needs to be repositioned in the classification tree, it is a simple matter to move the class, with its intact branches, to another node on the tree. We do this from time to time with the classification of living organisms.

Some of the recent changes in the taxonomy of living organisms have involved the highest classes in the hierarchy. The first division of the Eukaryotes was assigned to Class Bikonta and Class Unikonta (analogous to dicot and monocot division in Class Angiospermae).[63] Class Protoctista has been dropped from the formal taxonomy. Class Rhizaria was introduced. Class Microsporidia was moved from Class Protoctista to Class Fungi. Class Chlorophyta was moved from Class Protoctista to Class Archaeplastida. As you can imagine, positional changes in the upper hierarchy of the classification of living organisms involved much debate and turmoil in the scientific community. Once scientists agreed on the change, the tree of life was rearranged with a few bold strokes of the pen.

Unlike the case with uniparental classifications, it is virtually impossible to make sweeping changes in multiparental ontologies without starting again, from scratch. Class branches are insinuated in across multiple classes. A class cannot simply be cut and repositioned elsewhere. The more complex the ontology, the more difficult it is to modify its structure.

COMPLIANCE ISSUES

When it comes to complex standards, compliance is in the eye of the beholder. One vendor's concept of standard-compliant software might be entirely different from another vendor's concept. Standards organizations seldom have the time, manpower, money, or energy to ensure compliance with their standards; consequently, the implementations of standards are often nonstandard and incompatible with one another.

In large part, noncompliance is caused by the instability of modern standards. As we have seen, standards themselves may contain flaws related to the complexity of the technologies they model. When a technology outpaces the standard built for the technology, it may be impossible for businesses to adequately model all of their data and processes within the standard.

Small businesses may not have the manpower to keep abreast of every change in a complex standard. Large businesses may have the staff and the expertise to stay compliant, but they may lack the incentive. If they produce a product that works well and is believed, wrongly or not, to be compliant with a standard, then it may be in the best interest of the business to tolerate a degree of noncompliance. A vendor can lock-in customers to a corrupted and idiosyncratic rendition of a standard if their product offers a high level of functionality.

Compliance with specifications is, in general, much easier than compliance with standards. Specifications provide a syntax and a general method for describing data objects. In most cases, it is relatively easy to produce a program that determines whether a file conforms to a specification.

When a file conforms to the syntax of a specification, it is said to be well formed. When a file conforms to a document that describes how certain types of objects should be annotated (e.g., which tags should be used, the relationships among tags, the data value properties that can be assigned to tags, the inclusion of all required tags), then the file is said to be valid. A file that is fully compliant with a specification is said to be well formed and valid.

In the case of RDF files, a well-formed file would comply with RDF syntax rules. A valid file would conform with the classes and properties found in the RDF Schemas linked from within the RDF statements contained in the file.

INTERFACES TO BIG DATA RESOURCES

Any problem in Computer Science can be solved with another level of indirection. *Butler Lampson*

... except the problem of indirection complexity. *Bob Morgan*

Most Big Data resources do not provide a great deal of information about the content and operation of their systems. With few exceptions, the providers of Big Data expect their intended users to approach their resource with a skill set appropriate for their information domain. For example, a Big Data resource designed for military procurement officers might expect its users to be familiar with a host of specialized protocols dealing with the naming, description, pricing, and distribution of equipment. When a Big Data resource replaces a collection of printed materials (e.g., industry catalogs), then the resource will often be designed to offer an equivalent data representation and an equivalent service, without requiring its user base to learn an entirely new set of query skills, without developing a completely new set of data services, and without offering much in the way of explanatory text. Innovation, if it comes, often emerges gradually, as the resource matures.

Big Data managers often have a very specific idea of who will be using their resource and a very narrow idea of the range of questions that their resource must answer. With few exceptions, they see no need to embellish the resource with introspective powers that their users may never need. This being the case, interfaces to Big Data resources often come in one of several types.

1. *Direct user interfaces.* These interfaces permit individuals to submit simple queries, constructed within a narrow range of options, producing an output that is truncated to produce a manageable visual display. Google is an example. You never know what information is excluded from the indexed resource, or exactly how the search is conducted, and the output may or may not have the results you actually need. Regarding the actual query, it's limited to words and phrases entered into a box, and although it permits some innovative methods to specify the query, it does not permit you to enter hundreds of items at once, to search based on a user-invented algorithm, or to download the entire search output into a file. Basically, Google gives users the opportunity to enter a query according to a set of Google-specified query rules, and Google provides an output. What happens in the very short moment that begins when the query has been launched and ends when the reply is displayed is something that only Google fully understands. For most users, the Google reply may as well be conjured by magic.

2. *Programmer or software interfaces.* These are standard commands and instructions that a data service releases to the public and that individual developers can use to link to and interact with the service. The usual term applied to these interfaces is API (Application Programming Interface), but other related terms, including SaaS (Software as a Service), might also apply. Amazon is an example of a company that provides an API. Web developers can use the Amazon API to link to information related to specific Amazon products. Current information for the product can be displayed on the third-party Web site and a buyer's link can broker a purchase. The API enables transactions to be completed through interactions between the developer's software and the company's software.

3. *Autonomous agent interfaces.* These are programs that are launched into a network of communicating computers, carrying a query. The program contains communication and interface protocols that enable it to interrogate various databases. The response from a database is stored and examined. Depending on the information received, the autonomous agent might proceed to another database or may modify its interrogation of the first database. The agent continues to collect and process information, traveling to different networked databases in the process. At some point, the software program returns to the client (the user who initiated the query) with its collected output. Web crawlers, familiar to anyone who reviews Internet server logs, are somewhat primitive examples of partly autonomous software agents. They use an interface (Internet protocols) to visit servers, conducting an inventory of the contents and visiting other servers based on the addresses of links listed on Web pages. If a Big Data resource opens its data to programs that employ a compatible communications protocol (such as a Web services language; see Glossary item, Web service), then the problem of constructing a software agent becomes relatively straightforward. Opening a system to autonomous agents comes with risks. The consequences of opening a system to complex interactions with innumerable agents, each operating under its own set of instructions, are difficult, or impossible, to predict and control.[64]

6

Immutability and Immortality

You live your life forward, but you understand it backward. **Soren Kierkegaard**

BACKGROUND

Immutability is one of those issues, like identifiers and introspection, that seems unimportant until something goes terribly wrong. Then, in the midst of the problem, you realize that your entire information system was designed incorrectly, and there really is nothing you can do to cope.

Here is an example of an immutability problem. You are a pathologist working in a university hospital that has just installed a new, $600 million information system. On Tuesday, you released a report on a surgical biopsy, indicating that it contained cancer. On Friday morning, you showed the same biopsy to your colleagues, who all agreed that the biopsy was not malignant and contained a benign condition that simulated malignancy (looked a little like a cancer, but was not). Your original diagnosis was wrong, and now you must rectify the error. You return to the computer and access the prior report, changing the wording of the diagnosis to indicate that the biopsy is benign. You can do this because pathologists are granted "edit" access for pathology reports. Now, everything seems to have been set right. The report has been corrected, and the final report in the computer is the official diagnosis.

Unknown to you, the patient's doctor read the incorrect report on Wednesday, the day after the incorrect report was issued, and 2 days before the correct report replaced the incorrect report. Major surgery was scheduled for the following Wednesday (5 days after the corrected report was issued). Most of the patient's liver was removed. No cancer was found in the excised liver. Eventually, the surgeon and patient learned that the original report had been altered. The patient sued the surgeon, the pathologist, and the hospital.

You, the pathologist, argued in court that the computer held one report issued by the pathologist (following the deletion of the earlier, incorrect report) and that report was correct. Therefore, you said, you made no error. The patient's lawyer had access to a medical chart in which paper versions of the diagnosis had been kept. The lawyer produced, for the edification of the jury, two reports from the same pathologist, on the same biopsy: one positive for cancer, the other benign. The hospital, conceding that they had no credible defense, settled out of court for a very large quantity of money. Meanwhile, back in the hospital, a fastidious intern is deleting an erroneous diagnosis and substituting his improved rendition.

One of the most important features of serious Big Data resources (such as the data collected in hospital information systems) is immutability (see Glossary item, Serious Big Data). The rule is simple. Data is immortal and cannot change. You can add data to the system, but you can never alter data and you can never erase data. Immutability is counterintuitive to most people, including most data analysts. If a patient has a glucose level of 100 on Monday, and the same patient has a glucose level of 115 on Tuesday, then it would seem obvious that his glucose level changed between Monday and Tuesday. Not so. Monday's glucose level remains at 100. Until the end of time, Monday's glucose level will always be 100. On Tuesday, another glucose level was added to the record for the patient. Nothing that existed prior to Tuesday was changed.

IMMUTABILITY AND IDENTIFIERS

People change and forget to tell each other. Lillian Hellman

Immutability applies to identifiers. In a serious Big Data resource, data objects never change their identity (i.e., their identifier sequences). Individuals never change their names. A person might add a married name, but the married name does not change the maiden name. The addition of a married name might occur as follows:

18843056488 is_a		patient
18843056488 has_a		maiden_name
18843056488 has_a		married_name
9937564783 is_a		maiden_name
4401835284 is_a		married_name
18843056488 maiden_name		Karen Sally Smith
18843056488 married_name		Karen Sally Smythe

Here, we have a woman named Karen Sally Smith. She has a unique, immutable identifier, "18843056488." Her patient record has various metadata/data pairs associated with her unique identifier. Karen is a patient, Karen has a maiden name, and Karen has a married name. The metadata tags that describe the data that is associated with Karen include "maiden_name" and "married_name." These metadata tags are themselves data objects. Hence, they must be provided with unique, immutable identifiers. Though metadata tags are themselves unique data objects, each metadata tag can be applied to many other data objects. In the following example, the unique maiden_name and married_name tags are associated with two different patients.

9937564783 is_a	maiden_name
4401835284 is_a	married_name
18843056488 is_a	patient
18843056488 has_a	maiden_name
18843056488 has_a	married_name
18843056488 maiden_name	Karen Sally Smith
18843056488 married_name	Karen Sally Smythe
73994611839 is_a	patient
73994611839 has_a	maiden_name
73994611839 has_a	married_name
73994611839 maiden_name	Barbara Hay Wire
73994611839 married_name	Barbara Haywire

The point here is that patients may acquire any number of names over the course of their lives, but the Big Data resource must have a method for storing and describing each of those names and associating them with the same unique patient identifier. Everyone who uses a Big Data resource must be confident that all the data objects in the resource are unique, identified, and immutable.

By now, you should be comfortable with the problem confronted by the pathologist who changed his mind. Rather than simply replacing one report with another, the pathologist might have issued a modification report, indicating that the new report supersedes the earlier report. In this case, the information system does not destroy or replace the earlier report, but creates a companion report. As a further precaution, the information system might flag the early report with a link to the ensuant entry. Alternately, the information system might allow the pathologist to issue an addendum (i.e., add-on text) to the original report. The addendum could have clarified that the original diagnosis is incorrect, stating the final diagnosis is the diagnosis in the addendum. Another addendum might indicate that the staff involved in the patient's care was notified of the updated diagnosis. The parts of the report (including any addenda) could be dated and authenticated with the electronic signature of the pathologist. Not one byte in the original report is ever changed. Had these procedures been implemented, the unnecessary surgery, the harm inflicted on the patient, the lawsuit, and the settlement might have all been avoided.

The problem of updating diagnoses may seem like a problem that is specific for the health care industry. It is not. The content of Big Data resources is constantly changing; the trick is accommodating all changes by the addition of data, not by the deletion or modification of data. For example, suppose a resource uses an industry standard for catalog order numbers assigned to parts of an automobile. These 7-digit numbers are used whenever a part needs to be purchased. The resource may inventory millions of different parts, each with an order number annotation. What happens when the standard suddenly changes and all of the existing 7-digit numbers are replaced by 12-digit numbers? A well-managed resource will preserve all of the currently held information, including the metadata tags that describe the 7-digit standard, and the 7-digit order number for each part in the resource inventory. The new standard, containing 12-digit numbers, will have a different metadata tag from the prior standard, and the new metadata/data pair will be attached to the internal identifier for the part. This operation will work if the resource maintains its own unique identifiers for every data object held in the resource and if the data objects in the resource are associated with metadata/data pairs. All of these actions involve adding information to data objects, not deleting information.

In the days of small data, this was not much of a problem. The typical small data scenario would involve creating a set of data, all at once, followed soon thereafter by a sweeping analytic procedure applied against the set of data, culminating in a report that summarized the conclusions. If there was some problem with the study, a correction would be made, and everything would be repeated. A second analysis would be performed in the new and improved data set. It was all so simple.

A procedure for replicative annotations to accommodate the introduction of new standards and nomenclatures, as well as new versions of old standards and nomenclatures, would be one of the more onerous jobs of the Big Data curator (see Glossary item, Curator). Over the years, dozens of new or additional annotations could be required. It should be stressed that replicative annotations for nomenclatures and standards can be avoided if the data objects in the resource are not tied to any specific standard. If the data objects are well specified (i.e., providing adequate and uniform descriptions), queries can be matched against any standard or nomenclature on the fly (i.e., as needed, in response to queries). Such a method was discussed in Chapter 1.

Why is it always bad to change the data objects held in a Big Data resource? Though there are many possible negative repercussions to deleting data, most of the problems come down to data verification and time stamping (see Glossary items: Time stamp, Verification, and Validation). All Big Data resources must be able to verify that the data held in the resource conforms to a set of protocols for preparing data objects and measuring data values. The data in the resource is validated if it can be shown that the data fulfills its intended purposes, repeatably. When you change preexisting data, all of your efforts at resource verification are wasted because the resource that you once verified no longer exists. Aside from producing an unverifiable resource, you put the resource user into the untenable position of deciding which data to believe—the old data or the new data. Time stamping is another component of data objects. Events (e.g., a part purchased, a report issued, a file opened) have no meaning unless you know when they occurred. Time stamps must be unique and immutable for data objects. A single event cannot occur at two different times.

Big Data is forever. **Big Data managers must do what seems to be impossible; they must learn how to modify data without altering the original content.**

DATA OBJECTS

How do modern Big Data managers do the impossible? How do they modify data without altering the original values? This is accomplished with the miracle of data objects.

Small data deals with data values. Typically, the values are stored in a spreadsheet or a simple database in which a data item (the row in a spreadsheet) is assigned a list of values. The values of the spreadsheet or the database are numbers or character sequences; the value descriptors are the row and column designators. This cannot work with Big Data; the collections of data are too complex, too diverse, and everything is subject to change.

For Big Data, you need to think in terms of data objects, in which everything known about the object is encapsulated within the object. For example, a data object will contain one or more values, and each value will be annotated with descriptors (i.e., attached to metadata). The object will be assigned a unique identifier that distinguishes the object from every other object. The object will be assigned to one or more object classes of objects and will inherit the properties of each assigned class. Most importantly, the data object may contain assertions about the included data values, including addenda to the data (e.g., updates, transformations, mappings to nomenclatures, etc.) and the times that these additional values were created.

Introspection was reviewed in Chapter 4. Aside from providing a way to understand the organization and content held by a Big Data resource, introspection provides a way to fully understand each data object residing in the resource. With introspection, a user can review all of the data values held in the object, along with the times that these data objects were created. If the values were fully described with metadata, it would be possible to determine which values held in the data object are obsolete and which values have the preferred and current representation of the data.

In practical terms, how are data objects created and queried? There are many ways to implement data objects, but the easiest way to see the unifying principles behind data objects starts with an understanding of references, also known as pointers.

Consider the computer instruction:

$$x = 5$$

In most computer languages, this is equivalent to saying, in English, put the integer 5 into the variable x (i.e., assign 5 to x). For the computer, there is no x. The computer creates an address in memory to hold the integer 5. The variable x is a pointer to the address where the variable is stored. Every computation involves following a pointer to an address and accessing the data held within.

All object-oriented languages are based on using pointers to data. Once you have a pointer you can load all sorts of accessible information. Object-oriented languages associate complex objects with pointers and provide a variety of methods whereby the various data values associated with a data object can be updated, and all of the updates to the data object can be fully described and documented to produce a data object history.

In object-oriented languages, the methods available to a data object are determined by the class assignment for the object. The languages come with a library of class methods that can be applied to every data object that has been assigned to the class. The low-order mechanics of object methods (assigning pointers, finding pointers, accessing various parts of the data associated with specific pointers, performing basic operations on data values, etc.) are provided by the language and hidden from the programmer.[65]

Big Data resources need not be built as though they were object-oriented languages, but a few of the object-oriented tricks are worth preserving. Because it is impractical for a database to keep tabs on every modification on every data object, of every type, we create data objects that document and track their own content.

How these features of immutability will be implemented by Big Data resources is left to the data managers. In theory, all of these features can be simulated using a simple table, in which every row is a unique data object, and for which all of the necessary encapsulated data is splayed out along the length of the row. If the table were accessible to a program whose methods could search through each record, performing any and all operations needed to access the correct data values, then that would suffice. Likewise, a store of RDF triples, if well designed, could provide every requisite feature of data objects, as well as an opportunity for data object introspection (see Chapter 4). There is no reason to confine Big Data resources to any particular methodology.

LEGACY DATA

> We need above all to know about changes; no one wants or needs to be reminded 16 hours a day that his shoes are on. *David Hubel*

Every child believes, for a time, that the universe began with his own birth. Anything preceding his birth is unreal and of no consequence. Many Big Data resources have a similar disregard for events that preceded their birth. If events occurred prior to the creation of the Big Data resource, they have no consequence and can be safely ignored.

The problem here is that, for many domains, it is counterproductive to pretend that history starts with the creation of the Big Data resource. Take, for example, patents. Anyone seeking a patent must determine whether his claims are, in fact, novel, and this determination requires a search over existing patents. If the U.S. patent office decided one day to begin computerizing all applications, it would need to have some way of adding all of the patents dating back to 1790, when the first patent act of the U.S. Congress was passed. Some might argue that a good resource for U.S. patent data should include patents awarded within the original colonies; such patents date back to 1641.

Big Data creators often neglect legacy data—old data that may exist in obsolete formats, on obsolete media, without proper annotation, and collected under dubious circumstances. Old data often provides the only clues to time-dependent events. Furthermore, Big Data resources typically absorb smaller resources or merge into larger resources over time. If the added data is to have any practical value, then the managers of the resource must find a way to incorporate legacy data into the aggregated resource.

The health care industry is a prime example of Big Data in search of a legacy. President Barack Obama has set a goal for every American to have a secure medical record by 2014. If, in the year 2014, every American had a secure medical record, what might that record include? Let us consider the medical record for a hypothetical patient named Lily Livesy, age 92. None of her medical records, from birth to middle age, have survived the passage of time. Not only has Mary outlived her doctors; she has outlived most of her hospitals. Though she lived in one city all her life, several of the hospitals that administered her medical care have been closed, and the records destroyed. In the past 30 years, she has received medical care at various doctors' offices and in various departments in various hospitals. Some of these hospitals kept paper records; some had electronic records. Only one of the hospitals had anything that might be likened to an integrated hospital information system that aggregated transaction records produced by the various hospital departments (pharmacy, pathology, radiology, surgery, medicine, and so on). This hospital initiated a new electronic health record (EHR) system in the year 2013. Unfortunately, the new system is not compatible with the same hospital's prior information system, and the old records did not transfer to the new system. Consequently, in the year 2014, Lily Livesy, age 92, has one EHR, residing in one hospital's information system, with no contribution from any other medical facility, and this EHR contains a secure identifier, but no actual medical information. Her 92-year-long medical history is virtually blank.

Often, the utility of legacy data comes as an afterthought inspired by a preliminary analysis of contemporary data. If a cancer researcher notices that the incidence of a certain tumor is high, he or she would naturally want to know whether the incidence of the tumor has been increasing over the past 5 years, 10 years, 15 years, and so on. A forensic criminologist who collects a Combined DNA Index System (CODIS) signature on a sample of DNA might desperately need to check his sample against CODIS signatures collected over the past five decades. The most useful Big Data resources reach back through time.

History is replete with examples of old data driving new discoveries. A recent headline story explains how century-old tidal data plausibly explained the appearance of the iceberg that sank the Titanic on April 15, 1912.[66] Records show that several months earlier, in 1912, the moon, earth, and sun aligned to produce a strong tidal pull, and this happened when the moon was the closest to the earth in 1400 years. The resulting tidal surge was sufficient to break the January Labrador ice sheet, sending an unusual number of icebergs towards the open North Atlantic waters. The Labrador icebergs arrived in the commercial shipping lanes 4 months later, in time for a fateful rendezvous with the Titanic. Back in January 1912, when tidal measurements were being collected, nobody foresaw that the data would be examined a century later.

Legacy data plays a crucial role in correcting the current record. It is not unusual for people to rely on flawed data. If we knew the full history of the data, including how it was originally collected and how it was modified over time, we might avoid reaching erroneous conclusions. Several years ago, newspaper headlines drew attention to a modern manual for prisoner interrogation used by U.S. forces stationed in Guantanamo. It turned out that the manual was a republication of a discredited Chinese operations manual used during the Korean War. The chain of documentation linking the current manual back to the original source had been broken.[67] In another example of lost legacy data, a Supreme Court decision was based, in part, on flawed information; an earlier statute had been overlooked.[68] Had the legacy data been raised during deliberations, an alternate Supreme Court verdict may have prevailed. To know the history of a data source, we need access to the legacy data that documents the original sources of our data and permits us to trace the modifications of the data, over time.

DATA BORN FROM DATA

The chief problem in historical honesty isn't outright lying. It is omission or de-emphasis of important data. *Howard Zinn*

Imagine this scenario. A data analyst extracts a large set of data from a Big Data resource. After subjecting the data to several cycles of the usual operations (data cleaning, data reduction, data filtering, data transformation, and the creation of customized data metrics), the data analyst is left with a new set of data, derived from the original set. The data analyst has imbued this new set of data with some added value, not apparent in the original set of data.

The question is, "How does the data analyst insert his new set of derived data back into the original Big Data resource, without violating immutability?" The answer is simplicity itself—reinserting the derived data is impossible and should not be attempted. The transformed data set is not a collection of original measurements; it cannot be sensibly verified by the data manager of the Big Data Resource. The modifications guarantee that the data values will not fit into the data object model upon which the resource was created (see Glossary item, Data object model). There simply is no substitute for the original and primary data.

The data analyst should make her methods and her transformed data available for review by others. Every step involved in creating the new data set needs to be carefully recorded and explained, but the transformed set of data cannot be absorbed into the data model for the resource. The original Big Data resource from which the raw data was extracted can include a document containing the details of the analysis and the modified data set produced by the analyst. Alternately, the Big Data resource may provide a link to sources holding the modified data sets. These steps provide the public with an information trail leading from the original data to the transformed data prepared by the data analyst.

RECONCILING IDENTIFIERS ACROSS INSTITUTIONS

In many cases, the biggest obstacle to achieving Big Data immutability is data record reconciliation. When different institutions merge their data systems, it is crucial that no data be lost and all identifiers be sensibly preserved. Cross-institutional identifier reconciliation is the process whereby institutions determine which data objects, held in different resources, are identical (i.e., the same data object). The data held in reconciled identical data objects can be combined in search results, and the identical data objects themselves can be merged (i.e., all of the encapsulated data can be combined in one data object) when Big Data resources are combined or when legacy data is absorbed into a Big data resource.

In the absence of successful reconciliation, there is no way to determine the unique identity of records (i.e., duplicate data objects may exist across institutions) and data users will be unable to rationally analyze data that relates to or is dependent upon the distinctions among objects in a data set. For all practical purposes, without data object reconciliation, there is no way to understand data received from multiple sources.

Reconciliation is particularly important for health care agencies. Some countries provide citizens with a personal medical identifier that is used in every medical facility in the nation. Hospital A can send a query to Hospital B for medical records pertaining to a patient sitting in Hospital A's emergency room. The national patient identifier ensures that the cross-institutional query will yield all of Hospital B's data on the patient and will not include data on other patients.

In the United States, interhospital record reconciliations are all but impossible. The United States does not have a national patient identifier. Though the Health Insurance Portability and Accountability Act of 1996 mandated a unique individual identifier for health care purposes, the U.S. Congress has since opposed this provision. Specifically, the 1998 Omnibus Appropriations Act (Public Law 105-277) blocked funding for a final standard on unique health identifiers. It seems unlikely that a national patient identifier system will be deployed in the United States anytime soon. Reconciliation is needed whenever a patient needs to collect records from different institutions, when an institution is acquired by another institution, or when the legacy data from an abandoned information system is merged with the data in a newly deployed information system. It is obvious that reconciliation is one of the most vexing problems in the field of medical informatics.

Consider the common problem of two institutions trying to reconcile personal records (e.g., banking records, medical charts, dating service records, credit card information). When both institutions are using the same identifiers for individuals in their resources, then reconciliation is effortless. Searches on an identifier will retrieve all the information attached to the identifier, if the search query is granted access to the information systems in both institutions. However, multi-institutional or universal identifier systems are rare. If either of the institutions lacks an adequate identifier system, the data from the systems cannot be sensibly reconciled. Data pertaining to a single individual may be unattached to any identifier, attached to one or more of several different identifiers, or mixed into the records of other individuals. The merging process would fail, at this point.

Assuming both institutions have adequate identifiers, then the two institutions must devise a method whereby a new identifier is created, for each record, that will be identical to the new identifier created for the same individual's record, in the other institution. For example, suppose each institution happens to store biometric data (e.g., retinal scans, DNA sequences, fingerprints); then the institutions might agree on a way to create a new identifier validated against these unique markers. With some testing, they could determine whether the new identifier works as specified (i.e., either institution will always create the same identifier for the same individual, and the identifier will never apply to any other individual). Once testing is finished, the new identifiers can be used for cross-institutional searches.

Lacking a unique biometric for individuals, reconciliation between institutions is feasible, but difficult. Some combination of identifiers (e.g., date of birth, social security number, name) might be developed. Producing an identifier from a combination of imperfect attributes has its limitations (as discussed in detail in Chapter 2), but it has the advantage that if all the preconditions of the identifier are met, misidentification will be uncommon (i.e., two records with the same identifier will belong to the same person). In this case, both institutions will need to decide how they will handle the set of records for which there is no identifier match in the other institution. They may assume that some individuals will have records in both institutions, but their records were not successfully reconciled by the new identifier. They may also assume that the unmatched group contains individuals that actually have no records in the other institution. Dealing with unreconciled records is a nasty problem. In most cases, it requires a curator to slog through individual records, using additional data from records or new data supplied by individuals, to make adjustments, as needed.

ZERO-KNOWLEDGE RECONCILIATION

Though record reconciliation across institutions is always difficult, the task becomes truly Herculean when it must be done blindly, without directly comparing records. This awkward situation occurs quite commonly whenever confidential data records from different institutions must be checked to see if they belong to the same person. In this case, neither institution is permitted to learn anything about the contents of records in the other institution. Reconciliation, if it is to occur, must implement a zero-knowledge protocol—a protocol that does not convey knowledge in or about records.

In a prior publication, I proposed a zero-knowledge protocol for reconciling patient records across institutions.[69] Because the protocol itself is somewhat abstract and unintuitive, a physical analogy may clarify the methodology. Imagine two people each holding a box containing an item. Neither person knows the contents of the box that they are holding or of the box that the other person is holding. They want to determine whether they are holding identical items, but they don't want to know anything about the items. They work together to create two identically prepared imprint stamps. With eyes closed, each one pushes his deformable stamp against his item. By doing so, the stamp is imprinted with markings characteristic of the object's surface. The stamps are next examined to determine if the compression marks on the ridges are distributed identically in both stamps. If so, the items in the two boxes, whatever they may be, are considered to be identical. Not all of the markings need to be compared—just enough of them to reach a high level of certainty. It is theoretically possible for two different items to produce the same pattern of compression marks, but it is highly unlikely. After the comparison is made, the stamps are discarded.

This physical analogy demonstrates the power of a zero-knowledge protocol. Neither party knows the identity of his own item. Neither party learns anything about his item or the other party's item during the transaction. Yet, somehow, the parties can determine whether the two items are identical.

Here is how the zero-knowledge protocol is able to reconcile confidential records across institutions.

1. Both institutions generate a random number of a predetermined length, and each institution sends the random number to the other institution.
2. Each institution sums its own random number with the random number provided by the other institution. We will refer to this number as Random_A. In this way, both institutions have the same final random number, and neither institution has actually transmitted this final random number. The splitting of the random number was arranged as a security precaution.
3. Both institutions agree to create a composite representation of information contained in the record that could establish the human subject of the record. The composite might be a concatenation of the social security number, the date of birth, the first initial of the surname.
4. Both institutions create a program that automatically creates the composite representation for the record and immediately sums the signature with Random_A, the random number that was negotiated between the two institutions (steps 1 and 2). The sum of the composite representation of the record plus Random_A is a random number that we will call Random_B.

5. If the two records being compared across institutions belong to the same human subject, then Random_B will be identical in both institutions. At this point, the two institutions must compare their respective versions of Random_B in such a way that they do not actually transmit Random_B to the other institution. If they were to transmit Random_B to the other institution, then the receiving institution could subtract Random_A from Random_B and produce the signature string for a confidential record contained in the other institution. This would be a violation of the requirement to share zero knowledge during the transaction.

6. The institutions take turns sending consecutive characters of their versions of Random_B. For example, the first institution sends the first character to the second institution. The second institution sends the second character to the first institution. The first institution sends the third character to the second institution. The exchange of characters proceeds until the first discrepancy occurs or until the first eight characters of the string match successfully. If any of the characters do not match, both institutions can assume that the records belong to different human subjects (i.e., reconciliation failed). If the first eight characters match, then it is assumed that both institutions are holding the same Random_B string and that the records are reconciled.

Data record reconciliation is seldom impossible. In the somewhat extreme protocol described above, reconciliation occurs with neither institution providing the other institution with any of the information contained in confidential data records. As you might expect, a practical implementation of the protocol might carry a retinue of complexities, as discussed in the original article.[69] The point here is that it is possible to reconcile records from different institutions, from legacy collections, and from merged data sets within an institution, if you set your mind to the task.

THE CURATOR'S BURDEN

Who is responsible for all this immutability that haunts every Big Data resource? Most of the burden falls upon the data curator. The word "curator" derives from the Latin "curatus," the same root for "curative," and conveys that curators "take care of" things. In a Big Data resource, the curator must oversee the accrual of sufficiently annotated legacy and prospective data into the resource; must choose appropriate nomenclatures for annotating the data; must annotate the data; and must supplement records with updated annotations as appropriate, when new versions of nomenclatures, specifications, and standards are applied.

The curator is saddled with the almost impossible task of keeping current the annotative scaffold of the Big Data resource, without actually changing any of the existing content of records. In the absence of curation, all resources degenerate over time. We will return to the important tasks of the modern curator in Chapter 15.

CHAPTER

7

Measurement

Get your facts first, then you can distort them as you please. **Mark Twain**

BACKGROUND

Engineers have a saying: "You can only control what you can measure." When a scientist or engineer performs a small-scale experiment in his own laboratory, he can calibrate all of his instruments, make his own measurements, check and cross-check his measurements with different instruments, compare his results with the results from other laboratories, and repeat his measurements until he is satisfied that the results are accurate and valid. When a scientist or engineer draws information from a Big Data resource, none of his customary safeguards apply. In almost all cases, the data is too big and too complex to repeat. He cannot double-check each measured value. If there is a sample mix-up, the measurements will not correspond to the correct samples. If there is insufficient description of the experiments and the samples, a scientist may misconstrue the meaning of the measurements. Basically, scientists lose much of their customary control options when they use Big Data.

Lacking any of the standard controls on measurement, Big Data creators and analysts must develop a new set of strategies and tools to ensure that the data has meaning and that the meaning has a close relationship with reality. In many cases, data managers and data users must abandon preconceived "gold standards" and create a new set of measurements that embrace the strengths and limitations of Big Data.

COUNTING

> On two occasions I have been asked, "If you put into the machine wrong figures, will the right answers come out?" I am not able rightly to apprehend the kind of confusion of ideas that could provoke such a question. *Charles Babbage*

For the bulk of Big Data projects, analysis begins with counting. If you cannot count the data held in a Big Data resource, then you will derive little benefit from the resource. Systemic counting errors account for unreproducible or misleading results. Surprisingly, there is very little written about this issue in the Big Data literature. Presumably, the subject is considered too trivial for serious study. To rectify this oversight, this section describes, in some depth, the surprising intellectual challenges of Big Data counting.

Most people would agree that the simple act of counting data is something that can be done accurately and reproducibly, from laboratory to laboratory. Actually, this is not the case. Counting is fraught with the kinds of errors previously described in this chapter, plus many other hidden pitfalls. Consider the problem of counting words in a paragraph. It seems straightforward, until you start asking yourself how you might deal with hyphenated words. "De-identified" is certainly one word. "Under-represented" is probably one word, but sometimes the hyphen is replaced by a space and then it is certainly two words. How about the term "military-industrial," which seems as though it should be two words? When a hyphen occurs at the end of a line, should we force a concatenation between the syllables at the end of one line and the start of the next?

Slashes are a tougher nut to crack than hyphens. How should we count terms that combine two related words by a slash, such as "medical/pharmaceutical"—one word or two words? If we believe that the slash is a word separator (i.e., slashes mark the end of one word and the beginning of another), then we would need to parse Web addresses into individual words, for example, www.science.com/stuff/neat_stuff/super_neat_stuff/balloons.htm.

The Web address could be broken into a string of words, if the "." and "_" characters could be considered valid word separators. In that case, the single Web address would consist of 11 words: www, science, com, stuff, neat, stuff, super, neat, stuff, balloons, and htm. If we only counted words that match entries in a standard dictionary, then the split Web address would contain 8 words: science, stuff, neat, stuff, super, neat, stuff, and balloons. If we defined a word as a string bounded by a space or a part-of-sentence separator (e.g., period, comma, colon, semicolon, question mark, exclamation mark, end of line character), then the unsplit Web address would count as 1 word. If the word must match a dictionary term, then the unsplit Web address would count as zero words. So, which is it: 11 words, 8 words, 1 word, or 0 word?

This is just the start of the problem. How shall we deal with abbreviations?[70,71] Should all abbreviations be counted as one word or as the sum of words represented by the abbreviation? Is "U.S." one word or two words? Suppose, before counting words, the text is preprocessed to expand abbreviations (i.e., every instance of "U.S." becomes an instance of United States, and UCLA would count as four words). This would yield an artificial increase in the number of words in the document. How would the word counter deal with abbreviations that look like words, such as "mumps," which could be the name of a viral disease of childhood, or it could be an abbreviation for a computer language used by medical informaticians and expanded as "Massachusetts General Hospital Utility Multi-Programming System?"

How would we deal with numeric sequences appearing in the text? Should each numeric sequence be counted as a word? If not, how do we handle Roman numerals? Should "IV" be counted as a word, because it is composed of alphabetic characters, or should it be omitted as a word, because it is equivalent to the numeric value, "4"? When we encounter "IV," how can we be certain that we are parsing a Roman numeral? Could "IV," within the context of our document, represent the abbreviation for "intravenous?"

It is obvious that the number of words in a document will depend on the particular method used to count the words. If we use a commercial word-counting application, how can we know which word-counting rules are applied? In the field of informatics, the total number of words is an important feature of a document. The total word count often appears in the denominator of common statistical measurements. Counting words seems to be a highly specialized task. In Chapter 8, we will discuss estimators. My favorite estimator of the number of words in any plain-text file is simply the size of the file in bytes divided by 6.5, the average number of characters in a word plus one separator character.

The point here is that a simple counting task, such as word counting, can easily become complex. A complex counting task, involving subjective assessments of observations, seldom yields accurate results. When the criteria for counting change over time, then results that were merely inaccurate may devolve even further, into irreproducibility. An example of a counting task that is complex and objective is the counting of hits and errors in baseball. The rules for counting errors are subjective and based on the scorer's judgment of the intended purpose of the hit (e.g., sacrifice fly) and the expected number of bases reached in the absence of the error. The determination of an error sometimes depends on the outcome of the play after the presumptive error has occurred (i.e., on events that are not controlled or influenced by the error). Counting is also complex, with rules covering specific instances of play. For example, passed balls and wild pitches are not scored as errors—they are assigned to another category of play. Plays involving catchers are exempt from certain rules for errors that apply to fielders. It would be difficult to find an example of a counting task that is more complex than counting baseball errors.

Sometimes, counting criteria inadvertently exclude categories of items that should be counted. The diagnoses that appear on death certificates are chosen from a list of causes of death included in the International Classification of Diseases (ICD). Diagnoses collected from all of the death certificates issued in the United States are aggregated by the Centers for Disease Control and Prevention and published in the National Vital Statistics Report.[72] As it happens, "medical error" is not included as a cause of death in the ICD; hence, U.S. casualties of medical errors are not counted as such in the official records. Official tally notwithstanding, it is estimated that about one of every six deaths in the United States results from medical error.[72]

Big Data is particularly prone to counting errors, as data is typically collected from multiple sources, each with its own method for annotating data. In addition, Big Data may extend forwards and backwards in time, constantly adding new data and merging with legacy data sets. The criteria for counting data may change over time, producing misleading results. Here are a few examples of counts that changed radically when the rules for counting changed.

1. Beachy Head is a cliff in England with a straight vertical drop and a beautiful sea view. It is a favorite jumping off point for suicides. The suicide rate at Beachy Head dropped as sharply as the cliff when the medical examiner made a small policy change. From a certain moment on, bodies found at the cliff bottom would be counted as suicides only if their postmortem toxicology screen was negative for alcohol. Intoxicated subjects were pronounced dead by virtue of accident (i.e., not suicide), cutting by half the number of counted suicides.[73]

2. Sudden infant death syndrome (SIDS, also known as crib death) was formerly considered to be a disease of unknown etiology that caused infants to stop breathing and die, often during sleep. Today, most SIDS deaths are presumed to be due to unintentional suffocation from bedclothes, often in an overheated environment, and aggravated by a prone (i.e., face down) sleeping position. Consequently, some infant deaths that may have been diagnosed as SIDS in past decades are now diagnosed as unintentional suffocations. This diagnostic switch has resulted in a trend characterized by increasing numbers of infant suffocations and a decreasing number of SIDS cases.[74] This trend is, in part, artifactual, arising from changes in reporting criteria.

3. In the year 2000, nearly a half-century after the Korean War, the U.S. Department of State downsized its long-standing count of U.S. military Korean War deaths to 36,616 down from an earlier figure of about 54,000. The drop of 17,000 deaths resulted from the exclusion of U. S. military deaths that occurred during the Korean War in countries outside Korea.[75] The old numbers reflected deaths during the Korean War; the newer number reflects deaths occurring due to the Korean War. Aside from historical interest, the alteration indicates how collected counts may change retroactively.

4. Human life is flanked by two events, birth and death; both events are commemorated with a certificate. The death certificate is the single most important gauge of public health. They tell us the ages at which deaths occur and the causes of those deaths. With this information, we can determine the most common causes of death in the population, changes in the frequency of occurrences of the different causes of death, and the effect of interventions intended to increase overall life expectancy and reduce deaths caused by particular causes. Death certificates are collected on greater than 99% of individuals who die in the United States.[76] This data, vital to the health of every nation, is highly error prone, and the problems encountered in the United States seem to apply everywhere.[77,78] A survey of 49 national and international health atlases has shown that there is virtually no consistency in the way that death data is prepared.[79] Within the United States, there is little consistency among states in the manner in which the causes of death are listed.[19] Death data is Big Data, as it is complex (i.e., containing detailed, nonstandard information within death certificates), comes from many sources (i.e., every municipality), and arrives continually (i.e., deaths occur every minute), with many records (i.e., everyone dies eventually). The rules for annotating the data change regularly (i.e., new versions of the International Classification of Diseases contain different new terms and codes). The consistency of the data decreases as the Big Data grows in size and in time. Our basic understanding of how humans die, and our ability to measure the effect of potentially life-saving public health interventions, is jeopardized by our inability to count the causes of death.

GENE COUNTING

The Human Genome Project is a massive bioinformatics project in which multiple laboratories helped to sequence the 3 billion base pair haploid human genome (see Glossary item, Human Genome Project). The project began its work in 1990, a draft human genome was prepared in 2000, and a completed genome was finished in 2003, marking the start of the so-called postgenomics era. There are about 2 million species of proteins synthesized by human cells. If every protein had its own private gene containing its specific genetic code, then there would be about 2 million protein-coding genes contained in the human genome. As it turns out, this estimate is completely erroneous. Analysis of the human genome indicates that there are somewhere between 20,000 and 150,000 protein-coding genes. The majority of estimates come in at the low end (about 25,000 genes). Why are the current estimates so much lower than the number of proteins and why is there such a large variation in the lower and upper estimates (20,000 to 150,000)?

Counting is difficult when you do not fully understand the object that you are counting. The reason that you are counting objects is to learn more about the object, but you cannot always count an object accurately until you have already learned a great deal about the object. Perceived this way, counting is a bootstrapping problem. In the case of proteins, a small number of genes can account for a much larger number of protein species, because proteins can be assembled from combinations of genes, and the final form of a unique protein can be modified by so-called post-translational events (folding variations, chemical modifications, sequence shortening, clustering by fragments, etc.). The methods used to count protein-coding genes can vary.[80] One technique might look for sequences that mark the beginning and the end of a coding sequence, whereas another method might look for segments containing base triplets that correspond to amino acid codons. The former method might count genes that code for cellular components other than proteins, and the latter might miss fragments whose triplet sequences do not match known protein sequences.[81] Improved counting methods are being developed to replace the older methods, but a final number evades our grasp.

The take-home lesson is that the most sophisticated and successful Big Data projects can be stumped by the simple act of counting.

DEALING WITH NEGATIONS

A large portion of Big Data is categorical, not quantitative. Whenever counting categorical features, you need to know whether a feature is present or absent. Unstructured text has no specific format for negative assertions (i.e., statements indicating that a feature is absent or an assertion is false). Negations in unstructured data come into play during parsing routines wherein various features need to be counted.

If a computer program is seeking to collect, count, or annotate occurrences of a particular diagnosis included in a pathology report or a particular type of "buy" order on a financial transaction or the mention of a particular species of frog on a field report, there should be some way to distinguish a positive occurrence of the term (e.g., Amalgamated Widget is traded) from a negation statement (e.g., Amalgamated Widget is not traded). Otherwise, counts of the positive occurrences of trades would include cases that are demonstrably negative. Informaticians have developed a variety of techniques that deal with negations occurring in textual data.[82]

In general, negation techniques rely on finding a negation term (e.g., not present, not found, not seen) in proximity to an annotation term (e.g., a term that matches some term in a standard nomenclature or a term that has been cataloged or otherwise indexed for the data set onto which a markup tag is applied). A negated term would not be collected or counted as a positive occurrence of the term.

Examples of negation terms included in sentences are shown here:

He **cannot find** evidence for the presence of a black hole.
We **cannot find** support for the claim.
A viral infection **is not present**.
No presence of Waldo is noted.
Bigfoot is **not in evidence** in this footprint analysis.

It is easy to exclude terms that are accompanied by an obvious negation term. When terms are negated or otherwise nullified by terms that are not consistently characterized by a negative inference, the problem becomes complex.

Here is a short list of implied negations, lacking an unambiguous negation term, followed by the rewritten sentence that contains a negation:

"Had this been a tin control processor, the satellite would have failed."—The satellite did not fail.
"There is a complete **absence of** fungus."—Fungus is not present
"We **can rule out** the presence of invasive cancer."—Invasive cancer is not present.
"Hurricanes **failed to show**."—Hurricanes did not show.
"The witness **fails to** make an appearance."—The witness did not appear.
"The diagnosis is **incompatible with** psoriasis."—Psoriasis is not present.
"Drenching rain is **inconsistent with** drought."—Drought does not occur with drenching rain.
"There is **insufficient evidence** for a guilty verdict."—Not guilty.
"Accidental death **is excluded**."—Not an accidental death.
"A drug overdose **is ruled out**."—Not a drug overdose.
"**Neither fish nor** foul."—Not fish. Not foul.
"There is **zero evidence for** aliens in Hoboken."—Aliens have not been found in Hoboken.

In addition to outright negations, sentences may contain purposefully ambiguating terms, intended to prohibit readers from drawing any conclusion, positive or negative. For example, "The report is **inconclusive** for malignancy." How would this report be counted?

The point here is that, like everything else in the field of Big Data, the people who prepare and use resources must have a deep understanding of the contained data. They must also have a realistic understanding of the kinds of questions that can be sensibly asked and answered with the available data.

UNDERSTANDING YOUR CONTROL

In the small data realm, the concept of "control" is easily defined and grasped. Typically, a group is divided into treatment and control subgroups. Heterogeneity in the population (e.g., gender, age, health status) is randomly distributed into both groups so that the treatment and the control subgroups are, to the extent possible, indistinguishable from one another. If the treatment group receives a drug administered by syringe, suspended in a saline solution, then the control group might receive an injection of saline solution by syringe, without the drug. The idea is to control the control and the treatment groups so that they are identical in every way, save for one isolated factor. Measurable differences in the control and the treatment groups that arise after treatment are potentially due to the action of the one treatment factor.

The concept of "control" does not strictly apply to Big Data; the data analyst never actually "controls" the data. The data analyst does his best to make sense of the "uncontrolled" data that is provided.

In the absence of controlling an experiment, what can the data analyst do to exert some kind of data selection that simulates a controlled experiment? It often comes down to trying our best to find two populations, from the Big Data resource, that are alike in every respect but one—the treatment.

Let me relate a hypothetical situation that illustrates the special skills that Big Data analysts must master. An analyst is charged with developing a method for distinguishing endometriosis from nondiseased (control) tissue, using gene expression data. By way of background, endometriosis is a gynecologic condition wherein endometrial tissue that is usually confined to the endometrium (the tissue that covers the inside surface of the uterus) is found growing elsewhere: on the surfaces of the ovaries, the pelvic wall, and other organs found in the pelvic area. The analyst finds a public data collection that provides gene expression data on endometriosis tissues (five samples) and on control tissues (five samples). By comparing the endometriosis samples with the control samples, he finds a set of 1000 genes that are biomarkers for endometriosis (i.e., that have "significantly" different expression in the disease samples compared with the control samples).

Let us set aside the natural skepticism reserved for studies that generate 1000 new biomarkers from an analysis of 10 tissue samples. The analyst is asked the question, "What was your control tissue, and how was it selected and prepared for analysis?" The analyst indicates that he does not know anything about the control tissues. He points out that the selection and preparation of control tissues is a preanalytic task (i.e., outside the realm of influence of the data analyst). In this case, the choice of the control tissue was not at all obvious. If the control tissue were nonuterine tissue, taken from the area immediately adjacent to the area from which the endometriosis was sampled, then the analysis would have been comparing endometriosis with the normal tissue that covers the surface of pelvic organs (i.e., a mixture of various types of connective tissues). If the control consisted of samples of normal endometriotic tissue (i.e., the epithelium lining the endometrial canal), then the analysis would have been comparing an endometriosis with its normal counterpart. In either case, the significance and rationale for the study would have been very different, depending on the choice of controls.

In this case, as in every case, the choice and preparation of the control is of the utmost importance to the analysis that will follow. In a controlled study, every system variable but one, the variable studied in the experiment, is "frozen"—an experimental luxury lacking in Big Data. The Big Data analyst must somehow invent a plausible control from the available data. This means that the data analyst, and his close coworkers, must delve into the details of data preparation and must have a profound understanding of the kinds of questions that the data can answer. Finding the most sensible control and treatment groups from a Big Data resource can require a particular type of analytic mind that has been trained to cope with concepts drawn from many different scientific disciplines (see Chapter 15).

PRACTICAL SIGNIFICANCE OF MEASUREMENTS

The most savage controversies are those about matters as to which there is no good evidence either way. *Bertrand Russell*

Big Data provides statistical significance without necessarily providing any practical significance. Here is an example. Suppose you have two populations of people and you suspect that the adult males in the first population are taller than those from the second population. To test your hypothesis, you measure the heights of a random sampling (100 subjects) from both groups. You find that the average height of group 1 is 172.7 cm, while the average height of the second group is 172.5 cm. You calculate the standard error of the mean (the standard deviation divided by the square root of the number of subjects in the sampled population), and you use this statistic to determine the range in which the mean is expected to fall. You find that the difference in the average height in the two sampled populations is not significant, and you cannot exclude the null hypothesis (i.e., that the two sampled groups are equivalent, height-wise).

This outcome really bugs you! You have demonstrated a 2-mm difference in the average heights of the two groups, but the statistical tests do not seem to care. You decide to up the ante. You use a sampling of one million individuals from the two populations and recalculate the averages and the standard errors of the means. This time, you get a slightly smaller difference in the heights (172.65 for group 1 and 172.51 for group 2). When you calculate the standard error of the mean for each population, you find a much smaller number because you are dividing the standard deviation by the square root of one million (i.e., 1000), not by the square root of 100 (i.e., 10) that you used for the first calculation. The confidence interval for the ranges of the averages is much smaller now, and you find that the differences in heights between group 1 and group 2 are sufficient to exclude the null hypothesis with reasonable confidence.

Your Big Data project was a stunning success; you have shown that group 1 is taller than group 2, with reasonable confidence. However, the average difference in their heights seems to be about a millimeter. There are no real-life situations where a difference of this small magnitude would have any practical significance. You could not use height to distinguish individual members of group 1 from individual members of group 2; there is too much overlap among the groups, and height cannot be accurately measured to within a millimeter tolerance. You have used Big Data to achieve statistical significance, without any practical significance.

There is a tendency amongst Big Data enthusiasts to promote large data sets as a cure for the limited statistical power and frequent irreproducibility of small data studies. In general, if an effect is large, it can be evaluated in a small data project. If an effect is too small to confirm in a small data study, statistical analysis may benefit from a Big Data study by increasing the sample size and reducing variances. Nonetheless, the final results may have no practical significance, or the results may be unrepeatable in a small scale (i.e., real life) setting, or may be made invalid due to the persistence of biases that were not eliminated when the sample size was increased.

Cancer researchers are turning toward larger trials to overcome the statistical limitations of small studies. Erlotinib, sold as Tarceva by Genentech, OSI Pharmaceuticals, and Roche Pharmaceuticals, was approved by the Food and Drug Administration for the treatment of pancreatic cancer. It costs about $3500 per month and will improve survival by an average of 12 days.[83] The chief executive of OSI Pharmaceuticals projected that annual sales of Tarceva could reach $2 billion by 2011.[84] Large-scale clinical trials enabled researchers to determine that Erlotinib extended the survival of pancreatic cancer patients, but Big Data has not told us whether an average 12-day life extension delivers a practical benefit that exceeds costs.

The field of molecular biology has been moving toward high-throughput tests; these are automated and complex tests that produce huge sets of data for each experiment, often with thousands of measurements for a given biological sample. Much of the Big Data in the biology field consists of complex, multidimensional data collected from many different laboratories. Results from the past decade have indicated that polytelic tests may be difficult or impossible to reproduce between laboratories,[85–89] or the data is reproducible but of no biological relevance, or the data is dominated by random data values (i.e., noise) of no analytic benefit[90](see Glossary item, Polytely).

OBSESSIVE-COMPULSIVE DISORDER: THE MARK OF A GREAT DATA MANAGER

What do we really know about the measurements contained in Big Data resources? How can we know what these measurements mean and whether they are correct? Data managers approach these questions with three closely related activities: data verification, data validation, and data reproducibility.

Verification is the process that ensures that data conforms to a set of specifications. As such, it is a preanalytic process (i.e., done on the data, before it is analyzed).

Validation is the process that checks whether the data can be applied in a manner that fulfills its intended purpose. Validation often involves showing that correct conclusions can be obtained from a competent analysis of the data. For example, a Big Data resource might contain position, velocity, direction, and mass data for the earth and for a meteor that is traveling sunwards. The data may meet all specifications for measurement, error tolerance, data typing, and data completeness. A competent analysis of the data indicates that the meteor will miss the earth by a safe 50,000 miles, plus or minus 10,000 miles. If the asteroid smashes into the earth, destroying all planetary life, then an extraterrestrial observer might conclude that the data was verified, but not validated.

Reproducibility involves getting the same measurement over and over when you perform the test. Validation involves drawing the same conclusion over and over. Both reproducibility and validation are postanalytic tasks.

The methods used to verify and validate data, and to show that the results are reproducible, will vary greatly, depending on the data content, its method of preparation, and its intended purposes. The methods for documenting these procedures are less variable. Good managers will create a protocol for verifying the data held in the resource, and they will date and sign the protocol. In most cases, the protocol will be distributed and reviewed by a team or committee, and every reviewer should date and sign their approvals. When the protocol is modified, there should be a version number assigned to the newer protocol, and the same process of signatures and dates should be repeated for each modification. Competent data managers will make it their business to ensure that the protocols are followed and that each verification process is fully documented. The data manager should periodically review the protocol to determine if it needs revision. The data manager should review the verification studies and should determine what, if any, actions should be taken in response to the verification studies. If actions are taken, then a document must be generated detailing the actions taken and the results of such actions. Dates and signatures of participating and reviewing personnel must be included. A similar process is necessary for validation protocols and reproducibility protocols.

It all seems so tedious! Is it really necessary? Sadly, yes. Over time, data tends to degenerate: records are lost or duplicated, links become defunct, unique identifiers lose their uniqueness, the number of missing values increases, nomenclature terms become obsolete, and mappings between terms coded to different standards become decreasingly reliable. As personnel transfer, leave employment, retire, or die, the institutional memory for the Big Data resource weakens. As the number of contributors to a Big Data resource increases, controlling the quality of the incoming data becomes increasingly difficult. Data, like nature, regresses from order to disorder unless energy is applied to reverse the process. **There is no escape—every reliable Big Data resource is obsessed with self-surveillance.**

Simple but Powerful Big Data Techniques

Only theory can tell us what to measure and how to interpret it. **Albert Einstein**

BACKGROUND

It may come as something of a shock, but most Big Data analysis projects can be done without the aid of statistical or analytical software. A good deal of the value in any Big Data resource can be attained simply by looking at the data and thinking about what you've seen.

It is said that we humans have a long-term memory capacity in the petabyte range and that we process many thousands of thoughts each day. In addition, we obtain new information continuously and rapidly in many formats (visual, auditory, olfactory, proprioceptive, and gustatory). Who can deny that humans qualify, under the three v's (volume, velocity, and variety), as Big Data resources incarnate?

The late, great Harold Gatty was one of the finest Big Data resources of his time. Harold Gatty gained fame, in 1931, when he navigated an 8-day flight around the world. During World War II, he taught navigation and directed air transport for the Allies in the Pacific campaign. His most enduring legacy has been his book "Finding Your Way Without Map or Compass," in which he explains how to determine your location and direction, the time of day, the season of the year, the day of the month, and the approaching weather through careful observation and deduction.[91]

Location and direction can be established by observing the growth of branches on trees: upward-growing branches on the northern side of a tree, sideways-growing branches on the southern side of a tree. Open branches coalescing as pyramids pointing to the top of the tree are found in northern latitudes to catch lateral light; branches coalescing to form flat or round-topped trees are found in temperate zones to capture direct light. Broad-leafed branches are found in the tropics to shield heat and light. At sea, the number of seabirds in the sky can be estimated by latitude; the further away from the equator, the greatest number of seabirds. The paucity of seabirds in the tropics is a consequence of the fish population; the greatest numbers of fish are found in cold water in higher latitudes.

Gatty's book contains hundreds of useful tips, but how does any of this relate to Big Data? The knowledge imparted by Harold Gatty was obtained by careful observations of the natural world, collected by hundreds of generations of survivalists living throughout the world. In most cases, observations connected data values measured by one of the five human senses: the distinctive reflection of snow on an overhead cloud as seen from a distance, the odor of a herd of camel grazing at an oasis, the interval between a shout and its echo, the feel of the prevailing wind, or the taste of fresh water. All of these measurements produced a collective Big Data resource stored within human memory. The conclusions that Gatty and his predecessors learned were correlations (e.g., the full moon rises at sunset, the last quarter moon rises at midnight). Many samples of the same data confirmed the correlations.

Gatty cautions against overconfidence in correlations, insisting that navigators should never depend on a single observation "as it may be an exception to the general rule. It is the combined evidence of a number of different indications which strengthens and confirms the conclusions."[91]

In this chapter, you will learn to conduct preliminary analyses of Big Data resources without the use of statistical packages and without advanced analytical methods (see Glossary item, Deep analytics). Keen observational skills and a prepared mind are sometimes the only tools necessary to reach profoundly important conclusions from Big Data resources.

LOOK AT THE DATA

Before you choose and apply analytic methods to data sets, you should spend time studying your raw data. The following steps may be helpful.

1. **Find a free ASCII editor.** When I encounter a large data file, in plain ASCII format, the first thing I do is open the file and take a look at its contents. Unless the file is small (i.e., under about 20 megabytes), most commercial word processors fail at this task. They simply cannot open really large files (in the range of 100–1000 megabytes). You will want to use an editor designed to work with large ASCII files (see Glossary item, Text editor). Two of the more popular, freely available editors are Emacs and vi (also available under the name vim). Downloadable versions are available for Linux, Windows, and Macintosh systems. On most computers, these editors will open files of several hundred megabytes, at least.

If you are reluctant to invest the time required to learn another word processor, and you have a Unix or Windows operating system, then you can read any text file, one screen at a time, with the "more" command, for example, on Windows systems, at the prompt:

```
c:\>type huge_file.txt |more
```

The first lines from the file will fill the screen, and you can proceed through the file by pressing and holding the <Enter> key.

Using this simple command, you can assess the format and general organization of any file. For the uninitiated, ASCII data files are inscrutable puzzles. For those who take a few moments to learn the layout of the record items, ASCII records can be read and understood, much like any book.

Many data files are composed of line records. Each line in the file contains a complete record, and each record is composed of a sequence of data items. The items may be separated by commas, tabs, or some other delimiting character. If the items have prescribed sizes, you can compare the item values for different records by reading up and down a column of the file.

2. **Download and study the "readme" or index files, or their equivalent.** In prior decades, large collections of data were often assembled as files within subdirectories, and these files could be downloaded in part or in toto via ftp (file transfer protocol). Traditionally, a "readme" file would be included with the files, and the "readme" file would explain the purpose, contents, and organization of all the files. In some cases, an index file might be available, providing a list of terms covered in the files, and their locations, in the various files. When such files are prepared thoughtfully, they are of great value to the data analyst. It is always worth a few minutes time to open and browse the "readme" file. I think of "readme" files as treasure maps. The data files contain great treasure, but you're unlikely to find anything of value unless you study and follow the map.

In the past few years, data resources have grown in size and complexity. Today, Big Data resources are often collections of resources, housed on multiple servers. New and innovative access protocols are continually being developed, tested, released, updated, and replaced. Still, some things remain the same. There will always be documents to explain how the Big Data resource "works" for the user. It behooves the data analyst to take the time to read and understand this prepared material. If there is no prepared material, or if the prepared material is unhelpful, then you may want to reconsider using the resource.

3. **Assess the number of records in the Big Data resource.** There is a tendency among some data managers to withhold information related to the number of records held in the resource. In many cases, the number of records says a lot about the inadequacies of the resource. If the total number of records is much smaller than the typical user might have expected or desired, then the user might seek her data elsewhere. Data managers, unlike data users, sometimes dwell in a perpetual future that never merges into the here and now. They think in terms of the number of records they will acquire in the next 24 hours, the next year, or the next decade. To the data manager, the current number of records may seem irrelevant.

One issue of particular importance is the sample number/sample dimension dichotomy. Some resources with enormous amounts of data may have very few data records. This occurs when individual records contain mountains of data (e.g., sequences, molecular species, images, and so on), but the number of individual records is woefully low (e.g., hundreds or thousands). This problem, known as the curse of dimensionality, will be further discussed in Chapter 10.

Data managers may be reluctant to divulge the number of records held in the Big Data resource when the number is so large as to defy credibility. Consider this example. There are about 5700 hospitals in the United States, serving a population of about 313 million people. If each hospital served a specific subset of the population, with no overlap in service between neighboring hospitals, then each would provide care for about 54,000 people. In practice, there is always some overlap in catchment population, and a popular estimate for the average (overlapping) catchment for U.S. hospitals is 100,000. The catchment population for any particular hospital can be estimated by factoring in a parameter related to its size. For example, if a hospital hosts twice the number of beds than the average U.S. hospital, then one would guess that its catchment population would be about 200,000.

The catchment population represents the approximate number of electronic medical records for living patients served by the hospital (one living individual, one hospital record). If you are informed that a hospital, of average size, contains 10 million records (when you are expecting about 100,000), then you can infer that something is very wrong. Most likely, the hospital is creating multiple records for individual patients. In general, institutions do not voluntarily provide users with information that casts doubt on the quality of their information systems. Hence, the data analyst, ignorant of the total number of records in the system, might proceed under the false assumption that each patient is assigned one and only one hospital record. Suffice it to say that the data user must know the number of records available in a resource and the manner in which records are identified and internally organized.

4. **Determine how data objects are identified and classified.** The identifier and the classifier (the name of the class to which the data object belongs) are the two most important keys to Big Data information. Here is why. If you know the identifier for a data object, you can collect all of the information associated with the object, regardless of its location in the resource. If other Big Data resources use the same identifier for the data object, you can integrate all of the data associated with the data object, regardless of its location in external resources. Furthermore, if you know the class that holds a data object, you can combine objects of a class and study all of the members of the class. Consider the following example:

```
Big Data resource 1
    75898039563441 name                    G. Willikers
    75898039563441 gender                  male
Big Data resource 2
    75898039563441 age                     35
    75898039563441 is_a_class_member       cowboy
    94590439540089 name                    Hopalong Tagalong
    94590439540089 is_a_class_member       cowboy
Merged Big Data resource 1+2
    75898039563441 name                    G. Willikers
    75898039563441 gender                  male
    75898039563441 is_a_class_member       cowboy
    75898039563441 age                     35
    94590439540089 name                    Hopalong Tagalong
    94590439540089 is_a_class_member       cowboy
```

The merge of two Big Data resources combines data related to identifier 75898039563441 from both resources. We now know a few things about this data object that we did not know before the merge. The merge also tells us that the two data objects identified as 75898039563441 and 94590439540089 are both members of class "cowboy". We now have two instance members from the same class, and this gives us information related to the types of instances contained in the class.

The consistent application of standard methods for object identification and for class assignments, using a standard classification or ontology, greatly enhances the value of a Big Data resource (see Glossary item, Identification). A savvy data analyst will quickly determine whether the resource provides these important features.

5. **Determine whether data objects contain self-descriptive information.** Data objects should be well specified. All values should be described with metadata, all metadata should be defined, and the definitions for the metadata should be found in documents whose unique names and locations are provided (see Glossary item, ISO/IEC 11179). The data should be linked to protocols describing how the data was obtained and measured.

6. **Assess whether the data is complete and representative.** You must be prepared to spend many hours moving through the records; otherwise, you will never really understand the data. After you have spent a few weeks of your life browsing through Big Data resources, you will start to appreciate the value of the process. Nothing comes easy. Just as the best musicians spend thousands of hours practicing and rehearsing their music, the best data analysts devote thousands of hours to studying their data sources. It is always possible to run sets of data through analytic routines that summarize the data, but drawing insightful observations from the data requires thoughtful study.

An immense Big Data resource may contain spotty data. On one occasion, I was given a large hospital-based data set, with assurances that the data was complete (i.e., containing all necessary data relevant to the project). After determining how the records and the fields were structured, I looked at the distribution frequency of diagnostic entities contained in the data set. Within a few minutes I had the frequencies of occurrence of the different diseases, assembled under broad diagnostic categories. I spent another few hours browsing through the list, and before long I noticed that there were very few skin diseases included in the data. I am not a dermatologist, but I knew that skin diseases are among the most common conditions encountered in medical clinics. Where were the missing skin diseases? I asked one of the staff clinicians assigned to the project. He explained that the skin clinic operated somewhat autonomously from the other hospital clinics. The dermatologists maintained their own information system, and their cases were not integrated into the general disease data set. I inquired as to why I had been assured that the data set was complete when everyone other than myself knew full well that the data set lacked skin cases. Apparently, the staff were all so accustomed to ignoring the field of dermatology that it had never crossed their minds to mention the matter.

It is a quirk of human nature to ignore anything outside one's own zone of comfort and experience. Otherwise fastidious individuals will blithely omit relevant information from Big Data resources if they consider the information to be inconsequential, irrelevant, or insubstantial. I have had conversations with groups of clinicians who requested that the free-text information in radiology and pathology reports (the part of the report containing descriptions of findings and other comments) be omitted from the compiled electronic records on the grounds that it is all unnecessary junk. Aside from the fact that "junk" text can serve as important analytic clues (e.g., measurements of accuracy, thoroughness, methodologic trends, and so on), the systematic removal of parts of data records produces a biased and incomplete Big Data resource. In general, data managers should not censor data. It is the job of the data analyst to determine what data should be included or excluded from analysis, and to justify his or her decision. If the data is not available to the data analyst, then there is no opportunity to reach a thoughtful and justifiable determination.

On another occasion, I was given an anonymized data set of clinical data, contributed from an anonymized hospital (see Glossary item, Anonymization versus deidentification). As I always do, I looked at the frequency distributions of items on the reports. In a few minutes, I noticed that germ cell tumors, rare tumors that arise from a cell lineage that includes oocytes and spermatocytes, were occurring in high numbers. At first, I thought that I might have discovered an epidemic of germ cell tumors in the hospital's catchment population. When I looked more closely at the data, I noticed that the increased incidence occurred in virtually every type of germ cell tumor, and there did not seem to be any particular increase associated with gender, age, or ethnicity. Cancer epidemics raise the incidence of one or maybe two types of cancer and may involve a particular at-risk population. A cancer epidemic would not be expected to raise the incidence of all types of germ cell tumors, across ages and genders. It seemed more likely that the high numbers of germ cell tumors were explained by a physician or specialized care unit that concentrated on treating patients with germ cell tumors, receiving referrals from across the nation. Based on the demographics of the data set (the numbers of patients of different ethnicities), I could guess the geographic region of the hospital. With this information, and knowing that the institution probably had a prestigious germ cell clinic, I guessed the name of the hospital. I eventually confirmed that my suspicions were correct.

The point here is that if you take the time to study raw data, you can spot systemic deficiencies or excesses in the data, if they exist, and you may gain deep insights that would not be obtained by mathematical techniques.

7. **Plot some of the data.** Plotting data is quick, easy, and surprisingly productive. Within minutes, the data analyst can assess long-term trends, short-term and periodic trends, the general shape of data distribution, and general notions of the kinds of functions that might represent the data (e.g., linear, exponential, power series). Simply knowing that the data can be expressed as a graph is immeasurably reassuring to the data analyst.

There are many excellent data visualization tools that are widely available. Without making any recommendation, I mention that graphs produced for this book were made with Matplotlib, a plotting library for the Python programming language; and Gnuplot, a graphing utility available for a variety of operating systems. Both Matplotlib and Gnuplot are open source applications that can be downloaded, at no cost, and are available at sourceforge. net (see Glossary item, Open source).

Gnuplot is extremely easy to use, either as stand-alone scripts containing Gnuplot commands, or from the system command line, or from the command line editor provided with the application software. Most types of plots can be created with a single Gnuplot command line. Gnuplot can fit a mathematically expressed curve to a set of data using the nonlinear least-squares Marquardt–Levenberg algorithm.[92,93] Gnuplot can also provide a set of statistical descriptors (e.g., median, mean, standard deviation) for plotted sets of data.

Gnuplot operates from data held in tab-delimited ASCII files. Typically, data extracted from a Big Data resource is ported into a separate ASCII file, with column fields separated

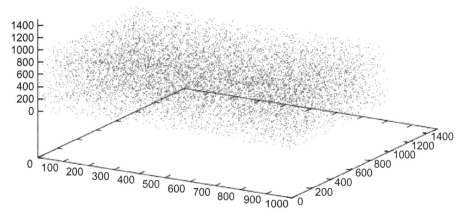

FIGURE 8.1 A plot of 10,000 random data points, in three coordinates.

with a tab character, and rows separated by a newline character. In most cases, you will want to modify your raw data before it is ready for plotting. Use your favorite programming language to normalize, shift, transform, convert, filter, translate, or munge your raw data as you see fit. Export the data as a tab-delimited file, named with a .dat suffix.

It takes about a second to generate a plot for 10,000 data points (see Figure 8.1).

The data for Figure 8.1 was created with a seven-line script using the Perl programming language, but any scripting language would have been sufficient.[19] Ten thousand data points were created, with the x, y, and z coordinates for each point produced by a random number generator. The point coordinates were put into a file named xyz_rand.dat. One command line in Gnuplot produced the graph shown in Figure 8.1:

```
splot 'c:\ftp\xyz_rand.dat'
```

It is often useful to compartmentalize data by value using a histogram. A histogram contains bins that cover the range of data values available to the data objects, usually in a single dimension. For this next example, each data object will be a point in three-dimensional space and will be described with three coordinates: x, y, and z. We can easily write a script that generates 100,000 points, with each coordinate assigned a random number between 0 and 1000. We can count the number of produced points whose x coordinate is 0, 1, 2, 3, and so on until 999. With 100,000 generated values, you would expect that each integer between 0 and 1000 (i.e., the 1000 bins) would contain about 100 points. Here are the histogram values for the first 20 bins.

107
97
101
87
105
107
85
113
100

106
110
104
108
98
103
68
93
93
111
107

We can create a histogram displaying all 1000 bins (see Figure 8.2).

Looking at Figure 8.2, we might guess that most of the bins contain about 100 data points. Bins with many fewer data points or many more data points would be hard to find. With another short script, we can compute the distribution of the numbers of bins containing all possible numbers of data points. Here is the raw data distribution (held in file x_dist.dat):

0 0 0 0 0 0 0 0 0 0 0 0 0 0 0 0 0 0 0 0 0 0 0 0 0 0 0 0 0 0 0 0 0 0 0 0 0 0 0 0

0 0 0 0 0 0 0 0 0 0 0 0 0 0 0 0 0 0 0 0 0 0 0 0 0 0 0 0 0 0 0 0 0 3 1 3 0 3 2 7 4

6 6 10 8 17 11 11 19 20 28 26 24 28 41 29 37 31 30 38 40 36 36 34 38 39 43 27 25

34 22 21 24 25 21 18 7 15 11 4 6 4 5 2 8 2 3 2 0 0 0 2 1 1 1 0 0 0 0 0 0 0 0 0 0

0 0 0 0 0 0 0 0 0 0 0 0 0 0 0 0 0 0 0 0 0 0 0 0 0 0 0 0 0 0 0 0 0 0 0 0 0 0 0 0

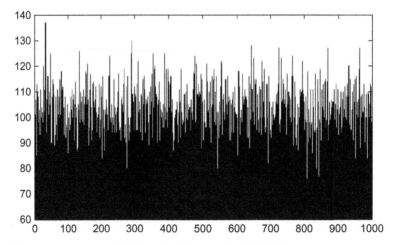

FIGURE 8.2 Histogram consisting of 1000 bins, holding a total of 100,000 data points whose x, y, and z coordinates fall somewhere between 0 and 1000.

What does this data actually show?

Zero bins contained 0 data points
Zero bins contained 1 data points
Zero bins contained 2 data points

.

.

.

Three bins contained 74 data points
One bin contained 75 data points
Three bins contained 76 data points
Zero bins contained 77 data points
Three bins contained 78 data points
and so on

The distribution is most easily visualized with a simple graph. The Gnuplot command producing a graph from our data is

```
plot 'x_dist.dat' smooth bezier
```

This simple command instructs Gnuplot to open our data file, "x_dist.dat," and plot the contents with a smooth lined graph. The output looks somewhat like a Gaussian distribution (see Figure 8.3).

We could have also created a cumulative distribution wherein the value of each point is the sum of the values of all prior points (see Figure 8.4). A minor modification of the prior Gnuplot command line produces the cumulative curve:

```
plot 'x_dist.dat' smooth cumulative
```

It is very easy to plot data, but one of the most common mistakes of the data analyst is to assume that the available data actually represents the full range of data that may occur. If the

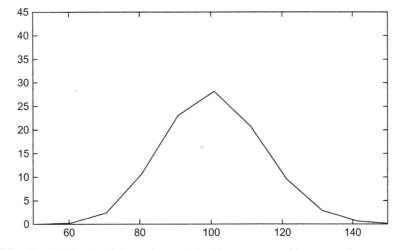

FIGURE 8.3 The distribution of data points per bin. The curve resembles a normal curve, peaking at 100.

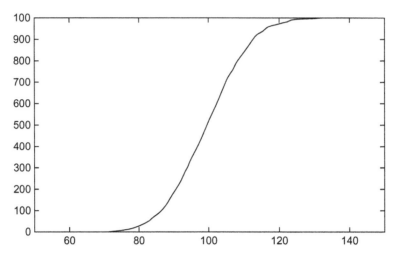

FIGURE 8.4 A cumulative distribution having a typical appearance of cumulative distribution for a normal curve.

data under study does not include the full range of the data, the data analyst will often reach a completely erroneous explanation for the observed data distribution.

Data distributions will almost always appear to be linear at various segments of their range (see Figure 8.5).

As demonstrated in Figure 8.5, an oscillating curve that reaches equilibrium may look like a sine wave early in its course and a flat line later on. In the larger oscillations, it may appear linear along the length of a half-cycle. Any of these segmental interpretations of the data will miss observations that would lead to a full explanation of the data.

An adept data analyst can eyeball a data distribution and guess the kind of function that might model the data. For example, a symmetric bell-shaped curve is probably a normal or Gaussian distribution. A curve with an early peak and a long, flat tail is often a power law distribution. Curves that are simple exponential or linear can also be assayed by visual inspection. Distributions that may be described by a Fourier series or a power series, or that can be segmented into several different distributions, can also be assessed (see Glossary items Power law, Power series, Fourier series, Fourier transform).

8. **Estimate the solution to your multimillion dollar data project on day 1.** This may seem difficult to accept, and there will certainly be exceptions to the rule, but the solution to almost every multimillion dollar analytic problem can usually be estimated in just a few hours, sometimes minutes, at the outset of the project. If an estimate cannot be attained fairly quickly, then there is a good chance that the project will fail. If you do not have the data for a quick-and-dirty estimate, then you will probably not have the data needed to make a precise determination.

We have already seen one example of estimation when we examined word-counting algorithms (see Chapter 7). Without bothering to acquire software that counts the words in a text file, we can get an approximation by simply dividing the size of the file (in bytes) by 6.5, the average number of characters contained in a word plus its separator character (space). Another example comes from the field of human epidemiology. The total number of humans on earth is about 7 billion. The total number of human deaths each year is about 60 million, roughly 1% of the living population. Modelers can use the 1% estimate for the percentage of people expected to die in a normal population. The same 1% estimate can be

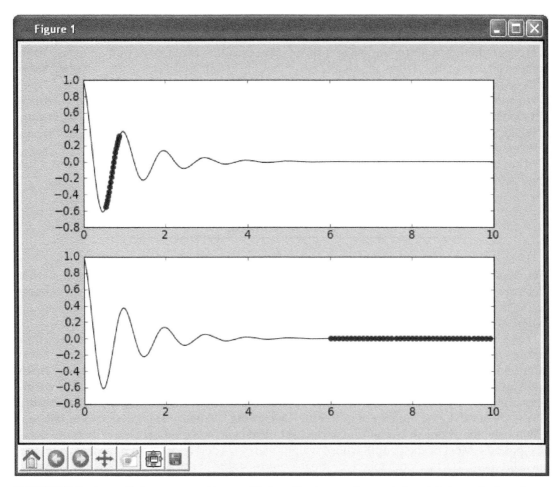

FIGURE 8.5 An oscillating wave reaching equilibrium. The top graph uses circle points to emphasize a linear segment for a half-cycle oscillation. The bottom graph of the same data emphasizes a linear segment occurring at equilibrium.

applied to the number of deaths from any cause compared to the number of deaths from all causes. In any field, adept data analysts apply simple estimators to their problems at hand.

The past several decades have witnessed a profusion of advanced mathematical techniques for analyzing large data sets. It is important that we have these methods, but in most cases, newer methods serve to refine and incrementally improve older methods that do not rely on powerful computational techniques or sophisticated mathematical algorithms.

As someone who was raised prior to the age of handheld calculators, personal computers, and smartphones, I was taught quick-and-dirty estimation methods for adding, subtracting, multiplying, and dividing lists of numbers. The purpose of the estimation was to provide a good idea of the final answer before much time was spent on a precise solution. If no mistake was introduced in either the estimate or the long calculation, then the two numbers would come close to one another. Conversely, mistakes in the long calculations could be detected if the two calculations yielded different numbers.

If data analysts go straight to the complex calculations, before they perform a simple estimation, they will find themselves accepting wildly ridiculous calculations. For comparison purposes, there is nothing quite like a simple and intuitive estimate to pull an overly eager analyst back to reality. Often, the simple act of looking at a stripped-down version of the problem opens a new approach that can drastically reduce computation time.[94]

In some situations, analysts will find that a point is reached when higher refinements in methods yield diminishing returns. When everyone has used their most advanced algorithms to make an accurate prediction, they may sometimes find that their best effort offers little improvement over a simple estimator.

The next sections introduce some powerful estimation techniques that are often overlooked.

DATA RANGE

Determine the highest and the lowest observed values in your data collection. These two numbers are often the most important numbers in any set of data—even more important than determining the average or the standard deviation. There is always a compelling reason, relating to the measurement of the data or to the intrinsic properties of the data set, to explain where and why the data begin and end.

Here is an example. You are looking at human subject data that includes weights. The minimum weight is a pound (the round-off weight of a viable but premature newborn infant). You find that the maximum weight in the data set is 300 pounds, exactly. There are many individuals in the data set who have a weight of 300 pounds, but no individuals with a weight exceeding 300 pounds. You also find that the number of individuals weighing 300 pounds is much greater than the number of individuals weighing 290 pounds. What does this tell you? Obviously, the people included in the data set have been weighed on a scale that tops off at 300 pounds. Most of the people whose weight was recorded as 300 will have a false weight measurement. Had we not looked for the maximum value in the data set, we would have assumed, incorrectly, that the weights were always accurate.

It would be useful to get some idea of how weights are distributed in the population exceeding 300 pounds. One way of estimating the error is to look at the number of people weighing 295 pounds, 290 pounds, 285 pounds, etc. By observing the trend, and knowing the total number of individuals whose weight is 300 pounds or higher, you can estimate the number of people falling into weight categories exceeding 300 pounds.

Here is another example where knowing the maxima for a data set measurement is useful. You are looking at a collection of data on meteorites. The measurements include weights. You notice that the largest meteorite in the large collection weighs 66 tons (equivalent to about 60,000 kg) and has a diameter of about 3 meters. Small meteorites are more numerous than large meteorites, but almost every weight category is accounted for by one or more meteorites, up to 66 tons. After that, nothing. Why do meteorites have a maximum size of about 66 tons?

A little checking tells you that meteors in space can come in just about any size, from a speck of dust to a moon-sized rock. Collisions with earth have involved meteorites much larger than 3 meters. You check the astronomical records and you find that the meteor that may have caused the extinction of large dinosaurs about 65 million years ago was estimated at 6 to 10 km (at least 2000 times the diameter of the largest meteorite found on earth).

There is a very simple reason why the largest meteorite found on earth weighs about 66 tons, while the largest meteorites to impact the earth are known to be thousands of times heavier. When meteorites exceed 66 tons, the impact energy can exceed the energy produced by an atom bomb blast. Meteorites larger than 66 tons leave an impact crater, but the meteor itself disintegrates on impact.

As it turns out, much is known about meteorite impacts. The kinetic energy of the impact is determined by the mass of the meteor and the square of the velocity. The minimum velocity of a meteor at impact is about 11 km/second (equivalent to the minimum escape velocity for sending an object from earth into space). The fastest impacts occur at about 70 km per second. From this data, the energy released by meteors, on impact with the earth, can be easily calculated.

By observing the maximum weight of meteors found on earth, we learn a great deal about meteoric impacts. When we look at the distribution of weights, you can see that small meteorites are more numerous than larger meteorites. If we develop a simple formula that relates the size of a meteorite with its frequency of occurrence, we can predict the likelihood of the arrival of a meteorite on earth, for every weight of meteorite, including those weighing more than 66 tons, and for any interval of time.

Here is another profound example of the value of knowing the maximum value in a data distribution. If you look at the distance from the earth to various cosmic objects (e.g., stars, black holes, nebulae), you will quickly find that there is a limit for the distance of objects from earth. Of the many thousands of cataloged stars and galaxies, none of them have a distance that is greater than 13 billion light years. Why? If astronomers could see a star that is 15 billion light years from earth, the light that is received here on earth must have traveled 15 billion light years to reach us. The time required for light to travel 15 billion light years is 15 billion years, by definition. The universe was born in a big bang about 14 billion years ago. This would imply that the light from the star located 15 billion miles from earth must have begun its journey about a billion years before the universe came into existence. Impossible!

By looking at the distribution of distances of observed stars and noting that the distances never exceed about 13 billion years, we can infer that the universe must be at least 13 billion years old. You can also infer that the universe does not have an infinite age and size; otherwise, we would see stars at a greater distance than 13 billion light years. If you assume that stars popped into the universe not long after its creation, then you can infer that the universe has an age of about 13 or 14 billion years. All of these deductions, confirmed independently by theoreticians and cosmologists, were made without statistical analysis by noting the maximum number in a distribution of numbers.

Sometimes fundamental discoveries come from simple observations on distribution boundaries. Penguins are widely distributed throughout the Southern Hemisphere. Outside of zoos and a few islands on the border of the Southern and Northern Hemispheres, penguins have never ventured into the northern half of this planet. In point of fact, penguins have never really ventured anywhere. Penguins cannot fly; hence they cannot migrate via the sky like most other birds. They swim well, but they rear their young on land and do not travel great distances from their nests. It is hard to imagine how penguins could have established homes in widely divergent climates (e.g., frigid Antarctic and tropical Galapagos).

Penguins evolved from an ancestral species, around 70 million years ago, that lived on southern land masses broken from the Pangaean supercontinent, before the moving continents arrived at their current locations. At this point, the coastal tips of South America and Africa, the western coast of Australia, and the length of Zealandia (from which New Zealand eventually emerged) were all quite close to Antarctica.

By observing the distribution of penguins throughout the world (knowing where they live and where they do not live), it is possible to construct a marvelous hypothesis in which penguins were slowly carried away when their ancient homeland split and floated throughout the Southern Hemisphere. The breakup of Pangaea, leading to the current arrangement of continents, might have been understood by noting where penguins live, and where they do not.

On occasion, the maxima or minima of a set of data will be determined by an outlier value (see Glossary item, Outlier). If the outlier were simply eliminated from the data set, you would have a maxima and minima with values that were somewhat close to other data values (i.e., the second-highest data value and the second-lowest data values would be close to the maxima and the minima, respectively). In these cases, the data analyst must come to a decision—to drop or not to drop the outlier. There is no simple guideline for dealing with outliers, but it is sometimes helpful to know something about the dynamic range of the measurements (see Glossary item, Dynamic range). If a thermometer can measure temperature from -20 to 140 degrees Fahrenheit and your data outlier has a temperature of 390 degrees Fahrenheit, then you know that the data must be an error; the thermometer does not measure above 140 degrees. The data analyst can drop the outlier, but it would be prudent to determine why the outlier was generated.

DENOMINATOR

Denominators are the numbers that provide perspective to other numbers. If you are informed that 10,000 persons die each year in the United States from a particular disease, then you might want to know the total number of deaths, from all causes. When you compare the death from a particular disease with the total number of deaths from all causes (the denominator), you learn something about the relative importance of your original count (e.g., an incidence of 10,000 deaths/350 million persons). Epidemiologists typically represent incidences as numbers per 100,000 population. An incidence of 10,000/350 million is equivalent to an incidence of 2.9 per 100,000.

Likewise, if you are using Big Data collected from multiple sources, your histograms will need to be represented as fractional distributions for each source's data, not as value counts. The reason for this is that a histogram from one source will probably not have the same total number of distributed values compared with a histogram created from another source. To achieve comparability among the histograms, you will need to transform values into fractions, by dividing the binned values by the total number of values in the data distribution, for each data source. Doing so renders the bin value as a percentage of total rather than a sum of data values.

Denominators are not always easy to find. In most cases, the denominator is computed by tallying every data object in a Big Data resource. If you have a very large number of data objects, the time required to reach a global tally may be quite long. In many cases, a Big Data resource will permit data analysts to extract subsets of data, but analysts will be forbidden to examine the entire resource. As a consequence, the denominator will be computed for the subset of extracted data and will not accurately represent all of the data objects available to the resource.

Big Data managers should make an effort to supply information that summarizes the total set of data available at any moment in time. Here are some of the numbers that should be available to analysts: the number of records in the resource, the number of classes of data objects in the resource, the number of data objects belonging to each class in the resource, the number of data values that belong to data objects, and the size of the resource in bytes.

There are many examples wherein data analysts manipulate the denominator to produce misleading results; one of the most outrageous examples comes from the emotionally charged field of crime reporting. When a crime is recorded at a police department, a record is kept to determine whether the case comes to closure (i.e., is either solved or is closed through an administrative decision). The simple annual closure rate is the number of cases closed in a year divided by the total number of cases occurring in the year. Analytic confusion arises when a crime occurs in a certain year, but is not solved until the following year. It is customary among some police departments to include all closures, including closures of cases occurring in preceding years, in the numerator.[95] The denominator is restricted to those cases that occurred in the given year. The thought is that doing so ensures that every closed case is counted and that the total number of cases is not counted more than once.

As it happens, including closures from cases occurring in prior years may be extraordinarily misleading when the denominator is decreasing (i.e., when the incidence of crime decreases). For example, imagine that in a certain year there are 100 homicides and 30 closures (a simple closure rate of 30%). In the following year, the murderers take a breather, producing a scant 40 homicides. Of those 40 homicides, only 10 are closed (a simple closure rate of 25%), but during this period, 31 of the open homicide cases from the previous year are closed. This produces a total number of current-year closures of $10 + 31$, or 41; yielding an impossible closure rate of $41/40$ or about 103%—not bad!

January is a particularly good month to find a closure rate that bodes well for the remainder of the year. Let's say that the homicide incidence does not change from year to year; that the homicide rate remains steady at 100 per year. Let's say that in year 1, 30 homicide cases are closed, yielding a simple closure rate of 30%. In the month of January in year 2, 9 homicides occur. This represents about one-twelfth of the 100 homicides expected for the year. We expect that January will be the month that receives the highest number of closures from the prior year's open-case pool. Let's say that in January there are 10 cases closed from prior year homicides, and that none of the homicides occurring in January were closed (i.e., 0% simple closure rate for January). We calculate the closure rate by taking the sum of closures $(10 + 0 = 10)$ and dividing by the number of homicides that occurred in January 9 to yield a closure rate of $10/9$ or a 111% closure rate.

Aside from yielding impossible closure rates, exceeding 100%, the calculation employed by many police departments provides a highly misleading statistic. Is there a method whereby we can compute a closure rate that does not violate the laws of time and logic, and that provides a reasonable assessment of crime case closures? Actually, there are many ways of approaching the problem. Here is a simple method that does not involve reaching back into cases from prior years or reaching forward in time to collect cases from the current year that will be solved in the future.

Imagine the following set of data for homicide cases occurring in 2012. There are 25 homicides in the data set. Twenty of the cases were closed inside the year 2012. The remaining cases are unclosed at the end of the calendar year. We know the date that each case occurred and the number of days to closure for each of the closed cases. For the 5 cases that were not closed, we know the number of days that passed between the time that the case occurred and the end of the year 2012, when all counting stopped.

Summary of 25 homicide cases

Days to closure: 001
Days to closure: 002
Days to closure: 002
Days to closure: 003
Days to closure: 005
Days to closure: 011
Days to closure: 023
Days to closure: 029
Days to closure: 039
Days to closure: 046
Days to closure: 071
Days to closure: 076
Days to closure: 083
Days to closure: 086
Days to closure: 100
Days to closure: 120
Days to closure: 148
Days to closure: 235
Days to closure: 276
Days to closure: 342
Unclosed at 10 days
Unclosed at 100 days
Unclosed at 250 days
Unclosed at 300 days
Unclosed at 320 days

The simple closure date is 20/25 or 80%. Now, let us plot the time until closure for cases (see Figure 8.6).

We see that all but 3 of the solved cases were solved within 150 days of the homicide occurrence. Of the 5 unclosed cases remaining at the end of 2012, 3 had not been solved in 250 days or more. These cases are highly unlikely to be solved. One had gone unsolved for only 10 days. This time period is so short that the likelihood that it will be solved is likely to be close to the simple closure rate of 80%. One case had gone unsolved for 100 days. Only 5 of the 20 solved cases were closed after 100 days, and this would represent about one-quarter (5/20) of the simple 80% closure rate.

Can we assign likelihoods of eventual closure to the five cases that were unclosed at the end of 2012?

Unclosed at 10 days—likelihood of eventual closure 80%
Unclosed at 100 days—likelihood of eventual closure $0.25 \times 0.80 = 20\%$
Unclosed at 250 days—likelihood of eventual closure 0%

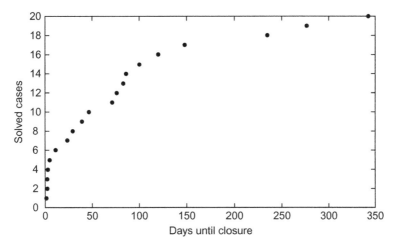

FIGURE 8.6 Time to closure of cases in 2012 for an imaginary set of data (see text).

Unclosed at 300 days—likelihood of eventual closure 0%
Unclosed at 320 days—likelihood of eventual closure 0%

The expected number of eventual closures from the 5 unclosed cases is $0.8 + 0.2 = 1$. This means that the predicted total closure rate for 2012 is 20 cases (the number of cases that were actually closed) $+ 1$ cases (the number of cases likely to be closed anytime in the future), or 21/25, or 84%. Without going into the statistical formalities for predicting likelihoods, we can summarize closure rates with two easily computed numbers: the simple closure rate and the predicted closure rate.

There are elegant statistical approaches, including Kaplan–Meier estimators,[96] which could provide a more rigorous analysis of the Washington, DC, homicide data. The point here is that reasonable estimations can be performed by simply studying the data and thinking about the problem. Big Data resources are in constant flux—growing into the past and the future. Denominators that make sense in a world of static measurements may not make sense in an information universe that is unconstrained by space and time.

FREQUENCY DISTRIBUTIONS

There are two general types of data: quantitative and categorical. Quantitative data refers to measurements. Categorical data is simply a number that represents the number of items that have a feature. For most purposes, the analysis of categorical data reduces to counting and binning.

Categorical data typically conforms to Zipf distributions. George Kingsley Zipf (1902–1950) was an American linguist who demonstrated that, for most languages, a small number of words account for the majority of occurrences of all the words found in prose. Specifically, he found that the frequency of any word is inversely proportional to its placement in a list of words, ordered by their decreasing frequencies in text. The first word in the frequency list will occur about twice as often as the second word in the list, three times as often as the third word in the list, and so on. Many Big Data collections follow a Zipf distribution (e.g., income distribution in a population, energy consumption by country, and so on).

Zipf's distribution applied to languages is a special form of Pareto's principle, or the 80/20 rule. Pareto's principle holds that a small number of causes may account for the vast majority of observed instances. For example, a small number of rich people account for the majority of wealth. This would apply to localities (cities, states, countries) and to totalities (the planet). Likewise, a small number of diseases account for the vast majority of human illnesses. A small number of children account for the majority of the behavioral problems encountered in a school. A small number of states hold the majority of the population of the United States. A small number of book titles, compared with the total number of publications, account for the majority of book sales. Much of Big Data is categorical and obeys the Pareto principle. Mathematicians often refer to Zipf distributions as Power law distributions (see Glossary items, Power law, Pareto's principle, Zipf distribution).

Let's take a look at the frequency distribution of words appearing in a book. Here is the list of the 30 most frequent words in the book and the number of occurrence of each word:

```
01 003977 the
02 001680 and
03 001091 class
04 000946 are
05 000925 chapter
06 000919 that
07 000884 species
08 000580 virus
09 000570 with
10 000503 disease
11 000434 for
12 000427 organisms
13 000414 from
14 000412 hierarchy
15 000335 not
16 000329 humans
17 000320 have
18 000319 proteobacteria
19 000309 human
20 000300 can
21 000264 fever
22 000263 group
23 000248 most
24 000225 infections
25 000219 viruses
26 000219 infectious
27 000216 organism
```

28 000216 host
29 000215 this
30 000211 all

As Zipf would predict, the most frequent word, "the," occurs 3977 times, roughly twice as often as the second most frequently occurring word, "and," which occurs 1689 times. The third most frequently occurring word, "class," occurs 1091 times, or very roughly one-third as frequently as the most frequently occurring word.

What can we learn about the text from which these word frequencies were calculated? As discussed in Chapter 1, "stop" words are high-frequency words that separate terms and tell us little or nothing about the informational content of text. Let us look at this same list with the "stop" words removed:

03 001091 class
05 000925 chapter
07 000884 species
08 000580 virus
10 000503 disease
12 000427 organisms
14 000412 hierarchy
16 000329 humans
18 000319 proteobacteria
19 000309 human
21 000264 fever
22 000263 group
24 000225 infections
25 000219 viruses
26 000219 infectious
27 000216 organism
28 000216 host

What kind of text could have produced this list? As it happens, these high-frequency words came from a book that I previously wrote entitled "Taxonomic Guide to Infectious Diseases: Understanding the Biologic Classes of Pathogenic Organisms."[49] Could there be any doubt that the list of words and frequencies came from a book whose subject is the classification of organisms causing human disease? By glancing at a few words, from a large text file, we gain a deep understanding of the subject matter of the text. The words with the top occurrence frequencies told us the most about the book, because these words are typically low frequency (e.g., hierarchy, protebacteria, organism). They occurred in high frequency because the text was focused on a narrow subject (i.e., infectious disease taxonomy).

A clever analyst will always produce a Zipf distribution for categorical data. A glance at the output always reveals a great deal about the contents of the data.

Let us go one more step, to produce a cumulative index for the occurrence of words in the text, arranging them in order of descending frequency of occurrence:

01 003977 0.0559054232618291 the
02 001680 0.0795214934352948 and

```
03 001091 0.0948578818634204 class
04 000946 0.108155978520622 are
05 000925 0.121158874300655 chapter
06 000919 0.134077426972926 that
07 000884 0.146503978183249 species
08 000580 0.154657145266946 virus
09 000570 0.162669740504372 with
10 000503 0.169740504371784 disease
11 000434 0.175841322499930 for
12 000427 0.181843740335686 organisms
13 000414 0.187663414771290 from
14 000412 0.193454974837640 hierarchy
15 000335 0.198164131687706 not
16 000329 0.202788945430009 humans
17 000320 0.207287244510669 have
18 000319 0.211771486406702 proteobacteria
19 000309 0.216115156456465 human
20 000300 0.220332311844584 can
21 000264 0.224043408586128 fever
22 000263 0.227740448143046 group
23 000248 0.231226629930558 most
24 000225 0.234389496471647 infections
25 000219 0.237468019904973 viruses
26 000219 0.240546543338300 infectious
27 000216 0.243582895217746 organism
28 000216 0.246619247097191 host
29 000215 0.249641541792010 this
30 000211 0.252607607748320 all

    .
    .
    .
    .
    .

8957 000001 0.999873485338356 acanthaemoeba
8958 000001 0.999887542522984 acalculous
8959 000001 0.999901599707611 academic
8960 000001 0.999915656892238 absurd
8961 000001 0.999929714076865 abstract
8962 000001 0.999943771261492 absorbing
8963 000001 0.999957828446119 absorbed
8964 000001 0.999971885630746 abrasion
8965 000001 0.999985942815373 abnormalities
8966 000001 1.000000000000000 abasence
```

In this cumulative listing, the third column is the fraction of the occurrences of the word along with the preceding words in the list as a fraction of all the occurrences of every word in the text.

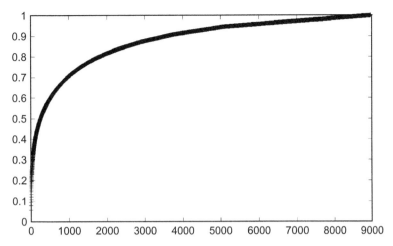

FIGURE 8.7 A cumulative frequency distribution of word occurrences from a sample text. Bottom coordinates indicate that the entire text is accounted for by a list of about 9000 different words. The steep and early rise indicates that a few words account for the bulk of word occurrences. Graphs with this shape are sometimes referred to as Zipf distributions.

The list is truncated after the 30th entry and picks up again at entry number 8957. There are a total of 8966 different, sometimes called unique, words in the text. The total number of words in the text happens to be 71,138. The last word on the list, "abasence," has a cumulative fraction of 1.0, as all of the preceding words, plus the last word, account for 100% of word occurrences. The cumulative frequency distribution for the different words in the text is shown in Figure 8.7. As an aside, the tail of the Zipf distribution, which typically contains items occurring once only in a large data collection, is often "mistakes." In the case of text distributions, typographic errors can be found in the farthest and thinnest part of the tail. In this case, the word "abasence" occurs just once, as the last item in the distribution. It is a misspelling for the word "absence."

Notice that though there are a total of 8957 unique words in the text, the first 30 words account for more than 25% of all word occurrences. The final 10 words on the list occurred only once in the text. When the cumulative data is plotted, we see a typical cumulative Zipf distribution, characterized by a smooth curve with a quick rise, followed by a long flattened tail converging to 1.0. Compare this with the cumulative distribution for a normal curve (see Figure 8.4). By comparing plots, we can usually tell, at a glance, whether a data set behaves like a Zipf distribution or like a Gaussian distribution.

MEAN AND STANDARD DEVIATION

Statisticians have invented two numbers that tell us most of what we need to know about data sets in the small data realm: the mean and the standard deviation. The mean, also known as the average, tells us the center of the bell-shaped curve, and the standard deviation tells us something about the width of the bell.

The average is one of the simplest statistics to compute: simply divide the sum total of data by the number of data objects. Though the average is simple to compute, its computation may not always be fast. Finding the exact average requires that the entire data set be parsed; a significant time waste when the data set is particularly large or when averages need to be recomputed frequently. When the data can be randomly accessed, it may save considerable time to select a subset of the data (e.g., 100 items), compute the average for the subset, and assume that the average of the subset will approximate the average for the full set of data.

In the Big Data realm, computing the mean and the standard deviation is often a waste of time. Big Data is seldom distributed as a normal curve. The mean and standard deviation have limited value outside of normal distributions. The reason for the non-normality of Big Data is that Big Data is observational, not experimental.

In small data projects, an experiment is undertaken. Typically, a uniform population may be split into two sets, with one set subjected to a certain treatment and the other set serving as a control. Each member of the treated population is nearly identical to every other member, and any measurements on the population would be expected to be identical. Differences among a population of nearly identical objects are distributed in a bell-shaped curve around a central average. The same is true for the control population. Statisticians use the magnitude of data points and their mean location to find differences between the treated group and the control group.

None of this necessarily applies to Big Data collections. In many instances, Big Data is non-numeric categorical data (e.g., presence or absence of a feature, true of false, yes or no, 0 or 1). Because categorical values come from many different objects, there is no special reason to think that the output will be distributed as a normal curve, as you might expect to see when a quantified measurement is produced for a population of identical objects.

In the prior section, we saw an example of a Zipf distribution, in which a few objects or classes of objects account for most of the data in the distribution. The remaining data values trail out in a very long tail (Figure 8.7). For such a distribution, the average and the standard deviation can be computed, but the numbers may not provide useful information. When there is no bell-shaped curve, the average does not designate the center of a distribution, and the standard deviation does not indicate the spread of the distribution around its average value.

Big Data distributions are sometimes multimodal, with several peaks and troughs. Multimodality always says something about the data under study. It tells us that the population is somehow nonhomogeneous. Hodgkin lymphoma is an example of a cancer with a bimodal age distribution (see Figure 8.8). There is a peak in occurrences at a young age, and another peak of occurrences at a more advanced age. This two-peak phenomenon can be found whenever Hodgkin lymphoma is studied in large populations.[19]

In the case of Hodgkin lymphoma, lymphomas occurring in the young may share diagnostic features with the lymphomas occurring in the older population, but the occurrence of lymphomas in two separable populations may indicate that some important distinction may have been overlooked: a different environmental cause, different genetic alterations of lymphomas in the two age sets, two different types of lymphomas that were mistakenly classified under one name, or there may be something wrong with the data (i.e., misdiagnoses, mix-ups during data collection). Big Data, by providing a large number of cases, makes it easy to detect data incongruities (such as multimodality) when they are present. Explaining the causes for data incongruities is always a scientific challenge.

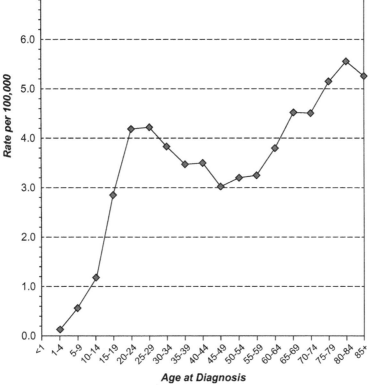

FIGURE 8.8   Number of occurrences of Hodgkin lymphoma in persons of different ages. There are two peaks, one at about 35 years of age and another at about 75 years of age. The distribution appears to be bimodal. *Source of graph: The National Cancer Institute's Surveillance Epidemiology End Results, available from http://seer.cancer.gov/.*[97]

The importance of inspecting data for multimodality also applies to black holes. Most black holes have mass equivalents under 33 solar masses. Another set of black holes are supermassive, with mass equivalents of 10 or 20 billion solar masses. When there are objects of the same type, whose masses differ by a factor of a billion, scientists infer that there is something fundamentally different in the origin or development of these two variant forms of the same object. Black hole formation is an active area of interest, but current theory suggests that lower mass black holes arise from preexisting heavy stars. The supermassive black holes presumably grow from large quantities of matter available at the center of galaxies. The observation of bimodality inspired astronomers to search for black holes whose masses are intermediate between black holes with near-solar masses and the supermassive black holes. Intermediates have been found and, not surprisingly, they come with a set of fascinating properties that distinguish them from other types of black holes. Fundamental advances in our understanding of the universe may sometimes follow from simple observations of multimodal data distributions.

The average behavior of a collection of objects can be applied toward calculations that would exceed computational feasibility if applied to individual objects. Here is an example. Years ago, I worked on a project that involved simulating cell colony growth using a Monte Carlo method (see Glossary item, Monte Carlo simulation).[98] Each simulation began with a single cell that divided, producing two cells, unless the cell happened to die prior to cell division. Each simulation applied a certain chance of cell death, somewhere around 0.5, for each cell, at each cell division. When you simulate colony growth, beginning with a single cell, the chance that the first cell will die on the first cell division would be about 0.5; hence there is about a 50% chance that the colony will die out on the first cell division. If the cell survives the first cell division, the cell might go through several additional cell divisions before it dies, by chance. By that time, there are other progeny that are dividing, and these progeny cells might successfully divide, thus enlarging the size of the colony. A Monte Carlo simulation randomly assigned death or life at each cell division, for each cell in the colony (see Glossary item, Monte Carlo simulation). When the colony manages to reach a large size (e.g., 10 million cells), the simulation slows down, as the Monte Carlo algorithm must parse through 10 million cells, calculating whether each cell will live or die, assigning two offspring cells for each simulated division, and removing cells that were assigned a simulated "death." When the computer simulation slows to a crawl, I found that the whole population displayed an "average" behavior. There was no longer any need to perform a Monte Carlo simulation on every cell in the population. I could simply multiply the total number of cells by the cell death probability (for the entire population), and this would tell me the total number of cells that survived the cycle. For a large colony of cells, with a death probability of 0.5 for each cell, half the cells will die at each cell cycle and the other half will live and divide, producing two progeny cells; hence the population of the colony will remain stable. When dealing with large numbers, it becomes possible to dispense with the Monte Carlo simulation and to predict each generational outcome with a pencil and paper.

Substituting the average behavior for a population of objects, rather than calculating the behavior of every single object, is called mean-field approximation (see Glossary item, Mean-field approximation). It uses a physical law telling us that large collections of objects can be characterized by their average behavior. Mean-field approximation has been used with great success to understand the behavior of gases, epidemics, crystals, viruses, and all manner of large population problems.

ESTIMATION-ONLY ANALYSES

The sun is about 93 million miles from the earth. At this enormous distance, light hitting the earth arrives as near-parallel rays, and the shadow produced by the earth is nearly cylindrical. This means that the shadow of the earth is approximately the same size as the earth itself. If the earth's circular shadow during a lunar eclipse has a diameter about 2.5 times the diameter of the moon itself, then the moon must have a diameter approximately 1/2.5 times that of the earth. The diameter of the earth is about 8000 miles, so the diameter of the moon must be about 8000/2.5 or about 3000 miles.

The true diameter of the moon is smaller, about 2160 miles. Our estimate is inaccurate because the earth's shadow is actually conical, not cylindrical. If we wanted to use a bit more trigonometry, we'd arrive at a closer approximation. Still, we arrived at a fair approximation of the moon's size from one simple division based on a casual observation made during a lunar eclipse. The distance was not measured; it was estimated from a simple observation. Credit for the first astronomer to use this estimation goes to the Greek astronomer Aristarchus of Samos (310 BCE-230 BCE). In this particular case, a direct measurement of the moon's distance was impossible. Aristarchus' only option was the rough estimate. His predicament was not unique. Sometimes estimation is the only recourse for data analysts.

A modern-day example wherein measurements failed to help the data analyst is the calculation of deaths caused by heat waves. People suffer during heat waves, and municipalities need to determine whether people are dying from heat-related conditions. If deaths occur, then the municipality can justifiably budget for supportive services such as municipal cooling stations, the free delivery of ice, increased staffing for emergency personnel, and so on. If the number of heat-related deaths is high, the governor may justifiably call a state of emergency.

Medical examiners perform autopsies to determine causes of death. During a heat wave, the number of deceased individuals with a heat-related cause of death seldom rises as much as anyone would expect.[99] The reason for this is that stresses produced by heat cause death by exacerbating preexisting nonheat-related conditions. The cause of death can seldom be pinned on heat. The paucity of autopsy-proven heat deaths can be relieved, somewhat, by permitting pathologists to declare a heat-related death when the environmental conditions at the site of death are consistent with hyperthermia (e.g., a high temperature at the site of death and a high body temperature of the deceased measured shortly after death). Adjusting the criteria for declaring heat-related deaths is a poor remedy. In many cases, the body is not discovered anytime near the time of death, invalidating the use of body temperature. More importantly, different regions may develop their own criteria for heat-related deaths (e.g., different temperature threshold measures, different ways of factoring night-time temperatures and humidity measurements). Basically, there is no accurate, reliable, or standard way to determine heat-related deaths at autopsy.[99]

How would you, a data estimator, handle this problem? It's simple. You take the total number of deaths that occurred during the heat wave. Then you go back over your records of deaths occurring in the same period, in the same geographic region, over a series of years in which a heat wave did not occur. You average that number, giving you the expected number of deaths in a normal (i.e., without heat wave) period. You subtract that number from the number of deaths that occurred during the heat wave and that gives you an estimate of the number of people who died from heat-related mortality. This strategy, applied to the 1995 Chicago heat wave, estimated that the number of heat-related deaths rose from 485 to 739.[100]

USE CASE: WATCHING DATA TRENDS WITH GOOGLE NGRAMS

Ngrams are ordered word sequences.
Ngrams for the prior sentence are:

Ngrams (1-gram)
are (1-gram)

ordered (1-gram)
word (1-gram)
sequences (1-gram)
Ngrams are (2-gram)
are ordered (2-gram)
ordered word (2-gram)
word sequences (2-gram)
Ngrams are ordered (3-gram)
are ordered word (3-gram)
ordered word sequences (3-gram)
Ngrams are ordered word (4-gram)
are ordered word sequences (4-gram)
Ngrams are ordered word sequences (5-gram)

Google has undertaken a Big Data effort to enumerate the ngrams collected from the scanned literature dating back to 1500. The public can enter their own ngrams into Google's Ngram Viewer and view a graph of the occurrences of the phrase, in published literature, over time. Figure 8.9 is the Google result for a search on the 2-gram "yellow fever."

We see that the term "yellow fever" (a mosquito-transmitted hepatitis) appeared in the literature beginning about 1800 (shortly after an outbreak in Philadelphia), with several subsequent peaks (around 1915 and 1945). The dates of the peaks correspond roughly to

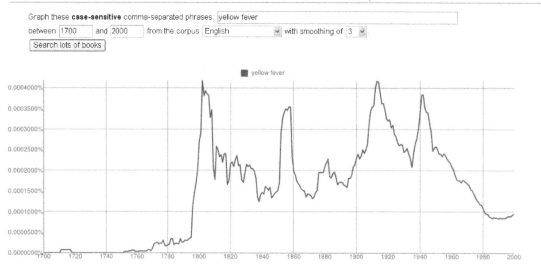

FIGURE 8.9   The frequency of occurrences of the phrase "yellow fever" in a large collection of literature from the years 1700 to 2000. The graph was automatically rendered by the Google Ngram Viewer.

outbreaks of yellow fever in Philadelphia (epidemic of 1793), New Orleans (epidemic of 1853), with U.S. construction efforts in the Panama Canal (1904–1914), and World War II Pacific outbreaks (about 1942). Following the 1942 epidemic, an effective vaccine was available, and the incidence of yellow fever, as well as the occurrences of the "yellow fever" 2-gram, dropped precipitously. In this case, a simple review of ngram frequencies provides an accurate chart of historic yellow fever outbreaks.

Sleeping sickness is a disease caused by a protozoan parasite transmitted by the tsetse fly, and endemic to Africa. The 2-gram search on the term "sleeping sickness" demonstrates a sharp increase in the frequency of occurrence of the term at the turn of the 20th century (see Figure 8.10). The first, and largest, peak, about the year 1900, coincided with a historic epidemic of sleeping sickness. At that time, a plague decimated the population of rinderpest, the preferred animal reservoir of the tsetse fly, resulting in an increase in human bites; hence an increase in sleeping sickness. Once again, the ngram data set has given us insight into a human epidemic.

Following the epidemic near the year 1900, the frequency of literary occurrences of "sleeping sickness" had a generally downwards trend, punctuated by a second, smaller peak about the time of World War II and a steady decline thereafter.

The Google Ngram Viewer supports simple lookups of term frequencies. For advanced analyses, such as finding co-occurrences of all ngrams against all other ngrams, data analysts would need to download the ngram data files, available at no cost from Google, and write their own programs suited to their tasks.

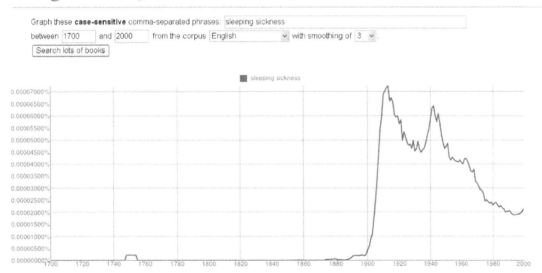

FIGURE 8.10 The frequency of occurrences of the term "sleeping sickness" in literature from the years 1700 to 2000. The graph was automatically rendered by the Google Ngram Viewer, available at http://books.google.com/ngrams.

USE CASE: ESTIMATING MOVIE PREFERENCES

Imagine you have all the preference data for every user of a large movie subscriber service, such as Netflix. You want to develop a system whereby the preference of any subscriber, for any movie, can be predicted. Here are some analytic options, listed in order of increasing complexity, omitting methods that require advanced mathematical skills.

1. **Ignore your data and use experts.** Movie reviewers are fairly good predictors of a movie's appeal. If they were not good predictors, they would have been replaced by people with better predictive skills. For any movie, go to the newspapers and magazines and collect about 10 movie reviews. Average the review scores and use the average as the predictor for all of your subscribers. This method assumes that there is not a large divergence in preferences, from subscriber to subscriber, for most movies.

You can refine this method a bit by looking at the average subscriber scores, after the movie has been released. You can compare the scores of the individual experts to the average score of the subscribers. Scores from experts that closely matched the scores from the subscribers can be weighted a bit more heavily than experts whose scores were nothing like the average subscriber score.

2. **Use all of your data, as it comes in, to produce an average subscriber score.** Skip the experts—go straight to your own data. In most instances, you would expect that a particular user's preference will come close to the average preference of the entire population in the data set, for any given movie.

3. **Lump people into preference groups based on shared favorites.** If Ann's personal list of top-favored movies is the same as Fred's top-favored list, then it's likely that their preferences will coincide. For movies that Ann has seen but Fred has not, use Ann's score as a predictor.

In a large data set, find an individual's top 10 movie choices and add the individual to a group of individuals who share the same top 10 list. Use the average score for members of the group, for any particular movie, as that movie's predictor for each of the members of the group.

As a refinement, find a group of people who share the top 10 and the bottom 10 scoring movies. Everyone in this group shares a love of the same top movies and a loathing for the same bottom movies.

4. **Focus your refined predictions.** For many movies, there really isn't much of a spread in ratings. If just about everyone loves "Star Wars," "Raiders of the Lost Ark," and "It's a Wonderful Life," then there really is no need to provide an individual prediction for such movies. Likewise, if a movie is universally loathed or universally accepted as an "average" flick, then why would you want to use computationally intensive models for these movies?

Most data sets contain easy and difficult data objects. There is seldom any good reason to develop predictors for the easy data. In the case of movie predictors, if there is very little spread in a movie's score, you can safely use the average rating as the predicted rating for all individuals. By removing all of the "easy" movies from your group-specific calculations, you reduce the total number of calculations for the data collection.

This method of eliminating the obvious has application in many different fields. As a program director at the National Cancer Institute, I was peripherally involved in efforts to predict cancer treatment options for patients diagnosed in different stages of disease. Traditionally, large numbers of patients, at every stage of disease, were included in a prediction model that employed a list of measurable clinical and pathological parameters (e.g., age and gender of patient, size of tumor, the presence of local or distant metastases). It turned out that early models produced predictions where none were necessary. If a patient had a tumor that was small, confined to its primary site of growth, and minimally invasive at its origin, then the treatment was always limited to surgical excision; there were no other options for treatment, and hence no reason to predict the best option for treatment. If a tumor was widely metastatic to distant organs at the time of diagnosis, then there were no available treatments that were known to cure the patient. By focusing their analyses on the subset of patients who could benefit from treatment, and for whom the best treatment option was not predetermined, the data analysts reduced the size and complexity of the data and simplified the problem.

9

Analysis

At this very moment, there's an odds-on chance that someone in your organization is making a poor decision on the basis of information that was enormously expensive to collect. **Shvetank Shah, Andrew Horne, and Jaime Capella**[101]

BACKGROUND

Here are the instructions for a foolproof fly swatter:

1. Place fly on flat surface.
2. Squash fly with stick, using a rapid downward force.

If you find these instructions amusing, then you will appreciate the fundamental challenge in every Big Data analysis project: collecting the data and setting it up for analysis. The analysis step itself is easy; preanalysis is the tricky part.

Data analysis is a well-established field, with thousands of books devoted to the topic. Many currently available analysis books are superb works, with each new book building upon a rich legacy of prior works.[102–106] Books devoted to preanalytic and postanalytic tasks are scarce. In the days of small data, the acquisition of data and the disposition of statistical results (i.e., submitting abstracts, writing grant reports, moving through the product development cycle) were all performed by professionals other than the mathematicians, computer scientists, and statisticians who analyzed the data. With the advent of Big Data, the data analyst often stands alone, and must somehow learn for herself how the data was obtained and how the results will be interpreted.

Analysis in the Big Data realm is fundamentally different from analysis for small data. This chapter focuses on how data must be prepared for analysis and what we learn about our data when we apply analytic methods.

ANALYTIC TASKS

Big Data performs many computational tasks, some of which are not directly involved in analytics (e.g., searching for specific data, searching for patterns of data, retrieving data, organizing the retrieved data by a ranking system). Data analysis involves drawing conclusions based on reviewing sets of data. These tasks can be somewhat arbitrarily divided into three areas: statistical analysis, modeling, and predictive analysis.

Statistical analysis is closely associated with hypothesis testing. The prototypical hypothesis question is, "If I have a control group and a treated group, how do I know when the treatment results in an effect that makes the treatment group measurably different from the control group?" Though statisticians cannot answer this fundamental question definitively, they provide some measure of confidence in an answer.

Modeling, as used in this book, is a description, using a mathematical equation or some logical language, to describe the behavior of a system or its objects. Examples would be a model for planetary motion, a model for interstate traffic, a model for enzymatic reactions, a model for cancer growth, a model for an ontology, and so on. In many cases, modeling equations will need to describe how different variables change, in relation to one another, over increments of time. Hence, many modeling equations involve differential calculus. Every computer scientist seems to have his or her own definition of modeling. Readers should not assume that the definition provided here will apply everywhere today, or anywhere, 10 years from today.

Predictive analysis is concerned with guessing how an individual, group, or data object will behave based on past outcomes or on the observed behaviors of similar individuals or groups. Predictive analytics relies on one concept: if thing A is similar to thing B, then thing A will most likely behave like thing B. Predictive analytics includes three types of algorithms: recommenders, classifiers, and clustering.[103]

CLUSTERING, CLASSIFYING, RECOMMENDING, AND MODELING

Reality is merely an illusion, albeit a very persistent one. *Albert Einstein*

Clustering Algorithms

Clustering algorithms are currently very popular. They provide a way of taking a large set of data objects that seem to have no relationship to one another and producing a visually simple collection of clusters wherein each cluster member is similar to every other member of the same cluster.

The algorithmic methods for clustering are simple. One of the most popular clustering algorithms is the k-means algorithm, which assigns any number of data objects to one of k clusters.[107] The number k of clusters is provided by the user. The algorithm is easy to describe and to understand, but the computational task of completing the algorithm can be difficult when the number of dimensions in the object (i.e., the number of attributes associated with the object) is large.

Here is how the algorithm works for sets of quantitative data.

1. The program randomly chooses k objects from the collection of objects to be clustered. We'll call each of these k objects a focus.
2. For every object in the collection, the distance between the object and all of the randomly chosen k objects (chosen in step 1) is computed.
3. A round of k clusters is computed by assigning every object to its nearest focus.
4. The centroid focus for each of the k clusters is calculated. The centroid is the point that is closest to all of the objects within the cluster. Another way of saying this is if you sum the distances between the centroid and all of the objects in the cluster, this summed distance will be smaller than the summed distance from any other point in space.
5. Steps 2, 3, and 4 are repeated, using the k centroid foci as the points for which all distances are computed.
6. Step 5 is repeated until the k centroid foci converge on a nonchanging set of k centroid foci (or until the program slows to an interminable crawl).

There are some serious drawbacks to the algorithm.

1. The final set of clusters will sometimes depend on the initial, random choice of k data objects. This means that multiple runs of the algorithm may produce different outcomes.
2. The algorithms are not guaranteed to succeed. Sometimes, the algorithm does not converge to a final, stable set of clusters.
3. When the dimensionality is very high, distances between data objects (i.e., the square root of the sum of squares of the measured differences between corresponding attributes of two objects) can be ridiculously large and of no practical meaning (see Glossary item, Curse of dimensionality). Computations may bog down, cease altogether, or produce meaningless results. In this case, the only recourse may require eliminating some of the attributes (i.e., reducing dimensionality of the data objects). Subspace clustering is a method wherein clusters are found for computationally manageable subsets of attributes. If useful clusters are found using this method, additional attributes can be added to the mix to see if the clustering can be improved.
4. The clustering algorithm may succeed, producing a set of clusters of similar objects, but the clusters may have no practical value. They may miss important relationships among the objects or might group together objects whose similarities are totally noninformative.

At best, clustering algorithms should be considered a first step toward understanding how attributes account for the behavior of data objects.

Classifier Algorithms

These algorithms assign a class (from a preexisting classification) to an object whose class is unknown.[107] The k-nearest neighbor algorithm is a simple and popular classifier algorithm. From a collection of data objects whose class is known, the algorithm computes the distances from the object of unknown class to the objects of known class. This involves a distance measurement from the feature set of the objects of unknown class to every object of known class (the test set). The distance measure uses the set of attributes that are associated with each object. After the distances are computed, the k-classed objects with the smallest distance to the object of unknown class are collected. The most common class in the nearest k-classed objects is assigned to the object of unknown class. If the chosen value of k is 1, then the object of unknown class is assigned the class of its closest classed object (i.e., the nearest neighbor).

The k-nearest neighbor algorithm is just one among many excellent classifier algorithms, and analysts have the luxury of choosing algorithms that match their data (e.g., sample size, dimensionality) and purposes.[108] Classifier algorithms differ fundamentally from clustering algorithms and from recommender algorithms in that they begin with an existing classification. Their task is very simple: assign an object to its proper class within the classification. Classifier algorithms carry the assumption that similarities among class objects determine class membership. This may not be the case. For example, a classifier algorithm might place cats into the class of small dogs because of the similarities among several attributes of cats and dogs (e.g., four legs, one tail, pointy ears, average weight 8 pounds, furry, carnivorous, etc.). The similarities are impressive, but irrelevant. No matter how much you try to make it so, a cat is not a type of dog. The fundamental difference between grouping by similarity and grouping by relationship will be discussed again later in this chapter.

Like clustering techniques, classifier techniques are computationally intensive when the dimension is high and can produce misleading results when the attributes are noisy (i.e., contain randomly distributed attribute values) or noninformative (i.e., unrelated to correct class assignment).

Recommender Algorithms

When a data object is very similar to another data object, the two objects are likely to behave similarly. Recommender techniques typically measure the distance between one data object (e.g., a potential customer) and other data items (e.g., customers who have bought a particular product or who have indicated a product preference). The data objects that are closest to one another will tend to have the same preferences and can serve as recommenders. Distances between data objects are measured with feature-by-feature comparisons using the Euclidean distance, the Mahalanobis distance, or whichever type of distance measurements seem appropriate (see Glossary items, Euclidean distance, Mahalanobis distance).

Modeling Algorithms

Modeling involves explaining the behavior of a system, often with a formula, sometimes with descriptive language. The formula for the data describes the distribution of the data and often predicts how the different variables will change with one another. Consequently, modeling comes closer than other Big Data techniques to explaining the behavior of data objects and of the system in which the data objects interact. Most of the great milestones in the physical sciences have arisen from a bit of data modeling supplemented by scientific genius (e.g., Newton's laws of mechanics and optics, Kepler's laws of planetary orbits, quantum mechanics). The occasional ability to relate observation with causality endows modeling with greater versatility and greater scientific impact than the predictive techniques (recommenders, classifiers, and clustering methods).

Unlike the methods of predictive analytics, which tend to rest on a few basic assumptions about measuring similarities among data objects, the methods of data modeling are selected from every field of mathematics and are based on an intuitive approach to data analysis. In many cases, the modeler simply plots the data and looks for familiar shapes and patterns that suggest a particular type of function (e.g., logarithmic, linear, normal, Fourier series, Power law, etc.). The modeler has various means of testing whether the data closely fits the model.

As one example of data modeling, let's look at the Fourier series. Periodic functions (i.e., functions with repeating trends in the data, including waveforms and periodic time series data) can be represented as the sum of oscillating functions (i.e., functions involving sines, cosines, or complex exponentials). This applies to periodic functions that are not shaped like a curve. In Figure 9.1, a square wave is represented as a single sine wave, a sum of 2 sine waves, 3 sine waves, up to 10 sine waves. A simple sine wave captures the periodicity and magnitude of the square wave, but it misses the right-angle corners. As the number of contributing sine waves increases, the approximation to the square wave improves. This indicates that when a set of data in periodic form is decomposed to a Fourier series, the form of the function can be approximated with a finite number of oscillating functions. Depending

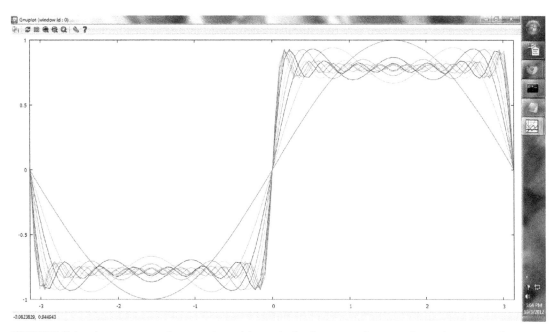

FIGURE 9.1 A square wave is approximated by a single sine wave, the sum of two sine waves, three sine waves, and so on. As more components are added, the representation of the original signal or periodic set of data is more closely approximated.

on the purposes of the data analyst, the first few components of the Fourier series may suffice to produce an adequate model of the data.

A transform is a mathematical operation that takes a function or a time series (e.g., values obtained at intervals of time) and transforms it into something else. An inverse transform will take the product of the transform and produce the original function. Transforms are useful when there are operations that can be performed on the transformed function, but not on the original function.

How can we take what we know about the Fourier series and use it as a transforming operation? Possibly the most popular and useful transform available to data analysts is the Fourier transform. The Fourier transform can be computed with great speed on modern computers, using a modified form known as the fast Fourier transform. Periodic functions and waveforms (periodic time series) can be transformed using this computational method. Operations on the transformed function can sometimes eliminate periodic artifacts or frequencies that occur below a selected threshold (e.g., noise). The transform can also separate signals into tracks (e.g., voice and instrumental tracks) and can find similarities between two signals. When the operations are complete, the inverse of the transform can be calculated and substituted for the original set of data.

DATA REDUCTION

There is something fascinating about science. One gets such a wholesale return of conjecture out of such a trifling investment of fact. *Mark Twain*

At first glance, it seems obvious that gravitational attraction is a Big Data problem. We know that gravitation between any two bodies is proportional to the product of their masses and inversely proportional to the square of the distance between them. If we want to predict the gravitational forces on an object, we would need to know the position and mass of every body in the universe. With this data, we would compute a force vector, from which we could determine the net gravitational influence of the universe upon the mass. Of course, this is absurd. If we needed all that data for our computation, physicists would be forever computing the orbit of the earth around the sun. We are lucky to live in a universe wherein gravity follows an inverse square distance rule, as this allows us to neglect the influences of heavenly bodies that are far away from earth and sun and of nearby bodies that have small masses compared with the sun. Any high school student can compute the orbits of the earth around the sun, predicting their relative positions millennia into the future.

Likewise, if we can see two galaxies in space and we notice that they are similar in shape and size and have a similar star density, then we can assume that they both produce about the same amount of light. If the light received on earth from one of those galaxies is four times that received by the other galaxy, we can apply the inverse square law for light intensity and infer that the brighter galaxy is probably twice as far from earth as the other galaxy. In this short analysis, we start with our observations on every visible galaxy in the universe. Next, we compare just two galaxies, and from this comparison we can develop general methods of analysis that may apply to the larger set of data.

The point here is that when Big Data is analyzed, it is seldom necessary to include every point of data in your system model. In the Big Data field, the most successful analysts will often be those individuals who are adept at simplifying the system model, thus eliminating unnecessary calculations.

Because Big Data is complex, you will often find that your data objects have high dimensionality; each data object is annotated with a large number of values. The types of values that are shared among all the different data objects are usually referred to as parameters. It is very difficult to make much sense of high dimensional data. It is always best to develop a filtering mechanism that expunges useless parameters. A useless parameter will often have one of these two properties.

1. **Redundancy.** If a parameter correlates perfectly with some other parameter, you know that you can safely drop one of the two parameters. For example, you may have some physiologic data on a collection of people, and the data may include weight, waist size, body fat index, weight adjusted by height, density, and so on. These measurements seem to be measuring about the same thing; are they all necessary? If several attributes closely correlate with one another, you might want to drop a few.

Association scores provide a measure of similarity between two variables (see Glossary item, Correlation distance). Two similar variables will rise and fall together. The Pearson correlation score is popular and can be easily implemented.[19,105] It produces a score that varies from −1 to 1. A score of 1 indicates perfect correlation; a score of −1 indicates perfect anticorrelation (i.e., one variable rises while the other falls). A Pearson score of 0 indicates lack of correlation. Other correlation measures are readily available.[109,110] Big Data analysts should not demure from developing their own correlation scores, as needed, to ensure enhanced speed or to provide a scoring measure that best serves their particular goals.

2. **Randomness.** If a parameter is totally random, then it cannot tell you anything meaningful about the data object and you can drop the parameter. There are many tests that measure randomness; most were designed to measure the quality of random number generators.[111] They can also be used to determine the randomness of data sets.

A simple but useful test for randomness can be achieved by putting your set of parameter values into a file and compressing the file. If the values of the parameter are distributed randomly, the file will not compress well, whereas a set of data that has a regular distribution (e.g., a simple curve, a Zipf-like distribution, or a distribution with a sharp peak) will compress down into a very small file.

As a simple illustration, I wrote a short program that created three files, each 10,000 bytes in length. The first file consisted of the number 1, repeated 10,000 times (i.e., 11111111...). The second file consisted of the numbers 0 through 9, distributed as a sequence of 1000 zeros followed by 1000 ones, followed by 1000 twos, and so on, up to 1000 nines. The final file consisted of the numbers 0 through 9 repeated in a purely random sequence (e.g., 285963222202186026084095527364317), extended to fill a file of 10,000 bytes. Each file was compressed with gunzip, which uses the DEFLATE compression algorithm, combining LZ77 and Huffman coding.

The uncompressed files (10,000 bytes) were compressed into the following file sizes:

compressed file size: 58 bytes for 10,000 consecutive "1"
compressed file size: 75 bytes for 1000 consecutive values of 0 through 9
compressed file size: 5092 bytes for a random sequence of 10,000 digits

In the third file, which consisted of a random sequence of digits, a small compression was achieved simply through the conversion from ASCII to binary representation. In general, though, a purely random sequence cannot be compressed. A data analyst can compare the compressibility of data values, parameter by parameter, to determine which parameters might be expunged, at least during the preliminary analysis of a large, multidimensional data set.

When random data are not omitted the unwary analyst may actually develop predictive models and classifiers based entirely on noise. This can occur because clustering algorithms and predictive methods, including neural networks, will produce an outcome from random input data (see Glossary item, Neural network). It has been reported that some published diagnostic tests have been developed from random data.[90]

Aside from eliminating redundant or random parameters, you might want to inspect the data and eliminate parameters that do not contribute in any useful way towards your analysis. For example, if you have the zip code for an individual, you will probably not need to retain the street address. If you have the radiologic diagnosis for a patient's chest X-ray, you might not need to retain the file containing the X-ray image unless you are conducting an image analysis project.

The process of reducing parameters applies to virtually all of the fields of data analysis, including standard statistical analysis. Names for this activity include feature reduction or selection, variable reduction and variable subset reduction, and attribute selection. There is sometimes a fine line between eliminating useless data parameters and cherry-picking your test set (see Glossary items, Cherry-picking, Second trial bias). It is important to document the data attributes you have expunged, and your reason for doing so. Your colleagues should be given the opportunity of reviewing all of your data, including the expunged parameters.

An example of a data elimination method is found in the Apriori algorithm. At its simplest, it expresses the observation that a collection of items cannot occur frequently unless each item in the collection also occurs frequently. To understand the algorithm and its significance, consider the items placed together in a grocery checkout cart. If the most popular combination of purchase items is a sack of flour, a stick of butter, and a quart of milk, then you can be certain that collections of each of these items individually, and all pairs of items from the list of three, must also occur frequently. In fact, they must occur at least as often as the combination of all three, because each of these smaller combinations are subsets of the larger set and will occur with the frequency of the larger set plus the frequency of their occurrences in any other item sets. The importance of the Apriori algorithm to Big Data relates to data reduction. If the goal of the analysis is to find association rules for frequently occurring combinations of items, then you can restrict your analysis to combinations composed of single items that occur frequently.[104,107]

After a reduced data set has been collected, it is often useful to transform the data by any of a variety of methods that enhance your ability to find trends, patterns, clusters, or relational properties that might be computationally invisible in the untransformed data set. The first step is data normalization, described in the next section. It is critical that data be expressed in a comparable form and measure. After the data is normalized, you can further reduce your data by advanced transformative methods.

One popular method for transforming data to reduce the dimensionality of data objects is multidimensional scaling, which employs principal component analysis[104](see Glossary item, Principal component analysis). Without going into the mathematics, principal component analysis takes a list of parameters and reduces it to a smaller list, with each component of the smaller list constructed from combinations of variables in the longer list. Furthermore, principal component analysis provides an indication of which variables in both the original and the new list are least correlated with the other variables. Principal component analysis requires operations on large matrices. Such operations are computationally intensive and can easily exceed the capacity of most computers.

As a final caveat, data analysts should be prepared to learn that there is never any guarantee that a collection of data will be helpful, even if it meets every criteria for accuracy and reproducibility. Sometimes the data you have is not the data you need. Data analysts should be aware that many of the advanced analytic methods, including clustering, neural networks, Bayesian methods, and support vector machines, may produce a result that does not take you any closer to a meaningful answer (see Glossary item, Support vector machine). The data analyst must understand that there is an important difference between a result and an answer.

NORMALIZING AND ADJUSTING DATA

When extracting data from multiple sources, recorded at different times, and collected for different purposes, the data values may not be directly comparable. The Big Data analyst must contrive a method to normalize or harmonize the data values.

1. **Adjusting for population differences.** Epidemiologists are constantly reviewing large data sets on large populations (e.g., local, national, and global data). If epidemiologists did not normalize their data, they would be in a constant state of panic. Suppose you are following long-term data on the incidence of a rare childhood disease in a state population. You notice that the number of people with the disease has doubled in the past decade. You are about to call the *New York Times* with the news when one of your colleagues taps you on the shoulder and explains that the population of the state has doubled in the same time period. The incidence, described as cases per 100,000 population, has remained unchanged. You calm yourself down and continue your analysis to find that the reported cases of the disease has doubled in a different state that has had no corresponding increase in state population. You are about to call the White House with the news when your colleague taps you on the shoulder and explains that the overall population of the state has remained unchanged, but the population of children in the state has doubled. The incidence as expressed as cases occurring in the target population has remained unchanged.

An age-adjusted rate is the rate of a disease within an age category, weighted against the proportion of persons in the age groups of a standard population. When we age adjust rates, we cancel out the changes in the rates of disease that result from differences in the proportion of people in different age groups.

Some of the most notorious observations on nonadjusted data come from the field of baseball. In 1930, Bill Terry maintained a batting average of 0.401, the best batting average in the National league. In 1968, Carl Yastrzemski led his league with a batting average of 0.301.

FIGURE 9.2   An image of the author (left) converted into a histogram representing the number of pixels that have a gray-scale value of 0, 1, 2, 3, and so on up to the top gray-scale value of 256. Each gray-scale value is a bin.

You would think that the facts prove that Terry's lead over his fellow players was greater than Yastrzemski's. Actually, both had averages that were 27% higher than the average of their fellow ballplayers of the year. Normalized against all the players for the year in which the data was collected, Terry and Yastrzemski tied.

2. **Rendering data values dimensionless**. Histograms express data distributions by binning data into groups and displaying the bins in a bar graph (see Figure 9.2). A histogram of an image may have bins (bars) whose heights consist of the number of pixels in a black-and-white image that fall within a certain gray-scale range.

When comparing images of different sizes, the total number of pixels in the images is different, making it impossible to usefully compare the heights of bins. In this case, the number of pixels in each bin can be divided by the total number of pixels in the image to produce a number that corresponds to the fraction of the total image pixels that are found in the bin. The normalized value (now represented as a fraction) can be compared between two images. Notice that by representing the bin size as a fraction, we have stripped the dimension from the data (i.e., a number expressed as pixels) and rendered a dimensionless data item (i.e., a purely numeric fraction).

3. **Converting one data type to another, more useful data type.** A zip code is an example of data formed by numeric digits that lack numeric properties. You cannot add two zip codes and expect to get any useful information from the process. However, every zip code has been mapped to a specific latitude and longitude at the center of the zip code region, and these values can be used as spherical coordinates from which distances between locations can be computed. It is often useful to assign geographic coordinates to every zip code entry in a database.

4. **Converting to a (0,1) interval.** Any set of data values can be converted into an interval between 0 and 1, wherein the original data values maintain their relative positions in the new interval. There are several simple ways to achieve the result. The most straightforward is to compute the range of the data by subtracting the smallest data value in your data set from the largest data value. To determine the location of any data value in the 0,1 range, simply subtract from it the smallest value in the data set and then divide the result by the range of the data. This tells you where your value is located, in a 0,1 interval, as a fraction of the range of the data.

Another popular method for converting data sets to a standard interval is to subtract the mean from any data value and divide by the standard deviation. This gives you the position of the data value expressed as its deviation from the mean as a fraction of the standard deviation. The resulting value is called the z score.

When comparing different data sets, it is important to normalize all of the data points to a common interval. In the case of multidimensional data, it is usually necessary to normalize the data in every dimension using some sensible scaling computation. This may include the methods just described (i.e., dividing by range or standard deviation or by substituting data with a dimensionless transformed value, such as a correlation measure).

5. **Weighting**. Weighting is a method whereby the influence of a value is moderated by some factor intended to yield an improved value. In general, when a data value is replaced by the sum of weighted factors, the weights are chosen to add to 1. For example, if you are writing your own smoothing function, in which each value in a data set is replaced by a value computed by summing contributions from itself and its immediate neighbors on the left and the right, you might multiply each number by one-third so that the final number is scaled to a magnitude similar to your original number. Alternately, you might multiply the number to the left and to the right by one-quarter and the original by one-half to provide a summed number weighted to favor the original number.

It is a shame that Big Data never comes with instructions. Data analysts are constantly required to choose a normalization method, and the choice will always depend on their intended use of the data. Here is an example. Three sources of data provide records on children that include an age attribute. Each source measures age in the same dimension, years. You would think that because the ages are all recorded in years, not months or decades, you can omit a normalization step. When you study the data, you notice that one source contains children up to the year 14, while another is cut off at age 12 and another stops at age 16. Suddenly, you are left with a difficult problem. Can you ignore the differences in the cut-off age in the three data sets? Should you truncate all of the data above age 12? Should you use all of the data, but weigh the data differently for the different sources? Should you divide by the available ranges for the data? Should you compute z scores? It all depends on what you are trying to learn from the data.

BIG DATA SOFTWARE: SPEED AND SCALABILITY

It's hardware that makes a machine fast. It's software that makes a fast machine slow. *Craig Bruce*

The Cleveland Clinic developed software that predicts disease survival outcomes from a large number of genetic variables. Unfortunately, the time required for these computations was unacceptable. As a result, the Cleveland Clinic issued a challenge to "to deliver an efficient computer program that predicts cancer survival outcomes with accuracy equal or better than the reference algorithm, including 10-fold validation, in less than 15 hours of real world (wall clock) time."[112] The Cleveland Clinic had a working algorithm, but it was not scalable to the number of variables analyzed.

The typical computer user has no patience for computational tardiness. When we submit a Google query, the output is collected from the totality of Web pages and we see the results immediately. We have come to expect every algorithm to operate in the blink of an eye. With Big Data, software may not scale to the size and complexity of the job.

Here are a few suggestions for achieving speed and scalability.

1. **Never assume that software is scalable.** A software application that works fine for a few megabytes of data may crawl or crash when confronted with a terabyte-sized file, or with millions of variables per record.

2. **Avoid turn-key applications.** A turn-key application may work well until the Big Data reaches a critical size, at which time the system slows or crashes. Turn-key applications tend to be monolithic and nonmodular, producing a "black box" mentality among users (see Glossary item, Black box). When one of the subsystems fails, it can be difficult or impossible to fix.

3. **Use small, efficient, and fast utilities.** Utilities are written to perform one task, optimally. For data analysts, utilities fit perfectly with the multistep paradigm of Big Data projects. A savvy data analyst will have hundreds of small utilities, most being free and open source products, that can be pulled, as needed. A utility can be tested with data sets of increasing size and complexity. If the utility scales to the job, then it can be plugged into the project. Otherwise, it can be replaced with an alternate utility or modified to suit your needs.

4. **Avoid unpredictable software.** Programs that operate with complex sets of input may behave unpredictably. It is important to use software that has been extensively tested by yourself and by your colleagues. After testing, it is important to constantly monitor the performance of software. This is especially important when using new sources of data, which may contain data values that have been formatted differently than prior data.

5. **When designing your own software, understand your algorithms and learn their limitations.** An algorithm that produces an inexact answer is always preferable to an algorithm that crashes under the load of a gigabyte of data. When your data runs too slowly, do not immediately look for a faster computer; most speed problems are due to design issues or to the selection of an algorithm that cannot scale. Do not look for a faster programming language. The difference in speed among the popular programming languages is not as great as their adherents might have you believe. Thinking deeply about what you really need to accomplish with your software will often lead you to a solution that will work with readily available hardware and programming languages.

6. **If you are conducting scientific research, you should avoid using proprietary software, even if it is reliable and scalable.** Proprietary software applications have their place in the realm of Big Data. They can be used to operate the servers, databases, and communications involved in building and maintaining the resource. They are often well tested and dependable. They do the job they were designed to do. However, in the analysis phase,

it may be impossible to fully explain your research methods if one of the steps is "Install the vendor's software and click on the 'Run' button." Data analysts should use open source software unless their proprietary software fully documents the algorithms and methods therein.

FIND RELATIONSHIPS, NOT SIMILARITIES

The creative act is the defeat of habit by originality. **George Lois**

The distinction between relationships among objects and similarities among objects is one of the most fundamental concepts in data analysis, yet it is commonly misunderstood. Relationships are the fundamental properties of an object that place it within a class of objects, each member of which has the same fundamental properties. A common set of relational properties distinguishes the ancestral classes of an object and the descendant classes of an object. Related objects tend to be similar to one another, but these similarities occur as the consequence of their relationships, not vice versa. For example, you may have many similarities to your father. You are similar to you father because you are related to him; you are not related to him because you are similar to him.

Here are two additional examples that stress the difference between relationship and similarity.

1. You look up at the clouds and you begin to see the shape of a lion. The cloud has a tail, like a lion's tail, and a fluffy head, like a lion's mane. With a little imagination, the mouth of the lion seems to roar down from the sky. You have succeeded in finding similarities between the cloud and a lion. If you look at a cloud and you imagine a tea kettle producing a head of steam, then you are establishing a relationship between the physical forces that create a cloud and the physical forces that produce steam from a heated kettle, and you understand that clouds are composed of water vapor.
2. You look up at the stars and you see the outline of a flying horse, Pegasus, or the soup ladle, the Big Dipper. You have found similarities upon which to base the names of celestial landmarks, the constellations. The constellations help you orient yourself to the night sky, but they do not tell you much about the physical nature of the twinkling objects. If you look at the stars and you see the relationship between the twinkling stars in the night sky and the round sun in the daylight sky, then you can begin to understand how the universe operates.

The distinction between grouping data objects by similarity and grouping data objects by relationship is sometimes lost on computer scientists. I have had numerous conversations with intelligent scientists who refuse to accept that grouping by similarity (e.g., clustering) is fundamentally different from grouping by relationship (i.e., building a classification).

Consider Figure 9.3, which contains 300 objects. Each object belongs to one of two classes, marked by an asterisk or by an empty box. The 300 objects naturally cluster into three groups. It is tempting to conclude that the graph shows three classes of objects that can be defined by their similarities, but we know from the outset that the objects fall into two classes, and we see from the graph that objects from both classes are distributed in all three clusters.

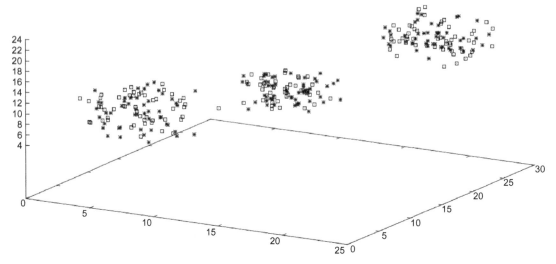

FIGURE 9.3 Spatial distribution of 300 objects represented by data points in three dimensions. Each data object falls into one of two classes, represented by an asterisk or an empty box. The data naturally segregates into three clusters. Objects of type asterisk and type box are distributed throughout each cluster.

Is this graph far-fetched? Not really. Suppose you have a collection of felines and canines. The collection of dogs might include Chihuahuas, St. Bernards, and other breeds. The collection of cats might include housecats, lions, and other species, and the data collected on each animal might include weight, age, and hair length. We do not know what to expect when we cluster the animals by similarities (i.e., weight, age, hair length), but we can be sure that short-haired cats and short-haired Chihuahuas of the same age will probably fall into one cluster. Cheetahs and greyhounds, having similar size and build, might fall into another cluster. The similarity clusters will mix together unrelated animals and will separate related animals.

For taxonomists, the importance of grouping by relationship, not by similarity, is a lesson learned the hard way. Literally 2000 years of misclassifications, erroneous biological theorizations, and impediments to progress in medicine and agriculture have occurred whenever similarities were confused with relationships. Early classifications of animals were based on similarities (e.g., beak shape, color of coat, number of toes). These kinds of classifications led to the erroneous conclusions that dolphins were fish and that the various juvenile forms of insects, nematodes, and thousands of species of animals were distinct organisms, unrelated to the adult form into which they would mature. The vast field of animal taxonomy was a hopeless and useless mess until taxonomists began to think very deeply about classes of organisms and the fundamental properties that accounted for the relationships among the classes.

Geneticists have also learned that sequence similarities among genes may bear no relationship to their functionalities, their inheritance from higher organisms, their physical locations, or to any biological process whatsoever. Geneticists use the term homology to describe the relationship among sequences that can be credited to descent from a common ancestral sequence. Similarity among different sequences can be nonhomologous, developing randomly in nonrelated organisms, or developing by convergence, through selection for genes that have common functionality. Sequence similarity that is not acquired from a common ancestral sequence seldom relates to the shared fundamental cellular properties that characterize inherited relationships. Biological inferences drawn from gene analyses are more useful when they are built upon phylogenetic relationships rather than on superficial genetic or physiologic similarities.[113]

It is my perception that the distinction between classification by similarity and classification by relationship is vitally important to the field of computer science and to the future of Big Data analysis. I have discussed this point with many of my colleagues, who hold the opposite view: that the distinction between similarity classification and relationship classification is purely semantic. There is no practical difference between the two methods. Regardless of which side you may choose, the issue is worth pondering for a few moments.

Two arguments support the opinion that classification is based on similarity measures. The first argument is that classification by similarity is the standard method by which relational classifications are built. The second argument is that relational properties are always unknown at the time that the classification is built. The foundation of every classification must be built on measurable features, and the only comparison we have for measurable features is similarity.

The first argument, based on common practice, has no scientific merit. It assumes that common practice must be correct, but determining the correctness of common practice is what we are trying to settle.

The second argument, that classification by relationship requires access to unobtainable knowledge, is a clever observation that hits on a weakness in the relational theory of classification. To build a classification, you must first know the relational properties that define classes, superclasses, and subclasses, but if you want to know the relationships among the classes, you must refer to the classification. It's another bootstrapping problem.

Building a classification is an iterative process wherein you hope that your tentative selection of relational properties and your class assignments will be validated over time. You build a classification by guessing which properties are fundamental and relational and by guessing which system of classes will make sense when all of the instances of the classes are assigned. A classification is often likened to a hypothesis that must be tested again and again as the classification grows.

Is it ever possible to build a classification by a hierarchical clustering algorithm based on measuring similarities among objects? The answer is a qualified yes, assuming that the object features that you have measured happen to be the relational properties that define the classes. A good example of this process is demonstrated by the work of Carl Woese and coworkers in the field of the classification of terrestrial organisms.[114] Woese compared ribosomal RNA sequences among organisms. Ribosomal RNA is involved in the precise synthesis of proteins according to instructions coded in genes. According to Woese, ribosomal RNA mutates slowly because it must be present in every terrestrial organism and it has scarcely any leeway in its functionality. Changes in the sequence of ribosomal RNA act like a chronometer for evolution. Using sequence similarities, Woese developed a brilliant classification of living organisms that has revolutionized evolutionary genetics. Woese's analysis is not perfect, and where there are apparent mistakes in his classification, disputations focus on the limitations of using similarity as a substitute for fundamental relational properties.[115,116]

The field of medical genetics has been embroiled in a debate, lasting well over a decade, on the place of race in science. Some would argue that when the genomes of humans from different races are compared, there is no sensible way to tell one genome from another on the basis of assigned race. The genes of a tall man and a short man are more different than the genes of an African-American man and a white man. Judged by genetic similarity, race has no scientific meaning.[117] On the other hand, every clinician understands that various diseases, congenital and acquired, occur at different rates in the African-American population than in the white population. Furthermore, the clinical symptoms, clinical outcome, and even the treatment of these diseases in African-American and white individuals will sometimes differ among ethnic or racial groups. Hence, many medical epidemiologists and physicians perceive race as a clinical reality.[118] The discord stems from a misunderstanding of the meanings of similarity and of relationship. It is quite possible to have a situation wherein similarities are absent, while relationships pertain. The lack of informative genetic similarities that distinguish one race from another does not imply that race does not exist. The basis for race is the relationship created by shared ancestry. The morphologic and clinical by-product of the ancestry relationship may occur as various physical features and epidemiologic patterns found by clinicians.

In the cancer field, measurements of tumor cells always demonstrate the same phenomenon—cancer cells differ from normal cells in virtually every measurable parameter. In this case, there is an overabundance of biological differences and a paucity of well-established cellular relationships with which to understand the biological differences. When we cluster different types of cancers based on similarity measures, we usually find that these clusterings are seldom repeatable. The problem has been that the similarities, when present, are not fundamentally related to the processes that account for the development of cancer cells or to the morphologic features observed by pathologists who use traditional microscopic techniques to examine cancerous tissues.[87,89,90,119,120]

Computer scientists may scoff at examples selected from the realm of biology and medicine. They might remark that biological systems are always messy; by using clean mathematical constructs, the distinction between relationships and similarities would simply disappear. Maybe not. In the past decade, I have programmed with object-oriented languages, particularly the Ruby programming language.[65,19] Everything in Ruby is an object, and every object belongs to a class. Methods are inherited through class lineage. Classes are defined by the methods they provide and the methods they inherit. No adept Ruby programmer would have any difficulty distinguishing between methods that apply to a class (i.e., available to every instance of the class) versus methods that apply to individual objects (so-called instance methods in Ruby). The idea of grouping objects belonging to different classes, based on shared instance methods, would be anathema to Ruby programmers. Doing so would defeat the purpose of object-oriented programming and would create chaos.

Fundamentally, all analysis is devoted to finding relationships among objects or classes of objects. All we know about the universe and the processes that play out in our universe can be reduced to simple relationships. In many cases, the process of finding and establishing relationships often begins with finding similarities, but it must never end there.

Special Considerations in Big Data Analysis

Those who ignore Statistics are condemned to reinvent it. **Brad Efron**

BACKGROUND

Big Data statistics are plagued by several intrinsic flaws. When the amount of data is sufficiently large, you can find almost anything you seek lurking somewhere within; the found observations may have statistical significance without having any significance in reality. Also, whenever you select a subset of data from an enormous collection, you may have no way of knowing the relevance of the data that you excluded. Most importantly, Big Data resources cannot be designed to examine every conceivable hypothesis. Many types of analytic errors ensue when a Big Data resource is forced to respond to questions that it cannot possibly answer. Over the past decade, a large literature has emerged to describe the pitfalls of Big Data statistics. The purpose of this chapter is to discuss these pitfalls and to provide general recommendations for the responsible use of analytic methods.

THEORY IN SEARCH OF DATA

Here's a riddle: "Which came first, the data or the data analyst?" The intuitive answer would be that data precedes the data analyst. Without data, there really is no reason for the data analyst to exist. In the Big Data universe, nothing is as it seems, and the data analyst commonly precedes the data. The analyst develops a question, a hypothesis, or a notion of what the facts "should be" and then goes about rummaging through the Big Data resource until he or she has created a data set that proves the point!

We cannot escape the dangerous practice of imposing models on selected sets of data. Historians, who have the whole of human history to study, are just as guilty as technical data analysts in this regard. Consider this hypothetical example: the United States is on the brink of a military intervention against entrenched and hostile revolutionaries on the other side of the globe. Two historians are asked to analyze the situation and render their opinions. The first historian compares the current crisis to the entrance of the United States into World War II. World War II worked out well for the United States. The first historian insists that World War II is a useful model for today's emergency and that we should engage our military against the current threat. The second historian says that the current crisis is very much like the crisis that preceded the Vietnam War. The Vietnam War did not turn out well for U.S. interests, and it would be best if we avoided direct military involvement in the current emergency. When you have all of history from which to choose, you can select any set of data that supports your biases. As humans, we do this all the time, whenever we make decisions.

Scientists have accused their peers of developing models for the purpose of reinforcing belief in their own favorite paradigms.[121] Big Data will not help advance science if analysts preferentially draw data to support their previously held biases.

One of the important tasks for Big Data analysts will involve developing methods for creating unbiased models from Big Data. In the meantime, there is no practical way to validate conclusions drawn from Big Data other than to test the hypothesis on additional data sets.

DATA IN SEARCH OF A THEORY

Without highly specified a-priori hypotheses, there are hundreds of ways to analyse the dullest data set. *John P A Ioannidis*[122]

In the prior section, the point was made that Big Data can be abused by data analysts if data is selected to confirm a hypothesis. In this section, the point is made that scientists must enter their analysis with a model theory; otherwise they will choose a hypothesis to fit their data, even if the hypothesis makes no sense.

Here's a good example. Suppose I am at a shooting range and shoot 10 shots at a bull's-eye target. I can measure the distance of each bullet from the center of the target, from which I would develop some type of score with which I could compare my marksmanship against that of others. Now, imagine shooting 10 shots at a wall that has no target. I may find that six of the bullets clustered very close together. I could then superimpose the bullet holes onto a bull's-eye target, placing the center of the target over the center of the tight cluster of bullet holes. A statistician analyzing the data might find that the six tightly clustered bullet holes at the center of the bull's eye indicated that I scored very well and that it was highly likely that I had better aim than others (who had actually aimed at the target). Scientists who troll large data sets will always find clusters of data upon which they can hang a bull's eye. Statisticians provided with such data can be tricked into confirming a ridiculous hypothesis that was contrived to fit the data. This deceptive practice is referred to as moving the target to the bullet hole.

Big Data analysts walk a thin line. If they start their project with a preconceived theory, then they run the risk of choosing a data set the confirms their bias. If they start their project without a theory, then they run the risk of developing a false hypothesis that happens to fit the data.

Is there a correct approach to Big Data analysis? It is important to remember that a scientific theory is a plausible explanation of observations. Theories are always based on some set of preexisting principles that are generally accepted as truth. When a scientist approaches a large set of data, he or she asks whether a set of commonly held principles will extend to the observations in the current set of data. Reconciling what is known with what is observed accounts for much of the activity of scientists.

For Big Data projects, holding a prior theory or model is almost always necessary; otherwise, the scientist is overwhelmed by the options. Adequate analysis can be ensured if the following four conditions are met.

1. All of the available data is examined or a subset is prepared from a random sampling (i.e., no cherry-picking data to fit the theory).
2. The analyst must be willing to modify or abandon the theory if it does not fit the data.
3. The analyst must not believe that fitting the theory to the data validates the theory. Theories must be tested against multiple sets of data.
4. The analyst must accept that the theory may be wrong, even if it is validated. Validation is not proof that a theory is correct. It is proof that the theory is consistent with all of the observed data. A better theory may also be consistent with the observed data and may provide a true explanation of the observations.

One of the greatest errors of Big Data analysts is to believe that data models are tethered to reality—they seldom are. Models are made to express data sets as formulas. When the data are numeric representations of physical phenomenon, it may sometimes be possible to link the model to a physical law. For example, repeated measurements of force, mass, and acceleration observed on moving bodies might produce a formula that applies consistently at any time, any place, and with any object (i.e., $f = ma$). Most mathematical models are abstract and cannot be ranked as physical laws. At best, they provide a quick glimpse of an ephemeral reality.

The Gaussian copula function provides a cautionary tale (see Glossary item, Gaussian copula function). This formerly honored and currently vilified formula, developed for Wall Street, calculated the risk of default correlation (the likelihood of two investment vehicles defaulting together) based on current market value of the vehicles, without factoring in historical data. The formula was easy to implement and became a favorite model for predicting risk in the securitization market. Though the Gaussian copula function had its detractors, it soon became the driving model on Wall Street. In about 2008, the function stopped working— then came the 2008 market collapse. In some circles, the Gaussian copula function is blamed for the disaster.[123]

OVERFITTING

Overfitting occurs when a formula describes a set of data very closely, but does not predict the behavior of comparable data sets. In overfitting, the formula is said to describe the noise of the system rather than the characteristic behavior of the system. Overfitting occurs with models that perform iterative approximations on training data, coming closer and closer to the training data set with each iteration. Neural networks are an example of a data modeling strategy that is prone to overfitting. In general, the bigger the data set, the easier it is to overfit the model.

Overfitting is discovered by testing your predictor or model on one or several new sets of data.[124] If the data is overfitted, the model will fail with the new data. It can be heartbreaking to spend months or years developing a model that works like a charm for your training data and for your first set of test data (collected from the same data set as your training data), but fails completely for a new set of data.

Overfitting can sometimes be avoided by evaluating the model before it has been fitted to a mathematical formula, often during the data reduction stage (see Glossary item, Data reduction). There are a variety of techniques that will produce a complex formula fitted to all your variables. It might be better to select just a few variables from your data that you think are most relevant to the model. You might try a few mathematical relationships that seem to describe the data plotted for the subset of variables. A formula built from an intuitive understanding of the relationships among variables may sometimes serve much better than a formula built to fit a multidimensional data set.

BIGNESS BIAS

Every increased possession loads us with new weariness. *John Ruskin*

Because Big Data methods use enormous sets of data, there is a tendency to give the results much more credence than would be given to a set of results produced from a small set of data. This is almost always a mistaken belief. In fact, Big Data is seldom a complete or accurate data collection. You can expect most Big Data resources to be selective, intentionally or not, for the data that is included and excluded from the resource. When dealing with Big Data, expect missing values, missing records, "noisy" data, huge variations in the quality of records, plus any and all of the inadequacies found in small data resources. Nevertheless, the belief that Big Data is somehow more reliable and more useful than smaller data is pervasive in the science community. In the late 1990s, I was personally involved in high-level discussions regarding the development of new biomarkers for cancer. It was believed then, as it is often believed now, that the different types of cancers must contain biological markers to tell us everything we needed to know about their clinical behaviors. Such biomarkers would be used to establish the presence of a cancer, the precise diagnosis of the cancer, the stage of the cancer (i.e., the size and the extent of spread of the cancer), and to predict the response of the cancer to any type of treatment. By the turn of the century, there was a sense that useful cancer biomarkers were not forthcoming; the pipeline for new biomarkers had apparently dried up.[125–128] It is my perception that there was near-universal consensus that we were funding too many small and irreproducible studies; we needed big studies, producing lots of data, yielding valid results that could be quickly applied in clinical settings.

In the past decade, biomarker studies have seen enormous growth: more funding, bigger studies, data-intensive methodologies for biomarker development (e.g., genomics, proteomics, metabolomics), large clinical trials, and the advent of Big Data resources. More than a decade has passed, but there has been virtually no progress in the field of biomarkers.[122] When a new potential biomarker is discovered using advanced methodology, it is seldom validated when the study is repeated in another laboratory with the same methodology or when examined with a different methodology.[89,129] An article published in 2010 asserted that despite enormous efforts, only a few predictive markers have proven useful to guide breast cancer therapy; basically, molecular profiling has not been shown to have more clinical value than standard histologic methods (i.e., looking at tissues under a microscope).[130] Not only have there been a paucity of new, validated biomarkers, the availability of large data sets has served to discredit some of the biomarkers that were previously held in high esteem.[131,132]

What has happened? Where did the field of Big Data biomarker research go wrong? The problem was simple: we thought that the problem was insufficient data, but the problem was biological. We started by assuming that simple and informative biomarkers must exist and that we could find these biomarkers if we had lots of data pertaining to the biological systems in which they operated. The problem is that we do not know very much about highly complex disease systems; nor do we know much about collecting useful data about these systems. We basically know very little about biomarkers. When you do not know what you are doing, it seldom helps to throw Big Data at the problem.

A little joke illustrates a subtle and often-neglected bias in data analysis. A young man is chatting with a nonagenarian. "What is the secret to longevity?" the young man asks. The old man answers: "Every night, before you go to sleep, drink a hot cup of tea with a little honey. Do this every day for 90 years, and you will live to be a very old man. Guaranteed." If you think this joke is funny, then you understand the principle underlying time-window bias[133](see Glossary item, Time-window bias).

Here are two examples of time-window bias. Nobel laureates live longer than other scientists; scientists who want to live a long life should try their utmost to win a Nobel prize. Popes live longer than other clergymen. If you are a priest, and you want to live long, aim for the Papacy. Both these biases are based on time-window conditions. The Nobel prize committee typically waits decades to determine whether a scientific work is worthy of the Nobel prize, and the prize is only awarded to living scientists. Would-be Nobelists who die before their scientific career begins, and accomplished scientists who die before works are deemed Nobel-worthy, are omitted from the population of potential winners. The time-window surrounding winners skews the average longevity of Nobel winners upwards. Likewise, the Papal conclave is not in the habit of seating fresh-faced youths on the Papal throne. Time-window bias is just one of a general class of biases wherein conclusions are invalidated by the preconditions imposed on the studies.

When a study is done on a very large number of people, or with a very large number of samples, with a large volume of data, there is a tendency to accept the results, even when the results defy intuition. Let us examine how time-window bias can be a particularly subtle intruder in Big Data studies. In 2007, a study using the enormous patient data set held by the U.S. Veterans Administration Medical Centers reported that the use of statins reduced the risk of developing lung cancer by about half.[134] The study, which involved nearly half a million patients, showed that the reduction in cancer risk held whether patients were smokers or nonsmokers. The highest reduction in lung cancers (77%) occurred in people who had taken statins for 4 years or longer.[134]

The importance of this study cannot be overestimated. Lung cancer is the most common cause of cancer deaths in the United States. A 77% reduction in lung cancer incidence would prevent the cancer deaths of about 123,000 U.S. residents, each year. This number is equivalent to the total number of cancer deaths attributed each year to prostate cancer, breast cancer, and colon cancer combined.[135] The findings were as unintuitive as they were exciting. Statins are widely used drugs that reduce the blood levels of cholesterol and various other blood lipids. There is nothing known about statins that would lead anyone to suspect that this drug would lower the incidence of lung cancer.

In 2011, a second study, by another group of researchers, was published on the effect of statins on lung cancer incidence. This study was also big, using about 133,000 patients. The results failed to show any effect of statins on lung cancer incidence.[136] That same year, a third study, using a population of about 365,000 people, also failed to find any influence of statins on the incidence of lung cancer.[137] According to the authors of the third study, time-window bias accounted for the discrepancy. By placing the condition that patients receive 4 years of statin therapy before comparing them against patients who did not receive statin therapy, the first study selected against people who developed cancer during or preceding the 4-year statin regimen.

Let us go back to the joke that began the topic of time-window bias: "If you drink tea every night for 90 years, you'll live to be an old man." Now let's rephrase it, for a time-window biased statin experiment: "If you take a statin every day for 4 years without developing lung cancer, then I can guarantee that you'll have a 4-year zone in which lung cancer does not occur".

The original study involved a large set of complex clinical data collected on about a half-million human subjects. The study protocol was authorized by a multisite institutional review board. The data was analyzed by a team of scientists. The submitted manuscript was peer-reviewed under the editorial direction of a prestigious medical journal. In the end, the results could not be validated, despite the best efforts of two teams of researchers using hundreds of thousands of human subjects. Big Data is very persuasive. The same biases that are caught in peer review for a small data study may evade the reviewer's notice when they occur in a Big Data study.

Still unconvinced that bigness bias is a real concern for Big Data studies? In the United States, our knowledge of the causes of death in the population is based on death certificate data collected by the Vital Statistics Program of the National Center for Health Statistics. Death certificate data is notoriously faulty.[77–79] In most cases, the data in death certificates is supplied by clinicians, at or near the time of the patient's death, without the benefit of autopsy results. In many cases, the clinicians who fill out the death certificate are not trained to fill out the cause of death form, often mistaking the mode of death (e.g., cardiac arrest, cardiopulmonary arrest) with cause of death (e.g., the disease process leading to cardiac arrest or cardiopulmonary arrest), thus nullifying the intended purpose of the death certificate. Thousands of instructional pages have been written on the proper way to complete a death certificate. Nonetheless, these certificates are seldom completed in a consistent manner. Clinicians become confused when there are multiple, sometimes unrelated, conditions that contribute to the patient's death or when the cause of death is not obvious. Though the death certificates are standardized throughout the United States, there are wide variations, from state to state, in the level of detail provided on the forms.[19] Despite all this, the venerable death certificate is the bedrock of vital statistics. What we know, or think we know, about the causes of death in the U.S. population is based on an enormous repository, collected since 1935, of death certificates.

Why do we believe death certificate data when we know that death certificates are highly flawed? Again, it is the bigness factor that prevails. There seems to be a belief, based on nothing but wishful thinking, that if you have a very large data set, bad measurements will cancel themselves out, leaving a final result that comes close to a fair representation of reality. For example, if a clinician forgets to list a particular condition as a cause of death, another physician will mistakenly include the condition on another death certificate, thus rectifying the error.

The cancel-out hypothesis puts forward the delightful idea that whenever you have huge amounts of data, systemic errors cancel out in the long run, yielding conclusions that are accurate. Sadly, there is neither evidence nor serious theory to support this hypothesis. If you think about it, you will see that it makes no sense. One of the most flagrant weaknesses is the fact that it is impossible to balance something that must always be positive. Every death certificate contains a cause of death. You cannot balance a false positive cause of death with a false negative cause of death; there is no such thing as a negative cause of death. The same applies to numeric databases. An incorrect entry for 5000 pairs of shoes cannot be balanced by a separate incorrect entry for negative 5000 pairs of shoes; there is no such thing as a negative shoe (see Glossary item, Negative study bias).

Perhaps the most prevalent type of bigness bias relates to the misplaced faith that complete data is representative data. Certainly, you might think, if a Big Data resource contains every measurement for a data domain, then biases imposed by insufficient sampling are eliminated. Danah Boyd, a social media researcher, draws a sharp distinction between Big-ness and Whole-ness.[138] She gives the example of a scientist who is exploring a huge data set of tweets collected by Twitter. If Twitter removes tweets containing expletives, tweets composed of nonword character strings, tweets containing highly charged words, or tweets containing certain types of private information, then the resulting data set, no matter how large it may be, is not representative of the population of tweeters. If the tweets are available as a set of messages, without any identifier for senders, then the compulsive tweeters (those who send hundreds or thousands of tweets) will be overrepresented and the one-time tweeters will be underrepresented. If each tweet was associated with an account and all the tweets from a single account were collected as a unique record, then there would still be the problem created by tweeters who maintain multiple accounts. Basically, when you have a Big Data resource, the issue of sample representation does not disappear—it becomes more complex (see Glossary item, Simpson's paradox). For Big Data resources lacking introspection and identifiers, data representation becomes an intractable problem.

TOO MUCH DATA

Intuitively, you might think that the more data you have at your disposal, the more you can learn about the system that you are studying. This is not always the case. There are circumstances when more data simply takes you further and further from the solution you seek. As a trivial example, consider the perennial task of finding a needle in a haystack. As you add more hay, you make the problem harder to solve. You would be much better off if the haystack were small, consisting of a single straw, behind which lies your sought-after needle.[139]

Great difficulties arise when the dimensionality of the data (i.e., the number of measured attributes for each data object) increases. The problem is known to mathematicians by the harrowing name of "the curse of dimensionality"! Basically, as the number of attributes for a data object increases, the multidimensional space encompassing the attributes becomes sparsely populated and the distances between any two objects, even the closest neighbors, becomes absurdly large. When you have thousands of dimensions, the space that holds the objects is so large that clustering becomes incomputable and meaningless. The curse applies to any algorithm that compares data objects on their distances from one another; this would include searching based on similarity.[140] Your simplest recourse may be dimension reduction (see Chapter 9).

In the field of molecular biology, the acquisition of whole genome sequencing on many individual organisms, representing hundreds of different species, has brought a flood of data, but many of the most fundamental questions cannot be answered when the data is complex and massive. Evolutionary biologists have invented a new term for a class of sequence data: "nonphylogenetic signal." The term applies to DNA sequences that cannot yield any useful conclusions related to the evolutionary position of an organism.

Evolutionary geneticists draw conclusions by comparing DNA sequences in organisms, looking for similar, homologous regions (i.e., sequences that were inherited from a common ancestor). Because DNA mutations arise stochastically over time (i.e., at random locations in the gene and at random times), unrelated organisms may attain the same sequence in a chosen stretch of DNA, without inheritance through a common ancestor. Such occurrences could lead to false inferences about the relatedness of different organisms. When mathematical phylogeneticists began modeling inferences for gene data sets, they assumed that most class assignment errors would be restricted to a narrow range of situations. This turned out not to be the case. In practice, errors due to nonphylogenetic signals occur due to just about any mechanism that causes DNA to change over time (e.g., random mutations, adaptive convergence).[141,142] There seems to be too much genetic information, and mathematical biologists are working feverishly on a solution. For now, the practical solution seems to involve moving away from purely automated gene analyses and using a step-by-step approach involving human experts who take into account independently acquired knowledge concerning the relationships among organisms and their genes.

FIXING DATA

Every data analyst understands that data, like the family pet, is apt to get dirty. For dirty data, there are always three choices: correct it, delete it, or leave it be.[143] For those in a quandary over which action to take, the general rule is that if a value is impossible, you cannot leave it—you must change it or delete it. Less obvious is the action taken when a value is extreme, but comes within the realm of possibility. The extreme outlier, if true, can sometimes be the most important data value in the collection.

Who is in charge of fixing the data in an extracted data set? Short answer: anyone but the data manager. In the case of genomic data, most of the data cleaning will be done by the experimentalist or, more precisely, by the instruments that measure the data. When an instrument registers the amount of fluorescence emitted by a hybridization spot on a gene array, the concentration of sodium in the blood, or virtually any of the measurements that we receive as numeric quantities, the output is produced by an algorithm executed by the instrument. Preprocessing of data is commonplace in the universe of Big Data, and data managers should not labor under the false impression that the data received is "raw." Modifications to the data extracted from the resource also occur a posteriori, in the data analyst's laboratory. The data analyst will decide how to deal with missing data values, impossible data values, and outliers (see Glossary items, Missing Data, Outlier). The data analyst will choose from a variety of available techniques to reduce the dimensionality of data (see Glossary item, Dimensionality). The data analyst will be responsible for explaining and documenting his or her modifications to the extracted data.

The data manager is responsible for data verification, not data cleaning. Data verification is the process that ensures that the data was collected, annotated, identified, stored, and made accessible in conformance with a set of approved protocols established for the resource (see Chapter 13). In other words, the data manager does not verify that the data is correct; the data manager verifies that the data was collected correctly.

DATA SUBSETS IN BIG DATA: NEITHER ADDITIVE NOR TRANSITIVE

> If you're told that a room has 3 people inside, and you count 5 people exiting the room, a mathematician would feel compelled to send in 2 people to empty it out. *Anonymous*

Simpson's paradox is a well-known problem for statisticians. The paradox is based on the observation that findings that apply to each of two data sets may be reversed when the two data sets are combined.

One of the most famous examples of Simpson's paradox was demonstrated in the 1973 Berkeley gender bias study.[144] A preliminary review of admissions data indicated that women had a lower admissions rate than men:

Number of men applicants: 8442. Percent applicants admitted: 44%
Number of women applicants: 4321. Percent applicants admitted: 35%

A nearly 10% difference is highly significant, but what does it mean? Was the admissions office guilty of gender bias?

A closer look at admissions, department by department, showed a very different story. Women were being admitted at higher rates than men in almost every department. The department-by-department data seemed incompatible with the combined data.

The explanation was simple. Women tended to apply to the most popular and oversubscribed departments, such as English and History, that had a high rate of admission denials. Men tended to apply to departments that the women of 1973 avoided, such as mathematics, engineering, and physics. Men tended not to apply to the high occupancy departments that women preferred. Though women had an equal footing with men in departmental admissions, the high rate of women rejections in the large, high-rejection departments accounted for an overall lower acceptance rate for women at Berkeley.

Simpson's paradox demonstrates that data is not always additive. It also shows us that data is not transitive; you cannot make inferences based on subset comparisons. For example, in randomized drug trials, you cannot assume that if drug A tests better than drug B, and drug B tests better than drug C, then drug A will test better than drug C.[145] When drugs are tested, even in well-designed trials, the test populations are drawn from a general population specific for the trial. When you compare results from different trials, you can never be sure whether the different sets of subjects are comparable. Each set may contain individuals whose responses to a third drug are unpredictable. Transitive inferences (i.e., if A is better than B, and B is better than C, then A is better than C) are unreliable.

Simpson's paradox has particular significance for Big Data research, wherein data samples are variously recombined and reanalyzed at different stages of the analytic process.

ADDITIONAL BIG DATA PITFALLS

There is a large literature devoted to the pitfalls of data analysis. It would seem that all of the errors associated with small data analysis will apply to Big Data analysis. There are, however, a collection of Big Data errors that do not apply to small data, such as the following.

1. **The misguided belief that Big Data is good data.** Big Data comes from many different sources, produced by many different protocols, and must undergo a series of tricky annotations. A Big Data resource may contain a set of data that is superior in every way to previous collections of comparable data. Nonetheless, data analysts can never assume that the data is accurate. The good analyst validates his or her original analysis with alternate sources of data and alternate analytic methods.
2. **Classification bias.** If you are studying the properties of a class of records (e.g., records of individuals with a specific disease or data collected on a particular species of fish), then any analysis of the data, no matter how large the data set, will be biased if your class assignments are erroneous (e.g., if the disease was misdiagnosed or if you mistakenly included other species of fish in your collection). Classification can be difficult when the classes are poorly defined, not based on a well-understood set of scientific principles, or assembled through an analytic technique that happens to be imperfect. For example, imagine that we have developed a predictive model, based on Big Data analytics, for Alzheimer's disease. If the model preferentially predicts very mild cases of Alzheimer's dementia, thus missing cases of severe dementia, then the overall prognosis of Alzheimer's disease in the general population will improve artifactually because there will be an increase in mild (i.e., improved prognosis) cases in the population. The predictive tool would be credited with improving the prognosis of Alzheimer's diseases, though it contributed nothing to treatment or outcome. Big Data analysts may assume, incorrectly, that their biased classifier has merit.
3. **Complexity bias.** The data in Big Data resources comes from many different sources. Data from one source may not be strictly comparable to data from another source. The steps in data selection, including data filtering and data transformation, will vary among analysts.

Together, these factors create a complex analytic environment for all Big Data studies that does not apply to small data studies.

4. **Statistical method bias.** Statisticians can apply different statistical methods to the data and arrive at any of several different conclusions. Statistical method biases are particularly dangerous for Big Data. The standard statistical tests that apply to small data and to data collected in controlled experiments may not apply to Big Data. Analysts are faced with the unsatisfying option of applying standard methods to nonstandard data or of developing their own methodologies for their Big Data project. History suggests that given a choice, scientists will adhere to the analysis that reinforces their own scientific prejudices.[146]

5. **Ambiguity bias.** Big Data analysts want to believe that complex systems are composed of simple elements, having well-defined attributes and functions. Clever systems analysts can develop algorithms that can predict the behavior of complex systems, when the elements of the system are understood. We learn from biological systems that the elements of complex systems cannot always be described, and the functionality of the elements may change, from one moment to the next.

Consider the very simple case of enzymatic activity. Inside a test tube, we can determine an enzyme's activity. The changing levels of substrate (i.e., a chemical participating in a reaction) and product (i.e., a chemical produced by a reaction), in the presence of the enzyme, can be measured with great precision. We can vary the amount of substrate and product and enzyme in the system and measure the ensuing changes. We can create a system and fully describe the system that we created. When we move from the test tube to the human cell, we may encounter intractable problems. Cells are complex systems in which many different metabolic pathways are operating simultaneously. A metabolic pathway is a multistep chemical process involving more than one enzyme and various additional substrate and nonsubstrate chemicals. Depending on the conditions within a cell, a single enzyme may participate in several different metabolic pathways. For example, alterations in the Lamin-B receptor are responsible for two clinically distinct conditions: Pelger–Huet anomaly and Hydrops-ectopic calcification–"moth-eaten" skeletal dysplasia. The two disparate conditions can be accounted for by the two unrelated physiologic functions of the Lamin-B receptor. It functions to preserve nuclear chromatin structure, and mutations may produce the Pelger–Huet anomaly wherein the structures of certain types of nuclei are abnormal.[147] The Lamin-B receptor also plays a role in cholesterol biosynthesis, resulting in disturbances of bone growth.[148]

Recent studies have shown that inherited behavior is not fully determined by the genetic sequence of DNA. There are many different elements that modify and control genetic expression, and these elements do not have simple functionality.[149] When complex cells are perturbed from their normal, steady-state activities, the rules that define cellular behavior become complex and more difficult to predict.[150] Big Data analysts, working with highly complex systems, cannot assume that the elements of their system have nonambiguous functionality.

Despite all the potential biases, Big Data offers us an opportunity to validate predictions based on small data studies. **As a ready-made source of observations, Big Data resources may provide the fastest, most economical, and easiest method to "reality test" limited experimental studies.** Testing against external data sets, on independently collected data objects, is an excellent way of validating predictors.[151,152]

Stepwise Approach to Big Data Analysis

The purpose of computing is insight, not numbers. **Richard Hamming**

BACKGROUND

At this point, you may feel completely overwhelmed by the complexities of Big Data resources. It may seem that analysis is humanly impossible. The best way to tackle a large and complex project is to divide it into smaller, less intimidating tasks. Of course, every analysis project is unique, and the steps involved in a successful project will vary. Nonetheless, a manageable process, built on techniques introduced in preceding chapters, might be helpful. My hope is that as Big Data resources mature and the methods for creating meaningful, well-annotated, and verified data become commonplace, some of the steps listed in this chapter can be eliminated. Realistically though, it is best to assume that the opposite will occur—more steps will be added.

STEP 1. A QUESTION IS FORMULATED

It takes a certain talent to ask a good question. Sometimes, a question, even a brilliant question, cannot be answered until it is phrased in a manner that clarifies the methods by which the question can be solved. For example, suppose I am interested in how much money is spent, each year, on military defense in the United States. I could probably search the Internet and find the budget for the Department of Defense in the year 2011. The budget for the Department of Defense would not reflect the costs associated with other agencies that have a close relationship with the military, such as intelligence agencies and the State Department. The Department of Defense budget would not reflect the budget of the Veterans Administration (an agency that is separate from the Department of Defense). The budget for the Department of Defense might include various items that have no obvious relationship to military defense. Because I am asking for the "annual" budget, I might need to know how to deal with projects whose costs are annualized over 5, 10, or 15 years. If large commitments were made, in 2005, to pay for long-term projects, with increasing sums of money paid out over the next decade, then the 2011 annual budget may reflect payouts on 2005 commitments. A 2011 budget may not provide a meaningful assessment of costs incurred by 2011 activities. After a little thought, it becomes obvious that the question "How much money is spent, each year, on military defense in the United States?" is complex and probably cannot be answered by any straightforward method.

At this point, it may be best to table the question for a while and to think deeply about what you can reasonably expect from Big Data. Many analysts start with the following general question: "How can this Big Data resource provide the answer to my question?" A more fruitful approach may be "What is the data in this resource trying to tell me?" The two approaches are quite different, and I would suggest that data analysts begin their analyses with the second question.

STEP 2. RESOURCE EVALUATION

Every good Big Data resource provides users with a detailed description of its data contents. This might be done through a table of contents or an index, or through a detailed "readme" file, or a detailed user license. It all depends on the type of resource and its intended purposes. Resources should provide detailed information on their methods for collecting and verifying data, and their protocols supporting outsider queries and data extractions. Big Data resources that do not provide such information generally fall into two categories: (1) highly specialized resources with a small and devoted user base who are thoroughly familiar with every aspect of the resource and who do not require guidance, or (2) bad resources.

Before developing specific queries related to your research interest, data analysts should develop queries designed to evaluate the range of information contained in the resource. For example, the Surveillance, Epidemiology, and End Results (SEER) database contains deidentified records on millions of cancers occurring in the United States since the mid-1970s.[76,153] When you query the database for the types of cancers included, you find that the two most common cancers of humans, basal cell carcinoma and squamous cell carcinoma of skin, are not included in the data. Together, the occurrences of these two cancers are equal to the occurrences of every other type of cancer combined. The SEER program does not collect data on these cancers because there are just too many of them; individuals may develop several such cancers on sun-exposed skin. In addition, these cancers are seldom lethal and are not generally recorded by the cancer registries that feed their data to the SEER database. A data analyst cannot draw conclusions about the totality of cancers when he or she uses a Big Data resource that omits the two most common cancers of humans. In fact, the SEER database excludes a great deal of information that might be of interest to data analysts. For example, the SEER database does not include most precancers (i.e., early stage cancers), thus limiting studies examining the progression rates of precancerous stages to fully invasive cancers.

Big Data resources may contain systemic biases. For example, PubMed contains abstracted data on about 20 million research articles. Research articles are published on positive findings. It is very difficult for a scientist to publish a paper that reports on the absence of an effect or the nonoccurrences of a biological phenomenon. PubMed has a positive result bias. The preferential exclusion or inclusion of specific types of data is very common, and data analysts must try to identify such biases.

Every Big Data resource has its blind spots—areas in which data is missing, scarce, or otherwise unrepresentative of the data domain. Often, the Big Data managers are unaware of such deficiencies. In some cases, Big Data managers blame the data analyst for "inventing" a deficiency that pertains exclusively to unauthorized uses of the resource. When a data analyst wishes to use a Big Data resource for something other than its intended purposes (e.g., using PubMed to predict National Institutes of Health funding priorities over the next decade, using the Netflix query box to determine what kinds of actors appear in zombie movies), then the Big Data manager may be reluctant to respond to the analyst's complaints.

Simply because you have access to large amounts of data does not imply that you have all the data you would need to draw a correct conclusion.

STEP 3. A QUESTION IS REFORMULATED

If you can dream—and not make dreams your master. *from If (poem), by Rudyard Kipling*

Data does not always answer the exact question you started with. After you have assessed the content and design of your Big Data resource(s), you will want to calibrate your question to your available data sources. In the case of our original question, from Step 1, we wanted to know how much money is spent, each year, on military defense in the United States; if we are unable to answer this question, we may be able to answer questions related to the budget sizes of individual government agencies that contribute to military spending. If we knew the approximate portion of each agency budget that is devoted to military spending, we might be able to produce a credible total for the amount devoted to military activities, without actually finding the exact answer.

After exploring the resource, the data analyst learns the kinds of questions that can best be answered with the available data. With this insight, he or she can reformulate the original set of questions.

STEP 4. QUERY OUTPUT ADEQUACY

Big Data resources can often produce an enormous output in response to a data query. When a data analyst receives a large amount of data, particularly if the output is vast, he or she is likely to assume that the query output is complete and valid. A query output is complete when it contains all of the data held in the Big Data resource that answers the query, and a query output is valid if the data in the query output yields a correct and repeatable answer.

A Google query is an example of an instance wherein query output is not seriously examined. When you enter a search term and receive millions of "hits," you may tend to assume that your query output is adequate. When you're looking for a particular Web page or an answer to a specific question, the first output page on your initial Google query may meet your needs. A thoughtful data analyst will want to submit many related queries to see which queries produce the best results. The analyst may want to combine the query outputs from multiple related queries and will almost certainly want to filter the combined outputs to discard response items that are irrelevant. The process of query output examination is often arduous, requiring many aggregation and filtering steps.

After satisfying yourself that you've taken reasonable measures to collect a complete query output, you will still need to determine whether the output you have obtained is fully representative of the data domain you wish to analyze. For example, you may have a large query output file related to the topic of poisonous mushrooms. You've aggregated query outputs on phrases such as "mushroom poisoning," "mushroom poisons," "mushroom poison," "mushroom toxicity," and "fungal toxins." You pared down queries on "food poisoning" to include only mushroom-related entries. Now you want to test the output file to see if it has a comprehensive collection of information related to your topic of interest. You find a nomenclature of mushrooms, and you look for the occurrence of each nomenclature term in your aggregated and filtered output file. You find that there are no occurrences in your output of many of the types of mushrooms listed in the mushroom nomenclature, including mushrooms known to be toxic. In all likelihood, this means that the Big Data resource simply does not contain the level of detail you will need to support a thorough data analysis on topics related to poisonous mushrooms.

There is no standard way of measuring the adequacy of a query output; it depends on the questions you want to answer and the analytic methods you will employ. In some cases, a query output will be inadequate because the Big Data resource simply does not contain the information you need; at least not in the detail you need the information. In other cases, the Big Data resource contains the information you need, but does not provide a useful pathway by which your query can access the data. Queries cannot thoroughly access data that is not fully annotated, assigned to classes, and constructed as identified data objects.

Data analysts must be prepared to uncover major flaws in the organization, annotation, and content of Big Data resources. When a flaw is found, it should be promptly reported to the data manager for the resource. A good data manager will have a policy for accepting error reports, conducting investigations, instituting corrections as necessary, and documenting every step in the process.

STEP 5. DATA DESCRIPTION

Is the output data numeric or is it categorical? If it is numeric, is it quantitative? For example, telephone numbers are numeric, but not quantitative. If the data is numeric and quantitative, then your analytic options are many. If the data is categorical information (e.g., male or female, true or false), then the analytic options are limited. The analysis of categorical data is first and foremost an exercise in counting; comparisons and predictions are based on the number of occurrences of features.

Are all of your data objects comparable? Big Data collects data objects from many different sources, and the different data objects may not be directly comparable. The objects themselves may be annotated with incompatible class hierarchies (e.g., one data object described as a "chicken" may be classed as "Aves," while another "chicken" object may be classed as "food"). One data object described as "child" may have the "age" property divided into 3-year increments up to age 21. Another "child" object may have "age" divided into 4-year increments up to age 16. The data analyst must be prepared to normalize assigned classes, ranges of data, subpopulations of wildly different sizes, different nomenclature codes, and so on.

After the data is normalized and corrected for missing data and false data, you will need to visualize data distributions. Be prepared to divide your data into many different groupings and to plot and replot your data with many different techniques (e.g., histograms, smoothing convolutions, cumulative plots, etc.). Look for general features (e.g., linear curves, nonlinear curves, Gaussian distributions, multimodal curves, convergences, nonconvergences, Zipf-like distributions). Visualizing your data with numerous alternate plotting methods may provide fresh insights and will reduce the likelihood that any one method will bias your objectivity.

STEP 6. DATA REDUCTION

An irony of Big Data analysis is that the data analyst must make every effort to gather all of the data related to a project, followed by an equally arduous phase during which the data analyst must cull the data down to its bare essentials.

There are very few situations wherein all of the data contained in a Big Data resource is subjected to analysis. Aside from the computational impracticalities of analyzing massive amounts of data, most real-life problems are focused on a relatively small set of local observations drawn from a large number of events that are irrelevant to the problem at hand. The process of extracting a small set of relevant data from a Big Data resource is referred to by a variety of names, including data reduction, data filtering, and data selection. The reduced data set that you will use in your project should obey the courtroom oath "the whole truth, and nothing but the truth."

Methods for reducing the dimensionality of data are described in Chapter 9. As a practical point, when the random and redundant variables have been expunged, the remaining data set may still be too large for a frontal computational attack. A good data analyst knows when to retreat and regroup. If something cannot be calculated to great precision on a large number of variables and data points, then it should be calculated with somewhat less precision with somewhat fewer variables and fewer data points. Why not try the small job first and see what it tells you?

STEP 7. ALGORITHMS ARE SELECTED, IF ABSOLUTELY NECESSARY

Algorithms are perfect machines. They work to produce consistent solutions; they never make mistakes; they need no fuel; they never wear down; they are spiritual, not physical. Every computer scientist loves algorithms.

If you peruse the titles of books in the Big Data field, you will find that most of these books are focused on data analysis. They focus on parallel processing, cloud computing (see Glossary item, Cloud computing), high-power predictive analytics, combinatorics methods, and the like. It is very easy to believe that the essential feature of Big Data that separates it from small data relates to algorithms. My experience is that we have a great many brilliant algorithms that will serve most of our Big Data analytic needs. The typical Big Data analyst will spend most of his or her career trying to collect and organize data. Algorithms are a small piece of the puzzle.

As algorithms become more and more clever, they become more and more enigmatic. Fewer and fewer people truly understand how they work. Some of the most popular statistical methods defy simple explanation, including p values and linear regression[104,154] (see Glossary items, Linear regression, p value). When a scientist submits an article to a journal, he or she can expect the journal editor to insist that a statistician be included as a coauthor. It is so easy to use the wrong statistical method that editors and reviewers do not trust nonstatisticians to conduct their own analyses. The field of Big Data comes with a dazzling assortment of analytic options. Who will judge that the correct method is chosen, that the method is implemented properly, and that the results are interpreted correctly?

If an analyst does not require advanced algorithms, avoidance may be a reasonable recourse. Analysts should consider the following options.

1. **Stick with simple estimates.** If you have taken to heart the suggestion in Chapter 8, to estimate your answers early in project development, then you have already found simple estimators for your data. Consider this option: keep the estimators and forget about advanced algorithms. For many projects, estimators can be easily understood by project staff and will provide a practical alternative to exact solutions that are difficult to calculate and impossible to comprehend.

2. **Pick better metrics, not better algorithms.** Sabermetrics is a sterling example of analysis using simple metrics that are chosen to correlate well with a specific outcome—a winning ballgame. In the past several decades, baseball analysts have developed a wide variety of new performance measurements for baseball players. These include base runs, batting average on balls in play, defense-independent pitching statistics, defense-independent earned run average, fielding independent pitching, total player rating, batter–fielder wins, total pitcher index, and ultimate zone rating. Most of these metrics were developed empirically, tested in the

field, literally, and optimized as needed. They are all simple linear metrics that use combinations of weighted measures on data collected during ballgames. Though sabermetrics has its detractors, everyone would agree that it represents a fascinating and largely successful effort to bring objective numeric techniques to the field of baseball. Nothing in sabermetrics involves advanced algorithms. It is all based on using a deep understanding of the game of baseball to develop a set of simple metrics that can be easily calculated and validated.

3. **Micromanage your macrodata.** Much of the success of Big Data is attained by making incremental, frequent changes to your system in response to your metrics. An example of successful micromanagement for Big Data is the municipal CompStat model, used by police departments and other government agencies.[155,156] A promising metric is chosen, such as emergency 911 call response time, and a team closely monitors the data on a frequent basis, sometimes several times a day. Slow 911 response times are investigated, and the results of these investigations typically generate action items intended to correct systemic errors. When implemented successfully, the metric improves (e.g., the 911 response time is shortened) and a wide range of systemic problems are solved. Micromanaging a single metric can improve the overall performance of a department.

Departments with imagination can choose very clever metrics upon which to build an improvement model (e.g., time from license application to license issuance, number of full garbage cans sitting on curbs, length of toll booth lines, numbers of broken street lights, etc.). It is useful to choose the best metrics, but the choice of the metric is not as important as the ability to effectively monitor and improve the metric.

As a personal aside, I have used this technique in the medical setting and found it immensely effective. During a period of about 5 years at the Baltimore VA Medical center, I had access to all the data generated in our pathology department. Using a variety of metrics, such as case turn-around time, cases requiring notification of clinician, cases positive for malignancy, and diagnostic errors, our pathologists were able to improve the measured outcomes. More importantly, the process of closely monitoring for deficiencies, quickly addressing the problem, and reporting on the outcome of each correction produced a staff that was sensitized to the performance of the department. There was an overall performance improvement.

Like anything in the Big Data realm, the data micromanagement approach may not work for everyone, but it serves to show that great things may come when you carefully monitor your Big Data resource.

4. **Let someone else find an algorithm for you; crowd source your project.** There is a lot of analytic talent in this world. Broadcasting your project via the Web may attract the attention of individuals or teams of researchers who have already solved a problem isomorphic to your own or who can rapidly apply their expertise to your specific problem.[157]

5. **Offer a reward.** Funding entities have recently discovered that they can solicit algorithmic solutions, offering cash awards as an incentive. For example, the InnoCentive organization issues challenges regularly, and various sponsors pay awards for successful implementations[112](see Glossary item, Predictive modeling contests).

6. **Develop your own algorithm that you fully understand.** You should know your data better than anyone else. With a little self-confidence and imagination, you can develop an analytic algorithm tailored to your needs.

STEP 8. RESULTS ARE REVIEWED AND CONCLUSIONS ARE ASSERTED

When the weather forecaster discusses the projected path of a hurricane, he or she will typically show the different paths projected by different models. The forecaster might draw a cone-shaped swath bounded by the paths predicted by the several different forecasting models. A central line in the cone might represent the composite path produced by averaging the forecasts from the different models. The point here is that Big Data analyses never produce a single, undisputed answer. There are many ways of analyzing Big Data, and they all produce different solutions.

A good data analyst should interpret results conservatively. Here are a few habits that will keep you honest and will reduce the chances that your results will be discredited.

1. **Never assert that your analysis is definitive.** If you have analyzed the Big Data with several models, include your results for each model. It is perfectly reasonable to express your preference for one model over another. It is not acceptable to selectively withhold results that could undermine your theory.
2. **Avoid indicating that your analysis provides a causal explanation of a physical process.** In most cases, Big Data conclusions are descriptive and cannot establish physical causality. This situation may improve as we develop better methods to make reasonable assertions for causality based on analyses of large, retrospective data sets.[158,159] In the meantime, the primary purpose of Big Data analysis is to provide a hypothesis that can be subsequently tested, usually through experimentation, and validated.
3. **Disclose your biases.** It can be hard to resist choosing an analytic model that supports your preexisting opinion. When your results advance your own agenda, it is important to explain that you have a personal stake in the outcome or hypothesis. It is wise to indicate that the data can be interpreted by other methods and that you would be willing to cooperate with colleagues who might prefer to conduct an independent analysis of your data. When you offer your data for reanalysis, be sure to include all of your data: the raw data, the processed data, and step-by-step protocols for filtering, transforming, and analyzing the data.
4. **Do not try to dazzle the public with the large number of records in your Big Data project.** Large studies are not necessarily good studies, and the honest data analyst will present the facts and the analysis without using the number of data records as a substitute for analytic rigor.

STEP 9. CONCLUSIONS ARE EXAMINED AND SUBJECTED TO VALIDATION

Sometimes you gotta lose "til you win." *from* Little Miss *(song) by Sugarland*

Validation involves demonstrating that the assertions that come from data analyses are reliable. You validate an assertion (which may appear in the form of a hypothesis, a statement about the value of a new laboratory test, or a therapeutic protocol) by showing that you draw the same conclusion repeatedly in comparable data sets.

Real science can be validated, if true, and invalidated, if false. Pseudoscience is a pejorative term that applies to scientific conclusions that are consistent with some observations, but which cannot be confirmed or tested with additional data. For example, there is a large body of information that would suggest that the earth has been visited by flying saucers. The evidence comes in the form of eyewitness accounts, numerous photographs, and vociferous official denials of these events suggesting some form of cover-up. Without commenting on the validity of UFO claims, it is fair to say that these assertions fall into the realm of pseudoscience because they are untestable (i.e., there is no way to prove that flying saucers do not exist) and there is no definitive data to prove their existence (i.e., the "little green men" have not been forthcoming).

Big Data analysis always stands on the brink of becoming a pseudoscience. Our finest Big Data analyses are only valid to the extent that they have not been disproven. A good example of a tentative and clever conclusion drawn from data is the Titius–Bode law. Titius and Bode developed a simple formula that predicted the locations of planets orbiting a star. It was based on data collected on all of the planets known to Johann Daniel Titius and Johann Elert Bode, two 18th-century scientists. These planets included Mercury through Saturn. In 1781, Uranus was discovered. Its position fit almost perfectly into the Titius–Bode series, thus vindicating the predictive power of their formula. The law predicted a fifth planet, between Mars and Jupiter. Though no fifth planet was found, astronomers found a very large solar-orbiting asteroid, Ceres, at the location predicted by Titius and Bode. By this time, the Titius–Bode law was beyond rational disputation. Then came the discoveries of Neptune and Pluto, neither of which remotely obeyed the law. The data had finally caught up to the assertion. The Titius–Bode law was purely descriptive—not based on any universal physical principles. It served well for the limited set of data to which it was fitted. Today, few scientists remember the discredited Titius-Bode law.

Let us look at a few counterexamples. Natural selection is an interesting theory, published by Charles Darwin in 1859. It was just one among many interesting theories aimed at explaining evolution and the origin of species. The Lamarckian theory of evolution preceded Darwin's natural selection by nearly 60 years. The key difference between Darwin's theory and Lamarck's theory comes down to validation. Darwin's theory has withstood every test posed by scientists in the fields of geology, paleontology, bacteriology, mycology, zoology, botany, medicine, and genetics. Predictions based on Darwinian evolution dovetail perfectly with observations from diverse fields. The Lamarckian theory of evolution, proposed well before DNA was established as the genetic template for living organisms, held that animals passed experiences to succeeding generations through germ cells, thus strengthening intergenerational reliance on successful behaviors of the parent. This theory was groundbreaking in its day, but subsequent findings failed to validate the theory. Neither Darwin's theory nor Lamarck's theory could be accepted on its own merits. Darwin's theory is correct, as far as we can know, because it was validated by scientific progress that occurred over the ensuing 150 years. The validation process was not rewarding for Lamarck.

The value of big data is not so much to make predictions, but to test predictions on a vast number of data objects. Scientists should not be afraid to create and test their prediction models in a Big Data environment. Sometimes a prediction is invalidated, but an important conclusion can be drawn from the data anyway. Failed predictions often lead to new, more successful predictions.

12

Failure

Program testing can be a very effective way to show the presence of bugs, but is hopelessly inadequate for showing their absence. **Edsger Dijkstra**

BACKGROUND

There are many ways in which a complex system can be broken. In 2000, a Concorde crashed on takeoff from Charles de Gaulle Airport, Paris. The Concorde was a supersonic transport jet, one of the most advanced and complex planes ever built. Some debris left on the runway had flipped up and torn a tire and some of the underside of the hull. All passengers were killed.

Big Data resources are complex; they are difficult to build and easy to break. After they break, they cannot be easily fixed.

Most Big Data failures do not result from accidents. Most failures occur when a Big Data resource is never completed or never attains an acceptable level of performance. What goes wrong? Let us run down the reasons for failure that have been published in blogs, magazine articles, and books on the subject of Big Data disappointments: inappropriate selection and use of human resources (wrong leadership, wrong team, wrong people, wrong direction, wrong milestones, wrong deadlines), incorrect funding (too little funding, too much funding, incorrect allocation of resources, wrong pay scales, wrong incentives), legal snags (patent infringements, copyright infringements, inept technology transfer, wrong legal staff, inadequate confidentiality and privacy measures, untenable consent forms, poor contracts with unhelpful noncompete clauses, noncompliance with applicable laws and regulations, inadequate financial records and poor documentation of protocol compliances), bad data (inaccurate and imprecise data, data obtained without regard to established protocols, data that is not fully specified, unrepresentative data, data that is not germane to the purpose of the resource), and poor data security (purposely corrupted data, data stolen by malevolent entities, data inadvertently copied and distributed by staff, noncompliance with internal security policies, poor internal security policies). The list goes on. Generally, we see failure in terms of our own weaknesses: funders see failure as the result of improper funding, managers see failure as the result of poor management, programmers see deficiencies in programming methods, informaticians see deficiencies in metadata annotations, and so on. The field of Big Data is young; the most senior members of a Big Data team are little more than newbies, and there's plenty of room for self-doubt.

It may be useful to accept every imaginable defect in a Big Data project as a potential cause of failure. For convenience sake, these defects can be divided into two general categories: (1) failures due to design and operation flaws in Big Data resources and (2) failures due to improper analysis and interpretation of results. Analytic and interpretive errors were discussed in Chapter 10. This chapter deals with the problems that arise when Big Data resources are poorly planned and operated.

FAILURE IS COMMON

> The most likely way for the world to be destroyed, most experts agree, is by accident. That's where we come in; we're computer professionals. We cause accidents. *Nathaniel Borenstein*

Big Data resources are new arrivals to the information world. With rare exceptions, database managers are not trained to deal with the layers of complexity found in Big Data resources. It is hard to assemble a team with the composite skills necessary to build a really good Big Data resource. At this time, many data managers are reflexively acquiring new software applications designed to deal with Big Data collections. Far fewer data managers are coming to grips with the fundamental concepts discussed in earlier chapters (e.g., identifier systems, introspection, metadata annotation, immutability, and data triples). It may take several decades before these fundamental principles sink in and Big Data resources reach their highest potential.

In the field of hospital informatics, costs run very high. It is not unusual for large, academic medical centers to purchase information systems that cost in excess of $500 million. Bad systems are costly and failures are frequent.[160-162] About three-quarters of hospital information systems are failures.[163] Successfully implemented electronic health record systems have not been shown to improve patient outcomes.[164] Based on a study of the kinds of failures that account for patient safety errors in hospitals, it has been suggested that hospital information systems will not greatly reduce safety-related incidents.[72] Clinical decision support systems, built into electronic health record systems, have not had much impact on physician practice.[165] These systems tend to be too complex for a hospital staff to master and are not well utilized.

The United Kingdom's National Health Service embarked on a major overhaul of its information systems, with the goal of system-wide interoperability and data integration. After investing $17 billion dollars, the project was ditched when members of Parliament called the effort "unworkable."[166–168]

Failures are not always irreversible. The 1992 crash of the London ambulance dispatch system was a setback to advanced computer control systems. A new system had been deployed on October 16, 1992. Almost immediately, emergency calls went unacknowledged or were lost. Completed jobs were uncleared, resulting in ambulances that were unengaged yet unavailable. Dozens of deaths resulted from a sudden cessation of services. The following day, the new system was terminated. Four years later, after many investigative studies, a new system was implemented; this one worked.[169]

It is difficult to determine the failure rate of Big Data projects. Organizations herald their triumphs but hide their misadventures. There is no registry of Big Data projects that can be followed to determine which projects fail over time. There is no formal designation "Big Data project" that is bestowed on some projects and withheld from others. Furthermore, we have no definition for failure, as applied to Big Data. Would we require a project to be officially disbanded, with all funds withdrawn, before we say that it is defunct? Or would we say that a Big Data project has failed if it did not meet its original set of goals? If a Big Data resource is built, and operates as planned, can we say that it has failed if nobody actually uses the resource? With these caveats in mind, it is believed that the majority of information technology projects fail, and that failure is positively correlated with the size and cost of the projects.[170] It is claimed that public projects costing hundreds of billions of dollars have failed quietly, without raising much attention.[171] Big Data projects are characterized by large size, high complexity, and novel technology, all of which aggravate any deficiencies in management, personnel, or process practices.[170]

FAILED STANDARDS

Don't be afraid of missing opportunities. Behind every failure is an opportunity somebody wishes they had missed. *Lily Tomlin*

Most standards fail. Examples are easy to find. Open Systems Interconnection was a seven-layer protocol intended as the Internet standard. It was backed by the U.S. government and approved by the International Organization for Standardization (ISO) and the International Electrotechnical Commission. It has been supplanted by the Transmission Control Protocol/Internet Protocol, preferred by Unix. Simply because a standard has been developed by experts, backed by the U.S. government, and approved by an international standards organization, there is no guarantee that it will be accepted by its intended users.

Even the best standards seldom meet their expectations. Consider the metric system. It is used throughout the world, and it is generally acknowledged as a vast improvement over every preceding measurement standard. Nonetheless, in the United States, our height is measured in feet and inches, not meters and centimeters, and our weight is measured in pounds, not kilograms. Here in the United States, it would be difficult to find a bathroom scale marked with metric graduations. The next time you look at your calendar, remember that about half the world uses a solar calendar. Most of the other half uses a lunar calendar. Some base their calendars on a combination of solar and lunar observations. We may all agree that the world spins on its axis, but every assertion that follows is controversial and nonstandardized.

In the realm of format standards (e.g., for documents, images, sound, movies), there are hundreds of standards. Some of these standards were developed for specific devices (e.g., cameras, image grabbers, word processors) and served a specific purpose in a small window of time. Today, most of these standard formats are seldom used. A few dozen remain popular. New mathematical methods for describing large binary data objects are sure to bring new image standards (see Glossary item, BLOB).

Every new programming language is born with the hope that it will be popular and immortal. In the past half-century, well over 2000 programming languages have been devised. Most of these languages are seldom used and often forgotten. In 1995, Ada 95 became an American National Standards Institute/ISO standard programming language, a distinction held by only a few programming languages. The U.S. National Institute of Standards announced that Ada would be used by federal departments and agencies in software applications that involve control of real-time or parallel processes, very large systems, and systems with requirements for very high reliability.[172] The official announcement was entitled "Announcing the Standard for ADA." The programming language, Ada, was named for Ada Lovelace (1815–1852), who wrote the first computer program (an algorithm for computing Bernoulli numbers) for Charles Babbage's prototype computer (the so-called analytic engine). Every Ada programmer knows that Ada is not an acronym; they bristle whenever Ada is spelled with all uppercase letters. The official announcement of "ADA" as a U.S. government standard may have foreshadowed the disasters that followed.

On June 4, 1996, the maiden flight of the French Ariane 5 exploded 37 seconds after launch. A software exception occurred during a data conversion from a 64-bit floating point to 16-bit signed integer value. The data conversion instructions (in Ada code) were not protected from causing an Operand Error.[173]

On September 23, 1999, the United States launched the Mars Climate Orbiter, which crashed on impact on the red planet. An official investigation by the Mars Climate Orbiter Mishap Investigation Board concluded that the crash occurred due to a software glitch that arose when English units of measurement were used in the software when metric units were supplied as input.[174] The flight software was coded in Ada.

Ada is a fine programming language, but declaring it a government standard could not guarantee error-free implementations, nor could it guarantee its popularity among programmers. Following its ascension to standards status, the popularity of Ada declined rapidly. Today, I know only one person who programs in Ada.

The most successful standards are specifications that achieved popularity before they achieved the status of "standard." The best of these filled a need, enjoyed broad use, had few or no barriers to implementation (e.g., free and easy to use), and had the bugs ironed out (i.e., did not require excessive modifications and version updates). The most unsuccessful standards are those prepared by a committee of special interests who create the standard ab initio (i.e., without a preexisting framework), without a user community, and without a proven need. The altogether worst standards seem to be those that only serve the interests of the standards committee members.

Robert Sowa has written a useful essay entitled "The Law of Standards."[175] His hypothesis is, "Whenever a major organization develops a new system as an official standard for X, the primary result is the widespread adoption of some simpler system as a de facto standard for X." He gives many examples. The PL/I standard, developed by IBM, was soon replaced by Fortran and COBOL. The Algol 68 standard was replaced by Pascal. Ada, promoted by the U.S. Department of Defense, was replaced by C. The OS/2 operating system produced by IBM was replaced by Windows.

For small data projects and for software applications, the instability of data standards is not a major problem. Small data projects are finite in length and will seldom extend beyond the life span of the standards implemented within the project. For software designers, a standard implemented within an application can be replaced in the next upgrade. Any costs are passed onto the licensed user. Instability in standards serves the interests of software developers by coercing customers to purchase upgrades that comply with the new versions of included standards.

For Big Data resources, instability in standards is always bad news. A failed standard may invalidate the data model for the resource—undoing years of work. How can the data manager cope with failed standards? Over 20 years ago, I was approached by a pathologist who was tasked with annotating his diagnostic reports with a standard vocabulary of diseases. The principal options at the time were International Classification of Diseases (ICD), Systematized Nomenclature of Medicine (SNOMED), and Medical Subject Headings (MeSH) produced by the National Library of Medicine. The ICD seemed too granular (i.e., not enough names of diseases). SNOMED was constantly changing; newer versions were incompatible with older versions and he worried that annotations under an old version of SNOMED could not be integrated into the newer hospital information systems. MeSH was a well-curated public nomenclature, analogous to the Dewey Decimal System for the health informatics community, but it was not widely adopted by the pathology community.

I suggested all of his options were untenable. His best bet, under the circumstances, was to write his reports in simple, declarative sentences, using canonical diagnostic terms (i.e., terms expressed in a form suitable for a nomenclature). Simplified sentences could be easily parsed into constituent parts and accurately translated or mapped to any chosen vocabulary, as needed.[176]

Consider the following sentence: "The patient has an scc, and we see invasion to the subcutaneous tissue, all the way to the deep margins, but the lateral margins are clear." This sentence, which is understandable to a clinician or a fellow pathologist, would not be understandable to a computer program. Among other impediments, a computer would not know that the abbreviation "scc" corresponds to the diagnostic term "squamous cell carcinoma." A computer that has an index list matching abbreviations to terms may falsely map the abbreviation to the wrong expansion term (e.g., small cell carcinoma rather than squamous cell carcinoma).

The complex sentence could be rewritten as six declarative statements:

Diagnosis: squamous cell carcinoma.
Invasion is present.
Invasion extends to subcutaneous tissue.
Margin is involved.
Tumor extends to deep margin.
Tumor does not extend to lateral margins.

It would be relatively easy to write a computer program that could autocode these very simple sentences. Every surgical pathology case entered in the hospital information system could be coded again and again, using any new version of any nomenclature.

We could go one step further, expressing every statement as a triple consisting of an identifier, a metadata term, and a data value. In a Big Data resource, an extremely simple data model might retain compatibility with any new data standard. If all of the data in the resource is available as simple triples, and if the model provides a method whereby data objects can be assigned to classes, then every data object can be fully specified. Specified data objects, expressed as a simple triples, can be ported into any old or new data standard, as needed.

For example, consider the following triples:

    2847302084 weight "25 pounds"
    2847302084 instance_of 8909851274
    8909851274 class_name "dog"
    8909851274 subclass_of 7590293847
    7590293847 class_name "canine"

This tells us that the data object identified as 2847302084 weighs 25 pounds and is an instance of class 8909851274 of dogs. The dog class is a subclass of 7590293847, the class of canines. We can use triples to express any information we might ever collect, and we can relate every triple to other classes of triples, to produce a data model. The triples we collect can be converted into more complex ontology languages (such as RDF, OWL, or DAML/OIL) because all of our data objects are well specified. Furthermore, our data can be ported into new standards created for specific types of data included in our resource. For example, if we needed to create a document for a veterinary department, in a standard format, we could collect our triples containing data on dogs, and we could produce a report, in a standard format, that lists everything we know about each dog.

It is best to keep in mind two general principles of data management.

1. **Data objects can be well specified, without a standard.** You do not need to store your data in a format that is prescribed by a standard.
2. **Data standards are fungible.** If you know the rules for standards, you can write a program that converts to the standard, as needed.

In many instances, a simple, generic data model may free the Big Data manager from the problems that ensue when a data standard becomes obsolete.

COMPLEXITY

Complexity is the worst enemy of security. *Bruce Schneier*[177]

Big Data is complex, and complexity is dangerous. It is easy to write software that attains a level of complexity that exceeds anything encountered in the physical realm. Likewise, there is no limit to the complexity of operational methods, security standards, data models, and virtually every component of a Big Data resource. When a Big Data resource somehow manages to cope with complexity, it can be just a matter of time before key personnel leave, errors are introduced into the system, and a once-great resource grinds to a halt.

When errors occur in complex systems, they can be very difficult to detect. A case in point is the Toyota Lexus ES 350 sedan. Thousands of vehicle owners experienced unintended vehicle acceleration; the complex electronic control system was the chief suspect.[178] Beginning about 2002 and extending to the present, Toyota has devoted enormous resources trying to understand and solve the problem.[179] A host of agencies and authorities were involved in the investigation; first came the Department of Transportation and the National Highway Traffic Safety Administration. Then, owing to its expertise in software integrity, computer control systems, and electromagnetic interference, the National Aeronautics and Space Administration was called into the fray. Later, the National Academy of Sciences launched its own study of unintended acceleration in the auto industry. During these investigations, Toyota paid about $50 million in fines and recalled about nine million cars. The dust may never settle completely on this problem, but it now appears that most, if not all, problems were due to sticky pedals, driver error, or improperly placed floor mats; no errors were uncovered in the complex electronic control system.

The most vexing problems in software engineering involve "sometimes" errors; software that runs perfectly under most circumstances, but fails at apparently random intervals. Finding the source of the problem is virtually impossible because the most thorough evaluations will indicate that everything is working well. Sometimes the mistake occurs because of the chaotic and unpredictable quality of complex systems. Sometimes mistakes occur because the numbers get too big or too small (division by zero); sometimes the order by which events occur are unexpected, causing the system to behave oddly. In all these situations, finding the problem is very difficult and may have been avoided if the system had been less complex.

Concerning complex systems, this much can be said with certainty: there are many ways to break a complex system, and after a complex system is broken, it can be very difficult to determine the precise cause of the problem. Knowing this, you might expect that data managers try their best to reduce the complexity of their resources. Actually, no. For most resources, increasing complexity is the normal state because it is easier to solve problems with more complexity than with more simplicity.

Every Big Data project should be designed for simplicity. The design team should constantly ask, "Can we achieve this functionality with less complexity?" When the complexity cannot be reduced for a desired level of functionality, a trade-off might be reached. The team is justified in asking, "Do we need this level of functionality? Might we achieve a reduced but adequate level of functionality with a less complex system?" After the design phase, every addition and every modification to the system should be examined for complexity. If complexity needs to be added to the system, then the team must analyze the consequences of the increased complexity.

WHEN DOES COMPLEXITY HELP?

As a rule, software systems do not work well until they have been used, and have failed repeatedly, in real applications. *Dave Parnas*

There are times when complexity is necessary. Think of the human mind and the human body. Our achievements as individuals and as a species come as the result of our complexity.

This complexity was achieved over 4 billion years of evolution, during which time disadvantageous traits were lost and advantageous traits were retained. The entire process was done incrementally. The complexity of a Big Data resource is created in a moment. We do not have 4 billion years to debug the system. When can complexity be permitted in a Big Data resource? There are several scenarios.

1. **When approximate or locally accurate solutions are not acceptable.** In the case of weather forecasting, the purpose is to attain predictions of ever-increasing accuracy. Each new forecasting model contains more and more parameters than the prior model, requires more computing power, and is expected to provide accurate forecasts that extend further and further into the future. Complex models that do not yield greater accuracy than simpler models are abandoned. The whole process mimics evolution.

2. **When complexity is achieved incrementally.** Many of the most important devices implemented in society are complex (televisions, computers, smartphones, jet airplanes, magnetic resonance imagers). They all started as simpler devices, with complexity added incrementally. These complex devices did not require 4 billion years to evolve, but they did require the intense participation of many different individuals, teams, corporations, and users to attain their current utility.

The venerable U-2 U.S. spy plane is an example of incrementally achieved complexity. The U-2 was born in the 1950s and designed as a cold war spy plane. Despite its advanced age, the U-2 has stubbornly resisted obsolescence by incrementally increasing its complexity and utility. Today, it is still in service, with a functionality far greater than anything imaginable when it was created.[180] The value of incremental complexity has been emulated in some modern Big Data technologies.[181]

3. **When your model really needs to match, item by item, the complexity of the real system that it is modeling.** Biologists have learned in the past decade that cellular processes are much more complex than they had originally imagined. Genes are controlled by interactions with other genes, with RNA, with proteins, and with chemical modifications to DNA. Complex chemical interactions that occur in the cell's nucleus and the cytoplasm have made it impossible to find simple genetic variants that account for many biologic processes. The entire field of gene research has shifted to accommodate previously unanticipated complexities that have thwarted our earlier analyses.[149] Our progress in disease biology, developmental biology, and aging seems to hinge on our willingness to accept that life is complex and cannot be reduced to a sequence of nucleotides in a strand of DNA.

Albert Einstein wrote, "Everything should be made as simple as possible, but not simpler." There are occasions when we cannot "wish away" complexity. The best we can do is to prepare a model that does not amplify the irreducible complexity that exists in reality.

WHEN REDUNDANCY FAILS

At first blush, it would be hard to argue that redundancy, in the context of information systems, is a bad thing. With redundancy, when one server fails, another takes up the slack;

if a software system crashes, its duplicate takes over; and when one file is lost, it is replaced by its backup copy. It all seems good.

The problem with redundancy is that it makes the system much more complex. Operators of a Big Data resource with built-in redundancies must maintain the operability of the redundant systems in addition to the primary systems. More importantly, the introduction of redundancies introduces a new set of interdependencies (i.e., how the parts of the system interact), and the consequences of interdependencies may be difficult to anticipate.

In recent memory, the most dramatic example of a failed redundant system involved the Japanese nuclear power plant at Fukushima. The plant was designed with redundant systems. If the power failed, a secondary power generator would kick in. On March 11, 2011, a powerful earthquake off the shore of Japan produced a tidal wave that cut the nuclear reactor's access to the electric power grid. The backup generators were flooded by the same tidal wave. The nuclear facilities were cut off from emergency assistance; also due to the tidal wave. Subsequent meltdowns and radiation leaks produced the worst nuclear disaster since Chernobyl.

As discussed previously in this chapter, on June 4, 1996, the first flight of the Ariane 5 rocket self-destructed, 37 seconds after launch. There was a bug in the software, but the Ariane had been fitted with a backup computer. The backup was no help; the same bug that crippled the primary computer put the backup computer out of business.[182] The lesson here, and from the Fukushima nuclear disaster, is that redundant systems are often ineffective if they are susceptible to the same destructive events that caused failure in the primary systems.

Computer software and hardware problems may occur due to unanticipated interactions among software and hardware components. Redundancy, by contributing to system complexity and by providing an additional opportunity for components to interact in an unpredictable manner, may actually increase the likelihood of a system-wide crash. Cases have been documented wherein system-wide software problems arose due to bugs in the systems that controlled the redundant subsystems.[182]

A common security measure involves backing up files and storing the backup files off-site. If there is a fire, flood, or natural catastrophe at a site or if the site is sabotaged, then the backup files can be withdrawn from the external site and eventually restored. The drawback of this approach is that the backup files create a security risk. In Portland, Oregon, in 2006, 365,000 medical records were stolen from a health service provider organization.[183] The thief was an employee who was simply given the backup files and instructed to store them in his home as a security measure. In this case, the theft of identified medical records was a command performance. The thief complied with the victim's request to be robbed as a condition of his employment. At the very least, the employer should have encrypted the backup files before handing them over to an employee.

Nature takes a middle-of-the-road approach on redundancy. Humans evolved to have two eyes, two arms, two legs, two kidneys, and so on. Not every organ comes in duplicate. We have one heart, one brain, one liver, and one spleen. There are no organs that come in triplicate. Human redundancy is subject to some of the same vulnerabilities as computer redundancy. A systemic poison that causes toxicity in one organ will always cause equivalent toxicity in its contralateral twin.

SAVE MONEY; DON'T PROTECT HARMLESS INFORMATION

Big Data managers tend to be overprotective of the data held in their resources, a professional habit that can work in their favor. In many cases, though, when data is of a purely academic nature, contains no private information, and is generally accessible from alternate sources, there really is no reason to erect elaborate security barriers.

I was involved in one project where the data holders could not be deterred from instituting a security policy wherein data access would be restricted to preapproved users. Anyone wishing to query the database would first submit an application, which would include detailed information about themselves and their employer. Supplying this information was a warm-up exercise for the next step. The application required users to explain how they intended to use the resource, providing a description of their data project.

The submitted application would be reviewed by a committee composed primarily of members of the Big Data team. A statistician would be consulted to determine if the applicant's plan was feasible.

The data team could not seem to restrain their enthusiasm for adding layers of complexity to the security system. They decided that access to data would be tiered. Some users would be given less access to data than other users. No users would be given free access to the entire set of data. No user would have access to individual deidentified records—only aggregate views of record data. A system would be designed to identify users and to restrict data access based on the user's assigned access status.

These security measures were unnecessary. The data in the system had been rendered harmless via deidentification and could be distributed without posing any risk to the data subjects or to the data providers. The team seemed oblivious to the complexities carried by a tiered access system. Bruce Schneier, a widely cited security expert, wrote an essay entitled "A Plea for Simplicity: You Can't Secure What You Don't Understand."[177] In this essay, he explained that as you add complexity to a system, the system becomes increasingly difficult to secure. I doubted that the team had the resources or the expertise to implement a complex, multitiered access system for a Big Data resource. I suspected that if the multitiered access system were actually put into place, the complexity of the system would render the resource particularly vulnerable to attack. In addition, the difficulty of access to the system would discourage potential users.

Security planning always depends on the perception of the value of the data held in the resource (e.g., Is the data worth money?) and the risks that the data might be used to harm individuals (e.g., through identity theft). In many cases, the data held in Big Data resources has no intrinsic monetary value and poses no risks to individuals. The value of most Big Data resource is closely tied to its popularity. A resource used by millions of people provides opportunities for advertising and attracts funders and investors.

Regarding the release of potentially harmful data, it seems prudent to assess from the outset whether there is a simple method by which the data can be rendered harmless. In many cases, deidentification can be achieved through a combination of data scrubbing and expunging data fields that might conceivably tie a record to an individual. If your data set contains no unique records (i.e., if every record in the system can be matched with another record, from another individual, for which every data field is identical), then it is impossible to link any given record to an individual. In many cases, it is a simple matter to create an enormous data set wherein every record is matched by many other records that contain the same informational fields. This process is sometimes referred to as record ambiguation.[184]

Sometimes a Big Data team is compelled to yield to the demands of their data contributors, even when those demands are unreasonable. An individual who contributes data to a resource may insist upon assurances that a portion of any profit resulting from the use of their contributed data will be returned as royalties, shares in the company, or some other form of remuneration. In this case, the onus of security shifts from protecting the data to protecting the financial interests of the data providers. When every piece of data is a source of profit, measures must be put into place to track how each piece of data is used and by whom. Such measures are often impractical and have great nuisance value for data managers and data users. The custom of capitalizing on every conceivable opportunity for profit is a cultural phenomenon, not a scientific imperative. Perhaps our future Big Data resources will be less profit driven.

AFTER FAILURE

In 2001, funds were appropriated to develop the National Biological Information Infrastructure. This Big Data project was a broad cooperative effort intended to produce a federated system containing biological data from many different sources, including federal and state government agencies, universities, natural history museums, private organizations, and others. The data would be made available for studies in the field of resource management. On January 15, 2012, the resource was officially terminated due to budget cuts. A Web site announcement sits vigil, like a tombstone, marking the passage of an ambitious and noble life (see Figure 12.1).

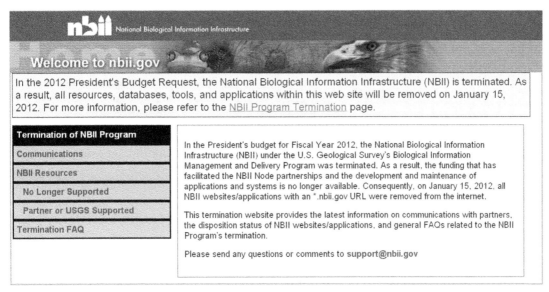

FIGURE 12.1   A U.S. government Web site announcing the demise of the National Biological Information Infrastructure project in 2012.

Like the humans who create the resources, Big Data lives for a time and then it dies. Humans often carry life insurance or savings to pay the costs of burial and to manage the distribution of an estate. In most cases, no preparations are made for the death of Big Data. One day it is there, and the next day it is gone.

Abandonware is a term that is most often applied to software developed under a grant. When the grant funding ceases, the software is almost always abandoned. Nobody assumes the responsibility of tying up loose ends, finding and removing bugs, distributing the software, or using the software in new projects. This is the typical case for software developed for a Big Data resource. The original programmers scramble to find new jobs; nobody remains who can understand their code.

The data in the failed resource either slips into the bit void or becomes legacy data, stored on disks, shelved, and forgotten. Legacy data can be resurrected, but it seldom happens.

The identifier system and the data model for the resource are almost always lost to posterity. All those charts and all those registration numbers simply disappear.

Here are two precautions that can salvage some of the pieces of a failed Big Data project.

1. **Write good utilities.** Software applications can be envisioned as utilities with a graphic user interface. One software application may have the functionality of three or four utilities (e.g., spreadsheet plus graph plotter plus statistics suite, with the graphic user interface of a word processor). When a Big Data resource is built, it will usually be accessed under an umbrella application. This application will support user queries, while shielding the user from the complexities of the data and the mechanics of passing the query over multiple, networked servers. When a Big Data resource is terminated, applications with a user interface to the resource retain no value. However, the small utility programs built into the application may have enormous value to the builders of the next generation of related Big Data resources. The best applications are modularized—built from working parts that can be extracted and used as utilities. Utilities that apply generally to many data-related projects are valuable assets.

2. **Pay up front to preserve your legacy data and your identifiers.** Big Data resources are very expensive. It makes sense to put aside funds to preserve the data in the event of failure. Data means nothing unless it is properly identified; hence, the data held in a Big Data resource must be preserved with its identifiers. If the data is identified and well annotated, it will be possible to reintegrate the data objects into a successor resource.

Preserving legacy data is particularly important in hospital information systems, which have a very high failure rate.[162] Hospitals and medical centers should set aside money, in an escrow fund, for this purpose.

USE CASE: CANCER BIOMEDICAL INFORMATICS GRID, A BRIDGE TOO FAR

In a software project team of 10, there are probably 3 people who produce enough defects to make them net negative producers. Gordon Schulmeyer

Some governments do an excellent job at analyzing their own failures. After the Ariane 5 exploded 37 seconds after launch on its maiden space flight, the French government issued the results of its investigation.[173] When the Mars Climate Orbiter crashed on Mars, the U.S. government issued a report on its investigation.[174] The world might be a better place if we, as individuals, published our own investigative reports when we disappoint our friends and coworkers or fail to meet our personal goals; but self-accountability has never been a human strength.

In 2004, the National Cancer Institute launched an ambitious project, known as the Cancer Biomedical Informatics Grid (caBIG), aimed at developing standards for annotating and sharing biomedical data and tools for data analysis. An unusual aspect of this government project was that it had its own business model "to create a front end that will make caBIG attractive for others to invest in and take on responsibility for downstream events."[3] Further, it was "anticipated at the time that the caBIG effort would evolve into a self-sustaining community."[3]

When the effort was launched, its goals seemed relatively modest, but over the next 6 years, the scope of the project grew; it eventually covered software interoperability and Web-based services for sharing and analyzing data produced by virtually every biomedical specialty, from gene sequencing to radiology imaging to tissue specimens.

For a time, the project received generous support from academia and industry. In 2006, the Cancer Biomedical Informatics Grid was selected as a laureate in Computerworld's Honors program.[185] Computerworld described the project as "effectively forming a World Wide Web of cancer research," with "promises to speed progress in all aspects of cancer research and care." The great promises of the project came with a hefty price tag. By 2010, the National Cancer Institute had sunk at least $350 million into the effort.[3] Though the project was ambitious, there were rumblings in the cancer informatics community that very little had been achieved. In view of past and projected costs, an ad hoc committee was assigned to review the program.

In a report issued to the public in 2011, the committee found that the project had major deficiencies and suggested a yearlong funding moratorium.[3] Soon thereafter, the project leader left the National Cancer Institute, and the caBIG was terminated.[4]

The ad hoc committee report went into considerable detail to explain the deficiencies of the program. Their observations serve as a general warning for overly ambitious Big Data efforts:

> The caBIG program has grown rapidly without adequate prioritization or a cost-effective business model, has taken on a continuously increasing and unsustainable portfolio of development and support activities, and has not gained sufficient traction in supporting critical cancer research community needs. The working group interviews indicate that the program has developed some extremely expensive software solutions that have not been adopted in a meaningful way by the NCI designated Cancer Centers, have competed unnecessarily with existing solutions produced by industry leaders that hold a 60% to 70% market share in the NCI-designated Cancer Centers, and ultimately have created an enormous long-term maintenance, administration, and deployment load for the NCI that is financially unsustainable.[3]

Regarding analysis tools, the working group found that

> the level of impact for most of the tools has not been commensurate with the level of investment. For example, many tools, such as caArray ($9.3 M), have been developed at significant expense and without a clear justification, particularly since a number of similar commercial and open software tools already existed. It is indeed noteworthy and a lesson for the future that the more widely adopted Life Sciences tools have their roots in projects that were already fairly successfully developed by academic research institutions, whereas most of the caBIG-initiated projects have been less successful and, ironically, much more expensive. Similarly, enormous effort was devoted to the development of caGRID ($9.8 M), an environment for grid-based cloud

computing, but the working group did not find evidence that it has empowered a new class of tools to "accelerate the discovery of new approaches for the detection, diagnosis, treatment, and prevention of cancer" as envisioned.[3]

The working group found that the project participants were attracted to new technological innovations, even when those innovations provided no advantages:

> In particular, the interviews suggest that the strategic goals of the program were determined by technological advances rather than by key, pre-determined scientific and clinical requirements. Thus, caBIG ended up developing powerful and far-reaching technology, such as caGRID, without clear applications to demonstrate what these technologies could and would do for cancer research.[3]

Regarding the value of new technology, the working group "struggled to find projects that could not have been implemented with alternative less expensive or existing technologies and software tools."[3]

I was a program director at the National Cancer Institute during the first 2 years of the project and had a front-row seat for the caBIG pageant. At the time, I thought that the project was too big, too complex, too ambitious, that it served too many interests (the intramural community at National Institutes of Health, the extramural community of academic researchers, a profusion of industry contractors, and the office of the director at the National Cancer Institute), enlisted the assistance of too many people, had too much money, was lavished with too much hype, had initiated too many projects, and that the program directors operated with insufficient accountability. In a word, I was envious.

In the case of the Cancer Biomedical Informatics Grid, hindsight would suggest that the project may have benefited from the following.

1. **Start small.**[186] Projects should begin with a relatively small number of highly dedicated and energetic people. Studies have shown that as more and more money and personnel are added to a software project, the chances of success drop precipitously.[187] When you stop and think about it, most of the great programming languages, some of the most important operating systems, the design of the Internet, the language of the World Wide Web, computer hardware advances, innovational corporations, and virtually all of the great algorithms in computer science were created by one individual or a small group of people (usually less than five).

Some Big Data projects are necessarily large. The Human Genome Project, touted as one of the largest and most successful Big Data projects in human history, involved hundreds of scientists. But when it came down to organizing the pieces of data into a coherent sequence, the job fell to one man. In a report published by the Center for Biomolecular Science and Engineering at U.C. Santa Cruz, Jim Kent "developed in just 4 weeks a 10,000-line computer program that assembled the working draft of the human genome."[188] Kent's assembly was celebrated at a White House ceremony on June 26, 2000.[188]

The Cancer Biomedical Informatics Grid began with teams of workers: contractors, government employees, academics, and advisors from various related informatics projects. The project sprang into existence too big to build.   •

2. **Complete your initial goals.** Projects that are closely tied to a community (the cancer research community in the case of caBIG) tend to expand their goals based on the interests of enthusiastic community members. It is very common for project managers to be approached by individuals and small groups of people asking that their pet projects be added

to the list of project goals. Requests that come from powerful and influential members of the community cannot be ignored. Somehow project managers must placate their constituents without losing focus on their original goals. It is not sufficient to show that the resource is managing to do a lot of different things; managers must be able to complete their critical goals. Failing to do so was a problem for caBIG. As a counterexample, consider the amazing success of Google. Today, we enjoy the benefits of Google Earth, Google Maps, Google Books, and so on. The Google designers started with a simple, albeit large and all-encompassing, search engine. Projects were added after the search engine had been created and popularized.

3. **Do not try to do everything yourself.** There is a tendency today for large projects to seek representation in every ongoing effort that relates in any way to the project. For example, a standards effort in the cancer community might send representatives to every committee and standards project in the general area of health technology interoperability. Likewise, narrowly focused standards efforts (e.g., gene array specifications, microscopy specifications) often attract representatives from large corporations and from other standards committees. The push toward internecine activity is based on the belief that the ultimate goal of software interoperability and data integration can only be achieved by broadening the level of participation. In practice, these interchanges make it difficult for project managers to achieve any kind of focus. Each workday is diluted with debriefings on other projects, conferences, and committee meetings.

Life is about balance. Managers need to have some sense of what is happening in the world outside of their own project, but they must not digress from their own goals. In many cases, careful attention to the Big Data fundamentals (e.g., specifying data fully, identifying and classifying data objects, achieving introspection) should suffice in creating a functional resource that can operate with other resources. Data is fungible; a well-specified data model can often be ported to other formats, other standards, and other specifications, as needed.

4. **Do not depend on things that you cannot depend on.** This tautology should never be forgotten or trivialized. It is quite common for Big Data resources to choose hardware, software, standards, and specifications that cannot possibly serve their needs. Oblivious to reality, they will choose a currently popular, but flawed methodology, hoping some miracle will save them. So strong is this belief that things will somehow "work out" that virtually every type of project proposal (e.g., grant application, business proposal, book deal) contains a hidden deus ex machina; an implied request that the reviewer suspend his disbelief. Allowing for human nature, some grant reviewers extend a "one-miracle per grant" policy. An applicant can ask for one miracle, but no more.

After caBIG was terminated, Barry Smith, a big thinker in the rather small field of ontology, wrote an editorial entitled "CaBIG Has Another Fundamental Problem: It Relies on 'Incoherent' Messaging Standard."[189] In his editorial, Smith suggested that HL7, a data model specification used by caBIG, could not possibly work and that it had proven to be a failure by those people who actually tried to implement the specification and use it for its intended purposes.[189] At about the same time that caBIG was being terminated, the $17 billion interoperability project undertaken by the U.K.'s National Health Service was scuttled. This failed program had been called "the world's biggest civil information technology program."[166] Back in 2001, a report published by the NHS Information Authority cited fundamental flaws in HL7.[190] These flaws included intrinsic difficulties in establishing a workable identifier system. The report concluded that despite these problems, choosing HL7 was strategically correct, as it was the only data model with a process of continual review and update.[190] At the time, everyone was hoping for a miracle. The miracle did not come for caBIG; nor had it come for the U.K.'s interoperability project. No one can say to what degree, if any, HL7 flaws contributed to the downfall of these projects, but flaws in the data model could not have been very helpful.

5. **Use existing, thoroughly tested open source technologies wherever possible.** There is a healthy appetite among information technologists for new and improved technologies. Though this preference may serve well for small and short-term projects, it is often counterproductive for Big Data efforts. All Big Data projects are complex, and there is seldom room to compound complexities by tossing innovative software into the mix. Unless there is a compelling reason to use new technology, it is usually much safer to use older technology that is adequate for the tasks. Stable open source solutions, particularly when there is an active community that supports the software, are often the best choice. Aside from cost considerations (most open source software is free), there is the added benefit of longevity. Unlike commercial software, which can be discontinued or replaced by applications that are incompatible with installed versions, open source software tends to stay viable. In the case of caBIG, the working group indicated that the project chose new technologies when older technologies would suffice.

6. **Avoid developing solutions for problems that nobody really cares about.** I have a colleague who works in the field of computer-aided diagnosis, an interesting field that has not yet garnered widespread acceptance in the medical community. Apparently, clinicians still prefer to reach their diagnoses through their own efforts, without the aid of computer software.[191] Perhaps, he thought, the aid of a computer program might be appreciated in areas where physicians were in short supply, such as developing countries. He thought that it would be useful to find a market for computer-aided diagnostic software somewhere in Africa. Of course, health care limitations in developing countries are often basic availability issues (e.g., access to hospitals, beds, antibiotics, sterile materials, equipment, and so forth). Access to diagnostic computer programs, developed on clinical data sets collected on U.S. patients, may not be "what the doctor ordered."

In the case of caBIG, the working group found that caBIG was developing powerful new technologies for which there was no apparent need. It is only human nature to want to make a difference in the world. For Big Data project managers, it is sometimes best to wait until the world asks you for your input.

7. **A Big Data resource should not focus its attention on itself.** Big data projects often involve a great number of people. Those involved in such efforts may come to believe that the resource itself has an intrinsic value that exceeds the value of its rendered services.[192] Experience would indicate that most users, even avid users, are not interested in the details. The couch potato may sit transfixed in front of his television for hours on end, but he is not likely to pursue an interest in the technologies underlying signal transmissions, liquid crystal screens, or high-definition image construction. Likewise, the public has no interest in knowing any of the protocols and models that underlie a Big Data resource. As someone who was asked to review caBIG manuscripts, it was my impression that journal articles emanating from this effort were self-congratulatory pieces describing various aspects of the project, in details that would have meaning only to the other team members on the project.[193]

Program managers should never forget that a Big Data resource is all about the data and how the data is analyzed. The resource itself, rightly or wrongly, should not be the focus of public attention.

Legalities

In 2031, lawyers will be commonly a part of most development teams. **Grady Booch**

BACKGROUND

I am not a lawyer, and this chapter is not intended to provide legal advice to the readers. It is best to think of this chapter as an essay that covers the issues that responsible managers of Big Data resources worry about all of the time. When I was a program director at the National Institutes of Health, I worked on resources that collected and analyzed medical data. My colleagues and I worked through the perceived legal risks that encumbered all of our projects. For the most part, our discussions focused on four issues: (1) responsibility for the accuracy of the contained data; (2) rights to create, use, and share the data held in the resource; (3) intellectual property encumbrances incurred from the use of standards required for data representation and data exchange; and (4) protections for individuals whose personal information is used in the resource. Big Data managers contend with a wide assortment of legal issues, but these four problems, that never seem to go away, will be described in this chapter.

RESPONSIBILITY FOR THE ACCURACY AND LEGITIMACY OF CONTAINED DATA

The contents of small data resources can be closely inspected and verified. This is not the case for Big Data. Because Big Data resources are constantly growing and because the sources of the data are often numerous and not strictly controlled, it is a safe bet that some of the data is incorrect. The reflexive position taken by some data managers can be succinctly stated as "It's not my problem!"

To a small extent, measures taken to improve the quality of data contained in a Big Data resource will depend on how the data will be used. Will the data be used for mission-critical endeavors? In the medical realm, will the data be used to make diagnostic or treatment decisions? These contingencies raise the stakes for Big Data resources, but the data manager's responsibility is largely the same, regardless of the intended use of the resource. Every Big Data resource must have in place a system whereby data quality is constantly checked, errors are documented, corrective actions are taken, and improvement is documented. Without a quality assurance plan, the resource puts itself in great legal jeopardy. In addition to retaining legal counsel, data managers would be wise to follow a few simple measures.

1. **Make no unjustified claims**. It is important that statements issuing from the resource, including claims made in advertisements and informational brochures and verbal or written communications with clients, should never promise data accuracy. People who insist on accuracy should confine their attention to small data resources. If your Big Data resource has made no effort to ensure that the data is true and accurate, then you owe it to your users to indicate as much.
2. **Require your outside sources to indicate that they have taken measures to provide accurate data.** Sources should have their own operation protocols, and these protocols must be made available to the manager of the Big Data resource.
3. **Have procedures in place ensuring that the data provided by outside sources is accurately represented within the resource.** This is particularly important when the data is reformatted and reannotated to conform to the data model for the Big Data resource.
4. **Warn your data users that their analytic results, based on the resource's data, must be validated against external data sources.** It may seem obvious to you that conclusions drawn from the analyses of Big Data are always tentative. You would expect any data analyst to validate their findings against data from other sources. Sometimes data analysts need to be protected from their own naïveté, necessitating an explicit warning.
5. **Open your verification procedures to review—preferably public review.** Users find it unsettling to read exculpatory verbiage in user licenses expressing that the data provider cannot guarantee the accuracy of the data and cannot be held liable for any negative consequences that might arise from the use of the data. At the very least, data managers should reassure their users that reasonable measures have been taken to verify the data contained in the resource. Furthermore, those measures should be available for public review.
6. **Provide a method by which complainants can be heard.** This may actually be one of those rare instances when the immutability of a Big Data resource is broken. If material is known to be illegal or if the material is a potential danger to individuals, then it may be necessary to expunge the data (i.e., violate data immutability, discussed in Chapter 6).

When Big Data resources are used to influence the governmental process, special regulatory conditions may apply. The U.S. government passed the Data Quality Act in 2001 as part of the FY 2001 Consolidated Appropriations Act (Pub. L. No. 106-554). The act requires federal agencies to base their decisions on high-quality data and to permit the public to challenge and correct inaccurate data.[194] The drawback to this legislation is that science is a messy process, and data may not always attain a high quality. Data that fails to meet standards of quality may be rejected by government committees or may be used to abrogate policies that were based on the data.[195,196]

Similar data quality requirements apply to data used in the courtroom. In the case of Daubert v. Merrell Dow Pharmaceuticals, Inc., the U.S. Supreme Court ruled that trial judges must determine the relevance and adequacy of data-based evidence presented by expert witnesses. Judicial oversight is conducted through a pretrial review that "entails a preliminary assessment of whether the reasoning or methodology underlying the testimony is scientifically valid and of whether that reasoning or methodology properly can be applied to the facts in issue."[197]

Big Data managers must constantly strive to assure that the data contained in their resources are fully described and linked to the protocols through which the data was obtained. Any verification processes, through which data is entered and checked into the resource, may be reviewed by government committees and courts.

Data managers have a common lament: "I can't be held responsible for everything!" They have a point, but their inability to control everything does not relieve them of their responsibility to exercise a high degree of data diligence.

RIGHTS TO CREATE, USE, AND SHARE THE RESOURCE

Ownership is a purely mercantile concept; the owner of an item is the person who can sell the item. If you own a cow, then you can sell the cow. Once the cow is sold, you no longer own the cow; the cow has a new owner. This simple ownership arrangement does not work well for Big Data. Data can be copied ad infinitum. In virtually all cases, financial transactions that involve the transfer of data do not actually result in the loss of the data by the provider. The data provider continues to hold the data after the transaction has transpired. In the Big Data universe, Big Data is not "owned" in the usual sense of the word; data is intangible. This explains why the term "service" pops up so often in the information field (e.g., Internet Service Providers, Web Services, List Servers). Data is more often a service than an owned commodity.

Because Big Data comes from many sources, and has many different uses, and because data can be retrieved via federated queries across multiple resources (big and small), the customary laws pertaining to property rights can be difficult to apply.

Big Data managers need to know whether they have the right to acquire and distribute the data held in their resources. It may be easiest to think in terms of two separable issues: laws dealing with data acquisition and laws dealing with data distribution.

Information produced through a creative effort (e.g., books, newspapers, journal articles) usually falls under copyright law. This means that you cannot freely obtain and distribute these materials. Exceptions would include books that fall into the public domain (e.g., books produced by the federal government and books whose copyright term has expired). Other exceptions might include copyrighted material that fall under Fair Use provisions.[198] Fair Use provisions permit the distribution of copyrighted material if it is done solely for the public good, with no profit motive, and if it can be done in a way that does not financially harm the copyright holder (e.g., does not result in the loss of sales and royalties).

Most Big Data resources are primarily composed of raw data, along with annotations to the data. The data may consist of measurements of physical objects and events, and short informational attributes appended to abstract data objects. These types of data are generally not produced through a creative effort and would not fall under copyright law. In the United States, the most cited precedent relevant to data acquisition is Feist Publishing, Inc. v. Rural Telephone Service Co. When Rural Telephone Co. refused to license its alphabetized listing of names and telephone numbers to Feist Publishing, Inc., Feist proceeded to copy and use the data. Rural Telephone Co. claimed copyright infringement. The court ruled that merely collecting data into a list does not constitute a creative work and was not protected by copyright.

European courts differ somewhat from American courts with regard to data protection. Like their American counterparts, Europeans interpret copyright to cover creative works, not data collections. However, the 1996 European Database Directive instructs courts to extend sui generis (i.e., one of a kind or exceptional) protection to databases. In Europe, databases that may have required a significant investment of time, effort, and money cannot be freely copied for commercial use. The idea behind such a directive is to protect the investments made by database builders. By protecting the database owner, European law attempts to promote the creation of new Big Data resources, along with the commercial activities that follow.

Insofar as Big Data resources have international audiences, differences in database laws across different countries can be very frustrating for data managers who strive for legal clarity. Consequently, providers and users often develop their own solutions, as needed. Acquisition of commercial data (i.e., data that does not belong to the public domain), much like access to commercial software, is often arranged through legal agreements (e.g., licenses or contracts) between the data providers and the data users.

Regarding laws dealing with holding and distributing data, the Digital Millennium Copyright Act of 1998 (DMCA) applies in the United States. This law deals primarily with antipiracy security measures built into commercial digital products.[199] The law also contains a section (Title II) dealing with the obligations of online service providers who inadvertently distribute copyrighted material. Service providers may be protected from copyright infringement liability if they block access to the copyrighted material when the copyright holder or the holder's agent claims infringement. To qualify for liability protection, service providers must comply with various guidelines (i.e., the so-called safe harbor guidelines) included in the act. In most instances, compliant service providers would also be protected from infringement claims when their site links to other sites that contain infringing materials.

Whereas the DMCA provides some liability relief for inadvertent copyright infringers, the United States No Electronic Theft Act of 1997 (NET Act) makes possible the criminal prosecution of infringers who distribute copyrighted material for noncommercial purposes (i.e., for free).[200] In the early days of the Internet, there was a commonly held, but unfounded, belief that copyrighted material could be held and distributed without fear of legal retribution if no profit was involved. This belief, perhaps based on an overly liberal interpretation of the Fair Use provisions, came to an end with the NET Act.

Without delving into legal minutiae, here are a few general suggestions for data managers.

1. **Require your sources to substantiate their claim that the data is theirs to contribute.** Nobody should be submitting data that they do not own or that they do not have the right to distribute.

2. **Require your sources to indicate that the data was collected in a manner that does not harm individuals.** There should be no reasonable basis for concern that distributed data will be used to harm individuals.

3. **Use government data whenever feasible.** Much of the best data available to Big Data resources comes absolutely free from the U.S. government and other governments that have a policy of contributing their official data to the public domain. Big Data resources can freely copy and redistribute public domain government data. Links to the major sources of prepared U.S. government data are found at http://www.data.gov/. In addition, virtually all data collected by the government, including data collected through federal grants and data used to determine public actions, policies, or regulations, can be requested through the Freedom of Information Act.[201] Many countries provide their citizens with the right to acquire data that was generated with government (i.e., taxpayer) funds.

4. **Pay for legitimate data when feasible.** It seldom makes good sense to copy a data set into a Big Data resource if that data requires constant updating and curation. For example, a comprehensive list of restaurants, with their addresses and phone numbers, is always a work in progress. Restaurants open, close, move their locations, acquire new phone numbers, revise their menus, and modify their hours of operation. If there is a database resource that collects and updates this information, there may be little reason to replicate these activities within another data resource. It might make much more sense to license the database or to license access to the database. A federated data service, wherein queries to your Big Data resource are automatically outsourced to other databases, depending on the query subject, may make much more sense than expanding your resource to include every type of information. In many circumstances, the best and the safest method of using and distributing data may come from negotiating payments for external data.

COPYRIGHT AND PATENT INFRINGEMENTS INCURRED BY USING STANDARDS

As described in Chapter 5, the standards you use in your Big Data resource may be someone's intellectual property. The standards might be copyrighted. The uses of a standard may be patented. Licensing a standard can be expensive,[60] and the license for the standard may impose unwanted restrictions on the use of the standard. For example, a standard may be distributed under a license that prohibits you from distributing item identifiers (codes) and other components of the standard.

The building blocks of Big Data resources may hide intellectual property.[60,61] This is particularly true for software, which may contain subroutines or lines of code that fall under a claim within a patent. One day, you might receive a letter from a lawyer who represents a patent holder for a fragment of code included in a piece of software that has proven to be a valuable or irreplaceable asset to your resource. The letter may assert the patent and demand that you cease using the patent holder's intellectual property. More commonly, the letter will simply indicate that a conflict has arisen and will suggest that both parties (your Big Data resource and the patent holder) should seek a negotiated remedy. In either case, most Big Data resources will keep a law firm on retainer for such occasions. Do not despair; the ultimate goal of the patent holder is to acquire royalty payments, not to initiate a lawsuit.

Big Data resources are complex and contain many different types of data objects that may have been transformed, annotated, or formatted by many different methods. The uses of these methods may be restricted under licenses, contracts, and other legal contrivances. A few precautionary steps may help reduce your risks.

1. **Whenever possible, use free and open source standards, software, nomenclatures, and ontologies for all of your data annotations.**
2. **If you must use licensed materials, carefully read the "Terms of Use" in the agreement.** Licenses are written by lawyers who are paid to represent their client (the licensor). In most cases, the lawyer will be unaware of the special-use requirements of Big Data resources. The terms of use may preclude the customary activities of a Big Data resource (e.g., sharing data across networks, responding to large numbers of queries with annotated data, storing data on multiple servers in widely distributed geographic locations).
3. **Inventory your standards, software, nomenclatures, and ontologies.** For each item, write a description of any restrictions that might apply to your resource.
4. **Investigate on the Web.** See if there are any legal actions, active or settled, involving any of the materials you might use. Visit the U.S. Patent Office to determine whether there are patent claims on the uses of the standards, software, nomenclatures, and ontologies held in your resource. Most likely, your Big Data resource will send and receive data beyond the United States. Consult the World Intellectual Property Organization. Do not restrict your search to proprietary materials. Free and open source materials may contain embedded intellectual property and other encumbrances.
5. **Talk to your legal staff before you encounter legal hurdles.** Your law firm will need to be involved in virtually every aspect of the design and operation of your Big Data resource.

Big Data would greatly benefit from a universal framework supporting resource interoperability.[202] At present, every data manager must fend for herself.

PROTECTIONS FOR INDIVIDUALS

Data managers must be familiar with the concept of tort. Tort relates to acts that result in harm. Tort does not require an illegal act; it only requires a harm and a person or entity who contributes to the harm and who is liable for the damages. Tort works like this: if you are held liable for harm to another entity, then you must compensate the victim to an extent that makes the victim whole (i.e., back to where they were before suffering harm). If the victim makes a case that the harm resulted from negligence or due to conditions that could have been corrected through customary caution, then punitive fees can be added to the victim's award.

The punitive fees can greatly exceed the restorative fees. Consequently, it behooves every data manager to constantly ask himself whether his Big Data resource can result in harm to individuals (i.e., the users of the data or the subjects of the data). Needless to say, Big Data managers must seek specialized legal advice to minimize tort-related risks.

In the Big Data universe, tort often involves the harms that befall individuals when their confidential data files have been breached. I was raised in Baltimore, not far from the community of Catonsville. Catonsville was the site of a 1968 protest against U.S. involvement in the Vietnam War. Nine antiwar activists stormed into a draft office, stole files, and publicly burned the files. The Catonsville 9 attained instant international notoriety. The number of files destroyed: 379. In the Big Data era, the ante has been upped by many orders of magnitude. Today, when records are stolen or destroyed, you can expect the numbers to be in the hundreds of thousands or the millions.[203]

In May 2006, 26.5 million records on military veterans were stolen, including Social Security numbers and birthdates. The records had been taken home by a data analyst employed by the Department of Veterans Affairs. His laptop, containing all this information, was stolen. A class action lawsuit was brought on behalf of the 26.5 million aggrieved veterans. Three years later, the Department of Veterans Affairs paid $20 million to settle the matter.[204] In the United Kingdom, a copy of medical and banking records on 25 million Britons were lost in the mail.[205] The error led to the sudden resignation of the chairman of Her Majesty's Revenue and Customs.[205]

There are occasions when security is broken, but no theft occurs. In these instances, resource managers may be unaware of the privacy breach for a surprisingly long period of time. Medical data collected on about 20,000 patients was posted on a public Web site in 2010. The data included patient names, diagnosis codes, and administrative information on admissions and discharges occurring in a 6-month period in 2009. The data stayed posted on a public Web site for about a year before a patient happened to see the data and reported the breach to the hospital.[206] Accidental breaches are common in many different fields.[207]

Today, health care organizations must report data breaches that affect more than 500 people. Hundreds of such breaches have been reported. These breaches cost the health care industry in excess of $6 billion annually, and the costs are increasing, not decreasing.[203] Other industries have data breaches but are not required to report incidents.

Industry costs do not reflect the personal costs in time, emotional distress, and money suffered by individuals coping with identity theft. In the Big Data field, everyone's deepest fear is identity theft. None of us wants to contemplate what may happen when another person has access to our financial accounts or gains the opportunity to create new accounts under the stolen identity.

Security issues are inseparable from issues related to privacy and confidentiality. There is a field of information science that deals exclusively with security issues, and this book cannot attempt to suggest a detailed approach to a problem whose threats and responses are constantly changing. Every Big Data resource must develop thoughtful and realistic measures to safeguard their data. There are, however, a few commonsense measures that will reduce the likelihood of identification theft.

1. **Don't collect or provide information that will link an individual to his or her data record unless you really need the information.** If you do not have information that links a

record to a named individual, then you cannot inadvertently expose the information. Names, Social Security numbers, credit card numbers, and birthdates constitute the core information sought by identity thieves. Big Data resources should seriously consider whether these pieces of information need to be stored within the resource. Does your resource really need to collect Social Security numbers and credit card numbers? Can the person's name be adequately replaced with an internal identifier? Do you need a birthdate when a birth year might suffice? When these data items are necessary, do they need to be included in data records that are accessible to employees?

2. **Work with deidentified records whenever possible.** Deidentification may not be a perfect way to render records harmless, but it takes you very close to your goal. A thoughtfully deidentified data set has quite limited value to identity thieves.

3. **All files should be encrypted whenever possible.** Most breaches involve the theft of unencrypted records. Decryption is quite difficult and far beyond the technical expertise of most thieves.

4. **Backup data should be encrypted, inventoried, and closely monitored.** Backup data is a vulnerability. Thieves would be just as happy to steal your backup data as your original data. Because theft of backup data does not result in a system crash, such thefts can go undetected. It is very important to secure your backup data and to deploy a system that monitors when backup data is removed, copied, misplaced, destroyed, or otherwise modified.

CONSENT

For data managers who deal with medical data or with any data whose use puts human subjects at risk, consent issues will loom as a dominant legal issue. The reason why consent is a consuming issue for data managers has very little to do with its risks; the risks associated with obtaining improper consent are very small. Consent issues are important because consenting data can be incredibly expensive to implement. The consent process can easily consume the major portion of the data manager's time, and cost-effective implementations are difficult to achieve.

In the context of Big Data, informed consent occurs when a human agrees to accept the risk of harm resulting from the collection and use of their personal data (see Glossary item, Informed consent). In principle, the consent transaction is simple. Someone involved with the Big Data resource approaches a person and indicates the data that he would like to collect for the data project. He indicates the harms that may occur if the data is collected. If relevant, he indicates the measures that will be taken to minimize the risk of harm. The human subject either signs or does not sign the consent form. If the subject signs the form, his data is included in the Big Data resource.

It is important that data managers understand the purpose of the consent form so that it is not confused with other types of legal agreements between data owners and data contributors. The consent form is exclusively devoted to issues of risk to human subjects. It should not be confused with a commercial agreement (i.e., financial incentives for data use), with an intellectual property agreement (i.e., specifying who controls the uses of the data), or with scientific assessment of the project (i.e., determining how the data is to be used and for which specific purposes).

The term "informed consent" is often misinterpreted to mean that the patient must be fully informed of the details of the Big Data effort with a somewhat detailed list of all the possible uses of their personal data. The "informed" in "informed consent" refers to knowledge of the risks involved in the study, not the details of the study itself. It is counterproductive to fill a consent form with detailed information related to the expected uses of data if it distracts from the primary purpose of the form—to explain the risks.

What are the risks to human subjects in a Big Data project? With virtually no exceptions, Big Data risks are confined to two related consequences: loss of confidentiality and loss of privacy.

The concepts of confidentiality and of privacy are often confused, and it is useful to clarify their separate meanings. Confidentiality is the process of keeping a person's secret. Privacy is the process of ensuring that the person will not be annoyed, betrayed, or harmed as a result of his decision to give you his secret. For example, if you give me your unlisted telephone number in confidence, then I am expected to protect this confidentiality by never revealing the number to other persons. I may also be expected to protect your privacy by never using the telephone number to call you unnecessarily at all hours of the day and night (i.e., annoying you with your private information). In this case, the same information object (i.e., your unlisted telephone number) is encumbered by confidentiality (i.e., keeping the unlisted number secret) and privacy (i.e., not using the unlisted number to annoy you).

Both confidentiality and privacy are important areas of concern for Big Data managers. The theft of Big Data can involve millions of records. Because data theft typically involves taking a copy of the data without actually destroying any of the data in the resource, it is quite possible for large data thefts to go unnoticed.

To cover confidentiality risks, the consent form could indicate that personal information will be collected, but that measures will be taken to ensure that the data will not be linked to your name. In many circumstances, that may be all that is needed. Few patients really care if anyone discovers that their gallbladder was removed in 1995. When the personal information is of a highly sensitive nature, the consent form may elaborate on the security measures that ensure confidentiality.

The risk of losing privacy is a somewhat more subtle risk than the loss of confidentiality. In practical terms, for a Big Data project, loss of privacy occurs when the members of the Big Data resource come back to the human subject with a request for additional information or with information regarding the results of the study. The consent form should indicate any constraints that the Big Data resource has put into place to ensure that subjects are not annoyed with unwelcome future contacts by members of the project. In some cases, the Big Data project will anticipate the need to recontact human subjects (i.e., to invade their privacy). In this case, the consent form must contain language informing the subjects that privacy will not be fully protected. In many cases, subjects do not particularly care one way or the other. They are happy to participate in projects that will benefit society and they do not mind answering a phone call at some future time. The problem for the Big Data resource comes if and when subjects have a change of heart and they decide to withdraw consent. How does one provide important information to an individual, when the individual has withdrawn consent?

Obtaining consent from human subjects carries its own administrative and computational challenges—many of which are unanticipated by Big Data managers. Consent-related tasks include the following.

1. **Creating a legally valid consent form.** There are many ways to write a bad consent form. The most common mistake is inserting consent clauses among the fine-print verbiage of broader legal documents (e.g., contracts, agreements, licenses). This is a bad mistake for several reasons. The validity of informed consent can be challenged if an individual can claim that his understanding of risk was obfuscated by the inclusion of distracting and irrelevant text. The consent form should be devoted to a single topic: consent.

The consent form should be written in language that the average person can understand. In many cases, particularly in medical settings, informed consent should be read aloud by an individual who is capable of explaining difficult passages in the consent document.

Consent forms should not contain exculpatory clauses. For example, the consent form should not contain language expressing that the Big Data resource cannot be held liable for harm resulting from the use of the consenter's data. Neither should the form ask signers to waive any of their normal rights.

The consent form should have a signature section, indicating an affirmative consent. Certain types of informed consent may require the signature of a witness, and consent protocols should have provisions for surrogate signatures (e.g., of a parent or legal guardian). It is common for consent forms to provide an opportunity for subjects to respond in the negative (i.e., to sign a statement indicating that consent is denied). Doing so is seldom a good idea, for several reasons. First, a negative (nonaffirmative) statement is not legally required and there are no circumstances for which a nonaffirmative statement has any practical value. Second, individuals should not feel compelled to respond in any way to the consent form. If they freely choose to give consent, they can sign the form. If they do not wish to give consent, they should not be coerced to sign their names to a statement of denial. Third, a nonaffirmative statement can produce great confusion in the future when an individual consents to having the same medical record used for another project or when the individual has a change of heart and decides to provide consent for the same project.

The consent form should reveal circumstances that might influence a person's decision to provide consent. For example, if the investigators have a commercial interest in the outcome of the study, that information should be included in the consent form. It is reasonable for individuals to fear that they might suffer harm if the investigators have something to gain by a particular outcome of an experiment or analysis.

Traditionally, consent is not open-ended. Consent generally applies to a particular project that is conducted over a specified period of time. Consent ends when the project ends. There has been a trend to lengthen the window of time to which consent applies to accommodate projects that might reasonably be expected to extend over many years. For example, the Framingham study on heart disease has been in progress for more than 60 years.[208] If the Big Data project intends to use consented data for an indefinite period, as it often does, the consent form must clarify this condition.

Most importantly, the consent form should carefully describe the risks of participation. In the case of Big Data analyses, the risks are typically confined to loss of confidentiality or loss of privacy.

2. **Obtaining informed consent.** The U.S. Census is an established project that occurs every decade. The methods and the goals of the census have been developed over many decades. About 600,000 census workers are involved; their jobs are to obtain signed census forms from about 250 million individuals. The cost of each census is about $14 billion. Keeping these

numbers in your mind, imagine that you are a Big Data manager. You maintain and operate a global Big Data resource, with data on over 2 billion individuals (eight times the population of the United States). You are informed by your supervisor that a new project will require you to obtain informed consent on the resource's catchment population. You are told that you will be assigned 10 additional part-time workers to help you. You are given a budget of $100,000 for the project. When you complain that you need more help and a larger budget, you are told that you should use the computational power of the Big Data resource to facilitate the effort. You start looking for another job.

There are no easy ways to obtain informed consent. Popular marketing techniques that use automated or passive affirmations cannot be used to obtain informed consent. For example, opt-out forms in which human subjects must take an action to be excluded from participating in a potentially harmful data collection effort are unacceptable. Informed consent must be affirmative. Forms should not be promissory (i.e., should not promise a reward for participation). Informed consent must be voluntary and uncompensated.

Consent must be obtained without coercion. Individuals cannot be denied customary treatment or access to goods and services if they refuse to grant consent. There are circumstances in which the choice of a person who seeks informed consent may be considered coercive. A patient might feel threatened by a surgeon who waves a research-related consent form in his or her face minutes before a scheduled procedure. Big Data managers must be careful to obtain consent without intimidation.

The consent form must be signed. This means that a Web page submission is unacceptable unless it can be reasonably determined that the person providing the consent is the same person who is listed in the submitted Web page. This would usually necessitate an authenticated password, at minimum. Issues of identity theft, password insecurity, and the general difficulty of managing electronic signatures make Web-based consent a difficult process.

The process of obtaining consent has never been easy. It cannot be fully automated because there will always be people whose contact information (e.g., email accounts) is invalid or who ignore all attempts at contact. To this date, nobody has found an inexpensive or labor-free method for obtaining informed consent from large numbers of individuals.

3. **Preserving consent.** After consent has been obtained, it must be preserved. This means that the original paper document or a well-authenticated electronic document, with a verified signature, must be preserved. The consent form must be linked to the particular record for which it applies and to the protocol or protocols for which the consent applies. An individual may sign many different consent forms, for different data uses. The data manager must keep all of these forms safe and organized. If these documents are lost or stolen, then the entire resource can be jeopardized.

4. **Ensuring that the consent status is kept confidential.** The consent forms themselves are potential sources of harm to patients. They contain information related to special studies or experiments or subsets of the population that include the individual. The consent form also contains the individual's name. If an unauthorized person comes into possession of consent forms, then the confidentiality of the individuality would be lost.

An irony of Big Data research is that the potential harm associated with soliciting consent may be greater than the potential harm of participating as a subject in a Big Data project.

5. **Determining whether biases are introduced by the consent process.** After all the consents have been collected, someone must determine whether the data has been biased.

The data analyst would ask: "Is the group of people who provide consent in any way different from the group of people who refuse to provide consent? If so, will differences between the consenters and the nonconsenters bias analytic outcomes?" A data analyst might look for specific differences among the consented and unconsented group in features that are relevant to the question under study. For example, for a medical disease study, are there differences in the incidence of the disease between the consenting group and the nonconsenting group? Are there differences in the ages at which the disease occurs in consenters and nonconsenters?

6. **Creating a process whereby reversals and modifications of consent can be recorded and flagged.** In most cases, consent can be retracted. Retraction is particularly important in long or indefinite studies. The data manager must have a way of tracking consents and documenting a new consent status. For any future use of the data, occurring after the consent status has been retracted, the subject's data records must not be available to the data analyst.

7. **Maintaining records of consent actions**. Tracking consent data is extremely difficult. Here are a few consent-related activities that Big Data managers must record and curate: "Does each consent form have an identifier?" "Does each consent form link to a document that describes the procedure by which the consent form was approved?" "If paper consent forms were used, can the data manager find and produce the physical consent document?" "Was the consent restricted, permitting certain uses of the data and forbidding other types of data uses?" "Is each consent restriction tagged for tracking?" "If the consent form was signed, is there a protocol in place by which the signature is checked to determine authenticity?" "Does the data manager have a recorded policy that covers situations wherein subjects cannot provide an informed consent (e.g., infants, patients with dementia)?" "Does the resource have protocols for using surrogate signatures for children and subjects who have guardians or assignees with power of attorney?" "Does the Big Data resource have policies that exclude classes of individuals from providing informed consent?" "Is there a protocol to deal with subjects who withdraw consent or modify their original consent?" "Does the resource track data related to consent withdrawals and modifications?"

8. **Educating staff on the liberties and limitations of consented research.** Many Big Data managers forget to train their staff on legal matters, including consent-related issues. Information technologists may erect strong mental barriers to exclude the kinds of legal issues that obfuscate the field of data law. Data managers have no choice but to persevere. It is unlikely that factors such as staff indifference and workplace incompetence will serve as mitigating factors when the award is calculated for a successful tort claim.

UNCONSENTED DATA

There are enormous technical difficulties and legal perils in the consent process. Is there some way of avoiding the whole mess?

I have worked for decades in an information-centric culture that has elevated the consent process to an ethical imperative. It is commonly held that the consent process protects individuals from harm and data managers from liability. In the opinion of many of my colleagues, all confidential data on individuals should be consented into the database, unless there is a very good reason to the contrary.

After many years of dealing with the consent issue, I have reached a very different conclusion. To my way of thinking, consent should be avoided, if feasible; it should only be used as a last resort. In most circumstances, it is far preferable for all concerned to simply render data records harmless and to use them without obtaining consent. As the dependence on consent has grown over the past few decades, several new issues, all having deleterious societal effects, have arisen.

1. Consent can be an unmerited revenue source for data managers. When consent must be obtained on thousands or millions of individuals, the consenting costs can actually exceed the costs of preparing and using the data. When these costs are passed on to investors or to taxpayers (in the case of public Big Data resources), it raises the perceived importance and the general cash flow for the resource. Though data managers are earnest and humble, as a rule, there are some managers who feel comfortable working in a high-stakes project, where there is ample money to spread around. Tasks related to the consent process cost money, without materially contributing to the research output. Because funding institutions must support consenting efforts, grant writers for Big Data projects can request and receive obscenely large awards, when consent is required.
2. The act of obtaining consent is itself a confidentiality risk. The moment you ask for consent, you're creating a new security weakness because the consent form contains sensitive information about the subject and the research project. The consent form must be stored and retrieved as needed. As more and more people have access to copies of the consent forms, the risk of a confidentiality breach increases.
3. Consent issues may preoccupy data managers, diverting attention from other responsibilities. There is a limit to the number of problems anyone can worry about. If half of your research effort is devoted to obtaining, storing, flagging, and retrieving consent forms, you are less likely to pay attention to other aspects of the project. One of the chief lessons of this book is that, at the current time, most of our Big Data resources teeter on the brink of failure. The consent process can easily push a resource over the brink.
4. Consented research has been used for unintended purposes. Once you have received permission to use personal data in a consented study, the data remains forever. Scientists can use this data freely, for any purpose, if they deidentify the data or if the original consent form indicates that the data might be used for future unspecified purposes. The latter option fueled the Havasupai lawsuit, discussed in the final section of this chapter.

Consent can be avoided altogether if the data in the resource has been rendered harmless. Data managers taking the unconsented path to data use need to ask themselves the following question. "Can I devise a way by which the data can be used, without risk to the individual?" The purpose of the consent form is to provide individuals with the choice to decline the risks associated with the use of their data in the Big Data resource. If there are no risks, there is usually no need to obtain consent. Exceptions exist. Regulations that restrict the use of data for designated groups of individuals may apply. Data confidentiality and privacy concerns are among the most difficult issues facing Big Data resources. Basing policy on the advice of legal counsel is always wise.

The widespread use and public distribution of data records is a sort of Holy Grail for data miners. Medical records, financial transactions, and collections of private electronic communications conducted over air and wire all contribute to the dark matter of the information universe. Everyone knows that this hidden data exists (we each contribute to these data collections), that this hidden data is much bigger than the data that we actually see, and that this data is the basic glue that binds the information universe. Nonetheless, most of the data created for the information universe is considered private. Private data is controlled by a small number of corporations who guard their data against prying eyes, while they use the data, to the extent allowed by law, to suit their own agendas. Why isn't this data deidentified using methods discussed earlier (Chapter 2) and distributed for public review and analysis? Here are some of the reasons.

1. All of the commercially available deidentification/scrubbing software is slow. It cannot cope with the exabytes of information being produced each year.
2. None of the commercially available deidentification/scrubbing software does a perfect job. These software applications merely reduce the number of identifiers in records; they leave behind an irreducible number of identifying information.
3. If deidentification/scrubbing software actually performed as claimed, removing every identifier and every byte of unwanted data from electronic records, some records might be identified through the use of external database resources that establish identities through nonidentifying details contained in records (vida infra).
4. Big Data managers are highly risk averse and would rather hoard their data than face the risk, no matter how unlikely, of a possible tort suit from an aggrieved individual.
5. Big Data managers are comfortable with restricted data sharing through legal instruments such as data use agreements (see Glossary item, Data sharing). Through such agreements, selected sets of data extracted from a Big Data resource are provided to one or a few entities who use the data for their own projects and who do not distribute the data to other entities.
6. Data deidentification methods, like many of the useful methods in the information field, can be patented. Some of the methods for deidentification have fallen under patent restriction or have been incorporated into commercial software that is not freely available to data managers.[45] For some data managers, royalty and license costs are additional reasons for abandoning the deidentification process.
7. Big Data managers are not fully convinced that deidentification is possible, even under ideal circumstances.

It may seem impossible, but information that is not considered identifying may actually be used to discover the name of the person linked to deidentified records. Mischievous schemes to thwart the deidentification process all work through one simple trick: access to an external database that contains identified information linked to nonidentifying data. Here is an example whereby the trick works: suppose I have a data set composed of deidentified records that includes a field for gene variants and another field for criminal record. The data resource is being used for many analytic purposes, including efforts to determine whether there is an association between certain gene variants and certain types of criminal behavior. Let us imagine that there is a public database containing identified records that contain the same kinds of gene variant data (see Glossary item, Public data). This public database is used for genealogy studies. All of the identified records in this database were obtained from volunteers who wished to participate in studies that might help identify their own ancestors.

A savvy data analyst compares the gene variant records from the deidentified (criminal) database with the gene variant records in the identified (genealogy) database. When he finds a match in gene variants, he acquires the name associated with the gene variant in the public database, and that name will correspond with the person whose criminal record is included in the deidentified database.

Basically, deidentification is easy to break when deidentified data can be linked to a name in an identified database containing fields that are included in both databases. This is the common trick underlying virtually every method designed to associate a name with a deidentified record.

There are many variants to the trick. In the example provided, it may be impossible to find an exact match between the gene variants in the deidentified database and the gene variants in the identified database. In this case, close matches to a group of records all identified with the same surname may provide all the information that is needed to establish a unique individual's identity.

Data managers who provide deidentified data sets to the public must worry whether there is, or ever will be, an available identified database that can be used to link fields, or combinations of fields, to their deidentified data, and thus linking their records to the names of individuals. This worry weighs so heavily on data managers and on legal consultants for Big Data resources that there are very few examples of publicly available deidentified databases. Everyone in the field of Big Data is afraid of the legal repercussions that will follow when the confidentiality of their data records is broken.

GOOD POLICIES ARE A GOOD POLICY

Discussions of privacy and confidentiality seem to always focus on the tension that results when the interests of the data holders conflict with the interests of the data subjects. These issues are often intractable because each side has a legitimate claim to their own preferences (businesses need to make profit and individuals need some level of privacy).

At some point, every Big Data manager must create a privacy policy and abide by his or her own rules. It has been my experience that legal problems arise when companies have no privacy policy, have a privacy policy that is not well documented, have a privacy policy that is closed to scrutiny, have a fragmented privacy policy, or fail to follow their own policy. If the company is open with its policy (i.e., permits the policy to be scrutinized by the public) and willing to change the policy if it fails to adequately protect individuals from harm, then the company is not likely to encounter any major problems.

Privacy protection protocols do not need to be perfect. They do, however, need to be followed. Companies are much more likely to get into trouble for ignoring their own policies than for following an imperfect policy. For a policy to be followed, the policy must be simple. Otherwise, the employees will be incapable of learning the policies. Unknowable policies tend to be ignored by the unknowing staff.

Every Big Data project should make the effort to produce a thoughtful set of policies to protect the confidentiality of its records and the privacy of data subjects. These policies should be studied by every member of a Big Data project, and should be modified as needed, and be reviewed at regular intervals. Every modification and review should be documented. Every breach or failure of every policy must be investigated, promptly, and the results of the investigation, including any and all actions taken, must be documented.

If you are a Big Data manager endowed with an overactive imagination, it is possible to envision all types of unlikely scenarios in which confidentiality can be breached. Nobody is perfect, and nobody expects perfection from any human endeavor. Much of law is based on a standard of "reasonableness." Humans are not expected to be held to an unreasonable standard. As an example, the privacy law that applies to hospitals and health care organizations contains 390 occurrences of the string "reasonable."[33] A reasonable approach to confidentiality and privacy is all that can be expected from a complex human endeavor.

USE CASE: THE HAVASUPAI STORY

For those who seek consent for research, the case of the Havasupai Tribe v. Arizona Board of Regents holds us in thrall. The facts of the case play out over a 21-year period, from 1989 to 2010. In 1989, Arizona State University obtained genetic samples from several hundred members of the Havasupai tribe, a community with a high prevalence of Type II diabetes. In addition to their use in diabetes research, the informed consent indicated the samples might be used for research on "behavioral and medical disorders," not otherwise specified. The researchers tried but failed to make headway linking genes sampled from the Havasupai tribe with cases of diabetes. The gene samples were subsequently used for ancillary studies that included schizophrenia and for studies on the demographic trends among the Havasupai. These ancillary studies were performed without the knowledge of the Havasupai. In 2003, a member of the Havasupai tribe happened to attend a lecture at Arizona State University on the various studies performed with the Havasupai DNA samples.

The Havasupai tribe was enraged. They were opposed to the use of their DNA samples for studies of schizophrenia or for the studies of demographic trends. In their opinion, these studies did not benefit the Havasupai and touched upon questions that were considered embarrassing and taboo, including the topic of consanguineous matings and the prevalence rates of mental illnesses within the tribe.

In 2004, the Havasupai tribe filed a lawsuit indicating lapses in the informed consent process, violation of civil rights, violation of confidentiality, and unapproved use of the samples. The case was dismissed on procedural grounds, but was reinstated by the Arizona Court of Appeals in 2008.[209]

Reinstatement of the case led to lengthy and costly legal maneuvers. Eventually, the case was settled out of court. Arizona State University agreed to pay individuals in the Havasupai tribe a total of $700,000. This award is considerably less than the legal costs already incurred by the university. Arizona State University also agreed to return the disputed DNA samples to the Havasupai tribe.

If the Havasupai tribe won anything in this dispute, it must have been a Pyrrhic victory. Because the case was settled out of court, no legal decision was rendered and no clarifying precedent was established.

Though I am not qualified to comment on the legal fine points, several of the general principles related to the acquisition and use of data are relevant and can be discussed as topics of general interest.

First, the purpose of an informed consent document is to list the harm that might befall the individual who gives consent as a consequence of his or her participation as a human subject. Consent relates only to harm; consent does not relate to approval for research. Laypersons should not be put into a situation wherein they must judge the value of research goals. By signing consent, the signator indicates that he or she is aware of the potential harm from the research and agrees to accept the risk. In the case of samples or data records contributed to a Big Data resource, consenters must be warned, in writing, that the data will be used for purposes that cannot be specified in the consent form.

Most consent is obtained to achieve one primary purpose, and this purpose is customarily described briefly in the consent form. The person who consents often wants to know that the risks that he or she is accepting will be compensated by some potential benefit to society. In the case of the Havasupai Tribe v. Arizona Board of Regents, the tribe sought to exert control over how their DNA would be used.[210] It would seem that the Havasupai tribe members believed that their DNA should be used exclusively for scientific efforts that would benefit the tribe. There is no ethical requirement that binds scientists to conduct their research for the sole benefit of one group of individuals. A good consent form will clearly state that research conducted cannot be expected to be of any direct value to the consenter.

Finally, the consent form should include **all** of the potential harms that might befall the consenter as a consequence of his or her participation. It may be impossible to anticipate every possible adverse consequence to a research participant. In this case, the scientists at Arizona State University did not anticipate that the members of the Havasuapai tribe would be harmed if their gene data was used for ancillary research purposes. I would expect that the researchers at Arizona State University do not believe that their research produced any real harm. The Havasupai tribal members believe otherwise. It would seem that the Havasupai believed that their DNA samples were abused and that their trust had been violated.

Had the original consent form listed all of the potential harms, as perceived by the Havasupai, then the incident could have been avoided. The Havasupai could have reached an informed decision weighing the potential benefits of diabetes research against the certain consequences of using their DNA samples for future research projects that might be considered taboo.

Why had the Havasupai signed their consent forms? Had any members of the Havasupai tribe voiced concerns over the unspecified medical and behavioral disorders mentioned in the consent form, then the incident could have been avoided.

In a sense, the Havasupai Tribe v. Arizona Board of Regents lawsuit hinged on a misunderstanding. The Havasupai did not understand how scientists use information to pursue new questions. The board of regents did not understand the harms that might occur when data is used for legitimate scientific purposes. The take-home lesson for data managers is the following: to the extent humanly possible, ensure that consent documents contain a complete listing of relevant adverse consequences. In some cases, this may involve writing the consent form with the assistance of members of the group whose consent is sought.

14

Societal Issues

The greatest enemy of knowledge is not ignorance, it is the illusion of knowledge. **Stephen Hawking**

BACKGROUND

Big Data, even Big Data used in science, is a social endeavor. The future directions of Big Data will be strongly influenced by social, political, and economic forces. Will scientists archive their experimental data in publicly accessible Big Data resources? Will scientists adopt useful standards for their operational policies and their data? The answers depend on a host of issues related to funding source (e.g., private or public), cost, and perceived risks. How scientists use data over the next few years may provide the strongest argument for or against the proliferation of Big Data resources.

HOW BIG DATA IS PERCEIVED

As preparation for writing this book, I spoke with many people, read a lot of blogs and magazine articles, and generally tried to understand how society perceives Big Data. The purpose of Big Data was rationalized under the following eight distinct hypotheses.

Gumshoe hypothesis: Hoarding information about individuals for investigative purposes. In this hypothesis, Big Data exists for private investigators, police departments, and snoopy individuals who want to screen, scrutinize, and invade the privacy of individuals for their own purposes. There is basis in reality to support this hypothesis. Investigators, including the Federal Bureau of Investigation, use Big Data resources, such as fingerprint databases, DNA databases, legal records, air travel records, arrest and conviction records, school records, home ownership records, genealogy trees, credit card transactions, financial transactions, Facebook pages, tweets, emails, and sundry electronic residua. The modern private eye has profited from Big Data, as have law enforcement officers. It is unsettling that savvy individuals have used Big Data to harass, stalk, and breach the privacy of other individuals. These activities have left some individuals dreading future sanctioned or unsanctioned uses of Big Data. The expectation that Big Data will serve to prevent crime, bring criminals to justice, and enhance the security of law-abiding citizens has not fully engaged the public consciousness.

Big Brother hypothesis: Collecting information about a population of individuals to control every member of the population. Modern governments obtain data from surveillance cameras, arrest records, wiretaps and sophisticated eavesdropping techniques, census records, tax records, accounting records, driving records, public health records, and a wide variety of information collected in the normal course of official operations. Much of the data collected by governments is mandated by law (e.g., census data, income tax data, birth certificates) and cannot be avoided. When a government sponsors Big Data collections, there will always be some anxiety that the Big Data resource will be used to control the public, reducing our freedoms of movement, expression, and thought. On the plus side, such population-wide studies may eventually reduce the incidence of crime and disease, make driving safer, and improve society overall.

Borg hypothesis: Collecting information about a population of individuals to learn everything about the population. I assume that if you are reading this book on Big Data, you most likely are a Star Trek devotee and understand that the Borg are a race of collectivist aliens who travel through galaxies, absorbing knowledge from civilizations encountered along the way. The conquered worlds are absorbed into the Borg "collective" while their scientific and cultural achievements are added to a Big Data resource. According to the Borg hypothesis, Big Data is the download of a civilization. Big Data analysts predict and control the activities of populations: how crowds move through an airport, when and where traffic jams are likely to occur, when political uprisings will occur, how many people will buy tickets for the next 3D movie production, or how fast the next flu epidemic will expand.

George Carlin hypothesis: A place to put all your stuff. The late great comedian George Carlin famously chided us for wasting our time, money, and consciousness on one intractable problem: "Where do we put all our stuff?" Before the advent of Big Data, electronic information was ephemeral; created and then lost. With cloud computing, search engines that encompass the Web, and protocols for retrieving our own information upon request, Big Data becomes an infinite storage attic. Your stuff is safe, forever, and it's available to you when you need it.

When the ancient Sumerians recorded buy–sell transactions, they used clay tablets. They used the same medium for recording novels, such as the Gilgamesh epic. These tablets have endured well over 4000 years. To this day, scholars of antiquity study and translate the Sumerian data sets. The safety, availability, and permanence of electronic "cloud" data is a hypothesis that will be tested over time.

Scavenger hunt hypothesis: Big Data is a collection of everything, created for the purpose of searching for individual items and facts. Find these: movies playing now at the local cineplex, Amtrak schedule for the northeast corridor of the United States, cost of tickets to a Broadway play, updated locations of spouse and children, average weight of male elephants, and in-air flight time to New Delhi. According to the scavenger hunt hypothesis, Big Data is everything you ever wanted to know about everything.

Egghead hypothesis: Collecting information to draw generalized scientific conclusions. To fully understand the beauty of the egghead hypothesis, a preliminary explanation of the purpose of science is in order.

Science is a method whereby we develop generalizations about the nature of our world and of the universe by observing individual objects in the universe under various naturally occurring or experimentally contrived conditions. For example, when an object such as an apple or a lead weight is dropped from a height, we can watch it fall, measure the time for the descent, determine that the apple and the lead weight dropped at the same rates throughout their respective descents, and develop a formula that relates the distance dropped to the square of the interval time for the drop. Once done, and confirmed on other objects, we know a great deal about how everything falls (not just one apple and one lead weight). We have moved from the specific (i.e., apple, lead weight) to the general (i.e., everything).

When a scientist extracts Big Data collected on a large set of individuals, his or her purpose is to quickly move from the level of specificity (i.e., a collection of identified data records) to the level of generality (i.e., general statements unconnected to individual records). For example, if a scientist is studying the incubation period for West Nile virus, when humans are infected by a mosquito bite, the scientist will want to collect as many infection records as possible, with detailed information documenting the time that infection occurred and the time that symptoms emerged. The records will be identified, at some time in the data collection process, with information that links the record to a particular person. The last thing that the scientist is interested in is the identity of the patient. The scientist is marching in a path that leads to the most general statement possible: "The incubation period for West Nile virus is 2 to 15 days."

To acquire the data for his or her studies, the scientist is willing, if not eager, to untether the data from the individual to whom the data applies. The scientist only needs to know that the record is unique (i.e., that he or she is not counting the same record over and over) and verified (i.e., that the data contained in the record was obtained through a process that ensures data integrity).

It is important to understand that Big Data is focused on complex, and individual, identified data records, while responsible science is focused on simplifying information to yield nonpersonal generalizations. This last point is stressed because the public should not need to fear that scientists have any interest in any individual's personal information.

The National Science Foundation has recently issued a program solicitation entitled "Core Techniques and Technologies for Advancing Big Data Science and Engineering"[10] This document encapsulates the egghead hypothesis of Big Data:

> The Core Techniques and Technologies for Advancing Big Data Science and Engineering (BIGDATA) solicitation aims to advance the core scientific and technological means of managing, analyzing, visualizing, and extracting useful information from large, diverse, distributed and heterogeneous data sets so as to: accelerate

the progress of scientific discovery and innovation; lead to new fields of inquiry that would not otherwise be possible; encourage the development of new data analytic tools and algorithms; facilitate scalable, accessible, and sustainable data infrastructure; increase understanding of human and social processes and interactions; and promote economic growth and improved health and quality of life. The new knowledge, tools, practices, and infrastructures produced will enable breakthrough discoveries and innovation in science, engineering, medicine, commerce, education, and national security—laying the foundations for U.S. competitiveness for many decades to come.[10]

Facebook hypothesis: A social archive that generates money. The underlying assumption here is that people want to use their computers to interact with other people (i.e., make friends and contacts, share thoughts, arrange social engagements, give and receive emotional support, and memorialize their lives). Some might dismiss social networks as a ruse whereby humans connect with their computers, while disconnecting themselves from committed human relationships that demand self-sacrifice and compassion. Still, a billion members cannot all be wrong, and the data collected by social networks must tell us something about what humans want, need, dislike, avoid, love, and, most importantly, buy. The Facebook hypothesis is the antithesis of the egghead hypothesis in that participants purposely add their most private thoughts and desires to the Big Data collection so that others will recognize them as unique individuals.

Nihilist hypothesis: Big Data does not exist as a definable field of endeavor; it represents what we have always done, but with more data. This last statement, which is somewhat of an antihypothesis, is actually prevalent among quite a few computer scientists. They would like to think that everything they learned in the final decades of the 20th century will carry them smoothly through the first decades of the 21st century. Many such computer scientists hold positions of leadership and responsibility in the realm of information management. They may be correct—time will either vindicate or condemn them.

Discourse on Big Data is hindered by the divergence of opinions on the nature of the subject. A proponent of the nihilist hypothesis will not be interested in introspection, identifiers, semantics, or any of the Big Data issues that do not apply to traditional data sets. Proponents of the George Carlin hypothesis will not dwell on the fine points of Big Data analysis if their goal is limited to archiving files in the Big Data cloud. If you read blogs and magazine articles on Big Data from diverse sources (e.g., science magazines, popular culture magazines, news syndicates, financial bulletins), you will find that the authors are all talking about fundamentally different subjects called by the same name: Big Data.

To paraphrase James Joyce, there are many sides to an issue; unfortunately, I am only able to occupy one of them. I closely follow the National Science Foundation's lead (vida supra). The focus for this chapter is the egghead hypothesis—using Big Data to advance science.

THE NECESSITY OF DATA SHARING, EVEN WHEN IT SEEMS IRRELEVANT

It's antithetical to the basic norms of science to make claims that cannot be validated because the necessary data are proprietary. *Michael Eisen*[211]

In the days of small data, scientists performed experiments, collected their data, and reported the results. In the Big Data era, scientists analyze data extracted from diverse resources. Sometimes the data is prepared to serve a particular scientific purpose. Sometimes the data serves unanticipated purposes. Here are a few examples of the latter, in chronologic order.

1. Tycho Brahe was a 16th-century astronomer who spent much of his life charting the planets and stars. When he died, circa 1600, he gave his charts to Johannes Keppler; legacy data in its most literal form. Kepler used the charts to develop three general laws describing the movement of planets. These laws assumed that the sun occupies the center of the universe. In 1687, Newton published his Principia, wherein Kepler's empiric laws were developed from basic physical principles—Newton's laws of motion.

2. In the early 17th century, the mathematical analysis of logarithms revolutionized computation. Practical applications of logarithms lacked a publicly available listing of numbers and their logs. Napier published the logarithm tables in 1614. A mere 8 years later, the slide rule was invented. By sharing his log tables with the world, one of the most successful tools for multiplication and division emerged. The slide rule was such a simple and elegant device that it was popular for about 150 years, until the early 1970s, when digital calculators were commoditized.

3. Vogel and Huggins, in 1879, published spectral data for hydrogen.[212] The hydrogen spectrum is observed as discrete spectral lines at characteristic wavelengths. Johann Jakob Balmer found an empirical formula that related the spectral wavelengths of hydrogen to a constant and to an increasing sequence of integers.[213] In 1913, Niels Bohr happened upon the Balmer equation and found a physical model for the equation, wherein spectral lines of different wavelengths were based on jumps of electrons orbiting the nucleus in quantized energy states. Thus the data shared by Vogel and Huggins led to the birth of quantum physics a quarter-century later.

4. Avandia is a diabetes drug manufactured by GlaxoSmithKline. Under pressure from a lawsuit unrelated to Avandia, the company posted its clinical data on Avandia to a public Web site.[214] In 2007, a Cleveland Clinic cardiologist, Dr. Steven Nissen, happened upon the site and analyzed the data. Data analysis by Dr. Nissen and coworkers indicated that the drug was cardiotoxic and posed serious risks for patients.[215] Regarding the pharmaceutical data site, Dr. Nissen said, "It was a treasure trove."[216]

5. Climate data has indicated that the average power of tropical cyclones has increased in the past few decades. Ocean temperature data collections indicate an increase in ocean temperatures during the same period.[217] Thus was born a new method for correlating the intensity of tropical storms and hurricanes with ocean temperatures. This specialized area of climatology, developing in the first decade of the 21st century, is new, unproven, and may lead nowhere. It shows, however, that shared data from different sources (e.g., hurricane data and ocean temperature data) may lead to new scientific paradigms.

6. Whimsical data may sometimes serve serious purposes. In 2009, a crowd-source database of dollar bill traffic was created by marking a large number of dollar bills and soliciting individuals to log in their locations and the serial numbers of the marked dollar bills if they received any. The database has been used to track and predict an influenza epidemic, based on the ability to analyze the migration data of hand-to-hand transactions, as modeled by the dollar exchange database.[218]

7. In 2012, astronomers discovered numerous planets revolving around stars in the Milky Way galaxy by reanalyzing sets of previously collected spectral data. The scientists looked for blue-shift/red-shift spectral wobbles produced by planets orbiting stars.[219] These new, exciting findings were made possible because the old data was stored and made available for reanalysis.

The past decade has witnessed a powerful movement among scientists to share data. The U.S. National Academy of Sciences has called for scientists to provide publishers with the primary data that supports the conclusions contained in their manuscripts.[220] The idea behind this requirement is that modern research is complex, data-intensive, expensive, and collaborative, with data contributed by multiple laboratories. It is seldom feasible to repeat experiments described in modern manuscripts. Without access to the primary data sets, there is no way to verify the experimental results or the final conclusions claimed in journal articles. Furthermore, without the primary data, colleagues cannot extend the research beyond the questions contained in the original manuscript. Sometimes, the most important purpose of a publication is to provide scientists with data for other studies (vida supra).

The National Institutes of Health (NIH) now requires NIH-funded researchers to submit their published manuscripts to the National Library of Medicine PubMed Central service for free and open public access. Along with the manuscripts, NIH-funded scientists are generally encouraged to submit all of the primary data supporting their conclusions. There is a growing trend for NIH grant applications to contain a section in which applicants describe their plans for sharing the data produced in the course of their funded research. As an example, here is an excerpt of NIH's instructions to applicants for Molecular Libraries Screening Centers Network (MLSCN) grants:

> It is, therefore, NIH's understanding that the usefulness of the data and resources generated by the MLSCN would be of maximal benefit to public health if they are treated as a community resource and made publicly available....Applicants' plans for maximizing the public use of the data and resources generated by the MLSCN network will be a major evaluation criterion for the pilot centers, and for applicants to become fully operational MLSCN centers. During the pilot MLSCN period, NIH will solicit opinions and collect additional data from the scientific and commercial sectors to allow an evaluation of whether the approaches described above are sufficient to ensure that screening data and resources generated by the MLSCN centers are broadly available. [221]

Academic and corporate cultures may have conflicting views of Big Data sharing; information is both a public asset and an instrument for profit (see Glossary item, Bayh-Dole Act). In a recent scientific conference in Lyon, France, scientists from Google and the University of Cambridge refused to share the primary data for their analysis of YouTube video preferences.[211] The chairman of the conference took the position that the conference should not accept papers for which the primary data was withheld. Huberman wrote, "If another set of data does not validate results obtained with private data.... How do we know if it is because they are not universal or the authors made a mistake?"[211]

A good scientist continuously questions his or her own beliefs, posing the following simple but incisive question: "Do I really know what I think I know?" Time and again, scientists have been tricked into believing ridiculous theories based on falsified data or on biased interpretations of data. Big Data provides a multitude of opportunities for scientific mischief (e.g., poor data, poor data annotation, cherry-picking data, poor analyses, distorted visualizations, skewed interpretations, and so on). The possibilities of a false or misleading outcome are so large that any scientific claim made on proprietary Big Data claims can be dismissed out of hand. In the realm of Big Data, scientific credibility is based on public access to the primary data and to all the protocols accounting for the collection, annotation, extraction, and analysis of the data.

The important topic of deidentification is often shoved aside in data-sharing discussions. About a decade ago, I attended a conference in which an information officer was lecturing a group on the topic of medical data warehousing. He boasted that his medical center had put terabytes of well-annotated data at his disposal. I asked if his institution had plans for deidentifying and sharing the data with the public, thus giving everyone a chance to use the data. I believe he winced, and then said, "It's very difficult to deidentify data, you know." I then asked if it was the policy of his institution to avoid projects that happen to be difficult. He indicated, quite diplomatically, that deidentification was a long-term goal, but other projects took priority.

There are many reasons for institutions and corporations to equivocate on the topic of deidentification. When forced to share against their will, such entities often resort to the following four disingenuous diversions.

1. "We're working on it." Large institutions are adept at dragging their feet. There is no need to show tangible progress; they only need to show a credible effort. It never ceases to amaze me that institutions will typically assign deidentification projects to the same computer scientists who insist that deidentification is impractical or impossible.
2. "Some of our data has been deidentified and released to the public." I call this practice deidentification in pieces. The data manager uses his or her imagination and skill to produce a selected set of deidentified records for user access. This practice seldom meets expectations; the preselected data never seems to be sufficient for the user's particular purposes. Aside from being paternalistic, this practice stifles creativity. Big Data should promote discovery by providing users with large, complex, and heterogeneous data that can be freely explored.
3. "We provide full access to our data to our staff." It is difficult to ascertain the number of private Big Data resources, but my perception is that most Big Data is closed to the public. The data that is available is sometimes restricted to a few staff members. Because employees are often required to restrict their research to activities that benefit their employer, the intellectual output from closed Big Data resources has limited scope and utility. Furthermore, primary data that supports published scientific conclusions must be made available to the public.[220] Assertions based on proprietary and undisclosed data have no scientific credibility.
4. "We provide access to our data to trusted individuals outside our institution." Private Big Data resources may open their data to selected individuals who are highly trusted or who are willing to enter a limited use agreement that promises data confidentiality. Proprietary Big Data resources may issue licenses to data users. The license stipulates the purposes to which the resource can be used and encumbers the licensee with various restraints, obligations, and fees. Licensing a Big Data resource is the most disingenuous form of data sharing.

Much has been written about the importance of distributing deidentified records to the public, but very little deidentified data has actually been publicly released. In 2010, the U.S. Office of Civil Rights held a workshop on deidentification in the health care industry.

I spoke at this conference and delivered a set of recommendations, which are provided here, verbatim:

> Healthcare institutions and health researchers need deidentification methods to exchange, aggregate, and analyze data. Data used in research and in public policy analysis will ultimately need to be disclosed to the public; otherwise, the quality of the data and the validity of research results, cannot be evaluated. Currently, some of the methods used to deidentify health data are held by patent or are otherwise encumbered as intellectual property (e.g., licensed software). Healthcare workers and scientists who would like to deidentify records often do not know the methods that are freely available to them, and cannot assess whether any particular method is encumbered. I recommend that HHS collect a variety of public domain algorithms and software implementations that can be used for the common tasks in data deidentification. These would include free-text scrubbing algorithms, methods to identify and remove safe harbor identifiers, statistically valid ambiguation and obfuscation methods, relevant encryption protocols, and methods to safely reconcile patient identifiers within and across institutions (e.g., zero knowledge protocols). The most important function of EHR software involves assigning a unique code to each patient (sometimes called the patient identifier), that is assigned to every transaction for the patient, and that is not used for any other patient, within a healthcare environment. Reliable methods for creating and assigning unique patient codes involve humans and software. I strongly suggest that HHS collect a variety of methods for assigning and maintaining unique patient codes. I also suggest that if EHR systems are reviewed by a federal agency, the key element of review should be the human/computer protocols for patient identifiers.[222]

REDUCING COSTS AND INCREASING PRODUCTIVITY WITH BIG DATA

We tend to think of Big Data exclusively as an enormous source of data: for analysis and for fact finding. Perhaps we should think of Big Data as a money saver—something that helps us do our jobs more efficiently and at reduced cost. It is easy to see how instant access to industry catalogs, inventory data, transaction logs, and communication records can improve the efficiency of businesses. It is less easy to see how Big Data can speed up scientific research, an endeavor customarily based on labor-intensive and tedious experiments conducted by scientists and technicians in research laboratories. For many fields of science, the traditional approach to experimentation has reached its fiscal and temporal limits; the world lacks the money and the time to do research the old-fashioned way. Everyone is hoping for something to spark the next wave of scientific progress, and that spark may be Big Data.

Here is the problem facing scientists today. Scientific experiments have increased in scale, cost, and time, but the incremental progress resulting from each experiment is no greater today than it was in the early 1960s. In the field of medicine, the 50-year progress between 1910 and 1960 greatly outpaced progress between 1960 and 2010. Modern science has reached a state of diminishing returns on investment.

By 1960, industrial science reached the level that we see today. In 1960, we had home television (1947), transistors (1948), commercial jets (1949), computers (Univac, 1951), nuclear bombs (fission in 1945, fusion in 1952), solar cells (1954), fission reactors (1954), satellites orbiting the earth (Sputnik I, 1957), integrated circuits (1958), photocopying (1958), probes on the moon (Lunik II, 1959), practical business computers (1959), and lasers (1960). Nearly all the engineering and scientific advances that shape the world today were discovered prior to 1960.

These engineering and scientific advancements pale in comparison to the advances in medicine that occurred between 1910 and 1960. In 1921, we had insulin. Over the next four decades, we developed antibiotics effective against an enormous range of infectious diseases, including tuberculosis. Civil engineers prevented a wide range of common diseases using a clean water supply and improved waste management. Safe methods to preserve food, such as canning, refrigeration, and freezing, saved countless lives. In 1941, Papanicolaou introduced the smear technique to screen for precancerous cervical lesions, resulting in a 70% drop in the death rate from uterine cervical cancer, one of the leading causes of cancer deaths in women. By 1947, we had overwhelming epidemiologic evidence that cigarettes caused lung cancer. The first polio vaccine and the invention of oral contraceptives came in 1954. By the mid-1950s, the sterile surgical technique was widely practiced, bringing a precipitous drop in post-surgical and postpartum deaths. The great achievements in molecular genetics from Linus Pauling, James D. Watson, and Francis Crick came in the 1950s.

If the rate of scientific accomplishment is dependent upon the number of scientists on the job, you would expect that progress would be accelerating, not decelerating. According to the National Science Foundation, 18,052 science and engineering doctoral degrees were awarded in the United States in 1970. By 1997, that number had risen to 26,847, nearly a 50% increase in the annual production of the highest level scientists.[223] The growing work force of scientists failed to advance science at rates achieved in an earlier era, with fewer workers, but not for lack of funding. In 1953, according to the National Science Foundation, the total U.S. expenditures on research and development were $5.16 billion, expressed in current dollar values. In 1998, that number rose to $227.173 billion, greater than a 40-fold increase in research spending.[223]

The beginning of the end of high-speed progress may have come in the late 1960s and early 1970s with the advent of successful clinical trials for highly effective chemotherapeutic agents effective against a wide range of childhood cancers. These advances were made using large, randomized, prospective clinical trials. Subjects in these trials would be followed for years to determine survival rates in the control population (i.e., treated with standard drugs) and the test population (i.e., treated with an experimental drug). The prospective, randomized control trial, performed on children with cancer, was so very successful that it served as the required standard for drug testing over the next half century.

The problem has been that very few of the drugs tested on adults with cancer have had the kind of curative successes that we see with the childhood tumors. Larger, longer, and increasingly expensive studies were conducted to demonstrate incremental improvements in chemotherapeutic regimens. Over the decades, it became evident that tumors occurring in adults had different responses to therapeutic agents depending on the stage of the tumor (i.e., whether it had spread from its site of origin and, if so, the extent of spread) and on the presence or absence of various biological features (e.g., cytogenetic abnormalities, tumor cell receptors). These observations inspired additional clinical trials for the different subtypes of cancers. These rarefied trials required longer accrual times (i.e., the time required to recruit a statistically sufficient number of subjects) and tended to produce only incremental improvements. Overall, most drug trials are therapeutic failures; no improved outcome is found. The relative inefficiency of clinical trials has contributed to the high cost of developing new treatments; at least $1 billion per drug.

The shift toward testing drugs on populations of subjects has drastically increased the number of potential clinical trials. **Funders of medical research are slowly learning that there simply is not enough money or time to conduct all of the clinical trials that are needed** to advance medical science at a pace that is remotely comparable to the pace of medical progress in the first half of the 20th century. Despite all the wonderful scientific discoveries that are reported in the popular press, the benefits will be slow to arrive.

Big Data provides a way to accelerate scientific progress by giving researchers data that can expand or bypass the clinical trial process. In fact, much of what we know about public health is based on the analysis of large data collections (e.g., death certificate data, Medicare and Medicaid data sets, and cancer data sets); none of this knowledge comes from prospective trial data. By reviewing millions of medical records and billions of medical tests, researchers can find subpopulations of patients with a key set of clinical features that would qualify them for inclusion in customized trials. The biological effects of drugs, and the long-term clinical outcomes, can be assessed retrospectively on medical records in Big Data resources. The effects of different types of drugs or different drugs of the same kind (i.e., drugs of the same chemical or biological class) can be compared by analyzing large numbers of treated patients.

Perhaps the most important scientific application of Big Data will be as a validation tool for small data experiments. All experiments, including the most expensive prospective clinical trials, are human endeavors and are subject to all of the weaknesses and flaws that characterize human behavior.[224–226] Like any human endeavor, experiments must be validated, and the validation of an experiment, if repeated in several labs, will cost more than the original study. Using Big Data, it may be feasible to confirm that experimental findings based on small, prospective studies are consistent with observations made on very large populations.[227] In some cases, confirmatory Big Data observations, though not conclusive in themselves, may enhance our ability to select the most promising experimental studies for further analysis. Moreover, in the case of drug trials, observations of potential side effects, nonresponsive subpopulations, and serendipitous beneficial drug activities may be uncovered in a Big Data resource.

In the past, statisticians have criticized using retrospective data in drug evaluations. There are just too many biases and opportunities to reach valueless or misleading conclusions. Today, there is a growing feeling that we just do not have the luxury of abandoning Big Data. Using these large resources may be worth a try if we use the best available data and the best analytical methods and if our results are interpreted by objective, competent experts.

Today, statisticians are finding opportunities afforded by retrospective studies for establishing causality, once considered the exclusive domain of prospective experiments.[158,159,228] One of the most promising areas of Big Data study, over the next decade or longer, will be in the area of retrospective experimental design. The incentives are high. Funding agencies and corporations should ask themselves, before financing any large research initiative, whether the study can be performed using existing data held in Big Data resources.[229]

PUBLIC MISTRUST

It ain't what you don't know that gets you into trouble. It's what you know for sure that just ain't so. *Mark Twain*

Much of the reluctance to share data is based on mistrust. Corporations, medical centers, and other entities that collect data on individuals will argue, quite reasonably, that they have a fiduciary responsibility to the individuals whose data is held in their repositories. Sharing such data with the public would violate the privacy of their clients. Individuals agree. Few of us would choose to have our medical records, financial transactions, and the details of our personal lives examined by the public.

Recent campaigns have been launched against the "database state." Data privacy organizations include NO2ID, a British campaign against ID cards and a National Identity Register. Other antidatabase campaigns include TheBigOptOut.org, which campaigns against involuntary participation in the United Kingdom medical record database, and LeaveThemKidsAlone, protesting fingerprinting in schools.

When the identifying information that links a record to a named individual is removed, then the residual data becomes disembodied values and descriptors. Deidentified data poses no threat to humans, but it has great value for scientific research. The public receives the benefits of deidentified medical data every day. This data is used to monitor the incidence and the distribution of cancer, detect emerging infectious diseases, plan public health initiatives, appropriate public assistance funds, manage public resources, and monitor industrial hazards. Deidentified data collected from individuals provides objective data that describes us to ourselves. Without this data, society is less safe, less healthy, less smart, and less civilized.

Those of us who value our privacy and our personal freedom have a legitimate interest in restraining Big Data. Yet, we must admit that nothing comes free in this world. Individuals who receive the benefits of Big Data should expect to pay something back. In return for contributing private records to Big Data resources, the public should expect resources to apply the strictest privacy protocols to their data. Leaks should be monitored, and resources that leak private data should be disciplined and rehabilitated. Noncompliant resources should be closed.

There are about a billion people who have Facebook accounts wherein they describe the intimate details of their lives. This private information is hanging in the cloud, to be aggregated, analyzed, and put to all manner of commercial purposes. Yet many of these same Facebook users would not permit their deidentified medical records to be used to save lives. It would be ideal if there were no privacy or confidentiality risks associated with Big Data. Unfortunately, zero risk is not obtainable. However, it is quite possible to reduce the risk of privacy violations to something far, far below the known risks of identity theft that occur with every charge card transaction, every cashed check, and every Facebook posting.

SAVING US FROM OURSELVES

Man needs more to be reminded than instructed. *Samuel Johnson*

Ever since computers were invented, there has been a push towards developing decision-making algorithms. The idea has been that computers can calculate better and faster than humans and can process more data than humans. Given the proper data and algorithms, computers can make decisions better than humans. In some areas, this is true. Computers can beat us at chess, they can calculate missile trajectories, and they can crack encryption codes.

They can do many things better and faster than humans. In general, the things that computers do best are the things that humans cannot do at all.

If you look over the past half century of computer history, computers have not made much headway in the general area of decision making. Humans continue to muddle through their days, making their own decisions. We do not appoint computers to sit in juries, doctors seldom ask a computer for their diagnostic opinions, computers do not decide which grant applications receive funding, and computers do not design our clothing. Despite billions of dollars spent on research on artificial intelligence, the field of computer-aided decision making has fallen short of early expectations.[191,230–232] It seems we humans still prefer to make our own choices, unassisted.

Although computers play a minor role in helping us make correct decisions, they can play a crucial role in helping us avoid incorrect decisions. In the medical realm, medical errors account for about 100,000 deaths and about a million injuries each year in the United States.[233] Can we use Big Data to avoid such errors? The same question applies to driving errors, manufacturing errors, construction errors, and any realm where human errors have awful consequences.

It really does not make much sense, at this early moment in the evolution of computational machines, to use computers to perform tasks that we humans can do very well. It makes much more sense to use computers to prevent the kinds of errors that humans commit because we lack the qualities found in computers.

Big Data resources hold medical records, lists of drug interactions, normal values, manufacturing specifications, costs of equipment, and material information sheets; all of the information needed to check for many different types of human errors. Here are a few examples wherein computers may reduce human errors.

1. Drug prescription errors. Computer systems can suspend prescriptions for which doses exceed expected values, for which known drug interactions contraindicate use, or for which abuse is suspected (e.g., multiple orders of narcotics from multiple physicians for a single patient).
2. Blood transfusion errors. A computer can check that a patient's scanned bracelet identifier matches the scanned transfusion blood bag, that the screened blood components are compatible with the screened blood of the patient, and that the decision to perform the transfusion meets standard guidelines established by the hospital.
3. Identification errors. As discussed at length in Chapter 2, identifying individuals is a complex process that should involve highly trained staff, particularly during the registration process. Biometrics may help establish uniqueness (i.e., determining that an individual is not registered under another identifier) and authenticity (i.e., determining that an individual is who he claims to be). Computer evaluation of biometric data (e.g., fingerprints, iris imaging, retinal scan, signature, etc.) may serve as an added check against identification errors.
4. Rocket launch errors. Computers can determine when all sensors report normally (e.g., no frozen o-rings), when all viewed subsystems appear normal (e.g., no torn heat shield tiles hanging from the hull), when all systems are go (e.g., no abnormalities in the function of individual systems), and when the aggregate system is behaving normally (e.g., no conflicts between subsystems). Rockets are complex, and the job of monitoring every system for errors is a Big Data task.

5. Motor vehicle accidents. With everything we know about electronic surveillance, geopositioning technology, traffic monitoring, vehicle identification, and drug testing, you might think that we would have a method to reduce motor vehicle fatalities. Big Data resources could collect, analyze, and react to data collected from highways. More than 32,000 people die each year from traffic accidents in the United States.

6. Data entry errors. Data entry error rates are exceedingly common and range from about 2% to about 30% of entries, depending on various factors, including the data type (e.g., numeric or textual) and length of the entry.[234,235] The check digit is an example of a very simple computational method for reducing entry errors. The check digit is a number that is computed from a sequence (e.g., charge card number) and appended to the end of the sequence. If the sequence is entered incorrectly, the check digit will not be compatible with the incorrectly entered number, in most instances. The check digit has proven to be a very effective method for reducing data entry errors for identifiers and other important short sequences. A wide variety of check-digit algorithms are available.

As society becomes more and more complex, humans become less and less capable of avoiding errors. Computers have their own limitations, and their judgment may be inferior to that of humans, but a warning from a computer may help humans avoid making some highly regrettable mistakes.

HUBRIS AND HYPERBOLE

> Intellectuals can tell themselves anything, sell themselves any bill of goods, which is why they were so often patsies for the ruling classes in nineteenth-century France and England, or twentieth-century Russia and America. *Lillian Hellman*

I know lots of scientists; the best of them lack self-confidence. They understand that their data may be flawed, their assumptions may be wrong, their methods might be inappropriate, their conclusions may be unrepeatable, and their most celebrated findings may one day be discredited. The worst scientists and physicians are just the opposite—confident of everything they do, or say, or think.[236]

The sad fact is that, among scientific disciplines, Big Data is probably the least reliable, providing major opportunities for blunders. Prior chapters covered limitations in measurement, data representation, and methodology. The biases encountered in every Big Data analysis were covered in Chapter 10. Apart from these limitations lies the ever-present dilemma that assertions based on Big Data analyses can sometimes be validated, but they can never be proven true. Confusing validation with proof is a frequently encountered manifestation of overconfidence.

Validation is achieved when a data-related hypothesis provides a correct answer, whenever the hypothesis is tested. It is tempting to infer that if you have tested a hypothesis over and over again, and it always passes your tests, then you've proven that the hypothesis is true. Not so.

If you want to attain proof, you must become a mathematician; mathematics is the branch of science devoted to truth. With math, you can prove that an assertion is true, you can prove that an assertion is false, and you can prove that an assertion cannot be proven to be true or false. Mathematicians have the monopoly on proving things. None of the other sciences have the slightest idea what they're doing when it comes to proof.

In nonmathematical sciences, such as chemistry, biology, medicine, and astronomy, assertions are sometimes demonstrably valid (true when tested), but assertions never attain the level of a mathematical truth (proven that it will always be true, and never false, forever). Nonetheless, we can do a little better than showing that an assertion is simply valid. We can sometimes explain why an assertion ought to be true for every test, now and forever. To do so, an assertion should have an underlying causal theory that is based on interactions of physical phenomena that are accepted as true. For example, $F = ma$ ought to be true because we understand the concepts of mass and acceleration, and we can see why the product of mass and acceleration produce a force. Furthermore, everything about the assertion is testable in a wide variety of settings.

Big Data analysts develop models that are merely descriptive (e.g., predicting the behavior of variables in different settings), without providing explanations in terms of well-understood causal mechanisms. Trends, clusters, classes, recommenders, and so on may appear to be valid over a limited range of observations, but may fail miserably in tests conducted over time with a broader range of data. Big Data analysts must always be prepared to abandon beliefs that are not actually proven.[237]

Finance has eagerly entered the Big Data realm, predicting economic swings, stock values, buyer preferences, the impact of new technologies, and a variety of market reactions, all based on Big Data analysis. For many financiers, accurate short-term predictions have been followed, in the long run, with absolutely ruinous outcomes. In such cases, the mistake was overconfidence—the false belief that their analyses will always be correct.[238]

In my own field of concentration—cancer research—there has been a major shift of effort away from small experimental studies toward large clinical trials and so-called high-throughput molecular methods that produce vast arrays of data. This new generation of cancer research costs a great deal in terms of manpower, funding, and the time to complete a study. The funding agencies and the researchers are confident that a Big Data approach will work where other approaches have failed. Such efforts may one day lead to the eradication of cancer—who is to say? In the interim, we have already seen a great deal of time and money wasted on huge, data-intensive efforts that have produced predictions that are unreproducible and no more valuable than a random throw of dice.[89,90,224,239,240]

Despite the limitations of Big Data, the creators of Big Data cannot restrain their enthusiasm. The following is an announcement from the National Human Genome Research Institute (NHGRI) concerning its own achievements:

> In April 2003, NHGRI celebrated the historic culmination of one of the most important scientific projects in history: the sequencing of the human genome. In addition, April 2003 marked the 50th anniversary of another momentous achievement in biology: James Watson and Francis Crick's Nobel Prize winning description of the DNA double helix and to mark these achievements in the history of science and medicine, the NHGRI, the NIH and the DOE held a month-long series of scientific, educational, cultural and celebratory events across the United States.[241]

In the years following this 2003 announcement, it has become obvious that the genome is much more complex than previously thought, that common human diseases are genetically complex, that the genome operates through mechanisms that cannot be understood by examining DNA sequences, and that much of the medical progress expected from the Human Genome Project will not be forthcoming anytime soon.[239,242,243] In a 2011 article, Eric Lander, one of the luminaries of the Human Genome Project, was quoted as saying "anybody who thought in the year 2000 that we'd see cures in 2010 was smoking something."[243] Monica Gisler and coworkers have hypothesized that large-scale projects create their own "social bubble," inflating the project beyond any rational measure.[244] It is important that Big Data proselytizers, myself included, rein in their enthusiasm.

15

The Future

Prediction is very difficult, especially if it's about the future. **Niels Bohr**

BACKGROUND

Big Data is a trendy subject. The name "Big Data" is likely to morph, before too long, into some other term, better suited for tomorrow's zeitgeist. When I selected the topics for this book, I tried my best to avoid names of currently popular software applications, methods, and programming tools. My goal was to focus on the enduring, fundamental principles underlying the construction and analysis of large and complex information systems. I'd like to think that 10 or 20 years from this book's publication date, new readers will benefit from the discussions contained herein. As proof of the timeless quality of this book, I am setting forth a list of assertions, inferred from its contents, that will apply to the Big Data field over the next two decades. Before doing so, I call the reader's attention to the following predictions, provided by some of the most brilliant and influential leaders in the field of computation:

"Two years from now, spam will be solved."
–Bill Gates, founder of Microsoft Corporation, 2004
"The problem of viruses is temporary and will be solved in two years."
–John McAfee, 1988
"Computer viruses are an urban legend."
–Peter Norton, 1988
"I don't know what the language of the year 2000 will look like, but I know it will be called Fortran."
–C.A.R. Hoare, 1982
"In the future, computers may weigh no more than 1.5 tonnes."
–*Popular Mechanics*, 1949
"I see little commercial potential for the Internet for at least ten years."
–Bill Gates, 1994
"There is no reason why someone would want a computer in their home."
–Ken Olson, president and founder of Digital Equipment Corporation, 1977.
"No one will need more than 637 kb of memory for a personal computer. 640 K ought to be enough for anybody."
–Bill Gates, 1981
"Heavier-than-air flying machines are impossible."
–Lord Kelvin, ca. 1895, British mathematician and physicist
"Radio has no future."
–Lord Kelvin, ca. 1897
"Well informed people know it is impossible to transmit the voice over wires and that were it possible to do so, the thing would be of no practical value."
–*The Boston Post*, 1865
"I think there is a world market for maybe five computers."
–Thomas Watson, chairman IBM, 1943.

Bearing in mind the limitations of past prophets, here is a list of questions concerning the future of Big Data and my responses.

Will Big Data, Being Computationally Complex, Require a New Generation of Supercomputers?

> Plus ca change, plus c'est la meme chose. *Old French saying ("The more things change, the more things stay the same.")*

Big Data analysis never involves throwing a lot of data into a computer and waiting for the output to pop out. With very few exceptions, data analysis follows a stepwise process of data extraction (in response to queries), data filtering (removing noncontributory data), data transformation (changing the form, properties, and appearance of the data), and data scaling (capturing the behavior of the data in a formula), usually ending in a rather simple and somewhat anticlimactic result. The most important task, the validation of conclusions, involves repeated tests, over time, on new data or data obtained from other sources. These activities do not require the aid of a supercomputer.

Reports of data-intensive and computationally demanding efforts on image data (e.g., Picasa) and personal ratings (e.g., Netflix) should be received with skepticism. Some analytic methods are both computationally difficult (e.g., requiring comparisons on all possible combinations of data values) and highly iterative (e.g., requiring repetitions over large sets of data when new data is added or when old data is updated). Most are neither. When an analytic process takes a very long time (i.e., many hours), the likelihood is that the analysts have chosen an inappropriate or unnecessary algorithm or they have opted for analyzing a full data set when a representative sampling with a reduced set of variables would suffice. Though upgrading to a supercomputer or parallelizing the computation over many different computers is a viable option for well-funded and well-staffed projects, it need not be necessary. Simply rethinking the problem will often lead to an approach suited to a desktop computer.

Desktop computers are becoming much more powerful than they actually need to be for most analytical pursuits. In 2012, desktop computers, using top-performance graphics processing units (GPU), can operate at about two teraflops (i.e., two trillion floating point operations per second). This is about the same speed as the top-rated supercomputers built in the year 2000. Originally designed purely for games and graphics projects, GPU now support standard programming operations.

If Big Data analytics do not require the use of supercomputers, why bother investing in the cost of developing these machines? There are several reasons. Probably the most important reason is that building faster and more powerful supercomputers is something that we do very well. Today, the top supercomputers in the world achieve a speed of about 20 petaflops (20 thousand trillion operations per second). You cannot knock success. Aside from that, there are a range of problems for which highly precise or specific solutions are desired. Some of these solutions have great scientific, political, or economic importance. Examples are weather forecasting (e.g., long-range and global forecasting), nuclear weapon simulations, decryption, and dynamic molecular modeling (e.g., protein folding, Big Bang expansion, supernova events, complex chemical reactions).[245] Supercomputers crunch structured, well-formed data applied against well-defined problems. Life in the Big Data universe is seldom this simple. Computational optimists fully expect the supercomputers of tomorrow to digest Big Data resources and produce answers to the profound economic, sociologic, and scientific questions that elude current analyses. In all likelihood, events will not proceed in this fashion.

Before closing this question, readers should be warned that my opinion is highly contestable. The National Science Foundation foresees a need for a high-performance computational infrastructure to support analytic projects whose computational requirements exceed the capacity of personal computers.[246] Time will tell.

Will Big Data Achieve a Level of Complexity That Exceeds Our Ability to Fully Understand or Trust?

Yes; that time has already arrived. One of the basic problems associated with Big Data analysis is that there are too many ways to select data, too many ways to compose a question, too many analytic options, and too many opportunities to interpret the data to fit an agenda. In the near future, you will see an increasing number of instances wherein experts, with access to the same Big Data resources, arrive at diametrically opposite conclusions; each insisting that his or her analysis is flawless.

Will We Need Armies of Computer Scientists Trained with the Most Advanced Techniques in Supercomputing?

According to an industry report prepared by McKinsey Global Institute, the United States faces a current shortage of 140,000–190,000 professionals adept in the analytic methods required for Big Data.[247] The same group estimates that the United States needs an additional 1.5 million data-savvy managers.[247]

Analysis is important; it would be good to have an adequate workforce of professionals trained in a variety of computationally intensive techniques that can be applied to Big Data resources. Nevertheless, there is little value in applying advanced computational methods to poorly designed resources that lack introspection and data identification. A high-powered computer operated by a highly trained analyst cannot compensate for opaque or corrupted data. Conversely, when the Big Data resource is well designed, the task of data analysis becomes relatively straightforward.

At this time, we have a great many analytic techniques at our disposal, and we have open source software programs that implement these techniques. Every university offers computer science courses and statistics courses that teach these techniques. We will soon reach a time when there will be an oversupply of analysts and an undersupply of well-prepared data. When this time arrives, there will be a switch in emphasis from data analysis to data preparation. The greatest number of Big Data professionals will be those people who prepare data for analysis.

Will Big Data Create New Categories of Data Professionals for Which There Are Currently No Training Programs?

> Computer Science is no more about computers than astronomy is about telescopes. *Edsger W. Dijkstra*

In the near future, millions of people will devote large portions of their careers towards the design, construction, operation, and curation of Big Data resources. Who are the people best equipped for these tasks?

Resource builders:
    Big Data designers and design analysts
    Big Data indexers
    Metadata experts
    Domain experts
    Cross-resource data integrators
    Ontologists and classification experts
    Software programmers
    Data curators, including legacy experts

    Data managers, including database managers
    Network specialists
    Security experts
Resource users:
    Data analysts
    Generalist problem solvers
    People with solid programming skills (not full-time programmers)
    Combinatorics specialists
    Data reduction, data-scaling specialists
    Data visualizers
    Freelance Big Data consultants
    Everyone else

All of the professionals listed as "resource builders" are well-established members of the general field of information technology. These professionals can be assigned to a Big Data project and they can apply their skills without a great deal of retraining, in most cases. Their biggest adjustment will involve developing a productive working relationship with their team members. The database manager must understand why metadata and semantics are important. The network manager must understand the importance of legacy data. Team training is crucial in Big Data efforts, and training will be concentrated on helping each member understand the roles played by the other members.

Among the professionals listed as "resource users," some are new or nonexistent at the moment. Data analysts, of course, have been around for a long time. As discussed, most data analysts carry a set of methods that they have used successfully on small data problems. No doubt they will apply the same methods to Big Data, with varying results. The data analysts will be the ones who learn, from trial and error, which methods are computationally impractical on large sets of data, which methods provide results that have no practical value, which methods are unrepeatable, and which methods cannot be validated. The data analysts will also be the ones who try new methods and report on their utility. Because so many of the analytic methods on Big Data are overhyped, it will be very important to hire data analysts who are objective, honest, and resistant to bouts of hubris.

The most important new professional is the "generalist problem solver," a term I use to describe people who have a genuine interest in many different fields, have a naturally inquisitive personality, and have a talent for seeing relationships where others do not. The data held in Big Data resources becomes much more valuable when information from different knowledge domains leads to associations that enlighten either field (e.g., veterinary medicine and human medicine, bird migration and global weather patterns, ecologic catastrophes and epidemics of emerging diseases, political upheaval and economic cycles, social media and wages in African nations). For these kinds of problems, someone needs to create a new set of cross-disciplinary questions that could not have been asked prior to the creation of Big Data resources.

Historically, academic training narrows the interests of students and professionals. Students begin their academic careers in college, where they are encouraged to select a major field of study sometime in their freshman year. In graduate school, they labor in a subdiscipline, within a rigidly circumscribed department. As postdoctoral trainees, they narrow their interests even further. By the time they become tenured professors, their expertise is so limited that they cannot see how other fields relate to their own studies. The world will always need people who devote their professional careers to a single subdiscipline, to the exclusion of everything else, but the future will need fewer and fewer of these specialists.[237]

My experience has been that cross-disciplinary approaches to scientific problems are very difficult to publish in scientific journals that are, with few exceptions, devoted to one exclusive area of research. When a journal editor receives a manuscript that employs methods from another discipline, the editor is apt to reject the paper, indicating that it belongs in some other journal. Even when the editor recognizes that the study applies to a problem within the scope of the journal, the editor would have a very difficult time finding reviewers who can evaluate a set of methods from another field.

To get the greatest value from Big Data resources, it is important to understand when a problem in one field has equivalence to a problem from another field. The baseball analyst may have the same problem as the day trader; the astrophysicist may have the same problem as the chemist. We need to have general problem solvers who understand how data from one resource can be integrated with the data from other resources and how problems from one field can be generalized to other fields and answered with an approach that combines data and methods from several different disciplines. It is important that universities begin to train students as problem solvers, without placing them into restrictive academic departments.

Regarding programming skills, let's get serious. You simply cannot do creative work using off-the-shelf software applications. You will always encounter situations wherein software applications fail to meet your exact needs. In these cases it is impractical to seek the services of a full-time programmer. Today, programming is quite easy. Within a few hours, motivated students can pick up the rudiments of popular scripting languages such as Perl, Python, Ruby, and R. With few exceptions, the scripts needed for Big Data analysis are simple and can be written in under 20 lines of code.[19,65,248] It is not necessary for Big Data users to reach the level of programming proficiency held by full-time programmers. Programming is one of those subjects for which a small amount of preparation will usually suffice.

Another new specialty within Big Data is the "combinatorics specialist." Much of Big Data analytics involves combinatorics, the evaluation, on some numeric level, of combinations of things. Often, Big Data combinatorics involves pairwise comparisons of all possible combinations of data objects, searching for similarities, or proximity (a distance measure) of pairs. The goal of these comparisons often involves clustering data into similar groups, finding relationships among data that will lead to classifying the data objects, or predicting how data objects will respond or change under a particular set of conditions. When the number of comparisons becomes large, as is the case with virtually all combinatoric problems involving Big Data, the computational effort may become massive. For this reason, combinatorics research has become somewhat of a subspecialty for Big Data mathematics. There are four "hot" areas in combinatorics. The first involves building increasingly powerful computers capable of solving combinatoric problems for Big Data. The second involves developing methods whereby combinatoric problems can be broken into smaller problems that can be distributed to many computers to provide relatively fast solutions to problems that could not otherwise be solved in any reasonable length of time. The third area of research involves developing new algorithms for solving combinatoric problems quickly and efficiently. The fourth area, perhaps the most promising area, involves developing innovative noncombinatoric solutions for traditionally combinatoric problems.

Data reduction, data scaling, and data visualization have been discussed in earlier chapters. There will be a need for professionals who develop strategies for reducing the computational requirements of Big Data and for simplifying the way that Big Data is organized and examined. For example, persons who developed the CODIS DNA identification system relieved forensic analysts from the prodigious task of comparing and storing, for each sampled individual, the 3 billion base pairs that span the length of the human genome. Instead, a selection of 13 short sequences can suffice to identify individual humans (see Glossary item, Combined DNA Index System). Likewise, classification experts drive down the complexity of their knowledge domain by collecting data objects into related classes with shared and inherited properties. Similarly, data modelers reduce complex systems to a set of mathematical expressions. Experts who can simplify Big Data will be in high demand and will be employed in academic centers, federal agencies, and corporations.

The final new professional among the Big Data users is the "freelance Big Data scientist." This occupation will be created de novo, specifically for Big Data. These will be self-employed professionals who have the skills to unlock the secrets that lie within Big Data resources. When they work under contract for large institutions and corporations, they may be called consultants or freelance analysts. When they sell their data discoveries on the open market, they may be called entrepreneurial analysts. They will be the masters of data introspection, capable of quickly determining whether the data in a resource can yield the answers sought by their clients.

Some of these Big Data freelancers will have expertise limited to one or several Big Data resources—expertise that may have been acquired as a regular employee of an institution or corporation in the years preceding his or her launch into self-employment. Freelancers will have dozens, perhaps hundreds, of small utilities for data visualization and data analysis. When they need help with a problem, the freelancer might enlist the help of fellow freelancers. Subcontracted alliances can be arranged quickly through Internet-based services. The need for bricks-and-mortar facilities, for institutional support, or for employers and supervisors, will diminish.

The freelancer will need to understand the needs of his clients and will be prepared to help the clients redefine their specific goals within the practical constraints imposed by the available data. When the data within a resource is insufficient, the freelancer would be the best person to scout alternate resources. Basically, freelance analysts will live by their wits, exploiting the Big Data resources for the benefit of themselves and their clients.

Will Standardized Methods for Data Representation Be Uniformly Adopted, Thus Supporting Data Integration and Software Interoperability Across Networked Big Data Resources?

No, not anytime soon. Data managers are adept at providing necessary data services for their corporations and agencies. New paradigms of data representation, including RDF and many of the concepts discussed in the earlier chapters of this book (e.g., immutability, introspection, deidentification), are considered disruptive technologies in some quarters. For many data managers, trained to protect their data from prying eyes, the concept of data sharing is disturbing. Because the fundamental principles of Big Data design require information managers to undergo major cultural adjustments, it is likely that change will come slowly—over decades, not years. In the meantime, Big Data resources will fulfill a limited number of important goals, but effortless data integration will come much later.

Will Big Data Be Accessible to the Public?

A futurist is never wrong today. *Unknown*

This is the most important question confronting the future of Big Data: will it be open (to the public) or closed (to all but the data owners)? I am sad to say that most indicators point to a future where valuable information is private information. Information available to the public will be a subset of existing data, selected to achieve a commercial or political agenda. The reasons are listed here.

1. Deception works. When you have a large quantity of data, it is possible to analyze and interpret the data to support virtually any conclusion that suits your fancy. The propaganda value of Big Data should not be underestimated. To achieve the greatest effect, it is important to restrict access to primary data. Otherwise, adversaries and skeptics will use the data to obtain a contradictory conclusion.
2. Truth costs. Somebody must pay for the huge costs in developing and operating Big Data resources. It is likely that the costs will be recouped from the users. This means that access to Big Data will be restricted to those who own the data or to those who have the resources to pay for the data.
3. End users will be unattached to the data. In many cases, end users will be shielded from any direct involvement with Big Data resources. Here is an example from a hypothetical future. A clinician, seeking to determine the proper drug and dosage for a patient based on the patient's genetic profile, may send an information request to a pharmacogenomic data corporation. The corporation keeps a database holding the genetic sequence of every individual in the country. It performs an analysis on its own data and recommends a drug and a dosage based on the analysis. The doctor receives the recommendation and writes a prescription for the patient. This scenario is not very different from current projections discussed in a workshop sponsored by the National Academy of Sciences.[249] The doctor is not directly involved in the clinical recommendation, blindly trusting that the Big Data owners are acting in the best interests of the patient.
4. Size limits access. It is impractical to download terabytes of data, but the Big Data resources of the future will hold data in the petabyte, exabyte, and higher ranges. The Big Data resources will be "out there" somewhere. Nobody, not even the Big Data managers, will have backup copies of Big Data resources. In the time that a copy could be produced, the resource would have changed. This means that when the data held in a Big Data resource is open to the public, any individual's access to the data will be limited to the small portion of the resource that can be downloaded onto a personal computer at a specific point in time. Basically, no two assessments of a resource will be the same because the resource is constantly changing, and downloads are just samples of the resource.

5. Big Data is a high-risk game. Owners of Big Data resources are risk averse. This is especially true if their investments are great, if the resource contains information that would be valuable to competitors, if stolen, or if the resource contains confidential information. When stakes are high, the easiest security measure involves limiting access to the data. As larger and larger Big Data resources are created, it is likely that the data owners will shut access to the public.

6. Humans enjoy privacy. Individuals who consent to have their personal information included in a data resource will often insist that the data be kept private (i.e., accessible to the data owner, but not accessible to anyone else). My experience is that people insist on data privacy, even when they are told that the data records will be deidentified, removing all links between the data and the identities of the contributors. A primal reluctance to share personal data, coupled with mistrust in data deidentification methods, will limit access to Big Data resources that hold human subject data.

It is said that an informed public makes informed decisions. If this is true, then access to Big Data should improve the world. Unfortunately, for all the aforementioned reasons, data that becomes publicly available may soon be restricted to aggregated subsets that may not be representative of a full data set. It is discouraging to contemplate that we may now be in the last hours of the golden age of Big Data access. The world desperately needs a new generation of enlightened Big Data experts.

Will Big Data Do More Harm Than Good?

There is no escaping the fact that more and more of your personal information resides in Internet databases, for example: your health, your home, details of your employment, your relatives, your friends, close encounters with the judicial system, financial accounts and transactions, your purchases, your consumer preferences, your memberships to organizations, where you live, where you have visited, who you know, and everything you have contributed to the Internet, such as emails, blogs, list server entries, and Facebook comments. The same applies to just about everyone else on the planet.

It would be relatively easy for a totalitarian government, with access to detailed data on every person within its borders, to exert enormous control over the lives of its citizens. This is a common fear that rises whenever the future of Big Data is discussed. The collection of camera surveillance data is a good example of Big Data's double-edged sword. A Big Data resource collects information from thousands of cameras installed on buildings and other high structures, covering every street and open space in a city. The purpose of the Big Data resource is to decrease the incidence of crime and to increase the likelihood of apprehending and convicting criminals when crimes occur. The same surveillance data that enhances our safety may reduce our sense of personal freedom by holding us accountable for our every public movement. The next time you walk down a public street and notice a camera attached to a cornice, you may ask yourself, who will have access to the data, what will they do with the data, and where are the cameras that you did not notice?

In the future, Big Data will gradually push aside various honored social and political traditions. There may not be much need for voting if we come to believe that political, economic, social, and ethical preferences for a population can be accurately predicted from Big Data.

People may feel less inclined to interact on a personal level within their local communities when they can choose their friends and create virtual communities of similar-minded people by analyzing profiles of individuals contained in Big Data resources.

It takes time and experience to sort the wheat from the chaff. Current trends in the Big Data field would suggest that the next several decades will be marked by abuses. Societal effects will be, in many cases, detrimental. Those who stand to benefit most from Big Data will be the powers that create and control the resources: corporations, data brokers, and governments. Many of the best things to come from Big Data are long-term goals: personalized medicine, complete and accurate electronic medical records, crime prevention, error reduction in industry, effective system safety protocols, global resource management, rational food distribution, and universal human rights. The greatest benefits from Big Data will fall upon a population that has not yet been born.

Can We Expect That Big Data Catastrophes Will Disrupt Vital Services, Cripple National Economies, and Destabilize World Politics?

We have already seen it happen. The 2008 global economic crisis was essentially a failure to analyze Big Data correctly.[123] In hindsight, the data was there, but the people we trusted to run the economy let us down: financial experts, the vaunted numerati, our oversight agencies, and our automatic control systems. They all failed us when we needed them to steer a true course. Nothing has happened before or since that would lead us to think that future disasters will not follow.

Big Data is here, whether we approve or not. Like the atom bomb, Big Data is important precisely because it can hurt us very badly if we are not careful.

Will Big Data Provide Answers to Important Questions That Could Not Otherwise Be Solved?

Most thoughtful scientists will admit that really good questions are rare. It takes brilliance to ask the right questions, at the right time in history. The value of a Big Data resource is that a good analyst can start to see connections between different types of data, and this may prompt the analyst to determine whether there is a way to describe these connections in terms of general relationships among the data objects. Big Data provides quantitative methods to describe relationships, but these descriptions must be transformed into experimentally verified explanations. This last step, which is as close as scientists get to a true answer, takes the scientist outside the confines of Big Data.

Technically, Big Data does not produce answers. At best, Big Data points us in the direction of answers and inspires new questions. At worst, Big Data pretends to give us answers when it cannot.

LAST WORDS

When you have access to Big Data, you feel liberated; when Big Data has access to you, you feel enslaved. Everyone is familiar with the iconic image, from Orwell's *1984*, of a totalitarian government that watches its citizens from telescreens.[250] The ominous phrase "Big Brother is watching you" evokes an important thesis of Orwell's masterpiece—that a totalitarian government can use an expansive surveillance system to crush its critics. Lest anyone forget, Orwell's book had a second thesis that was, in my opinion, more insidious and more disturbing than the threat of governmental surveillance. Orwell was concerned that governments could change the past and the present by inserting, deleting, and otherwise distorting the information available to citizens. In Orwell's *1984*, old reports of military defeats, genocidal atrocities, ineffective policies, mass starvation, and any ideas that might foment unrest among the proletariat could all be deleted and replaced with propaganda pieces. Such truth-altering activities were conducted undetected, routinely distorting everyone's perception of reality to suit a totalitarian agenda. **Aside from understanding the dangers inherent in a surveillance-centric society, Orwell was alerting us to the dangers inherent with mutable Big Data.**

In 2009, *The New York Times* reported on a young man who was the victim of identity theft in China.[251] Another person had stolen his official record containing his academic credentials. With his official file gone, the victim was unable to find work in his field; he was robbed of his future. Repercussions associated with stolen, missing, altered, fictitious, or flawed data are likely to become a major problem as we rely more and more on our Big Data resources.

One of the purposes of this book is to describe the potential negative consequences of Big Data if the data is not collected ethically, not prepared thoughtfully, not analyzed openly, and not subjected to constant public review and correction. The culture of Big Data is inchoate, at present. The future reality of our Big Data universe will be determined by some of the people who are reading this book today.

Glossary

Accuracy and precision Accuracy measures how close your data comes to being correct. Precision provides a measurement of reproducibility (i.e., whether repeated measurements of the same quantity produce the same result). Data can be accurate but imprecise. If you have a 10-pound object and you report its weight as 7.2376 pounds every time you weigh the object, then your precision is remarkable, but your accuracy is dismal.

Algorithm Algorithms are perfect machines. They never make mistakes; they need no fuel; they never wear down; they are spiritual, not physical. The ability to use Big Data effectively depends on the availability of appropriate algorithms. In the past half-century, many brilliant algorithms have been developed for the kinds of computation-intensive work required for Big Data analysis.[107,252]

Annotation Annotation involves describing data elements with metadata or attaching supplemental information to data objects.

Anonymization versus deidentification Anonymization is a process whereby all the links between an individual and the individual's data record are irreversibly removed. The difference between anonymization and deidentification is that anonymization is irreversible. There is no method for reestablishing the identity of the patient from anonymized records. Deidentified records can, under strictly controlled circumstances, be reidentified. Reidentification is typically achieved by entrusting a third party with a confidential list that maps individuals to deidentified records. Obviously, reidentification opens another opportunity of harming individuals if the confidentiality of the reidentification list is breached. The advantage of reidentification is that suspected errors in a deidentified database can be found and corrected if permission is obtained to reidentify individuals. For example, if the results of a study based on blood sample measurements indicate that the original samples were mislabeled, it might be important to reidentify the samples and conduct further tests to resolve the issue. In a fully anonymized data set, the opportunities of verifying the quality of data are highly limited.

Artificial intelligence Artificial intelligence is the field of computer science that seeks to create machines and computer programs that seem to have human intelligence. The field of artificial intelligence sometimes includes the related fields of machine learning and computational intelligence. Over the past few decades, the term "artificial intelligence" has taken a battering from professionals inside and outside the field—for good reasons. First and foremost is that computers do not think in the way that humans think. Though powerful computers can now beat chess masters at their own game, the algorithms for doing so do not simulate human thought processes. Furthermore, most of the predicted benefits from artificial intelligence have not come to pass, despite decades of generous funding. The areas of neural networks, expert systems, and language translation have not met expectations. Detractors have suggested that artificial intelligence is not a well-defined subdiscipline within computer science, as it has encroached into areas unrelated to machine intelligence and has appropriated techniques from other fields, including statistics and numerical analysis. Some of the goals of artificial intelligence have been achieved (e.g., speech-to-text translation), and the analytic methods employed in Big Data analysis should be counted among the enduring successes of the field.

ASCII ASCII is the American Standard Code for Information Interchange, ISO-14962-1997. The ASCII standard is a way of assigning specific 8-bit strings (a string of 0's and 1's of length 8) to alphanumeric characters and punctuation. There are 256 ways of combining 0's and 1's in strings of length 8, and this means there are 256 different ASCII characters. Uppercase letters are assigned a different ASCII character than their lowercase equivalents. UNICODE, an expansion of ASCII, with a greater binary string length per character, accommodates non-Latin alphabets. See Binary.

Bayh–Dole Act (Patent and Trademark Amendments of 1980, P.L. 96-517) Adopted in 1980, U.S. Bayh–Dole legislation and subsequent extensions gave universities and corporations the right to keep and control any intellectual property (including data sets) developed under federal grants. The Bayh–Dole Act has provided entrepreneurial opportunities for researchers who work under federal grants, but has created conflicts of interest that should be disclosed to human subjects during the informed consent process. It is within the realm of possibility that a researcher who stands to gain considerable wealth, depending on the outcome of the project, may behave recklessly or dishonestly to achieve his or her ends.

Big Data resource A Big Data collection that is accessible for analysis. Readers should understand that there are collections of Big Data (i.e., data sources that are large, complex, and actively growing) that are not designed to support analysis; hence, not Big Data resources. Such Big Data collections might include some of the older hospital information systems, which were designed to deliver individual patient records, upon request, but could not support projects wherein all of the data contained in all of the records was opened for selection and analysis. Aside from privacy and security issues, opening a hospital information system to these kinds of analyses would place enormous computational stress on the systems (i.e., produce system crashes). In the late 1990s and the early 2000s, data warehousing was popular. Large organizations would collect all of the digital information created within their institutions, and these data were stored as Big Data collections, called data warehouses. If an authorized person within the institution needed some specific set of information (e.g., emails sent or received in February, 2003; all of the bills paid in November, 1999), it could be found somewhere within the warehouse. For the most part, these data warehouses were not true Big Data resources because they were not organized to support a full analysis of all of the contained data. Another type of Big Data collection that may or may not be considered a Big Data resource is compilations of scientific data that are accessible for analysis by private concerns, but closed for analysis by the public. In this case, a scientist may make a discovery, based on her analysis of a private Big Data collection, but the data collection is not open for unauthorized critical review. In the opinion of some scientists, including myself, if the results of a data analysis are not available for review, the analysis is illegitimate; the Big Data collection is never consummated as a true Big Data resource. Of course, this opinion is not universally shared, and Big Data professionals hold various definitions for a Big Data resource.

Binary data All digital information is coded as binary data; strings of 0's and 1's. In common usage, the term "binary data" is restricted to digital information that is not intended to be machine interpreted as alphanumeric characters (text). Binary data includes images, sound files, and movie files. Text files, also called plain-text files or ASCII files, are constructed so that every consecutive eight-bit digital sequence can be mapped to an ASCII character. Proprietary word processor files store alphanumeric data in something other than ASCII format, and these files are also referred to as binary files; not as text files. See ASCII.

Binary large object See BLOB.

Binary sizes Binary sizes are named in 1000-fold intervals, as shown.

1 bit = binary digit (0 or 1)
1 byte = 8 bits (the number of bits required to express an ASCII character)
1000 bytes = 1 kilobyte
1000 kilobytes = 1 megabyte
1000 megabytes = 1 gigabyte
1000 gigabytes = 1 terabyte
1000 terabytes = 1 petabyte
1000 petabytes = 1 exabyte
1000 exabytes = 1 zettabyte
1000 zettabytes = 1 yottabyte

Black box In physics, a black box is a device with observable inputs and outputs, but what goes on inside the box is unknowable. The term is used to describe software, algorithms, machines, and systems whose inner workings are inscrutable.

BLOB A large assemblage of binary data (e.g., images, movies, multimedia files, even collections of executable binary code) that are associated with a common group identifier and that can, in theory, be moved (from computer to computer) or searched as a single data object. Traditional databases do not easily handle BLOBs. BLOBs belong to Big Data.

Cherry-picking The process whereby data objects are chosen for some quality that is intended to boost the likelihood that an experiment is successful, but which biases the study. For example, a clinical trial manager might prefer patients who seem intelligent and dependable, and thus more likely to comply with the rigors of a long and complex treatment plan. By picking those trial candidates with a set of desirable attributes, the data manager is biasing the results of the trial, which may no longer apply to a real-world patient population.

Classifier A classifier is a method or algorithm that takes a data object and assigns it to its proper class within a pre-existing classification. Classifier algorithms should not be confused with clustering algorithms, which group data objects based on their similarities to one another. See Recommenders and Predictive analytics.

Cloud computing According to the U.S. National Institute of Standards and Technology (NIST), cloud computing enables "ubiquitous, convenient, on-demand network access to a shared pool of configurable computing resources (e.g., networks, servers, storage, applications, and services) that can be rapidly provisioned and released with minimal management effort or service provider interaction."[253] As the NIST definition would suggest, cloud computing is similar to Big Data, but there are several features that are expected in one and not the other. Cloud computing typically offers an interface and a collection of in-cloud computational services. Cloud data is typically contributed by a large community, and the contributed data is deposited often for no reason other than to provide convenient storage. These features are not expected in Big Data resources. Perhaps the most important distinction between cloud computing and Big Data relates to mutability. Because cloud data is contributed by many different entities, for many purposes, nobody expects much constancy; data can be freely extracted from the cloud or modified in place. In the cloud, the greatest emphasis is placed on controlling computational access to cloud data, with less emphasis on controlling the content of the cloud. In contrast, Big Data resources are designed to achieve a chosen set of goals using a constructed set of data. In most cases, the data held in a Big Data resource is immutable. Once it is entered into the resource, it cannot be modified or deleted without a very good reason.

Combined DNA Index System (CODIS) A large database prepared from human DNA samples. In CODIS the DNA is extracted and 13 short tandem repeat fragments are selected from predetermined locations in the genome. The 13 fragments are sequenced, and the sequence data is stored in the CODIS database. The CODIS sequences are intended to uniquely identify individuals (or their identical twins). New DNA samples from the same individual should always match the stored CODIS sequence. CODIS is used primarily by law enforcement.

Confidentiality and privacy See Privacy and confidentiality.

Confounder Unanticipated or ignored factor that alters the outcome of a data analysis. Confounders are particularly important in Big Data analytics because most analyses are observational, based on collected parameters from large numbers of data records, and there is very little control over confounders. Confounders are less of a problem in controlled prospective experiments, in which a control group and a treated group are alike, to every extent feasible—only differing in their treatment. Differences between the control group and the treated group are presumed to be caused by the treatment, as the confounders have been eliminated. One of the greatest challenges of Big Data analytics involves developing new analytic protocols that reduce the effect of confounders in observational studies.

Correlation distance or correlation score The correlation distance provides a measure of similarity between two variables. Two similar variables will rise rise and fall together. The Pearson correlation score is popular and can be easily implemented.[19,105] It produces a score that varies from -1 to 1. A score of 1 indicates perfect correlation; a score of -1 indicates perfect anticorrelation (i.e., one variable rises while the other falls). A Pearson score of 0 indicates a lack of correlation. Other correlation measures can be applied to Big Data sets.[109,110]

Curator The word "curator" derives from the Latin curatus, the same root for "curative," and conveys that curators "take care of" things. In a Big Data resource, the curator must accrue legacy and prospective data into the resource, must ensure that there is an adequate protocol for verifying the data, must choose appropriate nomenclatures for annotating the data, must annotate the data, and must make appropriate adjustments to data annotations when new versions of nomenclatures are made available and when one nomenclature is replaced by another.

Curse of dimensionality As the number of attributes for a data object increases, the distance between data objects grows to enormous size. The multidimensional space becomes sparsely populated and the distances between any two objects, even the two closest neighbors, becomes absurdly large. When you have thousands of dimensions, the space that holds the objects is so large that distances between objects become difficult or impossible to compute, and computational results become useless for most purposes.

Data cleaning Synonymous with data fixing or data correcting, data cleaning is the process by which errors, inexplicable anomalies, and missing values are somehow handled. There are three options for data cleaning: correcting the error, deleting the error, or leaving it unchanged.[143] Data cleaning should not be confused with data scrubbing. See Data scrubbing.

Data manager This book uses "data manager" as a catch-all term, without attaching any specific meaning to the name. Depending on the institutional and cultural milieu, synonyms and plesionyms (i.e., near-synonyms) for data manager would include technical lead, team liaison, data quality manager, chief curator, chief of operations, project manager, group supervisor, and so on.

Data object A commonly used but somewhat inelegant definition for a data object is "the thing that the data values are about." In a medical record, the data object might be a patient and the data values might be the patient's blood chemistries. A well-specified data object has an identifier and is capable of encapsulating data values, metadata, and other self-descriptive data, such as the name of a class in which the data object holds membership. In the object-oriented paradigm, every data object is a member of a class and inherits the methods that belong to its class, as well as all of the methods of all the classes in its ancestral lineage. As a member of a class, it shares a set of class properties with the other members of its class. A class is itself a type of data object. Data objects are the subjects of meaningful assertions. See Meaning.

Data object model The data object model is a term defined for object-oriented programming languages, but it is often applied in vague ways to Big Data resources. In the context of Big Data, the term applies to the way that data objects are described and organized in the resource and to the manner in which objects interface to the resource for purposes of searching, retrieving, and exchanging whole data objects (e.g., records) and their data attributes (e.g., data values in the records). Those who read the Big Data literature extensively will find that this term is used in many different ways and is often confused with its plesionym, data modeling. See Modeling.

Data point The singular form of data is datum. Strictly speaking, the term should be datum point or datumpoint. Most information scientists, myself included, have abandoned consistent usage rules for the word "data." In this book, the term "data" always refer collectively to information, numeric or textual, structured or unstructured, in any quantity.

Data Quality Act Passed as part of the FY 2001 Consolidated Appropriations Act (Pub. L. No. 106-554), the act requires federal agencies to base their policies and regulations on high-quality data and permits the public to challenge and correct inaccurate data.[194] For an in-depth discussion, see Chapter 13.

Data reduction In almost all circumstances, it is impractical to work with all of the data in a Big Data resource. When the data analysis is confined to a set of data extracted from the resource, it may be impractical or counterproductive to work with every element of the collected data. In most cases, the data analyst will eliminate some or most of the data elements or will develop methods whereby the data is approximated. The term "data reduction" is sometimes reserved for methods that reduce the dimensionality of multivariate data sets. In this book, the term "data reduction" is applied to any method whereby items of data are excluded from a data set or are replaced by a simplified transformation or by a mathematical formula that represents values. Obviously, data reduction, if done unwisely, will create biases. See Mean-field approximations. See Dimensionality.

Data scrubbing A term that is very similar to data deidentification and is sometimes used improperly as a synonym for data deidentification. Data scrubbing refers to the removal, from data records, of identifying information (i.e., information linking the record to an individual) plus any other information that is considered unwanted. This may include any personal, sensitive, or private information contained in a record, any incriminating or otherwise objectionable language contained in a record, and any information irrelevant to the purpose served by the record. See Deidentification.

Data sharing Data sharing involves one entity sending data to another entity, usually with the understanding that the other entity will store and use the data. This process may involve free or purchased data, and it may be done willingly, or in compliance with regulations, laws, or court orders.

Deep analytics Jargon occasionally applied to the skill set needed for Big Data analysis. Statistics and machine learning are often cited as two of the most important areas of deep analytic expertise. In a recent McKinsey report, entitled "Big data: The next frontier for innovation, competition, and productivity," the authors asserted that the United States "faces a shortage of 140,000 to 190,000 people with deep analytical skills."[247]

Deidentification The process of removing all of the links in a data record that can connect the information in a record to an individual. This usually includes the record identifier, demographic information (e.g., place of birth), personal information (e.g., birthdate), biometrics (e.g., fingerprints), and so on. The process of deidentification will vary based on the type of records included in the Big Data resource. For an in-depth discussion, see Chapter 2. See Reidentification. See Data scrubbing.

Digital Millennium Copyright Act (DMCA) This act was signed into law in 1998. This law deals with many different areas of copyright protection, most of which are only peripherally relevant to Big Data. In particular, the law focuses on copyright protections for recorded works, particularly works that have been theft-protected by the copyright holders.[199] The law also contains a section (Title II) dealing with the obligations of online service providers who inadvertently distribute copyrighted material. Service providers may be protected from copyright infringement liability if they block access to the copyrighted material when the copyright holder or the holder's agent claims infringement. To qualify for liability protection, service providers must comply with various guidelines (i.e., the so-called safe harbor guidelines) included in the act.

Dimensionality The dimensionality of a data objects consists of the number of attributes that describe the object. Depending on the design and content of the data structure that contains the data object (i.e., database, array, list of records, object instance), the attributes will be called by different names, including field, variable, parameter, feature, or property. Data objects with high dimensionality create computational challenges, and data analysts typically reduce the dimensionality of data objects wherever possible. See Chapter 9.

DMCA See Digital Millennium Copyright Act

Dublin Core metadata The Dublin Core is a set of metadata elements developed by a group of librarians who met in Dublin, Ohio. It would be very useful if every electronic document were annotated with the Dublin Core elements. The Dublin Core Metadata is discussed in detail in Chapter 4. The syntax for including the elements is found at http://dublincore.org/documents/dces/.

Dynamic range Every measuring device has a dynamic range beyond which its measurements are without meaning. A bathroom scale may be accurate for weights that vary from 50 to 250 pounds, but you would not expect it to produce a sensible measurement for the weight of a mustard seed or an elephant.

Electronic medical record Abbreviated as EMR or EHR (electronic health record), the EMR is the digital equivalent of a patient's medical chart. Central to the idea of the EMR is the notion that all of the documents, transactions, and all packets of information containing test results and other information on a patient are linked to the patient's unique identifier. By retrieving all data linked to the patient's identifier, the EMR (i.e., the entire patient's chart) can be assembled instantly.

Euclidean distance Two points, $(x1, y1)$, $(x2, y2)$, in Cartesian coordinates are separated by a hypotenuse distance, that being the square root of the sum of the squares of the differences between the respective x axis and y axis coordinates. In n-dimensional space, the Euclidean distance between two points is the square root of the sum of the squares of the differences in coordinates for each of the n-dimensional coordinates. The significance of the Euclidean distance for Big Data is that data objects are often characterized by multiple feature values, and these feature values can be listed as though they were coordinate values for an n-dimensional object. The smaller the Euclidian distance between two objects, the higher the similarity to each other. Several of the most popular correlation and clustering algorithms involve pairwise comparisons of the Euclidean distances between data objects in a data collection.

Fourier series Periodic functions (i.e., functions with repeating trends in the data, including waveforms and periodic time series data) can be represented as the sum of oscillating functions (i.e., functions involving sines, cosines, or complex exponentials). The summation function is the Fourier series. See Fourier transform.

Fourier transform A transform is a mathematical operation that takes a function or a time series (e.g., values obtained at intervals of time) and transforms it into something else. An inverse transform takes the transform function and produces the original function. Transforms are useful when there are operations that can be more easily performed on the transformed function than on the original function. Possibly the most useful transform is the Fourier transform, which can be computed with great speed on modern computers using a modified form known as the fast Fourier transform. Periodic functions and waveforms (periodic time series) can be transformed using this method. Operations on the transformed function can sometimes eliminate periodic artifacts or frequencies that occur below a selected threshold (e.g., noise). The transform can be used to find similarities between two signals. When the operations on the transform function are complete, the inverse of the transform can be calculated and substituted for the original set of data.

Gaussian copula function A formerly honored and currently vilified formula developed for Wall Street that calculated the risk of default correlation (i.e., the likelihood of two investment vehicles defaulting together). The formula uses the current market value of the vehicles, without factoring in historical data. The formula is easy to implement and became a favorite model for calculating risk in the securitization market. The Gaussian copula function was the driving model on Wall Street. In about 2008, the function stopped working; soon thereafter came the 2008 global market collapse. In some circles, the Gaussian copula function is blamed for the disaster.[123]

Grid A collection of computers and computer resources that are coordinated to provide a desired functionality. The grid is the intellectual predecessor of cloud computing. Cloud computing is less physically and administratively restricted than grid computing. See Cloud computing.

Heterogeneous data Sets of data that are dissimilar with regard to content, purpose, format, organization, and annotations. One of the purposes of Big Data is to discover relationships among heterogeneous data sources. For example, epidemiologic data sets may be of service to molecular biologists who have gene sequence data on diverse human populations. The epidemiologic data is likely to contain different types of data values, annotated and formatted in a manner that is completely different from the data and annotations in a gene sequence database. The two types of related data, epidemiologic and genetic, have dissimilar content; hence they are heterogeneous to one another.

Human Genome Project The Human Genome Project is a massive bioinformatics project in which multiple laboratories contributed to sequencing the 3 billion base pair haploid human genome (i.e., the full sequence of human DNA). The project began its work in 1990, a draft human genome was prepared in 2000, and a completed genome was finished in 2003, marking the start of the so-called postgenomics era. All of the data produced for the Human Genome Project is freely available to the public.

Identification The process of providing a data object with an identifier or distinguishing one data object from all other data objects on the basis of its associated identifier. See Identifier.

Identifier A string that is associated with a particular thing (e.g., person, document, transaction, data object) and not associated with any other thing.[254] In the context of Big Data, identification usually involves permanently assigning a seemingly random sequence of numeric digits (0–9) and alphabet characters (a–z and A–Z) to a data object. The data object can be a class of objects. See Identification.

Immutability Immutability is the principle that data collected in a Big Data resource is permanent and can never be modified. At first thought, it would seem that immutability is a ridiculous and impossible constraint. In the real world, mistakes are made, information changes, and the methods for describing information changes. This is all true, but the astute Big Data manager knows how to accrue information into data objects without changing the preexisting data. Methods for achieving this seemingly impossible trick are described in Chapter 6.

Indexes Every writer must search deeply into his or her soul to find the correct plural form of "index." Is it "indexes" or is it "indices?" Latinists insist that "indices" is the proper and exclusive plural form. Grammarians agree, reserving "indexes" for the third person singular verb form: "The student indexes his thesis." Nonetheless, popular usage of the plural of "index," referring to the section at the end of a book, is almost always "indexes," the form used herein.

Informed consent Human subjects who are put at risk must provide affirmative consent if they are to be included in a government-sponsored study. This legally applies in the United States and most other nations and ethically applies to any study that involves putting humans at risk. To this end, researchers provide prospective human subjects with an "informed consent" document that informs the subject of the risks of the study and discloses foreseen financial conflicts among the researchers (see Glossary item, Bayh–Dole Act). The informed consent must be clear to laymen, must be revocable (i.e., subjects can change their mind and withdraw from the study, if feasible to do so), must not contain exculpatory language (e.g., no waivers of responsibility for the researchers), must not promise any benefit or monetary compensation as a reward for participation, and must not be coercive (i.e., must not suggest a negative consequence as a result of nonparticipation).

Integration This occurs when information is gathered from multiple data sets, relating diverse data extracted from different data sources. Integration can broadly be categorized as being pre-integrated or as being integrated on the fly. Pre-integration includes such efforts as absorbing new databases into a Big Data resource or merging legacy data with current data. On-the-fly integration involves merging data objects at the moment when the individual objects are parsed. This might be done during a query that traverses multiple databases or multiple networks. On-the-fly data integration can only work with data objects that support introspection. The two closely related topics of integration and interoperability are often confused with one another. An easy way to remember the difference is to note that *integration refers to data; interoperability refers to software.*

Intellectual property Data, software, algorithms, and applications that are created by an entity capable of ownership (e.g., humans, corporations, universities). The entity holds rights over the manner in which the intellectual property can be used and distributed. Protections for intellectual property may come in the form of copyrights, patents, and license agreements. Copyright applies to published information. Patents apply to novel processes and inventions. Certain types of intellectual property can only be protected by being secretive. For example, magic tricks cannot be copyrighted or patented, which is why magicians guard their intellectual property so closely. Intellectual property can be sold outright, essentially transferring ownership to another entity. In other cases, intellectual property is retained by the creator who permits its limited use to others via a legal contrivance (e.g., license, contract, transfer agreement, royalty, usage fee, and so on). In some cases, ownership of the intellectual property is retained, but the property is freely shared with the world (e.g., open source license, GNU license, FOSS license, Creative Commons license).

Introspection Well-designed Big Data resources support introspection, a method whereby data objects within the resource can be interrogated to yield their properties, values, and class membership. Through introspection, the relationships among the data objects in the Big Data resource can be examined and the structure of the resource can be determined. Introspection is the method by which a data user can find everything there is to know about a Big Data resource, without downloading the complete resource. For an in-depth discussion, see Chapter 4.

ISO/IEC 11179 The standard produced by the International Standards Organization (ISO) for defining metadata, such as XML tags. The standard requires that the definitions for metadata used in XML (the so-called tags) be accessible and should include the following information for each tag: Name (the label assigned to the tag), Identifier (the unique identifier assigned to the tag), Version (the version of the tag), Registration Authority (the entity authorized to register the tag), Language (the language in which the tag is specified), Definition (a statement that clearly represents the concept and essential nature of the tag), Obligation (indicating whether the tag is required), Datatype (indicating the type of data that can be represented in the value of the tag), Maximum Occurrence (indicating any limit to the repeatability of the tag), and Comment (a remark describing how the tag might be used).

KISS Acronym for Keep It Simple Stupid. With respect to Big Data, there are basically two schools of thought. The first is that reality is quite complex; the advent of powerful computers and enormous data collections allows us to tackle important problems, despite their inherent size and complexity. KISS represents a second school of thought: that big problems are just small problems that are waiting to be simplified.

k-means algorithm The k-means algorithm assigns any number of data objects to one of k clusters.[107] The algorithm is described fully in Chapter 9. The k-means algorithm should not be confused with the k-nearest neighbor algorithm.

k-nearest neighbor algorithm A simple and popular classifier algorithm that assigns a class (in a preexisting classification) to an object whose class is unknown.[107] The k-nearest neighbor is very simple. From a collection of data objects whose class is known, the algorithm computes the distances from the object of unknown class to k (a number chosen by the user) objects of known class. The most common class (i.e., the class that is assigned most often to the nearest k objects) is assigned to the object of unknown class. The k-nearest neighbor algorithm and its limitations are discussed in Chapter 9. The k-nearest neighbor algorithm, a classifier method, should not be confused with the k-means algorithm, a clustering method.

Large Hadron Collider (LHC) The LHC is the world's largest and most powerful particle accelerator, and is expected to produce about 15 petabytes (15 million gigabytes) of data annually.[255]

Linear regression A method for obtaining a straight line through a two-dimensional scatter plot. It is not, as it is commonly believed, a "best-fit" technique, but it does minimize the sum of squared errors (in the y axis values) under the assumption that the x axis values are correct and exact. This means that you would get a different straight line if you regress x on y rather than y on x. Linear regression is a popular method that has been extended, modified, and modeled for many different processes, including machine learning. Data analysts who use linear regression should be cautioned that it is a method, much like the venerable p value, that is commonly misinterpreted.[104] See p value.

Mahalanobis distance A distance measure based on correlations between variables; hence, it measures the similarity of the objects whose attributes are compared. As a correlation measure, it is not influenced by the relative scale of the different attributes. It is used routinely in clustering and classifier algorithms. See Euclidean distance.

MapReduce A method by which computationally intensive problems can be processed on multiple computers in parallel. The method can be divided into a mapping step and a reducing step. In the mapping step, a master computer divides a problem into smaller problems that are distributed to other computers. In the reducing step, the master computer collects the output from the other computers. Although MapReduce is intended for Big Data resources, holding petabytes of data, most Big Data problems do not require MapReduce.

Mean-field approximation A method whereby the average behavior for a population of objects substitutes for the behavior of each and every object in the population. This method greatly simplifies calculations. It is based on the observation that large collections of objects can be characterized by their average behavior. Mean-field approximation has been used with great success to understand the behavior of gases, epidemics, crystals, viruses, and all manner of large population phenomena.

Meaning In informatics, meaning is achieved when described data is bound to a unique identifier of a data object. "Jules J. Berman's height is five feet eleven inches" comes pretty close to being a meaningful statement. The statement contains data (five feet eleven inches), and the data is described (height). The described data belongs to a unique object (Jules J. Berman). If this data were entered into a Big Data resource, it would need a unique identifier to distinguish one instance of Jules J. Berman from all the other persons who are named Jules J. Berman. The statement would also benefit from a formal system that ensures that the metadata makes sense (e.g., what exactly is height and does Jules J. Berman fall into a class of objects for which height is an allowable property?) and that the data is appropriate (e.g., is 5 feet 11 inches an allowable measure of a person's height?). A statement with meaning does not need to be a true statement (e.g., the height of Jules J. Berman was not 5 feet 11 inches when Jules J. Berman was an infant). See Semantics.

Metadata Data that describes data. For example, in XML a data quantity may be flanked by a beginning and an ending metadata tag describing the included data. <age>48 years</age>. In the example, <age> is the metadata and "48 years" is the data.

Minimal necessary In the field of medical informatics, there is a concept known as "minimal necessary" that applies to shared confidential data.[33] It holds that when records are shared, only the minimum necessary information should be released. Information not directly relevant to the intended purposes of the study should be withheld.

Missing data Most complex data sets have missing data values. Somewhere along the line data elements were not entered, records were lost, or some systemic error produced empty data fields. Big Data, being large, complex, and composed of data objects collected from diverse sources, is almost certain to have missing data. Various mathematical approaches to missing data have been developed, commonly involving assigning values on a statistical basis; so-called imputation methods. The underlying assumption for such methods is that missing data arises at random. When missing data arises nonrandomly, there is no satisfactory statistical fix. The Big Data curator must track down the source of the errors and somehow rectify the situation. In either case, the issue of missing data introduces a potential bias, and it is crucial to fully document the method by which missing data is handled. In the realm of clinical trials, only a minority of data analyses bother to describe their chosen method for handling missing data.[256] See Data cleaning.

Modeling Modeling involves explaining the behavior of a system, often with a formula, sometimes with descriptive language. The formula for the data describes the distribution of the data and often predicts how the different variables will change with one another. Consequently, modeling comes closer than other Big Data techniques to explaining the behavior of data objects and of the system in which the data objects interact. The topic of modeling is discussed in Chapter 9. Data modeling is often confused with the task of creating a data object model. See Data object model.

Monte Carlo simulation This technique was introduced in 1946 by John von Neumann, Stan Ulam, and Nick Metropolis.[252] For this technique, the computer generates random numbers and uses the resultant values to simulate repeated trials of a probabilistic event. Monte Carlo simulations can easily simulate various processes (e.g., Markov models and Poisson processes) and can be used to solve a wide range of problems.[98,257] The Achilles heel of the Monte Carlo simulation, when applied to enormous sets of data, is that so-called random number generators may introduce periodic (nonrandom) repeats over large stretches of data.[38] What you thought was a fine Monte Carlo simulation, based on small data test cases, may produce misleading results for large data sets. The wise Big Data analyst will avail himself of the best possible random number generators and will test his outputs for randomness. Various tests of randomness are available.[111]

Multiple comparisons bias When you compare a control group against a treated group using multiple hypotheses based on the effects of many different measured parameters, you will eventually encounter statistical significance, based on chance alone. For example, if you are trying to determine whether a population that has been treated with a particular drug is likely to suffer a serious clinical symptom, and you start looking for statistically significant associations (e.g., liver disease, kidney disease, prostate disease, heart disease, etc.), then eventually you will find an organ in which disease is more likely to occur in the treated group than in the untreated group. Because Big Data tends to have high dimensionality, biases associated with multiple comparisons must be carefully avoided. Methods for reducing multiple comparison bias are available to Big Data analysts. They include the Bonferroni correction, the Sidak correction, and the Holm–Bonferroni correction.

Mutability Mutability refers to the ability to alter the data held in a data object or to change the identity of a data object. Serious Big Data is not mutable. Data can be added, but data cannot be erased or altered. Big Data resources that are mutable cannot establish a sensible data identification system and cannot support verification and validation activities. For a full discussion of mutability and immutability, as it applies to Big Data resources, see Chapter 9.

n3 See Notation 3.

Namespace A namespace is the metadata realm in which a metadata tag applies. The purpose of a namespace is to distinguish metadata tags that have the same name, but a different meaning. For example, within a single XML file, the metadata term "date" may be used to signify a calendar date, the fruit, or the social engagement. To avoid confusion, the metadata term is given a prefix that is associated with a Web document that defines the term within the document's namespace. See Chapter 4.

Negative study bias When a project produces negative results (fails to confirm a hypothesis), there may be little enthusiasm to publish the work.[258] When statisticians analyze the results from many different published manuscripts (i.e., perform a meta-analysis), their work is biased by the pervasive absence of negative studies.[259] In the field of medicine, negative study bias creates a false sense that every kind of treatment yields positive results.

Neural network A dynamic system in which outputs are calculated by a summation of weighted functions operating on inputs. Weights for the individual functions are determined by a learning process, simulating the learning process hypothesized for human neurons. In the computer model, individual functions that contribute to a correct output (based on the training data) have their weights increased (strengthening their influence to the calculated output). Over the past 10 or 15 years, neural networks have lost some favor in the artificial intelligence community. They can become computationally complex for very large sets of multidimensional input data. More importantly, complex neural networks cannot be understood or explained by humans, endowing these systems with a "magical" quality that some scientists find unacceptable. See Nongeneralizable predictor. See Overfitting.

Nomenclature A nomenclature is a specialized vocabulary, usually containing terms that comprehensively cover a well-defined field of knowledge. For example, there may be a nomenclature of diseases, celestial bodies, or makes and models of automobiles. Some nomenclatures are ordered alphabetically. Others are ordered by synonymy, wherein all synonyms and plesionyms (near-synonyms) are collected under a canonical (best or preferred) term. In many nomenclatures, grouped synonyms are collected under a code (unique alphanumeric string) assigned to the group. Nomenclatures have many purposes: to enhance interoperability and integration, to allow synonymous terms to be retrieved regardless of which specific synonym is entered as a query, to support comprehensive analyses of textual data, to express detail, to tag information in textual documents, and to drive down the complexity of documents by uniting synonymous terms under a common code. Sets of documents held in more than one Big Data resource can be harmonized under a nomenclature by substituting or appending a nomenclature code to every nomenclature term that appears in any of the documents. See Classification. See Vocabulary.

Nongeneralizable predictor Sometimes Big Data analysis can yield results that are true, but nongeneralizable (i.e., irrelevant to everything outside the set of data objects under study). The most useful scientific findings are generalizable (e.g., the laws of physics operate on the planet Jupiter or the star Alpha Centauri much as they do on earth). Many of the most popular analytic methods for Big Data are not generalizable because they produce predictions that only apply to highly restricted sets of data or the predictions are not explainable by any underlying theory that relates input data with the calculated predictions. Data analysis is incomplete until a comprehensible, generalizable, and testable theory for the predictive method is developed.

Notation 3 Also called n3. A syntax for expressing assertions as triples (unique subject + metadata + data). Notation 3 expresses the same information as the more formal RDF syntax, but n3 is compact and easy for humans to read. Both n3 and RDF can be parsed and equivalently tokenized (i.e., broken into elements that can be reorganized in a different format, such as a database record). See RDF.

Object-oriented programming In object-oriented programming, all data objects must belong to one of the classes built into the language or to a class created by the programmer. Class methods are subroutines that belong to a class. The members of a class have access to the methods for the class. There is a hierarchy of classes (with superclasses and subclasses). A data object can access any method from any superclass of its class. All object-oriented programming languages operate under this general strategy. The two most important differences among the object-oriented programming languages relate to syntax (i.e., the required style in which data objects call their available methods) and content (the built-in classes and methods available to objects). Various esoteric issues, such as types of polymorphism offered by the language, multiparental inheritance, and non-Boolean logic operations, may play a role in how expert programmers choose a specific language for a specific project. See Data object.

Object rank A generalization of PageRank, the indexing method employed by Google. Object ranking involves providing objects with a quantitative score that provides some clue to the relevance or the popularity of an object. For the typical object ranking project, objects take the form of a key word phrase. See Page rank.

One-way hash A one-way hash is an algorithm that transforms one string into another string (a fixed-length sequence of seemingly random characters) in such a way that the original string cannot be calculated by operations on the one-way hash value (i.e., the calculation is one way only). One-way hash values can be calculated for any string, including a person's name, a document, or an image. For any input string, the resultant one-way hash will always be the same. If a single byte of the input string is modified, the resulting one-way hash will be changed and will have a totally different sequence than the one-way hash sequence calculated for the unmodified string. One-way hash values can be made sufficiently long (e.g., 256 bits) that a hash string collision (i.e., the occurrence of two different input strings with the same one-way hash output value) is negligible. For an in-depth discussion of the uses of one-way hashes in Big Data resources, see Chapter 2.

Ontology An ontology is a collection of classes and their relationships to one another. Ontologies are usually rule-based systems (i.e., membership in a class is determined by one or more class rules). Two properties distinguish ontologies from classification. Ontologies permit classes to have more than one parent class and more than one child class. For example, the class of automobiles may be a direct subclass of "motorized devices" and a direct subclass of "mechanized transporters." In addition, an instance of a class can be an instance of any number of additional classes. For example, a Lamborghini may be a member of class "automobiles" and class "luxury items." This means that the lineage of an instance in an ontology can be highly complex, with a single instance occurring in multiple classes and with many connections between classes. Because recursive relations are permitted, it is possible to build an ontology wherein a class is both an ancestor class and a descendant class of itself. A classification is a highly restrained ontology wherein instances can belong to only one class and each class may have only one direct parent class. Because classifications have an enforced linear hierarchy, they can be easily modeled and the lineage of any instance can be traced unambiguously. See Classification.

Open access A document is open access if its complete contents are available to the public. Open access applies to documents in the same manner as open source applies to software.

Open source Software is open source if the source code is available to anyone who has access to the software.

Outlier Outliers are extreme data values. The occurrence of outliers hinders the task of developing models, equations, or curves that closely fit all the available data. In some cases, outliers are simply mistakes that can be ignored by the data analyst. In other cases, the outlier may be the most important data in the data set. There is no simple method to know the value of an outlier; it usually falls to the judgment of the data analyst. The importance of outliers to Big Data is that as the size of the data increases, the number of outliers also increases. Therefore, every Big Data analyst must develop a reasonable approach to dealing with outliers, based on the kind of data under study.

Overfitting Overfitting occurs when a formula describes a set of data very closely, but does not lead to any sensible explanation for the behavior of the data and does not predict the behavior of comparable data sets. In the case of overfitting, the formula is said to describe the noise of the system rather than the characteristic behavior of the system. Overfitting occurs frequently with models that perform iterative approximations on training data, coming closer and closer to the training data set with each iteration. Neural networks are an example of a data modeling strategy that is prone to overfitting.

p value The p value is the probability of getting a set of results that are as extreme or more extreme as the set of results observed, assuming that the null hypothesis is true (that there is no statistical difference between the results). The p value has come under great criticism over the decades, with a growing consensus that the p value is often misinterpreted, used incorrectly, or used in situations wherein it does not apply.[154] In the realm of Big Data, repeated samplings of data from large data sets will produce small p values that cannot be directly applied to determining statistical significance. It is best to think of the p value as just another piece of information that tells you something about how sets of observations compare with one another, not as a test of statistical significance.

Page rank PageRank is a method, popularized by Google, for displaying an ordered set of results (for a phrase search conducted over every page of the Web). The rank of a page is determined by two scores: the relevancy of the page to the query phrase and the importance of the page. The relevancy of the page is determined by factors such as how closely the page matches the query phrase and whether the content of the page is focused on the subject of the query. The importance of the page is determined by how many Web pages link to and from the page and by the importance of the Web pages involved in the linkages. It is easy to see that the methods for scoring relevance and importance are subject to many algorithmic variances, particularly with respect to the choice of measures (i.e., the way in which a page's focus on a particular topic is quantified) and the weights applied to each measurement. The reason that PageRank query responses can be completed very rapidly is that the score of a page's importance can be precomputed and stored with the page's Web address. Word matches from the query phrase to Web pages are quickly assembled using a precomputed index of words, the pages containing the words, and locations of the words in the pages.[260]

Parallel computing Some computational tasks can be broken down and distributed to other computers, to be calculated "in parallel." The method of parallel programming allows a collection of desktop computers to complete intensive calculations of the sort that would ordinarily require the aid of a supercomputer. Parallel programming has been studied as a practical way to deal with the higher computational demands brought by Big Data. Although there are many important problems that require parallel computing, the vast majority of Big Data analyses can be easily accomplished with a single, off-the-shelf personal computer. See MapReduce.

Pareto's principle Also known as the 80/20 rule, Pareto's principle holds that a small number of causes may account for the vast majority of observed instances. For example, a small number of rich people account for the majority of wealth. Likewise, a small number of diseases account for the vast majority of human illnesses. A small number of children account for the majority of the behavioral problems encountered in a classroom. A small number of states or provinces contain the majority of the population of a country. A small number of books, compared with the total number of published books, account for the majority of book sales. Sets of data that follow Pareto's principle are often said to follow a Zipf distribution, or a power law distribution. These types of distributions are not tractable by standard statistical descriptors. For example, simple measurements, such as average and standard deviation, have virtually no practical meaning when applied to Zipf distributions. Furthermore, the Gaussian distribution does not apply, and none of the statistical inferences built upon an assumption of a Gaussian distribution will hold on data sets that observe Pareto's principle. See Power law. See Zipf distribution.

Patent farming Also known as patent ambushing.[60] The practice of hiding intellectual property within a standard or device, at the time of its creation, is known as patent farming. After the property is marketed, the patent farmer announces the presence of his or her hidden patented material and presses for royalties—metaphorically harvesting his crop.

Pearson's correlation All similarity scores are based on comparing one data object with another, attribute by attribute, usually summing the squares of the differences in magnitude for each attribute, and using the calculation to compute a final outcome, known as the correlation score. One of the most popular correlation methods is Pearson's correlation, which produces a score that can vary from -1 to $+1$. Two objects with a high score (near $+1$) are highly similar. Pearson's correlation can be used to compare complex data objects that differ in size and content. For example, Pearson's correlation can compare two different books using the terms contained in each book and the number of occurrences of each term.[19]

Plesionymy Nearly synonymous words, or pairs of words that are sometimes synonymous; other times not. For example, the noun forms of "smell" and "odor" are synonymous. As verb forms, "smell" applies, but "odor" does not. You can smell a fish, but you cannot odor a fish. Smell and odor are plesionyms. Plesionymy is another challenge for machine translators.

Polysemy Polysemy occurs when a word has more than one distinct meaning. The intended meaning of a word can sometimes be determined by the context in which the word is used. For example, "she rose to the occasion" and "her favorite flower is the rose." Sometimes polysemy cannot be resolved, for example, "eats shoots and leaves."

Polytely From the Greek root meaning "many goals," polytely refers to problems that involve a large number of variables acting with one another in many different ways, where the rules of interaction may vary as times and conditions change. The outcome of such interactions may have many different consequences. Because Big Data is immense and complex, polytely is an important impediment to Big Data analysis.

Power law A mathematical relationship that applies to Zipf distributions.

Power series A power series of a single variable is an infinite sum of increasing powers of x, multiplied by constants. Power series are very useful because it is easy to calculate the derivative or the integral of a power series and because different power series can be added and multiplied together. When the high exponent terms of a power series are small, as happens when x is less than 1 or when the constants associated with the higher exponents all equal 0, the series can be approximated by summing only the first few terms. Many different kinds of distributions can be represented as a power series. Distributions that cannot be wholly represented by a power series may sometimes by segmented by ranges of x. Within a segment, the distribution might be representable as a power series. A power series should not be confused with a power law distribution. See Power law.

Precision and accuracy See Accuracy and precision.

Predictive analytics This term most often applies to a collection of techniques that have been used, with great success, in marketing. These are recommenders, classifiers, and clustering.[103] Though all of these techniques can be used for purposes other than marketing, they are often described in marketing terms: recommenders (e.g., predicting which products a person might prefer to buy), profile clustering (e.g., grouping individuals into marketing clusters based on the similarity of their profiles), and product classifiers (e.g., assigning a product or individual to a prediction category based on a set of features). See Recommender. See Classifier.

Predictive modeling contests Everyone knows that science is competitive, but very few areas of science have been constructed as a competitive game. Predictive analytics is an exception. Kaggle is a Web site that runs predictive-modeling contests. Their motto is "We're making data science a sport." Competitors with the most successful predictive models win prizes. Prizes vary from thousands to millions of dollars, and hundreds of teams may enter the frays.[261]

Principal component analysis A method for reducing the dimensionality of data sets. This method takes a list of parameters and reduces it to a smaller list of variables, with each component of the smaller list constructed from combinations of variables in the longer list. Furthermore, principal component analysis provides an indication of which variables in both the original and the new list are least correlated with the other variables. Principal component analysis requires matrix operations on large matrices. Such operations are computationally intensive and can easily exceed the capacity of most computers.[104]

Privacy and confidentiality The concepts of confidentiality and of privacy are often confused, and it is useful to clarify their separate meanings. Confidentiality is the process of keeping a secret with which you have been entrusted. You break confidentiality if you reveal the secret to another person. You violate privacy when you use the secret to annoy the person whose confidential information was acquired. If you give me your unlisted telephone number in confidence, then I am expected to protect this confidentiality by never revealing the number to other persons. I may also be expected to protect your privacy by never using the telephone number to call you at all hours of the day and night. In this case, the same information object (unlisted telephone number) is encumbered by confidentiality and privacy obligations.

Protocol A set of instructions, policies, or fully described procedures for accomplishing a service, operation, or task. Protocols are fundamental to Big Data. Data is generated and collected according to protocols. There are protocols for conducting experiments, and there are protocols for measuring the results. There are protocols for choosing the human subjects included in a clinical trial, and there are protocols for interacting with the human subjects during the course of the trial. All network communications are conducted via protocols; the Internet operates under a protocol [Transmission Control Protocol/Internet Protocol (TCP/IP)].

Public data, public databases A term that usually refers to data collections composed of freely available data or of public domain data that can be accessed via database services that are open to the public, such as a Web search engine. Here are a few Web sites that collect information on public Big Data resources: aws.amazon.com/datasets, www.data.gov, and www.google.com/publicdata/directory.

Public domain Data that is not owned by an entity. Public domain materials include documents whose copyright terms have expired, materials produced by the federal government, materials that contain no creative content (i.e., materials that cannot be copyrighted), or materials donated to the public domain by the entity that holds copyright. Public domain data can be accessed, copied, and redistributed without violating piracy laws. It is important to note that plagiarism laws and rules of ethics apply to public domain data. You must properly attribute authorship to public domain documents. If you fail to attribute authorship or if you purposely and falsely attribute authorship to the wrong person (e.g., yourself), then this would be an unethical act and an act of plagiarism.

Query The term "query" usually refers to a request, sent to a database, for information (e.g., Web pages, documents, lines of text, images) that matches a provided word or phrase (i.e., the query term). More generally, a query is a parameter or set of parameters that is submitted as input to a computer program, which searches a data collection for items that match or bear some relationship to the query parameters. In the context of Big Data, the user may need to find classes of objects that have properties relevant to a particular area of interest. In this case, the query is basically introspective, and the output may yield metadata describing individual objects, classes of objects, or the relationships among objects that share particular properties. For example, "weight" may be a property, and this property may fall into the domain of several different classes of data objects. The user might want to know the names of the classes of objects that have the "weight" property and the numbers of object instances in each class. Eventually, the user might want to select several of these classes (e.g., including dogs and cats, but excluding microwave ovens), along with data object instances whose weights fall within a specified range (e.g., 20 to 30 pounds). This approach to querying could work with any data set that has been well specified with metadata, but it is particularly important when using Big Data resources. See Introspection.

RDF See Resource Description Framework.

Recommender A collection of methods for predicting the preferences of individuals. Recommender methods often rely on one or two simple assumptions. (1) If an individual expresses a preference for a certain type of product and the individual encounters a new product that is similar to a previously preferred product, then he is likely to prefer the new product. (2) If an individual expresses preferences that are similar to the preferences expressed by a cluster of individuals and if the members of the cluster prefer a product that the individual has not yet encountered, then the individual will most likely prefer the product. See Predictive analytics. See Classifier.

Reflection A programming technique wherein a computer program will modify itself, at runtime, based on information it acquires through introspection. For example, a computer program may iterate over a collection of data objects, examining the self-descriptive information for each object in the collection (i.e., object introspection). If the information indicates that the data object belongs to a particular class of objects, the program might call a method appropriate for the class. The program executes in a manner determined by descriptive information obtained during runtime; metaphorically reflecting upon the purpose of its computational task. Because introspection is a property of well-constructed Big Data resources, reflection is an available technique to programmers who deal with Big Data. See Introspection.

RegEx Short for Regular Expressions, RegEx is a syntax for describing patterns in text. For example, if I wanted to pull all lines from a text file that began with an uppercase "B" and contained at least one integer and ended with a lowercase x, then I might use the regular expression "^B.*[0-9].*x$". This syntax for expressing patterns of strings that can be matched by prebuilt methods available to a programming language is somewhat standardized. This means that a RegEx expression in Perl will match the same pattern in Python, Ruby, or any language that employs RegEx. The relevance of Regex to Big Data is severalfold. Regex can be used to build or transform data from one format to another; hence creating or merging data records. It can be used to convert sets of data to a desired format; hence transforming data sets. It can be used to extract records that meet a set of characteristics specified by a user; thus filtering subsets of data or executing data queries over text-based files or text-based indexes. The big drawback to using RegEx is speed: operations that call for many Regex operations, particularly when those operations are repeated for each parsed line or record, will reduce software performance. Regex-heavy programs that operate just fine on megabyte files may take hours, days, or months to parse through terabytes of data.

Regular expressions See RegEx.

Reidentification A term casually applied to any instance whereby information can be linked to a specific person after the links between the information and the person associated with the information were removed. Used this way, the term reidentification connotes an insufficient deidentification process. In the health care industry, the term "reidentification" means something else entirely. In the United States, regulations define "reidentification" under the "Standards for Privacy of Individually Identifiable Health Information."[33] Reidentification is defined therein as a legally valid process whereby deidentified records can be linked back to their human subjects under circumstances deemed compelling by a privacy board. Reidentification is typically accomplished via a confidential list of links between human subject names and deidentified records, held by a trusted party. As used by the health care industry, reidentification only applies to the approved process of reestablishing the identity of a deidentified record. When a human subject is identified through fraud, through trickery, or through the deliberate use of computational methods to break the confidentiality of insufficiently deidentified records, the term "reidentification" would not apply.

Reification The process whereby the subject of a statement is inferred, without actually being named. Reification applies to human languages, programming languages, and data specification languages. Here is an example of reification in the English language: "He sat outside." The sentence does not identify who "he" is, but you can infer that "he" must exist and you can define "he" as the object that sat outside. In object-oriented programming languages, an object is reified without declaring it an instance of a class, when it accepts a class method. Likewise, in a specification, an object comes into existence if it is the thing that is being described in a statement (e.g., an RDF triple). Reifications bypass the normal naming and identification step, a neat trick that saves a little time and effort, often causing great confusion. See full discussion in Chapter 1.

Representation bias This occurs when the population sampled does not represent the population intended for study. For example, the population for which the normal range of prostate-specific antigen (PSA) was based was selected from a county in the state of Minnesota. The male population under study consisted almost exclusively of white men (i.e., virtually no African-Americans, Asians, Hispanics, etc.). It may have been assumed that PSA levels would not vary with race. It was eventually determined that the normal PSA ranges varied greatly by race.[262] The Minnesota data, though plentiful, did not represent racial subpopulations. A sharp distinction must drawn between Big-ness and Whole-ness.[138]

Resource Description Framework (RDF) A syntax within XML that formally expresses assertions in three components, the so-called RDF triple. The RDF triple consists of a uniquely identified subject plus a metadata descriptor for the data plus a data element. Triples are necessary and sufficient to create statements that convey meaning. Triples can be aggregated with other triples from the same data set or from other data sets as long as each triple pertains to a unique subject that is identified equivalently through the data sets. Enormous data sets of RDF triples can be merged or integrated functionally with other Big Data resources. See Notation 3. See Semantics. See Triples.

Second trial bias This can occur when a clinical trial yields a greatly improved outcome when it is repeated with a second group of subjects. In the medical field, a second trial bias arises when trialists find subsets of patients from the first trial who do not respond well to treatment, thereby learning which clinical features are associated with poor trial response (e.g., certain preexisting medical conditions, lack of a good home support system, obesity, nationality). During the accrual process for the second trial, potential subjects who profile as nonresponders are excluded. Trialists may justify this practice by asserting that the purpose of the second trial is to find a set of subjects who will benefit from treatment. With a population enriched with good responders, the second trial may yield results that look much better than the first trial. Second trial bias can be considered a type of cherry-picking. See Cherry-picking.

Selection bias See Cherry-picking.

Semantics The study of meaning. In the context of Big Data, semantics is the technique of creating meaningful assertions about data objects. A meaningful assertion, as used here, is a triple consisting of an identified data object, a data value, and a descriptor for the data value. In practical terms, semantics involves making assertions about data objects (i.e., making triples), combining assertions about data objects (i.e., merging triples), and assigning data objects to classes; hence relating triples to other triples. As a word of warning, few informaticians would define semantics in these terms, but I would suggest that most definitions for semantics would be functionally equivalent to the definition offered here. See Triples. See RDF.

Serious Big Data The 3V's (data volume, data variety, and data velocity) plus "seriousness." Seriousness is a tongue-in-cheek term that the author applies to Big Data resources whose objects are provided with an adequate identifier and a trusted time stamp and that provide data users with introspection, including pointers to the protocols that produced the data objects. Metadata in Big Data resources is appended with namespaces. Serious Big Data resources can be merged with other serious Big Data resources. In the opinion of the author, Big Data resources that lack seriousness should not be used in science, in legal work, in banking, and in the realm of public policy. See Identifier. See Trusted time stamp. See Introspection. See Namespace. See Merging.

Simpson's paradox When a correlation that holds in two different data sets is reversed when the data sets are combined, for example, baseball player A may have a higher batting average than player B for each of two seasons, but when the data for the two seasons are combined, player B may have the higher two-season average. Simpson's paradox has particular significance for Big Data research, wherein data samples are variously recombined and reanalyzed at different stages of the analytic process. For a full discussion, with examples, see Chapter 10.

Specification A method used for describing objects (physical objects such as nuts and bolts or symbolic objects such as numbers). Specifications do not require specific types of information and do not impose any order of appearance of the data contained in the document. Specifications do not generally require certification by a standards organization. They are generally produced by special interest organizations, and their legitimacy depends on their popularity. Examples of specifications are RDF, produced by the World Wide Web Consortium, and TCP/IP, maintained by the Internet Engineering Task Force.

Sponsor bias Are the results of big data analytics skewed in favor of the corporate sponsors of the resource? In a fascinating meta-analysis, Yank and coworkers asked whether the results of clinical trials, conducted with financial ties to a drug company, were biased to produce results favorable to the sponsors.[263] They reviewed the literature on clinical trials for antihypertensive agents and found that ties to a drug company did not bias the results (i.e., the experimental data), but they did bias the conclusions (i.e., the interpretations drawn from the results). This suggests that regardless of the results of a trial, the conclusions published by the investigators were more likely to be favorable if the trial was financed by a drug company. This should come as no surprise. Two scientists can look at the same results and draw entirely different conclusions.

Square kilometer array (SKA) SKA is designed to collect data from millions of connected radio telescopes and is expected to produce more than one exabyte (1 billion gigabytes) every day.[7]

String A string is a sequence of characters. Words, phrases, numbers, and alphanumeric sequences (e.g. identifiers, one-way hash values, passwords) are strings. A book is a long string. The complete sequence of the human genome (three billion characters, with each character an A, T, G, or C) is a very long string. Every subsequence of a string is another string.

Supercomputer Computers that can perform many times faster than a desktop personal computer. In 2012, the top supercomputers can perform in excess of a petaflop (i.e., 10 to the 15 power floating point operations per second). By my calculations, a 1 petaflop computer performs about 250,000 operations in the time required for my laptop to finish one operation.

Support vector machine (SVM) A machine-learning technique that classifies objects. The method starts with a training set consisting of two classes of objects as input. The SVA computes a hyperplane, in a multidimensional space, that separates objects of the two classes. The dimension of the hyperspace is determined by the number of dimensions or attributes associated with the objects. Additional objects (i.e., test set objects) are assigned membership in one class or the other, depending on which side of the hyperplane they reside.

Syntax Syntax is the standard form or structure of a statement. What we know as English grammar is equivalent to the syntax for the English language. If I write "Jules hates pizza," the statement would be syntactically valid but factually incorrect. If I write "Jules drives to work in his pizza," the statement would be syntactically valid but nonsensical. For programming languages, syntax refers to the enforced structure of command lines. In the context of triple stores, syntax refers to the arrangement and notation requirements for the three elements of a statement (e.g., RDF format or n3 format). Charles Mead distinctly summarized the difference between syntax and semantics: "Syntax is structure; semantics is meaning."[264]

Taxonomy The definition varies, but as used here, a taxonomy is the collection of named instances (class members) in a classification. When you see a schematic showing class relationships, with individual classes represented by geometric shapes and the relationships represented by arrows or connecting lines between the classes, then you are essentially looking at the structure of a classification. You can think of building a taxonomy as the act of pouring all of the names of all of the instances into their proper classes within the classification schematic. A taxonomy is similar to a nomenclature; the difference is that in a taxonomy, every named instance must have an assigned class.

Term extraction algorithm Terms are phrases, most often noun phrases, and sometimes individual words that have a precise meaning within a knowledge domain. For example, "software validation," "RDF triple," and "WorldWide Telescope" are examples of terms that might appear in the index or the glossary of this book. The most useful terms might appear up to a dozen times in the text, but when they occur on every page, their value as a searchable item is diminished; there are just too many instances of the term to be of practical value. Hence, terms are sometimes described functionally as noun phrases that have low-frequency and high information content. Various algorithms are available to extract candidate terms from textual documents. The candidate terms can be examined by a curator who determines whether they should be included in the index created for the document from which they were extracted. The curator may also compare the extracted candidate terms against a standard nomenclature to determine whether the candidate terms should be added to the nomenclature. For an in-depth discussion, see Chapter 1.

Text editor A text editor (also called an ASCII editor) is a software application designed to create, modify, and display simple unformatted text files. Text editors are different from word processors that are designed to include style, font, and other formatting symbols. Text editors are much faster than word processors because they display the contents of files without having to interpret and execute formatting instructions. Unlike word processors, text editors can open files of enormous size (e.g., gigabyte range).

Thesaurus A vocabulary that groups together synonymous terms. A thesaurus is very similar to a nomenclature. There are two minor differences: nomenclatures do not always group terms by synonymy and nomenclatures are often restricted to a well-defined topic or knowledge domain (e.g., names of stars, infectious diseases, etc.).

Time stamp Many data objects are temporal events, and all temporal events must be given a time stamp indicating the time that the event occurred, using a standard measurement for time. The time stamp must be accurate, persistent, and immutable. The Unix epoch time (equivalent to the Posix epoch time) is available for most operating systems and consists of the number of seconds that have elapsed since January 1, 1970, midnight, Greenwich Mean Time. The Unix epoch time can easily be converted into any other standard representation of time. The duration of any event can be calculated by subtracting the beginning time from the ending time. Because the timing of events can be maliciously altered, scrupulous data managers employ a protocol by which a time stamp can be verified (discussed in Chapter 4).

Time-window bias A bias produced by the choice of a time measurement. In medicine, survival is measured as the interval between diagnosis and death. Suppose a test is introduced that provides early diagnoses. Patients given the test will be diagnosed at a younger age than patients who are not given the test. Such a test will always produce improved survival simply because the interval between diagnosis and death will be lengthened. Assuming the test does not lead to any improved treatment, the age at which the patient dies is unchanged by the testing procedure. The bias is caused by the choice of timing interval (i.e., time from diagnosis to death). Survival is improved without a prolongation of life beyond what would be expected without the test. Some of the touted advantages of early diagnosis are the direct result of timing bias.

Triple In computer semantics, a triple is an identified data object associated with a data element and the description of the data element. In theory, all Big Data resources can be composed as collections of triples. When the data and metadata held in sets of triples are organized into ontologies consisting of classes of objects and associated properties (metadata), the resource can potentially provide introspection (the ability of a data object to be self-descriptive). This topic is discussed in depth in Chapter 4. See Introspection. See Data object. See Semantics. See Resource Description Framework.

Uniqueness In computational sciences, uniqueness is achieved when a data object is associated with a unique identifier (i.e., a character string that has not been assigned to any other object). A full discussion of uniqueness is found in Chapter 2. See Identifier.

Universally Unique Identifiers (UUID) A UUID is a protocol for assigning identifiers to data objects without using a central registry. UUIDs were originally used in the Apollo Network Computing System.[27] See Chapter 2.

UUID See Universally Unique Identifiers.

Validation This involves demonstrating that the conclusions that come from data analyses fulfill their intended purpose and are consistent.[265] You validate a conclusion (which may appear in the form of a hypothesis, or a statement about the value of a new laboratory test, or a therapeutic protocol) by showing that you draw the same conclusion repeatedly whenever you analyze relevant data sets, and that the conclusion satisfies some criteria for correctness or suitability. Validation is somewhat different from reproducibility. Reproducibility involves getting the same measurement over and over when you perform the test. Validation involves drawing the same conclusion over and over. See Verification and validation.

Variable In algebra, a variable is a quantity in an equation that can change, as opposed to a constant quantity that cannot change. In computer science, a variable can be perceived as a container that can be assigned a value. If you assign the integer 7 to a container named "x", then "x" equals 7 until you reassign some other value to the container (i.e., variables are mutable). In most computer languages, when you issue a command assigning a value to a new (undeclared) variable, the variable automatically comes into existence to accept the assignment. The process whereby an object comes into existence, because its existence was implied by an action (such as value assignment), is called reification. See Reification. See Dimensionality.

Verification and validation As applied to data resources, verification is the process that ensures that data conforms to a set of specifications. Validation is the process that checks whether the data can be applied in a manner that fulfills its intended purpose. This often involves showing that correct conclusions can be obtained from a competent analysis of the data. For example, a Big Data resource might contain position, velocity, direction, and mass data for the earth and for a meteor that is traveling sunwards. The data may meet all specifications for measurement, error tolerance, data typing, and data completeness. A competent analysis of the data indicates that the meteor will miss the earth by a safe 50,000 miles, plus or minus 10,000 miles. If the asteroid smashes into the earth, destroying all planetary life, then an extraterrestrial observer might conclude that the data was verified, but not validated.

Vocabulary This is a comprehensive collection of the words used in a general area of knowledge. The term "vocabulary" and the term "nomenclature" are nearly synonymous. In common usage, a vocabulary is a list of words and typically includes a wide range of terms and classes of terms. Nomenclatures typically focus on a class of terms within a vocabulary. For example, a physics vocabulary might contain the terms "quark, black hole, Geiger counter, and Albert Einstein"; a nomenclature might be devoted to the names of celestial bodies. See Nomenclature.

Web service A server-based collections of data, plus a collection of software routines operating on the data, that can be accessed by remote clients. One of the features of Web services is that they permit client users (e.g., humans or software agents) to discover the kinds of data and methods offered by the Web service and the rules for submitting server requests. To access Web services, clients must compose their requests as messages conveyed in a language that the server is configured to accept, a so-called Web services language.

WorldWide Telescope A Big Data effort from the Microsoft Corporation bringing astronomical maps, imagery, data, analytic methods, and visualization technology to standard Web browsers. More information is available at http://www.worldwidetelescope.org/Home.aspx.

eXtensible Markup Language (XML) A syntax for marking data values with descriptors (metadata). The descriptors are commonly known as tags. In XML, every data value is enclosed by a start tag, indicating that a value will follow, and an end tag, indicating that the value had preceded the tag, for example, <name>Tara Raboomdeay</name>. The enclosing angle brackets, "<>", and the end-tag marker, "/", are hallmarks of XML markup. This simple but powerful relationship between metadata and data allows us to employ each metadata/data pair as though it were a small database that can be combined with related metadata/data pairs from any other XML document. The full value of metadata/data pairs comes when we can associate the pair with a unique object, forming a so-called triple. See Triple. See Meaning.

Zipf distribution George Kingsley Zipf (1902–1950) was an American linguist who demonstrated that, for most languages, a small number of words account for the majority of occurrences of all the words found in prose. Specifically, he found that the frequency of any word is inversely proportional to its placement in a list of words, ordered by their decreasing frequencies in text. The first word in the frequency list will occur about twice as often as the second word in the list, three times as often as the third word in the list, and so on. Many Big Data collections follow a Zipf distribution (income distribution in a population, energy consumption by country, and so on). Zipf distributions within Big Data cannot be sensibly described by the standard statistical measures that apply to normal distributions. Zipf distributions are instances of Pareto's principle. See Pareto's principle.

References

1. Martin Hilbert M, Lopez P. The world's technological capacity to store, communicate, and compute information. Science 2011;332:60–5.
2. Schmidt S. Data is exploding: the 3 V's of big data. Business Computing World May 15, 2012.
3. An assessment of the impact of the NCI cancer Biomedical Informatics Grid (CaBIG). Report of the Board of Scientific Advisors Ad Hoc Working Group, National Cancer Institute, March, 2011. Available from: http://deainfo.nci.nih.gov/advisory/bsa/bsa0311/caBIGfinalReport.pdf; viewed January 31, 2013.
4. Komatsoulis GA. Program announcement to the CaBIG community. National Cancer Institute. Available from: https://cabig.nci.nih.gov/program_announcement; viewed August 31, 2012.
5. Freitas A, Curry E, Oliveira JG, O'Riain S. Querying heterogeneous datasets on the linked data web: challenges, approaches, and trends. IEEE Internet Computing 2012;16:24–33. Available from: http://www.edwardcurry.org/publications/freitas_IC_12.pdf; viewed September 25, 2012.
6. Drake TA, Braun J, Marchevsky A, Kohane IS, Fletcher C, Chueh H, et al. A system for sharing routine surgical pathology specimens across institutions: the Shared Pathology Informatics Network (SPIN). Hum Pathol 2007;38:1212–25.
7. Francis M. Future telescope array drives development of exabyte processing. Ars Technica April 2, 2012.
8. Markoff J. A deluge of data shapes a new era in computing. The New York Times December 15, 2009.
9. Harrington JD, Clavin W. NASA's WISE mission sees skies ablaze with Blazars. NASA Release 12-109, April 12, 2002.
10. Core techniques and technologies for advancing Big Data science. National Science Foundation program solicitation NSF 12-499, June 13, 2012. Available from: http://www.nsf.gov/pubs/2012/nsf12499/nsf12499.txt; viewed September 23, 2012.
11. Bianciardi G, Miller JD, Straat PA, Levin GV. Complexity analysis of the Viking labeled release experiments. Intl J Aeronautical Space Sci 2012;13:14–26.
12. Hayes A. VA to apologize for mistaken Lou Gehrig's disease notices, CNN August 26, 2009 Available from: http://www.cnn.com/2009/POLITICS/08/26/veterans.letters.disease; viewed September 4, 2012.
13. Hall PA, Lemoine NR. Comparison of manual data coding errors in 2 hospitals. J Clin Pathol 1986;39:622–6.
14. Berman JJ. Doublet method for very fast autocoding. BMC Med Inform Decis Mak 2004;4:16.
15. Berman JJ. Nomenclature-based data retrieval without prior annotation: facilitating biomedical data integration with fast doublet matching. In Silico Biol 2005;5:0029.
16. Swanson DR. Undiscovered public knowledge. Libr Q 1986;56:103–18.
17. Wallis E, Lavell C. Naming the indexer: where credit is due. The Indexer 1995;19:266–8.
18. Krauthammer M, Nenadic G. Term identification in the biomedical literature. J Biomed Inform 2004;37:512–26.
19. Berman JJ. Methods in medical informatics: fundamentals of healthcare programming in Perl, Python, and Ruby. Boca Raton, FL: Chapman and Hall; 2010.
20. Shah NH, Jonquet C, Chiang AP, Butte AJ, Chen R, Musen MA. Ontology-driven indexing of public datasets for translational bioinformatics. BMC Bioinform 2009;10(Suppl. 2):S1.
21. Cohen T, Whitfield GK, Schvaneveldt RW, Mukund K, Rindflesch T. EpiphaNet: an interactive tool to support biomedical discoveries. J Biomed Discov Collab 2010;5:21–49.
22. Swanson DR. Fish oil, Raynaud's syndrome, and undiscovered public knowledge. Perspect Biol Med 1986;30:7–18.
23. Reed DP. Naming and synchronization in a decentralized computer system. Doctoral Thesis, MIT; 1978.
24. Joint NEMA/COCIR/JIRA Security and Privacy Committee (SPC). Identification and allocation of basic security rules in healthcare imaging systems, September, 2002. Available from: http://www.medicalimaging.org/wp-content/uploads/2011/02/Identification_and_Allocation_of_Basic_Security_Rules_In_Healthcare_Imaging_Systems-September_2002.pdf; viewed January 10, 2013.
25. Kuzmak P, Casertano A, Carozza D, Dayhoff R, Campbell K. Solving the problem of duplicate medical device unique identifiers: High Confidence Medical Device Software and Systems (HCMDSS) workshop. Philadelphia,

PA; June 2-3, 2005. Available from: http://www.cis.upenn.edu/hcmdss/Papers/submissions/; viewed August 26, 2012.

26. Health Level 7 OID Registry. Available from: http://www.hl7.org/oid/frames.cfm; viewed August 26, 2012.

27. Leach P, Mealling M, Salz R. A Universally Unique IDentifier (UUID) URN namespace. Network Working Group, Request for Comment 4122, Standards Track. Available from: http://www.ietf.org/rfc/rfc4122.txt; viewed August 26, 2012

28. Berman JJ. Confidentiality for medical data miners. Art Intell Med 2002;26:25–36.

29. Patient Identity Integrity. A White Paper by the HIMSS Patient Identity Integrity Work Group, December 2009. Available from: http://www.himss.org/content/files/PrivacySecurity/PIIWhitePaper.pdf; viewed September 19, 2012.

30. Berman JJ. Biomedical informatics. Sudbury, MA: Jones and Bartlett; 2007.

31. Pakstis AJ, Speed WC, Fang R, Hyland FC, Furtado MR, Kidd JR, et al. SNPs for a universal individual identification panel. Hum Genet 2010;127:315–24.

32. Katsanis SH, Wagner JK. Characterization of the standard and recommended CODIS markers. J Foren Sci 2012;Aug 24.

33. Department of Health and Human Services . 45 CFR (Code of Federal Regulations), Parts 160 through 164. Standards for Privacy of Individually Identifiable Health Information (Final Rule). Fed Reg 2000;65(250):82461–510.

34. Department of Health and Human Services . 45 CFR (Code of Federal Regulations), 46. Protection of Human Subjects (Common Rule). Fed Reg 1991;56:28003–32.

35. Berman JJ. Concept-match medical data scrubbing: how pathology datasets can be used in research. Arch Pathol Lab Med 2003;127:680–6.

36. Berman JJ. Comparing de-identification methods. Available from: http://www.biomedcentral.com/1472-6947/6/12/comments/comments.htm; March 31, 2006 viewed January 31, 2013.

37. Knight J. Agony for researchers as mix-up forces retraction of ecstasy study. Nature 2003;425:109.

38. Sainani K. Error: what biomedical computing can learn from its mistakes. Biomed Comput Rev 2011Fall:12–9.

39. Palanichamy MG, Zhang Y. Potential pitfalls in MitoChip detected tumor-specific somatic mutations: a call for caution when interpreting patient data. BMC Cancer 2010;10:597.

40. Bandelt H, Salas A. Contamination and sample mix-up can best explain some patterns of mtDNA instabilities in buccal cells and oral squamous cell carcinoma. BMC Cancer 2009;9:113.

41. Harris G. U.S. Inaction lets look-alike tubes kill patients. The New York Times August 20, 2010.

42. Flores G. Science retracts highly cited paper: study on the causes of childhood illness retracted after author found guilty of falsifying data. The Scientist June 17, 2005.

43. Gowen LC, Avrutskaya AV, Latour AM, Koller BH, Leadon SA. Retraction of: Gowen LC, Avrutskaya AV, Latour AM, Koller BH, Leadon SA. Science. 1998 Aug 14;281(5379):1009-12. Science. 2003;300:1657.

44. Pearson K. The grammar of science. London: Adam and Black; 1900.

45. Berman JJ. Racing to share pathology data. Am J Clin Pathol 2004;121:169–71.

46. Scamardella JM. Not plants or animals: a brief history of the origin of kingdoms Protozoa, Protista and Protoctista. Intl Microbiol 1999;2:207–16.

47. Madar S, Goldstein I, Rotter V. Did experimental biology die? Lessons from 30 years of p53 research. Cancer Res 2009;69:6378–80.

48. Zilfou JT, Lowe SW. Tumor suppressive functions of p53. Cold Spring Harb Perspect Biol 200900:a001883.

49. Berman JJ. Taxonomic guide to infectious diseases: understanding the biologic classes of pathogenic organisms. Waltham: Academic Press; 2012.

50. Suggested Upper Merged Ontology (SUMO). The OntologyPortal. Available from: http://www.ontologyportal.org; viewed August 14, 2012.

51. de Bruijn J. Using ontologies: enabling knowledge sharing and reuse on the Semantic Web. Digital Enterprise Research Institute Technical Report DERI-2003-10-29, October 2003. Available from: http://www.deri.org/fileadmin/documents/DERI-TR-2003-10-29.pdf; viewed August 14, 2012.

52. Guarro J, Gene J, Stchigel AM. Developments in fungal taxonomy. Clin Microbiol Rev 1999;12:454–500.

53. Nakayama R, Nemoto T, Takahashi H, Ohta T, Kawai A, Seki K, et al. Gene expression analysis of soft tissue sarcomas: characterization and reclassification of malignant fibrous histiocytoma. Modern Pathol 2007;20:749–59.

54. Richard Cote R, Reisinger F, Martens L, Barsnes H, Vizcaino JA, Hermjakob H. The ontology lookup service: bigger and better. Nucleic Acids Res 2010;38:W155–60.

55. Neumann T, Weikum G. xRDF3X: Fast querying, high update rates, and consistency for RDF databases. Proceedings of the VLDB Endowment 2010;3:256–63.

56. Berman JJ. A tool for sharing annotated research data: the "Category 0" UMLS (Unified Medical Language System) vocabularies. BMC Med Inform Decis Mak 2003;3:6.

57. Kuchinke W, Ohmann C, Yang Q, Salas N, Lauritsen J, Gueyffier F, et al. Heterogeneity prevails: the state of clinical trial data management in Europe - results of a survey of ECRIN centres. Trials 2010;11:79.

58. Berman JJ, Edgerton ME, Friedman B. The Tissue Microarray Data Exchange Specification: a community-based, open source tool for sharing tissue microarray data. BMC Med Inform Dec Mak 2003;3:5.

59. Deutsch EW, Ball CA, Berman JJ, Bova GS, Brazma A, Bumgarner RE, et al. Minimum Information Specification For In Situ Hybridization and Immunohistochemistry Experiments (MISFISHIE). Nature Biotechnol 2008;26:305–12.

60. Gates S. Qualcomm v. Broadcom: The federal circuit weighs in on "patent ambushes". Available from: http://www.mofo.com/qualcomm-v-broadcom—the-federal-circuit-weighs-in-on-patent-ambushes-12-05-2008; December 5, 2008 viewed January 22, 2013.

61. Cahr D, Kalina I. Of pacs and trolls: how the patent wars may be coming to a hospital near you. ABA Health Lawyer 2006;19:15–20.

62. Duncan M. Terminology version control discussion paper: the chocolate teapot. Medical Object Oriented Software Ltd; September 15, 2009. Available from: http://www.mrtablet.demon.co.uk/chocolate_teapot_lite.htm; viewed August 30, 2012.

63. Cavalier-Smith T. The phagotrophic origin of eukaryotes and phylogenetic classification of Protozoa. Int J Syst Evol Microbiol 2002;52(Pt 2):297–354.

64. Jennings N. On agent-based software engineering. Art Intell 2000;117:277–96.

65. Berman JJ. Ruby programming for medicine and biology. Sudbury, MA: Jones and Bartlett; 2008.

66. Forsyth J. What sank the Titanic? Scientists point to the moon. Reuters March 7, 2012.

67. Shane S. China inspired interrogations at Guantanamo. The New York Times July 2, 2008.

68. Greenhouse L. In court ruling on executions, a factual flaw. The New York Times July 2, 2008.

69. Berman JJ. Zero-check: a zero-knowledge protocol for reconciling patient identities across institutions. Arch Pathol Lab Med 2004;128:344–6.

70. Booker D, Berman JJ. Dangerous abbreviations. Hum Pathol 2004;35:529–31.

71. Berman JJ. Pathology abbreviated: a long review of short terms. Arch Pathol Lab Med 2004;128:347–52.

72. Patient safety in American hospitals. HealthGrades; July, 2004. Available from: http://www.healthgrades.com/media/english/pdf/hg_patient_safety_study_final.pdf; viewed September 9, 2012.

73. Gordon R. Great medical disasters. New York: Dorset Press; 1986. p. 155–60.

74. Vital signs: unintentional injury deaths among persons aged 0-19 years; United States, 2000-2009. Morbidity and Mortality Weekly Report (MMWR). Centers for disease Control and Prevention. April 16, 2012;61:1–7.

75. Rigler T. DOD discloses new figures on Korean War dead. Army News Service May 30, 2000.

76. Frey CM, McMillen MM, Cowan CD, Horm JW, Kessler LG. Representativeness of the surveillance, epidemiology, and end results program data: recent trends in cancer mortality rate. JNCI 1992;84:872.

77. Ashworth TG. Inadequacy of death certification: proposal for change. J Clin Pathol 1991;44:265.

78. Kircher T, Anderson RE. Cause of death: proper completion of the death certificate. JAMA 1987;258:349–52.

79. Walter SD, Birnie SE. Mapping mortality and morbidity patterns: an international comparison. Intl J Epidemiol 1991;20:678–89.

80. Pennisi E. Gene counters struggle to get the right answer. Science 2003;301:1040–1.

81. How many genes are in the human genome? HumanGenome Project information; Available from: http://www.ornl.gov/sci/techresources/Human_Genome/faq/genenumber.shtml; viewed June 10, 2012.

82. Mitchell KJ, Becich MJ, Berman JJ, Chapman WW, Gilbertson J, Gupta D, et al. Implementation and evaluation of a negation tagger in a pipeline-based system for information extraction from pathology reports. MEDINFO 2004;2004:663–7.

83. Pollack A. Forty years' war: taking risk for profit, industry seeks cancer drugs. The New York Times September 2, 2009.

84. Berkrot B, Pierson R. OSI sees $2 billion Tarceva sales by 2011. Reuters Feb 23, 2006.

85. Irizarry RA, Warren D, Spencer F, Kim IF, Biswal S, Frank BC, et al. Multiple-laboratory comparison of microarray platforms. Nat Methods 2005;2:345–50.

86. Mathelin C, Cromer A, Wendling C, Tomasetto C, Rio MC. Serum biomarkers for detection of breast cancers: a prospective study. Breast Cancer Res Treat 2006;96:83–90.

87. Kolata G. Cancer fight: unclear tests for new drug. The New York Times April 19, 2010.

88. Begley CG, Ellis LM. Drug development: raise standards for preclinical cancer research. Nature 2012;483: 531–3.

89. Begley S. In cancer science, many 'discoveries' don't hold up. Reuters Mar 28, 2012.

90. Venet D, Dumont JE, Detours V. Most random gene expression signatures are significantly associated with breast cancer outcome. PLoS Comput Biol 2011;7:e1002240.

91. Gatty H. Finding your way without map or compass. Mineola: Dover; 1958.

92. Levenberg K. A method for the solution of certain non-linear problems in least squares. Q App Math 1944;2:164–8.

93. Marquardt DW. An algorithm for the least-squares estimation of nonlinear parameters. SIAM J Appl Math 1963;11:431–41.

94. Lee J, Pham M, Lee J, Han W, Cho H, Yu H, et al. Processing SPARQL queries with regular expressions in RDF databases. BMC Bioinform 2011;12(Suppl. 2):S6.

95. Thompson CW. The trick to D.C. police force's 94% closure rate for 2011 homicides. The Washington Post February 19, 2012.

96. Kaplan EL, Meier P. Nonparametric estimation from incomplete observations. J Am Statist Assn 1958;53:457–81.

97. SEER. Surveillance epidemiology end results. National Cancer Institute. Available from: http://seer.cancer.gov/; viewed April 22, 3013.

98. Berman JJ, Moore GW. The role of cell death in the growth of preneoplastic lesions: a Monte Carlo simulation model. Cell Prolif 1992;25:549–57.

99. Perez-Pena R. New York's tally of heat deaths draws scrutiny. The New York Times August 18, 2006.

100. Chiang S. Heat waves, the "other" natural disaster: perspectives on an often ignored epidemic. Global Pulse American Medical Student Association; 2006.

101. Shah S, Horne A, Capella J. Good data won't guarantee good decisions. Harv Bus Rev. April, 2012.

102. White T. Hadoop: the definitive guide. O'Reilly Media; 2009.

103. Owen S, Anil R, Dunning T, Friedman E. Mahout in action. Shelter Island, NY: Manning Publications Co; 2012.

104. Janert PK. Data analysis with open source tools. O'Reilly Media; 2010.

105. Lewis PD. R for medicine and biology. Sudbury: Jones and Bartlett Publishers; 2009.

106. Segaran T. Programming collective intelligence: building smart Web 2.0 applications. O'Reilly Media; 2007.

107. Wu X, Kumar V, Quinlan JR, Ghosh J, Yang Q, Motoda H, et al. Top 10 algorithms in data mining. Knowl Inf Syst 2008;14:1–37.

108. Zhang L, Lin X. Some considerations of classification for high dimension low-sample size data. Stat Methods Med Res 2011 Nov 23. Available from: http://smm.sagepub.com/content/early/2011/11/22/0962280211428387.long; viewed January 26, 2013.

109. Szekely GJ, Rizzo ML. Brownian distance covariance. Ann Appl Stat 2009;3:1236–65.

110. Reshef DN, Reshef YA, Finucane HK, Grossman SR, McVean G, Turnbaugh PJ, et al. Detecting novel associations in large data sets. Science 2011;334:1518–24.

111. Marsaglia G, Tsang WW. Some difficult-to-pass tests of randomness. J Stat Software 2002;7:1–8. Available from: http://www.jstatsoft.org/v07/i03/paper; viewed September 25, 2012.

112. Cleveland Clinic: build an efficient pipeline to find the most powerful predictors. Innocentive; September 8, 2011. https://www.innocentive.com/ar/challenge/9932794; viewed September 25, 2012.

113. Wu D, Hugenholtz P, Mavromatis K, Pukall R, Dalin E, Ivanova NN, et al. A phylogeny-driven genomic encyclopaedia of Bacteria and Archaea. Nature 2009;462:1056–60.

114. Woese CR, Fox GE. Phylogenetic structure of the prokaryotic domain: the primary kingdoms. PNAS 1977;74:5088–90.

115. Mayr E. Two empires or three? PNAS 1998;95:9720–3.

116. Woese CR. Default taxonomy: Ernst Mayr's view of the microbial world. PNAS 1998;95:11043–6.

117. Bamshad MJ, Olson SE. Does race exist? Sci Am 2003December:78–85.

118. Wadman M. Geneticists struggle towards consensus on place for 'race'. Nature 2004;431:1026.

119. Gerlinger M, Rowan AJ, Horswell S, Larkin J, Endesfelder D, Gronroos E, et al. Intratumor heterogeneity and branched evolution revealed by multiregion sequencing. N Engl J Med 2012;366:883–92.

120. Molyneux G, Smalley MJ. The cell of origin of BRCA1 mutation-associated breast cancer: a cautionary tale of gene expression profiling. J Mammary Gland Biol Neoplasia 2011;16:51–5.

121. Sainani K. Meet the skeptics: why some doubt biomedical models, and what it takes to win them over. Biomed Comput Rev 2012 June 5.

122. Ioannidis JP. Microarrays and molecular research: noise discovery? The Lancet 2005;365:454–5.

123. Salmon F. Recipe for disaster: the formula that killed Wall Street. Wired Magazine 17:03, February 23, 2009.

124. Ransohoff DF. Rules of evidence for cancer molecular-marker discovery and validation. Nat Rev Cancer 2004;4:309–14.

125. Innovation or stagnation: challenge and opportunity on the critical path to new medical products. U.S. Department of Health and Human Services, Food and Drug Administration; 2004.

126. Wurtman RJ, Bettiker RL. The slowing of treatment discovery, 1965-1995. Nat Med 1996;2:5–6.

127. Saul S. Prone to error: earliest steps to find cancer. The New York Times July 19, 2010.

128. Benowitz S. Biomarker boom slowed by validation concerns. J Natl Cancer Inst 2004;96:1356–7. Comment. Realistic assessment of the slowdown in translational science in the cancer field.

129. Abu-Asab MS, Chaouchi M, Alesci S, Galli S, Laassri M, Cheema AK, et al. Biomarkers in the age of omics: time for a systems biology approach. OMICS 2011;15:105–12.

130. Weigelt B, Reis-Filho JS. Molecular profiling currently offers no more than tumour morphology and basic immunohistochemistry. Breast Cancer Res 2010;12:S5.

131. Moyer VA. on behalf of the U.S. Preventive Services Task Force. Screening for prostate cancer: U.S. Preventive Services Task Force recommendation statement. Ann Intern Med 2011 May 21.

132. Ioannidis JP, Panagiotou OA. Comparison of effect sizes associated with biomarkers reported in highly cited individual articles and in subsequent meta-analyses. JAMA 2011;305:2200–10.

133. Shariff SZ, Cuerden MS, Jain AK, Garg AX. The secret of immortal time bias in epidemiologic studies. J Am Soc Nephrol 2008;19:841–3.

134. Khurana V, Bejjanki HR, Caldito G, Owens MW. Statins reduce the risk of lung cancer in humans: a large case-control study of US veterans. Chest 2007;131:1282–8.

135. Jemal A, Murray T, Ward E, Samuels A, Tiwari RC, Ghafoor A, et al. Cancer statistics, 2005. CA Cancer J Clin 2005;55:10–30.

136. Jacobs EJ, Newton CC, Thun MJ, Gapstur SM. Long-term use of cholesterol-lowering drugs and cancer incidence in a large United States cohort. Cancer Res 2011;71:1763–71.

137. Suissa S, Dellaniello S, Vahey S, Renoux C. Time-window bias in case-control studies: statins and lung cancer. Epidemiology 2011;22:228–31.

138. Boyd D. Privacy and publicity in the context of Big Data. Open Government and the World Wide Web (WWW2010). Raleigh, North Carolina; April 29, 2010. Available from: http://www.danah.org/papers/talks/2010/WWW2010.html; viewed August 26, 2012.

139. Li W. The more-the-better and the less-the-better. Bioinformatics 2006;22:2187–8.

140. Chavez E, Navarro G, Baeza-Yates R, Marroquin JL. Searching in metric spaces. ACM Comput Surveys 2001;33:273–321.

141. Philippe H, Brinkmann H, Lavrov DV, Littlewood DT, Manuel M, Worheide G, et al. Resolving difficult phylogenetic questions: why more sequences are not enough. PLoS Biol 2011;9:e1000602.

142. Bergsten J. A review of long-branch attraction. Cladistics 2005;21:163–93.

143. Van den Broeck J, Cunningham SA, Eeckels R, Herbst K. Data cleaning: detecting, diagnosing, and editing data abnormalities. PLoS Med 2005;2:e267.

144. Bickel PJ, Hammel EA, O'Connell JW. Sex bias in graduate admissions: data from Berkeley. Science 1975;187:398–404.

145. Baker SG, Kramer BS. The transitive fallacy for randomized trials: if A bests B and B bests C in separate trials, is A better than C? BMC Med Res Methodol 2002;2:13.

146. Tatsioni A, Bonitsis NG, Ioannidis JP. Persistence of contradicted claims in the literature. JAMA 2007;2517–26.

147. Ye Q, Worman HJ. Primary structure analysis and lamin B and DNA binding of human LBR, an integral protein of the nuclear envelope inner membrane. J Biol Chem 1994;269:11306–11.

148. Waterham HR, Koster J, Mooyer P, van Noort G, Kelley RI, Wilcox WR, et al. Autosomal recessive HEM/Greenberg skeletal dysplasia is caused by 3-beta-hydroxysterol delta(14)-reductase deficiency due to mutations in the lamin B receptor gene. Am J Hum Genet 2003;72:1013–7.

149. Ecker JR, Bickmore WA, Barroso I, Pritchard JK, Gilad Y, Segal E. Genomics: ENCODE explained. Nature 2012;489:52–5.

150. Rosen JM, Jordan CT. The increasing complexity of the cancer stem cell paradigm. Science 2009;324:1670–3.

151. Mallett S, Royston P, Waters R, Dutton S, Altman DG. Reporting performance of prognostic models in cancer: a review. BMC Med 2010;30:21.

152. Ioannidis JP. Is molecular profiling ready for use in clinical decision making? Oncologist 2007;12:301–11.

153. Fifty-six year trends in U.S. cancer death rates. In: SEER Cancer Statistics Review 1975–2005. National Cancer Institute. Available from: http://seer.cancer.gov/csr/1975_2005/results_merged/topic_historical_mort_trends.pdf; viewed September 19, 2012.

154. Cohen J. The earth is round (p < .05). Am Psychol 1994;49:997–1003.

155. Rosenberg T. Opinionator: armed with data, fighting more than crime. The New York Times May 2, 2012.

156. Hoover JN. Data, analysis drive Maryland government. Information Week March 15, 2010.

157. Howe J. The rise of crowdsourcing. Wired 2006;14:06.

158. Robins JM. The control of confounding by intermediate variables. Stat Med 1989;8:679–701.

159. Robins JM. Correcting for non-compliance in randomized trials using structural nested mean models. Commun Stat Theory Methods 1994;23:2379–412.

160. Lohr S. Google to end health records service after it fails to attract users. The New York Times Jun 24, 2011.

161. Schwartz E. Shopping for health software, some doctors get buyer's remorse. The Huffington Post Investigative Fund Jan 29, 2010. Available from: http://www.huffingtonpost.com/2010/01/29/shopping-for-health-softw_n_442653.html; viewed January 31, 2013.

162. Heeks R, Mundy D, Salazar A. Why health care information systems succeed or fail. Institute for Development Policy and Management, University of Manchester; June 1999. Available from: http://www.sed.manchester.ac.uk/idpm/research/publications/wp/igovernment/igov_wp09htm; viewed July 12, 2012.

163. Littlejohns P, Wyatt JC, Garvican L. Evaluating computerised health information systems: hard lessons still to be learnt. Br Med J 2003;326:860–3.

164. Linder JA, Ma J, Bates DW, Middleton B, Stafford RS. Electronic health record use and the quality of ambulatory care in the United States. Arch Intern Med 2007;167:1400–5.

165. Gill JM, Mainous AG, Koopman RJ, Player MS, Everett CJ, Chen YX, et al. Impact of EHR-based clinical decision support on adherence to guidelines for patients on NSAIDs: a randomized controlled trial. Ann Fam Med 2011;9:22–30.

166. Lohr S. Lessons from Britain's health information technology fiasco. The New York Times Sept. 27, 2011.

167. Dismantling the NHS national programme for IT. Department of Health Media Centre Press Release; September 22, 2011. Available from: http://mediacentre.dh.gov.uk/2011/09/22/dismantling-the-nhs-national-programme-for-it/; viewed June 12, 2012.

168. Whittaker Z. UK's delayed national health IT programme officially scrapped. ZDNet September 22, 2011.

169. Fitzgerald G, Russo NL. The turnaround of the London Ambulance Service Computer-Aided Dispatch system (LASCAD). Eur J Inform Syst 2005;14:244–57.

170. Kappelman LA, McKeeman R, Lixuan Zhang L. Early warning signs of IT project failure: the dominant dozen. Inform Syst Manag 2006;23:31–6.

171. Arquilla J. The Pentagon's biggest boondoggles. The New York Times March 12, 2011.

172. FIPS PUB 119-1. Supersedes FIPS PUB 119. 1985 November 8. Federal Information Processing Standards Publication 119-1 1995 March 13. Announcing the standard for ADA. Available from: http://www.itl.nist.gov/fipspubs/fip119-1.htm; viewed August 26, 2012.

173. Ariane 501 inquiry board report. Available from: http://esamultimedia.esa.int/docs/esa-x-1819eng.pdf; July 19, 1996 viewed August 26, 2012.

174. Mars Climate Orbiter. Mishap Investigation Board. Phase I Report. ftp://ftp.hq.nasa.gov/pub/pao/reports/1999/MCO_report.pdf; November 10, 1999.

175. Sowers AE. Funding research with NIH grants: a losing battle in a flawed system. The Scientist 1995;9:Oct. 16.

176. Pogson G. Controlled English: enlightenment through constraint. Language Technol 1988;6:22–5.

177. Schneier B. A plea for simplicity: you can't secure what you don't understand. Information Security November 19, 1999 Available from: http://www.schneier.com/essay-018.html; viewed September 3, 2012.

178. Vlasic B. Toyota's slow awakening to a deadly problem. The New York Times February 1, 2010.

179. Valdes-Dapena P. Pedals, drivers blamed for out of control Toyotas. CNN Money February 8, 2011.

180. Drew C. U-2 spy plane evades the day of retirement. The New York Times March 21, 2010.

181. Riley DL. Business models for cost effective use of health information technologies: lessons learned in the CHCS II project. Stud Health Technol Inform 2003;92:157–65.

182. Leveson NG. A new approach to system safety engineering. Self-published ebook; 2002.

183. Weiss TR. Thief nabs backup data on 365,000 patients. Computerworld January 26, 2006. Available from: http://www.computerworld.com/s/article/108101/Update_Thief_nabs_backup_data_on_365_000_patients; viewed August 21, 2012.

184. Noumeir R, Lemay A, Lina J. Pseudonymization of radiology data for research purposes. J Digit Imaging 2007;20:284–95.

185. The ComputerWorld honors program case study. Available from: http://www.cwhonors.org/case_studies/NationalCancerInstitute.pdf; viewed August 31, 2012.

186. Olavsrud T. How to avoid big data spending pitfalls. CIO May 08, 2012. Available from: http://www.cio.com/article/705922/How_to_Avoid_Big_Data_Spending_Pitfalls; viewed July 16, 2012.

187. The Standish Group Report: Chaos. Available from: http://www.projectsmart.co.uk/docs/chaos-report.pdf; 1995 viewed September 19, 2012.

188. The human genome project race. UC Santa Cruz Center for Biomolecular Science and Engineering; March 28, 2009. Available from: http://www.cbse.ucsc.edu/research/hgp_race.

189. Smith B. caBIG has another fundamental problem: it relies on "incoherent" messaging standard. Cancer Lett 2011;37(16).

190. Robinson D, Paul Frosdick P, Briscoe E. HL7 Version 3: an impact assessment. NHS Information Authority; 2001 March 23.

191. Eccles M, McColl E, Steen N, Rousseau N, Grimshaw J, Parkin D, et al. Effect of computerised evidence based guidelines on management of asthma and angina in adults in primary care: cluster randomised controlled trial. BMJ 2002;325:October 26.

192. Scheff TJ. Peer review: an iron law of disciplines. Self-published paper, published May 27, 2002. Available from: http://www.soc.ucsb.edu/faculty/scheff/23.html; viewed September 1, 2012.

193. Boyd LB, Hunicke-Smith SP, Stafford GA, Freund ET, Ehlman M, Chandran U, et al. The caBIG life science business architecture model. Bioinformatics 2011;27:1429–35.

194. Guidelines for ensuring and maximizing the quality, objectivity, utility, and integrity of information disseminated by federal agencies. Fed Reg 2002;67(36).

195. Sass JB, Devine Jr JP. The Center for Regulatory Effectiveness invokes the Data Quality Act to reject published studies on atrazine toxicity. Environ Health Perspect 2004;112:A18.

196. Tozzi JJ, Kelly Jr WG, Slaughter S. Correspondence: data quality act: response from the Center for Regulatory Effectiveness. Environ Health Perspect 2004;112:A18–9.

197. Cranor C. Scientific inferences in the laboratory and the law. Am J Public Health 2005;95:S121–8.

198. Copyright Act, Section 107, limitations on exclusive rights: fair use. Available from: http://www.copyright.gov/title17/92chap1.html; viewed September 18, 2012.

199. The Digital Millennium Copyright Act of 1998 U.S. Copyright Office Summary. Available from: http://www.copyright.gov/legislation/dmca.pdf; viewed August 24, 2012.

200. No Electronic Theft (NET) Act of 1997 (H.R. 2265). Statement of Marybeth Peters the Register of Copyrights before the Subcommittee on Courts and Intellectual Property Committee on the Judiciary. United States House of Representatives 105th Congress, 1st Session. September 11, 1997. Available from: http://www.copyright.gov/docs/2265_stat.html; viewed August 26, 2012.

201. The Freedom of Information Act. 5 U.S.C. 552. Available from: http://www.nih.gov/icd/od/foia/5usc552.htm; viewed August 26, 2012.

202. Greenbaum D, Gerstein M. A universal legal framework as a prerequisite for database interoperability. Nature Biotechnol 2003;21:979–82.

203. Perlroth N. Digital data on patients raises risk of breaches. The New York Times December 18, 2011.

204. Frieden T. VA will pay $20 million to settle lawsuit over stolen laptop's data. CNN January 27, 2009.

205. Mathieson SA. UK government loses data on 25 million Britons: HMRC chairman resigns over lost CDs. ComputerWeekly.com 20 November 20, 2007.

206. Sack K. Patient data posted online in major breach of privacy. The New York Times September 8, 2011.

207. Broad WJ. U.S. accidentally releases list of nuclear sites. The New York Times June 3, 2009.

208. Framingham Heart Study. Clinical Trials.gov. Available from: http://www.clinicaltrials.gov/ct/show/ NCT00005121; viewed October 16, 2012.

209. Appeal from the Superior Court in Maricopa County Cause No. CV2005-013190. Available from: http://www .azcourts.gov/Portals/89/opinionfiles/CV/CV070454.pdf; viewed August 21, 2012.

210. Informed consent and the ethics of DNA research. The New York Times April 23, 2010.

211. Markoff J. Troves of personal data, forbidden to researchers. The New York Times May 21, 2012.

212. Vogel HW. Monatsbericht der Konigl. Academie der Wissenschaften zu Berlin July 10, 1879.

213. Boorse HA, Motz L. The world of the atom, vol. 1. New York: Basic Books; 1966.

214. Harris G. Diabetes drug maker hid test data, files indicate. The New York Times July 12, 2010.

215. Nissen SE, Wolski K. Effect of rosiglitazone on the risk of myocardial infarction and death from cardiovascular causes. N Engl J Med 2007;356:2457–71.

216. Meier B. For drug makers, a downside to full disclosure. The New York Times May 23, 2007.

217. Roush W. The Gulf Coast: a victim of global warming? Technol Rev 2005 September 24.

218. McNeil DG. Predicting flu with the aid of (George) Washington. The New York Times May 3, 2009.

219. Khan A. Possible earth-like planets could hold water: scientists cautious. Los Angeles Times November 7, 2012.

220. Sharing publication-related data and materials: responsibilities of authorship in the life sciences. Washington, DC: The National Academies Press; 2003. Available from: http://www.nap.edu/openbook.php ?isbn=0309088593; viewed September 10, 2012.

221. Guidance for sharing of data and resources generated by the molecular libraries screening centers network (mlscn): addendum to rfa rm-04-017, NIH notice not-rm-04-014. Available from http://grants.nih.gov/ grants/guide/notice-files/NOT-RM-04-014.html; viewed September 19, 2012.

222. Berman JJ. De-identification. Washington, DC: U.S. Office of Civil Rights (HHS), Workshop on the HIPAA Privacy Rule's De-identification Standard; March 8-9, 2010. Available from: http://hhshipaaprivacy.com/assets/ 4/resources/Panel1_Berman.pdf; viewed August 24, 2012.

223. National Science Board. Science & Engineering Indicators. Arlington, VA: National Science Foundation; 2000 (NSB-00-1).

224. Bossuyt PM, Reitsma JB, Bruns DE, Gatsonis CA, Glasziou PP, Irwig LM, et al. Standards for reporting of diagnostic accuracy. The STARD statement for reporting studies of diagnostic accuracy: explanation and elaboration. Clin Chem 2003;49:7–18.

225. Ioannidis JP. Why most published research findings are false. PLoS Med 2005;2:e124.

226. Ioannidis JP. Some main problems eroding the credibility and relevance of randomized trials. Bull NYU Hosp Jt Dis 2008;66:135–9.

227. Pueschel M. National outcomes database in development. U.S. Medicine; 2000 December.

228. Cook TD, Shadish WR, Wong VC. Three conditions under which experiments and observational studies produce comparable causal estimates: new findings from within-study comparisons. J Policy Analy Manage 2008;27:724–50.

229. Bornstein D. The dawn of the evidence-based budget. The New York Times May 30, 2012.

230. Ledley RS, Lusted LB. Reasoning foundations of medical diagnosis. Science 1959;130:9–21.

231. Shortliffe EH. Medical expert systems: knowledge tools for physicians. West J Med 1986;145:830–9.

232. Heathfield H, Bose D, Kirkham N. Knowledge-based computer system to aid in the histopathological diagnosis of breast disease. J Clin Pathol 1991;44:502–8.

233. Grady D. Study finds no progress in safety at hospitals. The New York Times November 24, 2010.

234. Goldberg SI, Niemierko A, Turchin A. Analysis of data errors in clinical research databases. AMIA Annu Symp Proc 2008242–6.

235. Shelby-James TM, Abernethy AP, McAlindon A, Currow DC. Handheld computers for data entry: high tech has its problems too. Trials 2007;8:5.

236. Berner ES, Graber ML. Overconfidence as a cause of diagnostic error in medicine. Am J Med 2008;121:S2–S23.

237. Tetlock PE. Expert political judgment: how good is it? How can we know? Princeton: Princeton University Press; 2005.

238. Thaler RH. The overconfidence problem in forecasting. The New York Times August 21, 2010.

239. Janssens ACJW, vanDuijn CM. Genome-based prediction of common diseases: advances and prospects. Hum Mol Genet 2008;17:166–73.

240. Michiels S, Koscielny S, Hill C. Prediction of cancer outcome with microarrays: a multiple random validation strategy. The Lancet 2005;365:488–92.

241. Fifty years of DNA: from double helix to health, a celebration of the genome. National Human Genome Research Institute; April, 2003. Available from: http://www.genome.gov/10005139; viewed September 19, 2012.

242. Wade N. Scientist at work: David B. Goldstein, a dissenting voice as the genome is sifted to fight disease. The New York Times September 16, 2008.

243. Cohen J. The Human Genome, a decade later. Technol Rev 2011 Jan-Feb.

244. Gisler M, Sornette D, Woodard R. Exuberant innovation: The Human Genome Project. Cornell University Library; Mar 15, 2010. Available from: http://arxiv.org/ftp/arxiv/papers/1003/1003.2882.pdf; viewed September 22, 2012.

245. Anthony S. What can you do with a supercomputer? ExtremeTech 2012 March 15.

246. Dear colleague letter - US ignite: the next steps. National Science Foundation Announcement NSF 12-085, June 12, 2012.

247. Manyika J, Chui M, Brown B, Bughin J, Dobbs R, Roxburgh C, et al. Big data: the next frontier for innovation, competition, and productivity. McKinsey Global Institute; June 2011.

248. Berman JJ. Perl programming for medicine and biology. Sudbury, MA: Jones and Bartlett; 2007.

249. Olson S, Beachy SH, Giammaria CF, Berger AC. Integrating large-scale genomic information into clinical practice: workshop summary. Washington, DC: The National Academies Press; 2012.

250. Orwell G. 1984. Tiptree, UK: Signet; 1950.

251. LaFraniere S. Files vanished, young Chinese lose the future. The New York Times July 27, 2009.

252. Cipra BA. The best of the 20th century: editors name top 10 algorithms. SIAM News 2000;33(4).

253. Mell P, Grance T. The NIST definition of cloud computing. Recommendations of the National Institute of Standards and Technology. NIST Publication 800-145NIST September 2011.

254. Paskin N. Identifier interoperability: a report on two recent ISO activities. D-Lib Mag 2006;12:1–23.

255. Worldwide LHC Computing Grid. European Organization for Nuclear Research. Available from: http://public.web.cern.ch/public/en/lhc/Computing-en.html; 2008 viewed September 19, 2012.

256. Carpenter JR, Kenward MG. Missing data in randomised control trials: a practical guide. Available from: http://www.hta.nhs.uk/nihrmethodology/reports/1589.pdf; November 21, 2007 viewed June 28, 2011.

257. Berman JJ, Moore GW. Spontaneous regression of residual tumor burden: prediction by Monte Carlo Simulation. Anal Cell Pathol 1992;4:359–68.

258. McGauran N, Wieseler B, Kreis J, Schuler Y, Kolsch H, Kaiser T. Reporting bias in medical research - a narrative review. Trials 2010;11:37.

259. Dickersin K, Rennie D. Registering clinical trials. JAMA 2003;290:51.

260. Brin S, Page L. The anatomy of a large-scale hypertextual Web search engine. Comput Networks ISDN Syst 1998;33:107–17.

261. Stross R. The algorithm didn't like my essay. The New York Times June 9, 2012.

262. Sawyer R, Berman JJ, Borkowski A, Moore GW. Elevated prostate-specific antigen levels in black men and white men. Mod Pathol 1996;9:1029–32.

263. Yank V, Rennie D, Bero LA. Financial ties and concordance between results and conclusions in meta-analyses: retrospective cohort study. BMJ 2007;335:1202–5.

264. Mead CN. Data interchange standards in healthcare IT—computable semantic interoperability: now possible but still difficult, do we really need a better mousetrap? J Healthc Inf Manag 2006;20:71–8.

265. Committee on Mathematical Foundations of Verification, Validation, and Uncertainty Quantification; Board on Mathematical Sciences and Their Applications, Division on Engineering and Physical Sciences, National Research Council. Assessing the reliability of complex models: mathematical and statistical foundations of verification, validation, and uncertainty quantification. National Academy Press; 2012. Available from: http://www.nap.edu/catalog.php?record_id=13395; viewed January 29, 2013.

Index

Note: Page numbers followed by *f* indicate figures.

Printed and bound by CPI Group (UK) Ltd, Croydon, CR0 4YY

03/10/2024

01040327-0013